Teaching a Child to Read

Roger Farr   Nancy Roser

INDIANA UNIVERSITY   UNIVERSITY OF TEXAS, AUSTIN

TEACHING A CHILD TO READ

 Harcourt Brace Jovanovich, Inc.

NEW YORK   SAN DIEGO   CHICAGO   SAN FRANCISCO   ATLANTA

ISBN: 0-15-586650-8

Library of Congress Catalog Card Number: 78-71882

Printed in the United States of America

Cover illustrations by Edward Malsberg

Illustrations by Edward Malsberg appear on the following pages: 45, 101 (*center
drawings*), 103, 113, 120 (*top*), 121 (*top left*), 122 (*bottom*), 123–25, 130, 134,
135 (*top*), 137, 140, 143, 186–87, 200 (*top*), 202, 204–06, 207 (*top*), 208, 214–15,
223–25, 231, 234, 242, 326, 340–41, 391–92, 404–06.

Illustrations by Vantage Art, Inc., appear on the following pages: 29, 43, 50,
101–02, 104, 112 (*top*), 119, 120 (*bottom*), 121 (*top right, bottom*), 122 (*top*),
135 (*bottom left and right*), 136, 198, 200 (*bottom*), 201, 203, 207 (*bottom*), 241,
320–21, 327–28, 345–48, 351–54, 356, 360, 380, 387, 393.

Picture credits appear on page 497, which is a continuation of the copyright page.

This book is dedicated to all those children who taught us that they will learn to read when reading makes sense in their lives.

Preface

Teaching a child to read is an opportunity to give another human being a fuller and richer life. Our goals in this book are first to help the student understand what he or she needs to know in order to teach a child to read and then to provide the student with some of the knowledge to fulfill that need.

Although we have specifically written *Teaching a Child to Read* for the undergraduate teacher-education student, we believe that even experienced teachers will find some new teaching suggestions or a useful explanation of reading development. Our primary aim, however, has been to provide each teacher with a description of how to teach reading so that he or she can help children use and appreciate the printed word. To this end, rather than providing a complete review of the extensive research on reading, we have instead emphasized an application of this research to teaching situations. Thus we have included descriptions of our own as well as of others' teaching experiences.

By describing both classroom settings and children, we introduce the content of teaching a child to read as well as the theory for our teaching suggestions. We have tried to present practice and theory realistically intertwined. We hope that, after reading this text, the student will not be left with such questions as "Where does this information 'fit'?" or "How can awareness of this point affect children's learning or my teaching procedures?" We have described diagnostic teaching in real settings; our theories develop out of these practical settings; and controversies are placed in the perspective of suggested teaching procedures.

Our focus in planning the content has been on enabling the teacher to become a competent initiator, guide, and evaluator of a "tailor-made" reading program. We want to help the teacher plan and execute the individualization of the reading program. Some topics, such as "psycholinguistics and reading" or "the disabled reader," could have been included as separate chapters or sections, as they are in some other reading texts. However, here they are not treated separately—not because such topics are unimportant but rather because these topics need to be presented and discussed in the context of learning how to teach reading. These topics, as well as others, have therefore been incorporated in the total fabric of the text.

The book's ten chapters are organized into four units. Unit One, "Getting Started," includes an initial chapter on setting the stage for the prospective teacher; it outlines in broad strokes the context in which he or she will be expected to teach. We believe this chapter will help the student begin to understand what is needed to teach a child to read. The second chapter deals with the assessment that is essential for planning instruction. Assessment is discussed not just in terms of assessing a child's abilities but also in terms of available materials and the community's resources, for the latter two elements must be understood to plan an effective reading program. The third chapter describes the crucial process of getting a child started in learning to read. The emphasis of this chapter is on how to adjust the teaching to the development of each child, rather than on when to begin teaching.

Units Two and Three encompass the totality of teaching reading. While writing this book we were very concerned about dividing the discussion of word recognition and comprehension into separate units. We knew that we wanted to discuss each topic, but we also knew that word recognition and comprehension must not be separated when one actually teaches a child to read. Unit Two, "Recognizing Words," therefore emphasizes the use of context in teaching word-recognition behaviors. The descriptions of teaching phonics, structural analysis, and the development of a sight vocabulary, as well as the use of a dictionary, are related to purposeful reading experiences. In Unit Three, "Understanding the Context," the emphasis is on the three crucial aspects of developing a reader who will read to satisfy personal needs: establishing and building on a child's purpose, interests, and background; encouraging attentive, active reasoning while he or she is reading; and providing for the thoughtful application of what has been read.

Unit Four, "Planning the Program," includes a chapter on organizing materials, students, time schedules, and oneself to produce a reading program tailored to the needs of each child. The final chapter describes a number of reading programs and discusses how teachers may adopt and adapt these to their individual situations.

In preparing this book, a number of people have provided assistance and encouragement beyond the usual demands of their positions. We would like to take special note of the editorial guidance given by the staff of Harcourt Brace Jovanovich, particularly William J. Wisneski's encouragement—not only in getting this project started but also in keeping it going—and Lee Shenkman's very capable editorial leadership. We would also like to note the special contributions made by designer Anna Kopczynski and art editor Yvonne Steiner. Two teachers, critics, and constant reviewers of the manuscript to whom we are grateful are Paula Blomenberg and Bruce Tone. Our typist, Marcia McHargue, saw us through two, three, and even four revisions of many chapters.

ROGER FARR
NANCY ROSER

Contents

Getting Started

Recognizing Words

Understanding the Context

4 Planning the Program

Getting Started

Me? Teach a Child to Read?

Opening a textbook that offers to tell you how to teach children to read can be both an exciting and an intimidating experience: exciting because of the worlds of information and pleasure that await children in books; intimidating because (if you believe the popular press) others before you have failed at teaching all children to read. Indeed, schools are currently under intensive pressure to account for the children who enter and exit without some minimal level of literacy. According to some United States Office of Education statistics, 30 percent of American school children function below their capabilities in reading. In urban areas the percentages are even higher (Holloway, 1973). A concerned citizenry has clamored for an explanation: "Why can't our children read?" And some educators have responded:

"They are poor."
"They have moved too often."
"Their dialect is not the same as the textbooks'."
"They come from broken homes."
"They have some perceptual dysfunction."
"Nobody read to them."

And on and on. But as teachers, we are responsible for the achievements of our students. No longer can we "pass the buck." In the future, if the children can't read, *we* bear the blame.

try this ▶

Ask several classroom teachers to identify the children in their classrooms experiencing little success with learning to read. Then ask the teachers to tell you *why* these children are not achieving. Record what you hear. Pick as a winner anyone who answers: "I think I haven't yet reached him."

You probably concluded long ago that your reading skill is invaluable—even though what it is exactly, how it developed, and how it improved may be fuzzy in your memory. It may seem as though you have always read, for the process was so gradual, you could not point to a day or month and say, "This is when it happened." Perhaps it started with the Sunday comics and the day when you knew which ones you wanted read to you. Or perhaps you remember a favorite early teacher and recall that, somehow, by some seemingly magical turn of events, you learned to read in that classroom. It wasn't magical. Most children learn to read easily and without anguish—sometimes in spite of the "programs," "sequences," "objectives," "tapes," "kits," and "systems" designed to make the act look scientific and, yes, intimidating. Arthur Gates (1937), a noted scholar, researcher, and educator, wrote that learning to read

could be as natural as learning to talk. While there may not be a biological basis for reading as there is for speech, reading *can* and *is* being learned on laps, in cars, and at supermarkets. In fact, more children are learning to read today, and they are learning better, than ever before (Farr, Tuinman, and Rowls, 1974). But better is not good enough, for success in reading should mean total success. And no other factor will contribute more toward pupils' attainment of their full potential as readers than knowledgeable teachers.

Reading Is Another Way

In his book *The Student as Nigger,* Jerry Farber describes the emphasis placed on reading in schools and in society as a genuine case of "misplacement." Why learn to read, he asks, when effective functioning as a person is not in any way hindered by lack of this skill?

> If someone should choose to pass his life illiterate, there are other communications media accessible to him. He'll probably make out fine. He may even be able to teach the rest of us some things that print hides. (p. 37)

Rolland Callaway (1973) concurs, questioning the importance of reading in a multimedia culture, stressing the danger of teaching reading too early (before ages ten or eleven), and stating that reading should not be viewed as the only means for the development of a basic American culture. He advocates a "right not to read."

---

try this ▶

If you have access to children, select a few from various grade levels or of increasing ages. Prepare an informal question-response session to sample the children's reactions to:

what they think reading is
why they read (or listen to someone read)
how they feel about reading
their favorite book(s) and why

Share your information with your class.

In some ways Farber and Callaway are right: you can be a whole person—capable and involved, emoting and reflecting—without ever learning to read. Each of us can exist without reading (or without reading well); but by acquiring the skill, we have still one more option for a richer life—one more alternative to clarify our visions, expand our horizons, and reach outward. Certainly, learning to read is not an end in

The Reality?

Unfortunately, the happy prereading experiences that convince children that learning to read is a skill to be coveted don't always continue after instruction actually begins. Bruno Bettelheim reports some spontaneous reactions of fourth and fifth graders when asked to recollect how they reacted to being taught to read:

> One readily admitted that though he now liked reading, he still had a hard time reading aloud. The reason was that when in first grade he was asked to read aloud, he felt so ashamed to say such stupid things that he blocked; he simply could not do it; and henceforth he resented reading, preferring to do anything else in class.
>
> Another hated the stories he had to read because these were neither realistic nor fantastic. Stories, he thought, should either give a picture of what life was really like, or not pretend to do so. He would have had a much easier time learning to read, and enjoying it, had the stories been either true to life, describing how people really are, or truly fantastic, like fairy tales. He told me that he finally overcame his resentment of reading when he began to become acquainted with fairy tales, because then after he had read a story, he would contemplate its content "for a long while." These were meaningful experiences for him; those he read in class were not.
>
> When I asked in what sense the stories from which these children had learned to read were not "true to life," every one of the group was eager to talk, and each had some different objection. One was that in these stories there are only two age-groups: children of their own age, and adults, mostly parents; and both children and parents alike are depicted as insipid. But they wanted to see and read also stories about teenagers, and about old people. Another universal objection was that nobody in these stories showed their true feelings, such as being angry. Other complaints of these ten-year-olds were that there was no reason to learn to read that they could make out, because in the early grades they never learned anything through reading that they didn't already know, and knew much better and in greater detail than it was set out in the books from which they were supposed to learn great things. (1974, p. 16)

itself. We would not want to produce a nation of readers who could read, but chose not to, or who, when forced to read through necessity, did not enjoy it. Reading should be enjoyable and useful. It is one more way of gathering information that will be used in making decisions. The ability to communicate speedily and accurately is essential. In a rapidly advancing technological society, it becomes even more imperative to selectively retrieve, use, and transmit the masses of accumulating knowledge. Rather than a subject in the curriculum, reading is a valuable skill—one that offers alternatives capable of opening all facets of life.

And reading is also important because it is fun. Children who are introduced to reading in the laps of loving parents or grandparents, who hear stories over and over, who squeal when they have no words, and who delight in pictures and language already understand that reading is something special. Children who share books on the kindergarten rug, "pretend read," and request favorite stories already look on reading as a treat. For them, reading is an avenue to adventure, an imaginary trip, and an interaction with the human experience.

Learning to Read: Reflecting and Projecting

Prod your own memories of learning to read. It may help to clarify your own biases and prepare you to deal more objectively with the teacher you are becoming. Maybe we can help refresh that memory.

Spirit of reading past. The first days of school were etched in new crayons with points and scissors without them. Impressions include Mother's hand, rows of desks, strange faces, and a smiling teacher who showed you where to sit. Then it was book money, good-by Mother, and on your own. Perhaps you thought, "Today I learn to read." But it wasn't that day. First, you and your classmates had "reading readiness." You were given a book in which you drew lines, matched shapes, and sequenced pictures. When you finished that readiness book, teacher assigned you to groups. Remember? You could be a Robin, a Bluejay, or a Sparrow. When teacher called "Robins," you took the book you *could* mark in and the book you *couldn't* mark in and went to some little chairs in the corner. Teacher sat in a bigger chair, facing you and the other children. Teacher's book was like yours—only fatter.

Teacher said, "Open your books. What do you think this story is about?"

You *knew* what it was about because you had turned all the pages in the book on the day the teacher passed them out, so you put your hand up like the other children. But you didn't get called on.

"A bird," answered Tommy, "who builds a nest in a mailbox and hatches babies."

"Did you peek?" asked the teacher.

"No," said Tommy, "I guessed."

"Remember," said the teacher, "I asked you not to look ahead in our book."

"Yes," nod the children.

You nodded too, no doubt, vowing never to peek again, and hoping to forget what you saw.

"Here is a picture of the boy in our story," said the teacher. "Read the boy's name."

"Bob," (or Rick or Red or . . .) you chimed with the others. Learning to read was going to take some time.

Perhaps it was like that—Perhaps not. Perhaps you were excited about learning to read, or perhaps you already did read.

Across the hall in the other first grade, the teacher stood in front of the whole class to teach.

"Time for phonics," said that teacher. "Bee," intoned the teacher, "says buh, buh, buh."

"Cee," she continued, "says kuh, kuh, kuh."

And the children repeated, most likely unaware that they were learning to read.

Any memories stirred? Or any pain? If you haven't spent much time in an elementary school since those days of Robins, Bluejays, and sound drills, you will be interested in learning that many things have changed.

Spirit of reading present.   Entering school today, children are often greeted by quite a different physical environment. Mothers and fathers still arrive on the first day bearing the birth certificate. There are still new crayons and snubnosed scissors. Children still expect to learn to read on the first day of school. But gone are the rows of desks and often the reading circle chairs; they have been replaced by tables and chairs, open areas with brightly colored carpet, and corners designated as learning centers. There are still chalk and bulletin boards, along with the omnipresent cards of model manuscript letters. But now the walls fold back

to permit use of larger spaces, the windows are lower and larger, and supplies go into a box or dishpan rather than a desk.

Gone, too, are the static groups of Sparrows, Bluejays, and Robins. More likely, today's teacher has assessed the reading skill of each child, and, by taking the child's interests and background into account, has designed a reading program for the child—regardless of how the child compares with others in the class. Sometimes the teacher meets with the child in a group; often, however, the child reads alone to the teacher. All of the children are not reading from the same book; it is less likely that a story is read by the "fast group" while a slower child is waiting to get that far.

Today's child can move as rapidly through books as he or she wishes—no longer is there a "law" against looking ahead. The classroom library today is richer than was yours. Learning to read is, more often than not, a joyous, noncompetitive experience. Many skills can be practiced with a variety of creative learning aids, not all of which are dependent upon pencil and paper. Many of the learning aids are designed to be self-checking, enabling the child to select one from the shelves, practice a skill, check the work, and then reshelve it. The child often records his or her own progress on an individual learning record, or "learning contract," so that teacher and child can discuss progress when they next meet together. A learning contract can be like an individual game plan, filled with the events and activities of the day (including when the teacher will hear the child read).

Upon entering today's classroom, it is often difficult for the observer to determine what is going on. Children are spread over the carpet, working at tables, using learning centers. One may see the teacher at work but not hear an adult voice as the teacher moves about the room quietly giving aid as needed, checking, redirecting, teaching new skills, discussing a story, or guiding a project. In short, learning to read today is an active, meaningful, and individual process.

Sound like a dream? It often is. Too few teachers have moved far enough or fast enough to significantly change instructional practices. But improved teacher education and more awareness on the part of administrators has made this type of learning experience begin to take hold across the nation.

Spirit of reading future. Visionary educators look toward even greater changes in the coming decades. They predict many new and creative uses of the computer—for example, "diagnostic" teaching that will provide for the monitoring of brainwaves, resulting in instant analysis and

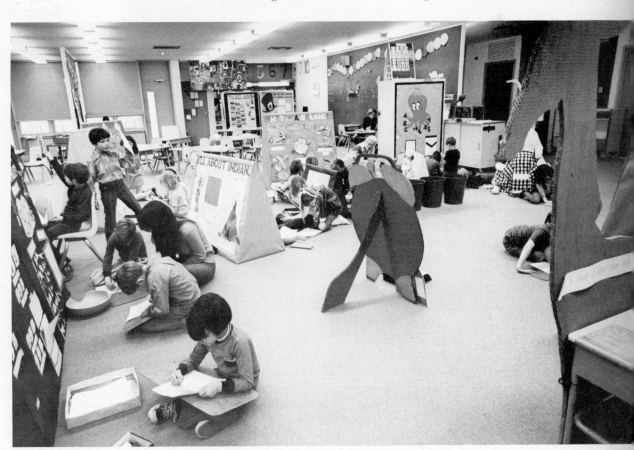

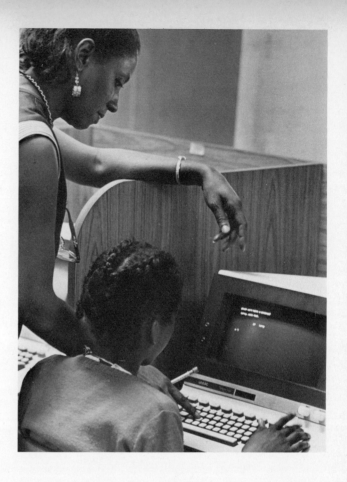

educational prescriptions. Breaking from the rigid lock-step approaches and highly linear programs that still predominate in some schools, future use of computer instruction can focus upon the interrelationship of information, new forms of sensory stimulation, and varied response modes. But regardless of the amount of reliance on advanced technology (or perhaps in spite of it), the classroom of the future should be a place where the limits of awareness and perception are expanded, as well as a place that fosters a closeness between students and teachers as learning takes place.

In the future classroom, there should be an emphasis on making learning real to children, relating reading with their life styles, needs, and interests. An outside observer may find the "program" even less apparent than before as children pursue reading through high-interest projects and self-defined problems. The concern of educators of the future will be to help their learners become thinkers, critical evaluators, questioners, and seekers. Good teaching has always been defined as the arousal and nourishment of curiosity and interest, coupled with the provision of a learning environment in which the child can offer and test solutions, knowledge, and skills (Chomsky, 1972). In the future, the number of educators who will subscribe to this goal and do something about it will make the critical difference. There may no longer be books designed specifically to teach reading. Teachers may be so well educated in the reading process, the learning to read process, and the teaching process that reading will be learned as a result of the natural curiosity of children. There will be important things going on in their world, and they won't be sheltered from the reality while they master some program's skills sequence.

The physical environment of the school of the future may be unrecognizable to twentieth-century learners; learning materials may be beyond our imaginations. Problems of arousing interest and of motivating students may, perhaps, be solved. Taking a cue from the alternative school movement of the past decade, the school of the future will be open to the community—not only full of parents and graduates, but interested community members of all ages.

Teachers of the future will have abandoned their futile quest for *the* best method of teaching reading and will focus instead on *a* method for each child. The future poses challenges to prepare learners for a changing world, but the key to the challenge is still in the hands of the teacher.

Three Processes Are a Key to the Challenge

Regardless of historical era, teachers have strived for the same goal—skilled readers—and have based their methods on their understanding of: (1) what they think reading is; (2) how they think children learn to read; and (3) how they think reading can best be taught.

What Is Reading?

All kinds of definitions and explanations of the reading process exist. Experts define, redefine, chart, model, and mull over what it means to read. Each of you reading this book has a somewhat different perception of the skill you possess and are exercising. At best, reading is a complex process. By examining some widely quoted definitions of reading in Figure 1–1, you will no doubt conclude that experts show considerable variance in what they believe reading is. We believe that persons interested in teaching children to read have a vested interest in arriving

try this ▶ What is your definition of reading at this point? Write it down and hang on to it. Perhaps you will find that it changes as your experiences dictate. Read it again when you have finished this text.

Figure 1–1

What Is Reading?

*Reading Is Interpretation of General Experience**

Frank Jennings (1965)

Reading begins with wonder at the world about us. It starts with the recognition of repeated events like thunder, lightning, and rain. It starts with the seasons and the growth of things. It starts with an ache that vanishes with food and water. It occurs when time is discovered. Reading begins with the management of signs of things. It begins when the mother, holding the child's hand, says that a day is "beautiful" or "cold." Or that the wind is "soft."

Reading is "signs and portents," the changing moon, the "changeless" sun and the "fixed" stars that move through the night. It was this for the man at the cave's mouth. It is this for us at the desk, the bench or control panel (p. 3).

* Categories for classification are taken from Emerald V. Dechant, *Improving the Teaching of Reading* (Englewood Cliffs, N.J.: Prentice-Hall, 1970), p. 15.

Reading Is Interpretation of Graphic Symbols

Rudolf Flesch (1955)

Reading means getting meaning from certain combinations of letters. Teach the child what each letter stands for and he can read (p. 3). Phonics is taught to the child, letter by letter, and sound by sound until he knows it—and when he knows it he knows how to read (p. 121).

Charles Fries (1962)

Learning to read, therefore, means developing a considerable range of habitual responses to a specific set of patterns of graphic shapes. The process of learning to read in one's native language is the process of transfer from the auditory signs for language signals, which the child has already learned, to the new visual signs for the same signals . . . But we . . . confuse the issue if we insist that this use of reading in stimulating and cultivating the techniques of thinking, evaluating, and so on constitutes the reading process. The abilities enumerated above are all abilities that are and must be developed through the uses of language (pp. 120–21).

Reading Is a Combination of 1 and 2

Ernest Horn (1937)

Reading includes those processes that are involved in approaching, perfecting and maintaining meaning through the use of the printed page (p. 152).

David Russell (1960)

Reading is a subtle and complex act. It involves, more or less simultaneously, the following: sensation of light rays on the retina of the eye reaching the brain, perception of separate words and phrases, functioning of the eye muscles with exact controls, immediate memory for what has just been read, remote memories based on the reader's experiences, interest in the content read, and organization of the materials, so that finally it can be used in some way. These various features operate more or less concurrently; but they can be analyzed in at least four overlapping stages: sensation, perception, comprehension, and utilization (p. 99).

Miles Tinker and Constance McCullough (1962)

Reading involves the recognition of printed or written symbols which serve as a stimuli for the recall of meanings built up through past experience, and the construction of new meanings through manipulation of concepts already possessed by the reader (p. 13).

Emerald Dechant (1970)

Reading is far more than recognition of the graphic symbols. It is much more than the mere ability to pronounce the words on the printed page; it is even more than the gaining of meaning from printed materials. The reader is stimulated by the writer's words, but in turn vests these words with his own meaning. Reading typically is the bringing of meaning *to* rather than the gaining of meaning *from* the printed page (p. 11).

E. Brooks Smith, Kenneth Goodman, and Robert Meredith (1970)

Reading is the active process of reconstructing meaning from language represented by graphic symbols (letters), just as listening is the active process of reconstructing meaning from the sound symbols (phonemes) of oral language (p. 247).

at their own definition of reading. Your own understanding of what you think it means to read will shape your teaching objectives and procedures. Helping you to acquire that definition and understanding is a goal of this book.

"If so many experts can't agree," you may ask, "why do I have to wrestle with a definition of reading?" A noted psycholinguist, Frank Smith, has answered the question eloquently:

> Many teachers are trained to be ignorant, to rely on the opinions of experts or superiors rather than on their own judgment. The questions I am asked after lectures to teachers (on the topic of reading) are always eminently practical—how should reading be taught, which method is best, and what should be done about a real life child of eight who has the devastating misfortune to read like a statistically fictitious child of six? Teachers do not ask the right kind of question—instead of asking what they should do, which can never be answered with the generality they expect, they should ask what they need to know in order to decide for themselves. (It is a monument to the efficiency of the brainwashing that teachers received during their training that they are practically immune to insult on the topic of their own intellectual capacity. The only time teachers express surprise or disbelief is when it is suggested that their own experience and intuition might be as good a guide for action as the dogma of some expert.) (1973, p. 46)

We wholeheartedly concur with Smith's argument and encourage you to accept his challenge. As you are guided toward your own definition of the reading process, you will arrive at your own decisions about what to teach and how to teach. You will find, however, that your own beliefs and biases will be modified as you explore, try out, innovate, and reflect.

Collective Wisdom

Perhaps one of the most comprehensive and exhaustive attempts to define reading was completed through a *convergence* technique—a method of assembling experts to "brain storm" and to reach consensus. The Gephart report provided a summary definition of reading:

> "Reading" is a term used to refer to an interaction by which meaning encoded in visual stimuli by an author becomes meaning in the mind of the reader. The interaction always includes three facets: (1) material to be read; (2) knowledge possessed by the reader; and (3) physiological and intellectual activities. The variability apparent when the interaction is viewed at different points in time is a result of the variability possible in each of the several facets. (1970, p. 172)

How Do Children Learn to Read?

Depending upon your definition of reading, children do learn to read in a variety of ways. If you believe that reading is information processing, for example, then your children will learn to read by *getting meaning from* and *bringing meaning to* their reading. Children will learn to depend upon the patterns that signal meaning and the grammar of spoken English. They will learn that reading is communicating with an author rather than correctly pronouncing all of the words. Conversely, if you believe that reading is learned by learning to interpret graphic symbols, children under your direction may learn to decode sound-symbol patterns as they progress in reading skill. Variations lie along a continuum of interpretations ranging from "Children learn to read by cracking the code" to "Children learn to read when their experiential background is in harmony with the author's." Fortunately, the children don't delay their learning while we try to figure out *how* they are learning. Ultimately, the value of any interpretation will be judged by whether or not those who are taught can use print effectively. Your definition of reading will dictate the way you will understand and interpret the process of learning to read. Within this text, we will offer examples of that learning-to-read process.

How Can Reading Best Be Taught?

No one knows *a* best way. Again, each definition of reading dictates (or at least suggests) a methodology. Collected experience and research results offer support for certain practices. But scientific Truths are unavailable. The best any text can offer is to share "what works" and to attempt to interpret why it works. And each text (including this one) is colored by the author's interpretation of what reading is and how he or she thinks children learn to read.

For each definition of reading offered in Figure 1–1, we could project implications for the process of learning to read if the author were teacher. We could hypothesize that children learning with Frank Jennings as their teacher may go walking in the woods, discover nature at work, and then talk, talk, talk about their experiences. We could project that Jennings' classroom would be a visually enriching and stimulating environment with a great deal of emphasis placed on sharing books, ideas, and experiences. This whole process of experience-building would frame Jennings' introduction to reading. Rudolf Flesch's classroom, on the other hand, would be replete with phonics materials. He would concentrate on helping children learn to read by perceiving letters, attaching representative speech sounds, and blending the sounds to produce words and—ultimately—independent readers. Kenneth Goodman's class might be involved with learning first to read their own language. Like Jennings' class, Goodman's might experience events to-

Take your own definition of reading and project the kind of class-room reading program that would grow from that definition.

Then, visit an elementary classroom during reading instruc-tion; try to inductively arrive at the definition of reading that is being acted upon in that room.

Compare your results.

gether—a field trip, a visiting pet, a science experiment. Goodman would encourage the subsequent natural exchange of conversation. He might take dictation from the children, believing that they would be able to learn to reproduce their own words, thoughts, and patterns more rapidly and with greater meaning attached than the thoughts and lan-guage patterns of other authors. Goodman would accept as "reading" a reconstruction of the thoughts and sentence sense of the material re-gardless of whether all words were "sounded out" correctly.

Of course, these projections are hypothetical, designed to illustrate how your definition of reading affects the learning-to-read process and the teaching process. The projections may also serve to underscore the earlier tenets that there may be no one best method, that many teachers representing a host of philosophies and definitions of reading succeed in helping children to read, and that the most successful teachers vary their methods to account for learner differences. This text, then, does not offer the answer, but simply describes "what has worked" for us and for others.

Overview of the Chapters

Teachers past and present have come to know children representing different sexes, races, ages, abilities, and interests. Each of these differ-ences has contributed to making each child unique. We hope that you will understand and value these differences. While understanding the differences in the children you teach will have bearing on the discussion throughout this text, Chapter 2, "Getting to Know Them: Assessment," will relate directly to these concerns.

"To begin or not to begin" has for too long been the question. Chap-ter 3, "At the Beginning: Reading Readiness," offers some suggestions on *how* to begin. In addition, some informal diagnostic and teaching activities are suggested.

Chapter 3 also focuses on planning instruction for the child just start-ing a reading program. The chapter's intent is to provide a base for the chapters that follow.

Children who are able to bring an interpretation to a symbolic (graphic) representation are exercising the skill of word perception or recognition. Skills of word recognition are difficult to separate. They are

analogous to the mixtures you have produced in chemistry labs. Unlike chemical compounds, the components of mixtures remain somewhat identifiable although smoothly blended; they could be reclaimed into separate entities only through some artificial process. So, only for the purposes of study and discussion have we separated the aspects of word recognition discussed in Chapters 4, 5, and 6. Chapter 4 presents the overview. Chapter 5 emphasizes the importance of the use of context as a word-recognition clue; while Chapter 6 describes methods for teaching the basic skills of word recognition.

More than understanding, reading comprehension implies the reasoning or thinking skills that the reader applies to the reading task. The background of experience permits the reader to interpret, to make judgments, and to detect subtleties of meaning, which are each a part of comprehension. The "subareas" of comprehension are another source of contention for experts who study the reading process. No matter how comprehension skills are categorized, however, most experts agree that to comprehend fully is to react to the author's thought, to formulate hypotheses, and to test those hypotheses against further reading. Helping children to comprehend fully and to become responsive to the printed word is the subject of Chapter 7, "Meaning is Reading: Comprehension," and Chapter 8, "Teaching Reading for Special Purposes."

The organization of the total day will affect the time and effort given to reading instruction. Students can assume some of the responsibility for their learning, but they must be taught to do so. Organizing the classroom and an introduction to materials are the subjects of Chapter 9.

Chapter 10, "Programs for Teaching Reading," describes the variety of programs that are available to the teacher of reading and presents selected samples of those materials.

The concerns: This introduction has served as the overview of the text and the challenge of the task. The text may be read in any order—back to front, skipping chapters, skimming, or poring; but right now, we can imagine that your concerns are predictable:

How do I begin?
Where do I begin?
How many days until school is out?

We can also imagine that you have within you the ingredients for success—high interest and great energy. Lacking these, your success is not guaranteed. With these, the course is still dubious, but your charts are more positive.

So, let us begin. . . .

REFERENCES

Bettelheim, Bruno. "Janet and Mark and the New Illiteracy." *Encounter* 43 (December 1974): 15–23.

Callaway, Rolland. "Social Perspectives on Reading: Politics." In *Social Perspectives on Reading*, edited by James B. Macdonald, pp. 3–14. Newark, Del.: International Reading Association, 1973.

Chomsky, Carol. "Stages in Language Development and Reading Exposure." *Harvard Educational Review*, 42 (February 1972): 1–33.

Dechant, Emerald V. *Improving the Teaching of Reading*. Englewood Cliffs, N.J.: Prentice-Hall, 1970.

Farber, Jerry. *The Student as Nigger*. New York: Pocket Books, 1969.

Farr, Roger; Tuinman, Japp; and Rowls, Michael. *Reading Achievement in the United States: Then and Now*. Prepared for Educational Testing Service under Contract OEC-71-3713 by the Reading Program Center of the Institute for Child Study. Bloomington, Ind.: Indiana University, August 1974.

Flesch, Rudolf. *Why Johnny Can't Read*. New York: Harper, 1955.

Fries, Charles C. *Linguistics and Reading*. New York: Holt, Rinehart and Winston, 1962.

Gates, Arthur. "The Necessary Mental Age for Beginning Reading. *Elementary School Journal* 37 (March 1937): 497–508.

Gephart, William J. *Application of the Covergence Technique to Basic Studies of the Reading Process*. Washington, D.C.: U.S. Department of Health, Education and Welfare, Office of Education, National Center for Educational Research and Development, 1970. Project No. 8–0737.

Holloway, Ruth Love. "The Worldwide Right to Read." In *Reading for All*, pp. 27–33. Proceedings of the Fourth IRA World Congress on Reading. Newark, Del.: International Reading Association, 1973.

Horn, Ernest. *Methods of Instruction in the Social Studies*. New York: Charles Scribner's Sons, 1937.

Jennings, Frank G. *This Is Reading*. New York: Teachers College Press, Columbia University, 1965.

Russell, David. *Children Learn to Read*. Boston: Ginn, 1960.

Smith, E. Brooks; Goodman, Kenneth; and Meredith, Robert. *Language and Thinking in the Elementary School*. New York: Holt, Rinehart and Winston, 1970.

Smith, Frank. "The Politics of Ignorance." In *The Politics of Ignorance: Point-counterpoint*, edited by Sister Rosemary Winkeljohann, pp. 43–55. Newark, Del.: ERIC/RCS and International Reading Association, 1973.

Tinker, Miles A., and McCullough, Constance. *Teaching Elementary Reading*. New York: Appleton-Century-Crofts, 1962.

FOR FURTHER READING

Clymer, Theodore. "What Is Reading? Some Current Concepts." In *Innovation and Change in Reading Instruction*, edited by Helen M. Robinson. Sixty-seventh Yearbook of the National Society for the Study of Education, pp. 7–29. Chicago: University of Chicago Press, 1968.

Guszak, Frank J. *Diagnostic Reading Instruction in the Elementary School*. New York: Harper and Row, 1972.

Harris, Larry, and Smith, Carl. *Reading Instruction Through Diagnostic Teaching*. New York: Holt, Rinehart and Winston, 1976.

Postman, Neil. "The Politics of Reading." *Harvard Educational Review* 40 (May 1970): 244–52.

Smith, Frank. "Twelve Easy Ways to Make Learning to Read Difficult and One Difficult Way to Make It Easy." In *Psycholinguistics and Reading*, edited by Frank Smith. New York: Holt, Rinehart and Winston, 1973.

Smith, Nila B. *American Reading Instruction*. Newark, Del.: International Reading Association, 1965.

Getting to Know Them: Assessment

One not-too-distant day in September you will enter a classroom expecting to develop the reading abilities of thirty children. Of course, these children won't be completely unknown to you. You will know a little about them from such sources as other teachers, parent reports, and school records. You will have some notions about both their behavior and how some can be expected to achieve. And, in assessing the data, you will have to decide how much credence to give these opinions and evaluations, since much information will have come from subjective judgments and is, therefore, tainted by the unique personality of the judge. For example, is Brenda really a slow learner, or is her notorious daydreaming the symptom of something else—boredom, perhaps? Is David really seeing how much of a disruptive influence he can be, or are his energies misdirected? Even if what you have heard or read about these children was perhaps valid for their previous class situations, a youngster's attitude, behavior, and performance can change in a new learning situation. You will be responsible for providing that new opportunity, and to do it, you will need as much relevant information as you can accrue for each child.

Since this initial assessment is logically among the first tasks you will perform as you prepare to teach children to read, the intent of this chapter is to aid you in gathering objective information that will help you appreciate them all as individual learners. The more objective the data-gathering process, the better the resultant information for making plans and decisions—and the better the teaching will "fit" the learner. No one expects or even desires that you set up some "individualized reading program" on the first day of school. That would mean putting the program ahead of its participants. Getting to know the children is the primary and continuous challenge. Without an understanding of the reading ability, the interests, and the personality of each child, you will have no basis for planning. And you won't be able to gather the information you need in just one setting; if you tried, you would have only a brief and perhaps inaccurate view of each child. You will be collecting information each time you talk with, listen to, and observe children. This continuous information gathering will alert you to the subtle, and not so subtle, changes in each child's development.

There are various types of information that you will want to collect in order to know each child and thus to teach effectively. For the sake of gathering the information, it will be treated separately here as: (1) information that reveals the child's interests, needs, problems, and motivations, and (2) information that indicates the child's reading ability. It will be your responsibility to acquire the various types of information, to record what you learn—mentally or in notes—and to build your instruction on what you learn.

There is a sequential development to this information gathering. Getting to know the children as individuals with special interests is a natural activity for beginning a new school year. The next step, determining each child's reading ability, is essential if you are to begin instruction at a level at which the child will have success. Both are basic to planning specific instruction to help increase the reading ability of each child.

Getting to Know the Child as a Person

There are several techniques that will enable you to learn about a child's interests, needs, problems, and motivations. Although some of the behaviors that you assess, observe, or hear reported will actually be fronts for the real problems or feelings they cloak, as you become more sensitive with practice, you may learn to recognize these as symptoms of the real problems. But most of what you learn can help to shape your instruction.

You can learn about children if you use such techniques as: (1) observation, (2) interest inventories, (3) interviews with the child, and (4) parent interviews. These sources of information are vital tools in uncovering the background and interests of the child; and, as you will see throughout the book, having that knowledge is absolutely essential in teaching the child to read for meaning and thus to grow as a reader. After discussing these techniques, informal record-keeping is demonstrated as a means of accruing what is learned from observation and interview. In a very practical sense, the records you keep will link what you learn from observations, inventories, and interviews and will serve to influence your teaching.

Learn by Observing

Just by looking around the classroom, the teacher gets a feeling for the range of differences among children: height, weight, shoe size, color, size of eyes, length of hair—characteristics that make each child unique. These are the physical (and often the most apparent) differences. Other differences, although less obvious, are even more important. They are the social differences demonstrated through such behaviors as the ease or difficulty of forming friendships, the frequency and nature of peer contact, the temerity or reticence of approach to learning activities, the degree of anxiety exhibited, or the aggressiveness or passivity demonstrated in a group situation. Some children cope more easily with stress, have patience for detail, indicate wide interests, and appear self-motivated; while others appear disinterested and seem to lack ability to attend to tasks for even short periods of time. Some appear to be troubled by problems that you may never discover, while on the surface they remain docile and cooperative; others may act out frustrations and actually be begging for attention. It is not our contention that the teacher can solve every personal problem; we do believe that attentive observation can better help the teacher understand, accept, and *teach*.

Generally, your observations can provide you with estimates of:

how the child feels about school
how the child interacts with peers and/or adults
how the child approaches new problem situations
to what extent the child exhibits qualities of self-confidence, curiosity, enthusiasm, self-directiveness, leadership, resourcefulness, and creativity

You should not approach the initial observation of your students as an attempt to gather detailed personality information about each child. Rather, you want to begin to know them, and to do so you need to give them opportunities to express themselves and to participate in all kinds of activities. For example, watch them as they play. Who are the leaders? Which children seem reluctant to participate? Or, as the children listen to a story, notice which children seem intrigued with the sequence of events, which children show excitement at a sudden turn of events, and, of course, which children just can't seem to sit still to listen to any story.

As children choose a free-time activity, note which head for the library corner, which head for the games, and which children choose to work on arts and crafts. It is also worth noting which children seem to be unable to find anything to do and drift from one activity to another.

Inventory Their Interests

You can systematically collect information about a child's needs and tastes with an interest inventory. Interest inventories are sets of questions or incomplete statements that the child is asked or encouraged to complete in order to find out such information as what the child does in his or her spare time and what school activities, television shows, books, heroes and heroines, and hobbies are favorites. Older or more capable children generally write responses to the questions, with follow-up discussion to expand on the written responses. Younger or less capable children are asked the questions orally during an informal chat. Often, brief notes are taken, but only if writing does not impede the free flow of conversation.

Sometimes a child's responses to an interest inventory uncover unique interests in hobbies, sports, or animals that, when linked with the instructional program, stimulate and aid learning. However, if interest inventories are administered in a dull, formal fashion or if the child is hesitant to reveal herself or himself in initial encounters, the resultant information will yield little of value to the teacher.

Although there are published interest inventories available, you should use one of them only if you have carefully reviewed it to be sure that it fits your students' ages, background experiences, or economic situations. It is also important to be aware that these inventories do not guarantee that children will necessarily be interested in reading what they say interests them.

For example, let's assume that Mr. Searcher administers an interest inventory to Paul, who describes an interest in cars. The teacher finds a book about a boy who helps his brother repair an old car and gives it to Paul. Paul should be able to read the book, but several days later Mr. Searcher learns that Paul started the book but quit reading because, "It's a dumb book." It turns out that Paul's interest was not in old cars but rather in sleek racing cars and the thrill of competition on the track. The inventory had not been sensitive or specific enough.

Using another information-gathering technique—the child interview—Mr. Searcher might have learned Paul's real interest. And it is worth noting that a teacher can also get good clues about real interests from careful observation during sharing sessions and informal peer group encounters. If you listen in the hallways, on the playground, and in the cafeteria, you will recognize that real and reported interests surface, change, and develop. And these interests will become apparent to you if you are a sharp observer and a good listener. The point here is that interest inventories—particularly published ones—can be less useful than what you can learn from a combination of informal observation techniques.

The teacher, then, is the best designer of an interest inventory. The teacher has the best indication of the range of children's interests and can easily revise any self-made assessment technique to increase its sensitivity.

Figure 2–1 suggests some sample questions from an interest inventory and gives you some idea of how one is prepared.

Figure 2–1 Sample Questions from an Interest Inventory

1. What sports do you like to play? (Circle your answers.) What sports do you like to watch? (Underline your answers.)

   Roller skating   Swimming
   Skiing   Bowling
   Football   Tennis
   Baseball   Basketball
   Boating   _____ (other)

2. Do you have pets? _____ What kinds? _____ Names? _____

3. Do you collect things? (Circle your answers.)

   Foreign money   Stamps   Postcards
   Rocks   Dolls
   Butterflies, insects   _____ (other)

4. Do you have hobbies or pastimes? (Circle your answers.)

   Writing   Cooking
   Making things   Hunting, fishing
   Collecting   Drawing, painting
   Dancing   Singing
   Playing an instrument   _____ (other)

5. If you could have one wish come true, what would it be?
   _____
   _____

6. What school subjects do you like best? _____
   _____

7. What is one of your favorite books? _____
   _____

8. Do you enjoy reading? _____

9. Do you like to have someone read to you? _____
   Who? _____

10. Other than at school, where do you read? _____
    _____

11. Can you remember the names of some books that you have read recently?
    _____

12. Do you have a library card? _____
    Do you use it? _____

13. Do you read (or look at) parts of any newspaper? _____
    What sections do you like best? (Circle your answers.)
    Sports   Front page
    Funnies   Editorials
    Stories   _____ (other)
    What magazines do you read (or look at)? _____
    _____

14. Do you have a favorite comic book? _____
    _____

15. Tell the name of a favorite movie? _____
    Why do you like it? _____

16. Name the TV program(s) you like best. _____
    _____
    _____

17. Name some places you have been or would like to go.
        Places I've Been   Places I'd Like to Go
    _____   _____
    _____   _____
    _____   _____

Interview the Child

As a teacher, you communicate continually with a child, but by arranging to talk with the child privately, you can ask questions that may provoke a very informative discussion. The interview can fill in gaps in the information you have gathered through less formal observation and build on the knowledge you gather through an interest inventory. The interview should be a free, friendly, and personal exchange of information. In a sense, interview schedules are handled much like the interest inventories. But the interview permits the teacher to share her or his own interests with the child. If the teacher describes personal interests and experiences, the child will likely be more expressive. The initial purpose for scheduling the interview may be the need to update

the child's cumulative record,* but the result of such interviews may encourage you to make this personal, uninterrupted encounter part of the ongoing schedule of activities. Some teachers leave a pencil and a pad or a small calendar in a place where children who need to talk can voluntarily sign up for some exclusive teacher time.

Interview the Parents

Parents can tell a teacher a great deal about their child's special interests, hobbies, and talents. Teachers who schedule time to talk with parents (either through home visits or during school hours) can learn how the child uses leisure time and relates and participates at home. Parent interviews frequently uncover concerns the parents would like to discuss, and these may explain pressures on the child or cue the teacher to concealed problems. The teacher who establishes rapport with parents cements a team approach to learning and opens channels for further communication throughout the year. When parents can sense the teacher's genuine concern for their child, they are willing—and even eager—to come back for further discussions.

---

* A cumulative record is usually maintained on each child in a school. Generally, this record contains such demographic information as the child's name, address, birthdate, parents' names and names of brothers and sisters. Sometimes the cumulative record also includes a health and school attendance record for the child as well as standardized achievement test information. These records are often maintained in the school principal's office.

It is important to remember that the interview—and all other data-gathering techniques as well—is valuable only insofar as it can be applied in a valid program.

For example, Jenny participated in class only when the teacher specifically called on her. She seemed disdainful of most classroom activities and of classmates who participated. Even when her teacher tried to encourage reading in books related to Jenny's interests, she balked. Her teacher noticed that Jenny liked animals and sensed that she would like to have a pet, so Jenny was made caretaker of the class hamster. At first, she expressed a lack of confidence; she was afraid she could not keep the hamster healthy. The teacher offered Jenny a small book on hamster care, but the child finally insisted that she really did not like hamsters.

Perplexed, her teacher invited Jenny's parents for a talk. She learned that Jenny—an only child—led a rather secluded life with no close friends in her neighborhood. "She becomes upset when she makes mistakes," Jenny's mother volunteered.

Jenny's teacher decided to involve Jenny in a project with two other children, giving them very clear and simple tasks at first. She praised Jenny for small steps and slowly added opportunities for increased success. Through a parent interview, the teacher got a clue that may be a very important beginning for the child. The teacher plans to find some interesting reading related to the project that Jenny can select as she becomes more involved and confident.

| Figure 2–2 | Suggestions for a Parent Interview |

1. Be prepared for the interview by being familiar with all the information you have available concerning the child and the instructional program.
2. Be certain to state your purpose (if you initiated the interview) and the nature of the information you are sharing and/or seeking.
3. Show respect and be sensitive to parent feelings.
4. Establish rapport as early as possible. One way to do this is by expressing your interest in the child.
5. Be sincere and honest.
6. Refrain from making value judgments of parents' statements.
7. Avoid technical jargon and be specific.
8. Rephrase what you say, if necessary, and address both parents equally.
9. Keep all information gained through the interview confidential.

Keep Informal Records

Using the four sources of information that have been discussed—observation, interest inventory, child interview, parent interview—you may be inclined to make mental notes of what you learn instead of written ones. This seems especially workable when you learn through observations. Eventually, however, some notation of what you learn, even through observation, should be put onto a record of the child's interests, needs, problems, and so on.

The child or parent interview is another instance where making mental notes is useful, since taking notes during an interview session might be interruptive. Afterward though, when the teacher has a chance, the important revelations that came from the interview ought to be recorded. Not only does this allow the teacher to refer to the record in planning future instruction but such information also has a way of indicating trends as it accumulates in an informal record.

Just as the information from observations and interviews is gathered together in some record-keeping system, the information about a child's interests and activities that is revealed through an interest inventory should also be recorded. Your notes and the child's responses can be summarized after you have had a chance to think about the information. For example, you may be able to discern an interest pattern from the inventory that runs through a child's choice of favorite television programs, comic strips, and after-school activities. If so, make a note of it.

One method for recording information is to keep a loose-leaf notebook for your class. Dividers can be used to make a separate section in the notebook for each child. Copies of record formats such as the one represented by Figure 2–3 and the one described on page 50 can be duplicated and kept for each child as you continuously gather and record information.

In addition to recording information about a child's interests, needs, and motivations, this record system can also be used to record information about a child's current reading level, specific reading skill needs, and growth in reading ability. How and what to observe in a child's reading will be discussed later in this chapter. At this point, the important thing to note is that a record-keeping system should contain what you want to remember about a child in order best to help him or her. Recording skill development and interests in one record system increases efficiency in planning reading instruction for a particular child.

Entries into your record system should be dated so you can determine changes and growth for each child. For example, are a child's interests changing; is another child becoming more or less of an active classroom participant; and how are the parent planning sessions helping? By periodically reviewing your records you can plan instruction that is directed to the changing and growing children in your classroom. These records reflect the ongoing informal assessments and become the blueprints for the instructional plans.

Some teachers find it useful to include both an objective description of a behavior and their interpretation or decision as to how to use the information. The reason for this is that if teachers record only observations, they may not try to understand the information and relate it to planning. On the other hand, if only interpretations of an observation are recorded, later misinterpretations are more likely.

Figure 2–3   Summary of Student Observations, Interviews, Interests

Name	Date	Source	Information	Decision
Donna	10/1	playground	can run! Looks like an outdoor leader	peer tutoring? more leadership opportunities
	10/5	classroom	expressed interest in Canadian vacation at Thanksgiving	find books! travel folders, maps, etc.
	11/1	Mrs. Hargrove (parent)	Donna needs "more classroom homework"	choose with Donna some learning games she'd like to take home
	11/7	interest inventory	favorite TV programs are sports, especially basketball; also spends many afternoons after school shooting baskets with several friends	could be a lead for reading materials
	11/10	interview with Donna	Donna spent a lot of time discussing her home life; she seems to be responsible for managing several younger siblings	stories dealing with various responsibilities faced by young girls may be an excellent possibility

This simple format allows the teacher to record information and then to consider its possible use.

It is also important to keep in mind that, like the reports a teacher gets on a child before ever teaching that child, the information the teacher gathers on the child is also somewhat subjective. As long as it is taken as a clue and not as truth, however, it is a valid attempt to learn and thus can be an important indicative reference.

One final caution must be added at this point. Informal record keeping for the sake of accumulating masses of data is an untenable way to get to know a child. For every scrap of information sought, there must be some positive, useful purpose. Does the information help you to understand the child better? Are you using the information to plan activities? To select reading materials? Do you merely record and put the record aside—or do you record and constantly refer to your records?

Informal record keeping is an excellent growth tool for the teacher. By regularly keeping records the teacher sharpens his or her skill in the following:

(1) capturing fleeting impressions in writing—turning objective descriptions into useful planning information

(2) noting clues or causes for behavior already recorded and relating the two

(3) judging details recorded from observation, inventories, and interviews both in the light of supporting or contradicting information and in the light of developing instructional needs—identifying patterns of behavior and analyzing their instructional implications

try this ▶

Observe a child—in a classroom and for several days, if possible—noting his or her behavior. Keep an informal record on the child, recording incidents that you think relate to how eagerly the child participates in activities and relates with peers. Note behavior that indicates interests the child may have.

Couple your observation with at least one of the following:

(1) an interview with the child about his or her interests

(2) the administration of an interest inventory. (You might want to construct your own inventory, use one another teacher has prepared, or use a published one.)

(3) an interview with one or both of the child's parents or guardians

Record the information you get from the second technique on the same record with the information from the observation. Then discuss the informal record you have started with some of your classmates to decide if you have learned enough to give any indications that might help you make such decisions as the topics the child might be interested in reading about.

Compare the information you gathered by each technique. Are the differences important? What seem to be the limitations of each technique?

Assessing the Child's Learning Environment

An important part of knowing about the children in your classroom is knowing their learning environment. This is important for two reasons. First, knowing the environment will help you to know better the children you will be teaching. Second, you need to know about the situation in which you will be teaching so you can make the most effective use of that situation. Informally taking stock of the environment should be an activity that is begun very early in the school year—preferably even before the first day of school.

What is the environment of the children? The learning environment is more than just the classroom and school building. The environment encompasses the instructional materials, the library, the other teachers, the attitudes of the administration, and a host of other factors. The learning environment also includes the community. What do the children do in their spare time? What recreational facilities are available? Do they have opportunities to interact after school? What are the things that the children seem to hold in esteem? Knowledge of the community from the adult's point of view is also important. What do the adults hope for from the schools? What do they believe about education? Where do the parents work? Where do they take their children for special trips? Or are they unable to take them on trips? Where are the adults apt to seek recreation?

Just as you have certain beliefs about the teaching of reading, you will work in a school and community that also have beliefs and biases. And the community has influenced its children's attitudes toward reading. Any area's economics, ethnic and racial mix, social advantages and limitations, and types of industry, for example, will all help determine what the children value and what their interests may be.

The school's facilities, the strength and availability of its library, and equipment can also influence learning. Other teachers in the school will provide the reading instruction for students in the grades preceding and following yours. A lifetime reader isn't nurtured in one school year; but, when you work in concert with a group of teachers who know and respect each other's beliefs, and who work with the parents and community, results can be achieved. You will want to study the school and the community to determine how to plan your program to complement rather than conflict with the child's environment.

In the sections that follow, we list and describe those things that we think are important for you to know about the child's environment. The first section deals with the immediate school environment; the second examines the community environment as viewed by the child and as viewed by the adult. Techniques for learning about the environment include observation and interview. You will want to talk with people, to ask questions, to listen, and to withhold judgments.

How the School Environment Affects Teaching and Learning

Your assessment of the school environment should help you provide the type of setting where children will learn to read because reading is part of their natural inquiry. In your initial information gathering, there are some key aspects of your school to consider.

The library.   The library potentially provides the most support for your reading program. One way to acquaint yourself with the library is to set aside some time on a weekly basis when you can go to the library and regularly review the books and materials. In addition, you may want to ask other teachers how they have utilized the services of the library and librarian. You can observe the reactions of the children when they visit the library, noting, for example, how they view it and use it. Discussions and observations such as these are valuable data-collecting procedures. They will begin to build your knowledge and appreciation of the library and how it can be used in your reading program.

Instructional materials.   In a very practical sense, materials make up an important part of the environment in any school. While we will discuss the need for and use of a variety of materials in Chapter 9, it is important to note here that in an initial assessment of the school, the teacher should quickly determine the availability of books and support materials and how they can be tapped for use inside and outside the classroom. We have already discussed assessing the resources of the library, but you also need to determine what books, equipment, and resource materials can be taken from the library (or other resource centers) and used for a period of time in your classroom.

Exactly what equipment will you have access to? Does your school provide phonographs, cassette tape recorders, film and filmstrip projectors with slide attachments, and so on? In many schools, teachers share such aids. In that case, you will have less flexibility in terms of planning, since the machines are not always nearby. To ensure having the equipment when you need it, you will need to plan ahead.

Not only should you be aware of the hardware (equipment) that is available but you should also acquaint yourself with the materials (software) that are available for use with them. The library may have a collection of filmstrips, slides, and records. Become familiar with check-out procedures from school and public libraries as well as from your state or regional education agencies. Check the typewriters that are available for your use. Is there a primary typewriter so that you can prepare materials for kindergarten and primary grades? These aids can help you to support and enrich your reading instruction.

Your classroom.   Examine your teaching space carefully in terms of its potential. How can it best be used? Is there space for a classroom library and a free-reading area? When there is a comfortable place for children to relax and read independently, they are most inclined to read. Can furniture in the room be arranged so there is room for different groups to be involved simultaneously without unduly disturbing others? Is there space where children can make puppets, construct dioramas, and paint pictures that deal with their reading selections? Having such facilities allows children to express their appreciation and comprehension

of reading materials in diverse ways. Organizing your classroom is discussed more extensively in Chapter 9.

Other teachers. Your professional colleagues are valuable sources of information about the school and its reading program. As you become acquainted with the school faculty, you should also be seeking answers to key questions that will influence the shape, scope, and expectations of your classroom instruction in reading. Familiarization with your fellow teachers' ideas and teaching strategies in reading will enable you to form a reading program that will complement theirs. You can also determine whether possibilities exist for team teaching or sharing instructional materials.

The administration. Administration refers to a large number of persons ranging from the principal of your particular school to the superintendent of the school district to the state department of education. Decisions made or not made by these persons can have direct bearing on your classroom program. You need to know the attitude of administrators toward reading instruction in the schools. Do they take an active interest? Have provisions been made for a curriculum guide in reading? Are there specific policies that are enforced?

Other resources. You need to become aware of other sources of aid and support that may be available to you. For example, there may be personnel employed to provide specialized diagnosis for children experiencing difficulty in reading. There may be a school reading teacher, a resource-room teacher with whom children evidencing various needs spend a portion of their day, and parent or teacher aides. By finding out early what help is available, you are most likely to make a smooth start.

Be aware, too, that the school staff—its secretaries, custodians, and cafeteria personnel—can support your teaching by helping you to use school facilities to their fullest.

How the Community Environment Affects Teaching and Learning

The division in the community in which you teach will be great. There will be families that represent many sociocultural backgrounds; the interests of various groups will differ; and the attitudes and values will certainly cover a wide spectrum. But the greatest differences will be between the community as seen from the children's eyes and that same community as seen through the eyes of the adults. You need to understand the community from both perspectives, although it will probably be more difficult for you to grasp that of the children. However, it is important that you understand both the differences in and the perspectives on your new community. For, if you are going to make reading a real activity for children, you need to know what their lives are like. You need to know what they experience so that your reading program can build on and enrich those experiences.

Another point to remember in attempting to understand a community is that you yourself are the product of a particular socioeconomic background that has influenced your values and expectations. Nevertheless, you need to be willing to understand, accept, and appreciate the backgrounds of a wide range of people.

Your study of the general community is not going to give you the information that you need for instructing individuals. The community or environment for each child is unique and you will need to learn about those individual differences as you get to know each child throughout the school year. What you can learn through a study of the community are the general values, interests, and activities of the children.

The child's point of view. We have all encountered the situation where we returned to our childhood surroundings after an absence to find that everything looked different. It is not always that the buildings, streets, stores, and neighbors have changed; it is that we are viewing that setting

from an entirely different perspective. You will need to be extremely perceptive and constantly observant to understand the difference in perspective of adult and child. Many adults are sure they understand what children believe. In fact, it is the rare adult who really is able to step out of his or her own adult world and view the world as a child. Usually such people are natural teachers.

Learning about the children's perspective on the community is very important. It will shape your selection of reading materials, the way you work with the children, and even the way you organize your classroom. Most important, it will help you to set realistic goals.

In assuming the child's point of view, there are four major aspects of their lives that you should examine. These factors are not discrete, but they will help you to discover important influences in the child's life as well as the vantage point from which he or she sees the community. You need to recognize, understand, and accept the child's language patterns, cultural patterns, attitudes, and interests.

How do you go about this task? Perhaps the best thing for you to do is to develop a list of questions that will guide your inquiry. The sample questions below may help you to generate your own list. Do the children use specific, unique phrases in their conversations? Do the children use unusual grammatical constructions? Do you know what these mean? Do the children use specific vocabulary words, such as slang expressions, that are unfamiliar to you? What holidays and other special days are of greatest importance to the children? Who are the children's heroes and heroines? On television? In the community? What makes a child a hero in the eyes of the other children? Where do the children spend their free time? Do the children join organized activities such as scouts, little league baseball, and others, or do they tend to plan their own activities? When? Where? What do the children see as their most important activities each day? What do they look forward to the most? There are obviously many other questions that could be added to this list. And any list of questions should reflect what you think is important to learn about in the children's lives.

The task of answering those questions is difficult. The best way is to listen to children and to observe them. Walking through a local park or along a street where they play can be very revealing. Ask them where they play each day and what they do. But don't pry or they will be put on guard or try to tell you what they think you want to hear.

The adult's point of view.   The importance of understanding the community as the child views it is obvious. You will be selecting certain materials and planning instruction as it relates to the life of the children. But why do you need to understand the community from the point of view of the adult?

The adult community greatly influences the school and the children. The children frequently reflect the attitudes of the adults. You will need to be responsive to those attitudes. Most important, perhaps, you need to know the kinds of experiences that the parents can and will provide for the children. Three factors that you should consider in examining the community include the following:

(1) cultural backgrounds
(2) attitudes toward education
(3) recreation

As in your study of the child's community, here, too, you will have many questions. A few might include: What are the predominant cultural and ethnic influences in the community? Do these provide any indication of the kinds of reading materials you might select? Do the parents generally support the school or are they antagonistic or intimidated by it? Is the community going through a transition period? Have the parents supported special bond issues? Do they attend parent meetings? Do they seem willing to provide extra help for their children at home? How do the parents view education? Have the parents been involved in establishing the goals for their schools? What do the parents do with and for their children in recreation time? Do they take the children on trips? Where do the adults spend their free time? Are there family activities?

By being aware of the community, you will know where to turn for help and the kind of help you can expect. You will know when there is a difference between the goals for reading as you have defined them and as the parents define them. You will know whether the parents have been expressing strong opinions about school philosophy, curriculum, or methodology. Your study of the adult community is important also, because you will serve the parents and the community.

Getting to Know the Child's Reading Ability: Three Levels of Reading

Another primary concern and first step toward using assessment to become a diagnostic* teacher of reading is to determine how well (or if) each child reads. "How well" can be defined as the level of the reading material the child can handle successfully. Not long ago, most teachers assumed that if they received a third-grade teaching assignment, they merely distributed the third-grade readers and their reading program had begun. The task was simply one of moving some third-graders more rapidly and some more slowly through the grade-level material. Perhaps a few children had to reread or complete last year's book. Thus, the teacher made the assigned text do for several levels of readers. A first-grade teacher had but to assume that once the children had completed the reading readiness workbook, they were on their way. The truth was that some children didn't need the readiness workbook and were mark-

---

* All teachers should be *diagnostic* teachers. That is, they need to assess students' achievements as a basis for planning instruction. Good teaching is diagnostic teaching and in this chapter the diagnostic aspects of teaching are emphasized.

ing time, others needed only parts of it, while still others weren't yet ready for it. Our point is this: reading materials must be adjusted to the reading level of each child; the child should not be forced to adjust to the reading materials. A class of children does not come to you needing only the application of one text—or even two or three books, for that matter. Passing out third-grade books to the third-grade class will not gear the program to the specific skills and abilities of all the children in that class.

A question that logically follows is this: How can I tell what material fits the child's reading level? A correlate question is: If the grade-level materials don't "fit," what can be done about it? The solution lies in acquiring the necessary skills to determine each child's reading level in order to decide what level of material could be used for instruction. Thus, to the best of his or her ability, the teacher can instruct individuals, using a variety of reading materials that fit the instructional reading levels of each child.

The instructional reading level is often described as the center of a continuum that encompasses a range of difficulty for a reader. The continuum goes from the level that is easy for the reader and that can be read *independently* to the reading level that becomes too difficult, or *frustrating,* for the reader.

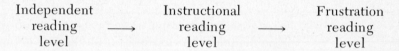

Independent level.   The child's independent reading level is determined by the material he or she handles with ease and efficiency. With material at an independent level, the child's oral reading sounds fluent, indicating that he or she not only recognizes words but is probably comprehending as well. Material at this level is a good choice for the child's free-time reading. Wide reading at the independent level enables the child to apply the skills he or she has acquired.

Instructional level.   The instructional reading level is defined as the level of material at which a child could most profitably read—that is, difficult enough so that some instruction is necessary, but easy enough so that the reading is not frustrating. Marjorie Johnson and Roy Kress state that the child reading at his instructional level "should encounter no more difficulty than can reasonably be expected to be overcome through good instruction" (1965, p. 9). This implies, of course, that a child may read the selection at his or her improved independent level after instruction occurs.

Frustration level.   The frustration level is the point at which the reading becomes too difficult for the child. Frustration is generally characterized by a drop in oral reading fluency, by many word-recognition errors, and by a concomitant drop in comprehension. In short, the child labors over the reading task. There may even be physical signs of frustration including lip movement, finger pointing, rhythmic body motion—kicking, tapping, swaying—and other manifestations of anxiety.

Not every reader has three reading levels.* Beginning readers may have no independent level; more capable readers may be independent at several levels. In such cases, the independent level is defined as the highest book level at which a child reads fluently and with little need for assistance (McCracken, 1967).

Determining the Instructional Level with Informal Reading Inventories

In determining the instructional reading level of a child, a teacher is, simply, finding a good "fit" of material for the child. To have the child read only at his or her independent level would not promote reading growth. To provide material that is too difficult is to frustrate the reader.

To arrive at the instructional level, the teacher has the child "try on" some materials for size—to see how they fit that individual reader. Two common techniques for doing this are an *Informal Reading Inventory* (IRI) and the *cloze technique.* Informal reading inventories are discussed here, and the cloze technique is discussed on page 71.

An informal reading inventory is a method or process of discovering the most appropriate level of materials for each child's reading instruction. An informal reading inventory usually consists of from 25- to 100-word selections chosen from each level of a particular graded or basal reading series.†

Some basal reader publishers provide IRI's with their evaluation materials. (See the example on pages 40–41.) In addition, there are several independently published versions available to the teacher (McCracken, 1966, and Silvaroli, 1973).

---

* Some authorities describe a fourth level, the capacity level. This is the level at which the child should have the ability to read if he or she were given appropriate reading instruction. The capacity level is usually determined by reading a story to a child and asking questions to determine how well the child has understood the story. We believe there are too many problems in assessing capacity and are very concerned that capacity can be taken as a self-fulfilling prophecy—or even worse, as an excuse for not helping a child become a more able reader. We believe you should determine a child's instructional reading level and, regardless of capacity, provide the child with the most appropriate instruction you can plan.

† Basal reading series traditionally had three preprimers, a primer, and a first-grade reader. These were followed by a 2^1 reader (first half of second grade), a 2^2 reader (second half of second grade), a 3^1 reader, a 3^2 reader, and one book for each of the fourth, fifth, and sixth grades. Currently, however, many publishing companies are leveling the books with number or letter designations—for example, levels one through seven, or A through H. Publishers' levels do not always correspond equivalently, and some teachers still feel a need to ask for a translation to the traditional "grading" system.

SAY: Find page 4 in your book. At the top are six rows of words. Let's see how well you know them. Start with the top row and tell me all the words in each row. If you don't know a word, just say "I don't know." See how quickly you can go. Ready. Start.

SAY: Below the words you just named and on the next page is a story told with pictures and with sentences that tell what the animals said. Each little picture shows who said the sentences beside it. Read the story to yourself, and find out how Kangaroo, the dentist, changed her ideas about lions. When you finish, close your book. Then I'll ask you some questions.

1.	school	am	day	play	take
2.	one	there	want	look	for
3.	my	at	now	be	out
4.	your	what	this	do	no
5.	work	of	that	run	where
6.	big	away	did	how	find

Lion   Frog   Kangaroo   Rabbit

 What can we do, Lion?

Kangaroo will not work on lions and tigers.

She is scared of big teeth.

 I have to get help for my teeth, Frog,

It's no fun to be sick.

 I have it! You can be a rabbit.

Kangaroo works on rabbits.

Get this rabbit <u>suit</u> on.

4

10   Level D • FOOTPRINTS

The material on these two pages is used by the teacher to help determine a child's reading level. The words in the box at the top of the page are read aloud by the child so the teacher can determine his or her word recognition. The story is read silently by the student and the teacher checks his or her comprehension by asking the questions in the left-hand margin (L indicates a literal question; C indicates a question that requires the child to draw conclusions, make inferences, or predict outcomes; D indicates a question to determine if the child has decoded a new word in context; M indicates a

QUESTIONS

L: Why wouldn't Kangaroo
work on lions and tigers?
(because they have big teeth)

C: What was the matter with
Lion? *(His teeth hurt.)*

D: How did Frog get Kangaroo
to look at Lion's teeth? *(He got
Lion to put on a rabbit suit.)*

M: Was Kangaroo still afraid
of big teeth after she fixed
Lion's teeth? *(No)* Why, or
why not? *(because Lion had a
nice smile and looked funny)*

L: How many of Lion's teeth
did Kangaroo pull out? *(none)*

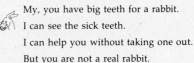 My, you have big teeth for a rabbit.

I can see the sick teeth.

I can help you without taking one out.

But you are not a real rabbit.

I can see that.

 I'm a lion.

And you do not work on lions.

I did have to get help.

Your big teeth didn't scare me, Lion.

And you have a nice smile now.

You are a funny-looking lion.

5

Level D • FOOTPRINTS   11

main-idea question). There are other stories and word recognition tasks that represent
the other instructional levels in the Houghton Mifflin program. Most basal reader publishers include some type of reading inventory—although there are many variations.

Informal Reading Inventory

In *The Informal Reading Inventory*, published by the International Reading Association, Johnson and Kress define an IRI:

> The term *informal reading inventory* is one in our language which expresses three fundamental concepts with three words. Consider first the basic noun in the title. This technique of evaluating a child's performance is an inventory in the sense that it is a detailed study of his whole performance in the reading area and those language and thinking functions related to reading. The second major concept is that of reading itself. In the label informal reading inventory, the function reading is widely conceived. The interest is not in mere pronunciation of words, but also in the manipulation of ideas which are represented by these words. Finally, the technique is an informal one in that specific methods are not standardized, and no norms have been established for performance to be compared with what other students can do (1965, p. 3).

Constructing Your Own IRI

If the basal series available to you don't include an informal reading inventory—or if you are not satisfied with those that are included—you can build your own. You may decide that your IRI would be more effective because you can best select passages that will capture and hold the interest of your readers.

To construct an IRI, passages are selected from each level of a basal series. The selections must make sense in and of themselves without being dependent for meaning upon preceding or subsequent material. Some builders of informal reading inventories select passages from both the beginning and near the end of a book in order to get an even closer estimate of fit. When only one passage is selected from a book, there is a chance that the particular passage may be easier or more difficult than the rest of the material in the book. When two passages are selected and used, the possibility of selecting unrepresentative material is reduced considerably. The selected passages may be marked directly in the book or may be photocopied or typed so that both teacher and student have a copy of the material.

An example of an IRI that a teacher might construct from a published basal series is given on pages 53–64, along with questions the teacher has written to assess comprehension at each of the difficulty levels.*

A step-by-step guide that will help you to build an informal reading inventory follows.

* A thorough discussion of question types that promote different kinds of thinking is included in Chapter 7.

Step one: Choosing the materials.   Choose a system of basal readers. Any standard system will do, but it makes sense to choose a series from which the child is likely to be reading.

Locate the basic texts from preprimer one through grade six.*

Step two: Choosing the selections.   Choose a selection from each book. Depending upon the difficulty of the series, either twenty-five to fifty words or one complete story (if it is shorter) is sufficient to take from each of the preprimers. Choose about fifty words from the primer and the first-reader level and one hundred words from each succeeding book. (You may choose two selections from each book—one from the beginning and one from near the end for an even closer approximation of reading level.)

Check to be certain that each paragraph makes sense—that is, it is a complete selection.

Lightly mark in the book the passages to be read. Put a paper clip on the page for ease of location and make a copy for yourself so that you can follow along and mark as the child reads. Or, you might want to copy the selected paragraphs from the books, using a photocopier, typewriter, or any other process that provides legibility. A photocopy has one distinct advantage, however: it retains the pictures and thus provides clues for the lower-level materials.

You will need a copy of the material because you will be keeping a record as the child reads to you.

Step three: Building the questions.   Write five to ten questions that will check the child's understanding of the passages.

Some guidelines for building questions:

Avoid questions requiring a simple "yes" or "no" answer. Such questions are guessed correctly half the time and they reveal little of a child's understanding of a story.

Try to question for main idea, important details, and predictions.

You may want to include a question requiring critical thinking or judgment.

Only you get a copy of the questions. They are usually asked orally after each passage is read, and the child's answers can be discussed. In fact, this discussion or the child's ability to retell the story often provides more insight into the child's understanding of the story than response to a question alone.

---

* If you are not sure of the reading levels of the books, consult the teacher's manual for each of the books.

Administering and Interpreting Your IRI

Administering an IRI should be a relaxed experience for you and the child. You should not approach the situation as if you were testing to determine a report-card grade or irrevocably labeling the child a third- or fourth-grade reader. Rather, you are trying to find a reading level that seems to be comfortable for the child—the best level to begin reading instruction.

You should remember that in administering an IRI you are trying to get an overall assessment of how well the child reads and understands various selections. The percentages given in Figure 2–6 (see page 49) for word recognition and comprehension are merely guides, and your judgment should be the final determination of the best instructional level for the child. The initial judgment of instructional level need not be perfectly on target for each reader. If you make a mistake and place a reader at the "wrong" level, you will discover the misjudgment when you hear the child read from that particular book and you can adjust the level immediately.

Beginning with the passage either at the preprimer level or at one level below the teacher's estimate of the child's independent reading level, the child reads either silently or orally. Most IRIs are administered by asking the child to read the selection orally. It is possible to have the passages read only silently; in that case, instructional reading level is determined only by the child's comprehension, since there is, of course, no way to record silent-reading word-recognition errors. Some teachers use two passages at each reading level and ask the child to read one orally and one silently.

For children who are likely to read at or below the third-grade level, it is better to have the passages read orally. For children reading from the third-grade level to the fifth-grade level, useful information can be obtained by having passages read both orally and silently. For children whose likely reading level is at or above the sixth-grade level, the selections should probably be read silently. Obviously, a more complete initial picture of a child's reading can be determined at all levels if the child reads two passages, one silently, one orally. However, this is not always feasible in terms of teacher time.

The discussion on the following pages is based on the assumption that you will be asking the child to read orally. We are using an oral example in order to discuss and explain the recording of word-recognition errors. As the child reads aloud, the teacher marks the child's oral reading errors (or miscues).* After reading, the child demonstrates his or

---

* *Miscue* is a term that has grown out of the research of Kenneth Goodman and his associates. The term *miscue* is used here to describe a child's oral reading errors such as leaving out a word, inserting an extra word, or mispronouncing a word. Goodman has demonstrated that these errors—or miscues, as he calls them—can be used to understand a child's reading. We prefer Goodman's use of *miscue* to the less positive term *error*, and will use it throughout this book.

her grasp (or comprehension) of the material by answering questions, by retelling the material, or through discussion with the teacher.

Here are some important points to remember in administering and interpreting an IRI.

When you are ready to administer the IRI, first talk easily with the child to make the atmosphere pleasant and relaxed, and thus ensure valid results.

Ask the child to read the first paragraph. Always give a purpose for reading.

Mark the miscues and symptoms as you hear them.

Mark the answers offered to comprehension questions or the detail recalled in retelling.

Stop when the reader sounds (or looks) frustrated.

Count the miscues and comprehension errors. Interpret reading levels using the percentages offered in Figure 2–6 (page 49) coupled with (or tempered by) your best judgments.

Learning a marking system to record miscues.   As many points in the list demonstrate, an important aspect of administering an IRI is the recording of the information it reveals. To record miscues, the teacher must learn and practice a system for marking them on the text as the child reads orally. Some of the more common miscues are:

A *substitution* occurs. A child substitutes another word or a portion of a word.

A word is *told* to the child after a reasonable pause (from five to ten seconds).

An *omission* occurs. Either a word, word part, phrase, or complete line is left out.

A word is *inserted* into the context by the reader even though it does not appear in print.

These miscues are further explained in Figure 2–4.

Figure 2–4 | Four Common Miscues—Their Markings and Interpretations

Miscue Type	Example
Substitution	Child reads *party* for *purple* in the phrase "the purple hat."
Word told	Child pauses before the word *purple* and says nothing; time elapses and finally you tell the word.
Omission	Child leaves out the word *purple* in the phrase.
Insertion	Child inserts the word *big* before "purple hat."

Recognizing some non-miscues. Some possible symptoms of oral-reading difficulty are usually *not* interpreted as miscues.

When the reader repeats words or phrases, it can signal the possibility that the material is becoming too difficult or that the reader is "revving up" on the recognized portion to gain momentum for an attack on the unknown. In the latter case, there is reason to recognize the behavior as a strength: the reader recognizes and is using the context. Repetitions are not generally counted as miscues; some authorities, however, recommend that the cumulation of several repetitions be counted as one miscue.

A reader who pauses before an unknown word and either waits to be told or attempts the word only with much sputtering and difficulty is demonstrating a symptom of oral-reading difficulty. Consistent hesitations make for awkward phrasing, reduced fluency, and, sometimes, less comprehension. The hesitations are not counted as miscues, but they give information that the child is having some difficulty reading the material.

A reader who switches the order of words may not necessarily be affecting the sense of the passage. When the reversal in word order does not affect the meaning, it indicates that the reader has understood the passage and has merely reordered the words into a syntax that is more familiar. (When word order changes do affect the meaning, the change

Mark It	*Interpret it*
party the (purple) hat Circle the word or portion of the word that is substituted. Write the substitution above the word(s) on which the miscue occurs.	Before counting the substitution as a miscue, consider whether the substitution fits the grammar and meaning of the context (syntax and semantics). Both *party* and *purple* describe the hat, and both are grammatically correct, but the meaning of the passage may be altered if the purple hat was not a party hat.
the ~~purple~~ hat Draw a line through the word that is told.	Count as a miscue when the word told is not a proper noun. Count the same word only once even though you may retell it.
the (purple) hat Circle the word (or words) that were omitted.	Count as a miscue only when the omission significantly alters the sense of the passage.
big the ∧ purple hat Write the inserted word above the area where it occurs and mark the insertion with a caret.	Count as a miscue only when the insertion significantly alters the meaning of the passage.

ought to be considered a miscue.) These non-miscues are further explained in Figure 2–5.

Recording comprehension responses. The reader's answers to the comprehension questions, which you have developed to accompany the selections read by the child, should be recorded as simply as possible. A plus mark (+) for each correct response is adequate. Incorrect answers should be noted; later, these errors can give you information about the question types that trouble the reader, ways in which the reader may interpret the questions, and why a reader may answer in a particular way. If a child answers part of a question, give credit for the amount of understanding the response seems to indicate to you, such as "½" or "¼." As you become more comfortable with the IRI as a process, you will be able to vary from the question-answer format to asking a reader to retell or discuss a passage. When you reach that stage of experience, you will probably subjectively judge the reader's understanding of the selection.

You may want to probe beyond the basic question to determine whether the child is not responding merely because of shyness or because the question has not been understood. You want to determine how much of the selection the child understands—not how many questions are answered absolutely correctly.

Figure 2–5 | Possible Symptoms of Oral-Reading Difficulty

Symptom	Mark It
Repetition	the rocking horse Draw a wavy line under the part that is repeated.
Hesitation	the rocking|horse Use parallel slash marks to indicate hesitation before words.
Reversal	the rocking|horse Use an inverted line to indicate change in word order.

Determining Reading Levels with the IRI

As we indicated earlier, the primary purpose for administering an IRI is to determine a student's instructional reading level (see Figure 2–6). This is done by determining the student's percentage of correct word recognition and comprehension for each of the passages read. Figure 2–7 shows how these percentages are calculated for one selection. For example, suppose the following passages were read with the accompanying results:

Difficulty Level of Passages	Percentage of Word Recognition	Percentage of Comprehension
P(primer)	98 percent	90 percent
1	100 percent	85 percent
2^1	95 percent	80 percent
2^2	90 percent	75 percent
3^1	80 percent	50 percent

If you had listened to a student read these passages, you probably would have stopped the reader after the 3^1 passage because at that level the student was experiencing frustration. Notice that the percentages above don't neatly fit the criteria from Figure 2–6; the percentages almost never do, and that is why your judgment is crucial. Your trained ear will also begin to help you determine when a student is reading at an instructional level.

In the particular example above, the student's frustration level may be 2^2 or 3^1; the instructional reading level may be 2^1, and the independent reading level is first grade. When determining reading levels, it is best to estimate to the lower level when there is doubt between two levels. The goal is to place each student at a level at which he or she can experience rapid success.

Figure 2–6 | Reading Levels that Can Be Determined Through an Informal Reading Inventory

Level	Description	Word Recognition	Comprehension
Independent	Highest level at which child can read without assistance; reading is smooth, efficient; child reads with ease	Recognizes 99 percent of the words	Answers 90 percent of accompanying questions
Instructional	Material is challenging but not too difficult; instruction should take place here	Recognizes 95 percent of the words	Answers 70 percent of accompanying questions
Frustration	Child is frustrated by the reading task; many errors; drop in fluency	Recognizes fewer than 90 percent of the words	Answers fewer than 50 percent of accompanying questions

The percentages provided here are only suggestions and should not be used in any absolute sense. An informal reading inventory should be a guide to instruction and not a device for labelling children. While researchers may study and debate the use of various percentage criteria, you should remember the goal is to determine the level at which the child can profit from instruction.

Figure 2–7 | Calculating Percentages of Word Recognition and Comprehension

Word Recognition — *Sample*

Take the number of miscues on a particular passage — 7
Divide by the number of words in the total passage — ÷100

$$100 \overline{)\,7.00}^{\,.07}$$

Subtract the quotient from 1.00

$$\begin{array}{r} 1.00 \\ -\ .07 \\ \hline .93 \end{array}$$ Word Recognition = 93 percent

Comprehension

Take the number of incorrect answers for a particular passage — 2
Divide by the number of questions — ÷ 10

$$10 \overline{)\,2.00}^{\,.20}$$

Subtract the quotient from 1.00

$$\begin{array}{r} 1.00 \\ -\ .20 \\ \hline .80 \end{array}$$ Comprehension = 80 percent

IRI Information Is Part of a Student's Record

After determining the independent and instructional reading level for a student, that information should be added to the informal record that the teacher is keeping for that child. Earlier, we mentioned that teachers should not continue compiling information on a learner when it is not contributing to reasonable instructional decisions. It is equally valid to stress that this information is not stored but should be actively retrieved and updated daily. As we noted in our discussion of records about interests, needs, problems, and motivations, some teachers find it helpful to use a loose-leaf notebook with a divider section for each child. Thus, for each child the teacher would record the interest inventory and an analysis of an informal reading inventory. Space would be left for continued use of the techniques of the informal reading inventory—hearing oral reading selections regularly, and systematically recording patterns of need—as well as for results of observations, interviews, and other records—books that the child has read, is reading, and so on.

Figure 2–8　　Keeping a Record System

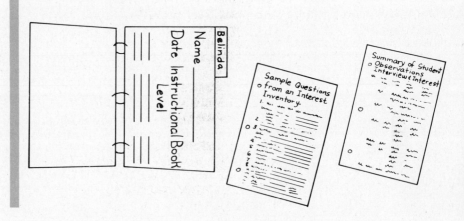

The advantages of systematic, informal record-keeping are:

(1) Flexibility—information can be collected when and if the teacher sees fit to do so.

(2) Usefulness—no information need be collected if it is not deemed instructionally useful in the specific reading program the teacher designs.

(3) Child-centeredness—information proceeds from the child to the selection and use of appropriate materials.

(4) Timeliness—information is current, because the process is continuous, rather than dependent upon beginning-and-end-of-the-year test scores.

(5) Accessibility—pertinent information for an individual child is always handy.

Questions about Assessing with the IRI

You may have questions about trying out an Informal Reading Inventory. We have tried to anticipate and to answer some of them.

Question	*Answer*
(1) What do I do if a miscue seems to be a function of dialect? (For example, the child omits endings, substitutes a different verb form, or produces a variant pronunciation?)	(1) Do *nothing* with dialect differences that appear in oral reading. If the reading act means communication, then we must not be concerned that every word be "pronounced correctly."
(2) What do I do with a miscue that makes sense? (For example, the story repeated *giant fish* several times and then dropped *giant* but the child inserted it.)	(2) Any miscue (insertion, omission, substitution) that retains the meaning and fits the grammatical structure of the passage should *not* be counted as a miscue.
(3) What do I do if word recognition approaches 100 percent accuracy, but the child's reading is labored and tedious?	(3) Stop. Informal reading inventories are not intended to be painful applications. Start instruction one level lower and concentrate on fluency.
(4) What do I do if word recognition indicates the child has reached frustration level, yet comprehension indicates he or she is still reading at an independent or instructional level?	(4) Stop when *either* word recognition or comprehension indicates frustration. Instruction can begin at the highest level where *neither* word recognition nor comprehension creates frustration.
(5) What if I put the child at the wrong instructional level?	(5) Relax. The IRI is not a test; it is a process. You will be employing these skilled listening techniques every time you hear a sample of the child's reading. You can adjust upward, downward, or horizontally into a more appropriate level.
(6) Can I tape record oral reading samples to make certain I catch everything?	(6) Certainly. But be sure that the reader is at ease with the presence of the recorder.

(7) How do I interpret the miscues and/or comprehension difficulties?

(7) See pages 65–71 of this chapter.

(8) How long should it take me to administer informal reading inventories to my entire class?

(8) It depends upon you and your class. You will get more skillful with more practice, and you will also get to be a better estimator of level. For example, a child who you know reads well doesn't have to start at level one or preprimer one. He or she can begin reading just below your estimate of the instructional level. Some teachers complete the initial inventories within a time span of two weeks to one month.

(9) What will I do with the other children while I am listening to one read?

(9) That depends, too. It depends upon whether you are using a silent or oral-reading inventory. (Silent-reading inventories can be administered in groups.) It also depends upon the maturity of your students and the kinds of activities they can do independently. The value of their independent activities depends upon the types of materials that are available to you.

The Teacher-Made IRI

On pages 53–64 is an example—from preprimer level to sixth-grade level—of a teacher-made informal reading inventory that was developed from the *Bookmark* series.* First, the inventory is presented (pages 53–64); then on pages 65–71 we shall give a sample interpretation of the inventory.

* Selections and art from *The Bookmark Reading Program,* 2d ed., by Margaret Early et al., reprinted and reproduced by permission of Harcourt Brace Jovanovich, Inc.; © 1974 by Harcourt Brace Jovanovich, Inc.

Selection 1

**Reading Level—
Preprimer 1**

Sun Up

The sun was up.
Sandy was up.
Bing was up.
The sun was up.
Good morning, sun.
Good morning, Sandy.
Good morning, Bing.
Good morning, Sandy and Bing.
Good morning, Bing and Sandy.
Bing was in the sun.
Sandy was in the sun.

Number of words ___43___

Student's percentage of word recognition _____

Student's percentage of comprehension _____

**Comprehension Questions
to Accompany Preprimer 1**

Who is this story about?
Were Sandy and Bing people? How do you know?
Where was Bing?
Where was Sandy?
What time of day do you think it is--morning or
    evening?

Some teachers like to pencil in the answers to the questions so they will be
immediately available.

From *Sun Up* by Margaret Early et al. (New York: Harcourt Brace Jovanovich, 1974), pp. 5–13.

Selection 2

Reading Level— Preprimer 2

In the Morning Sun

Bing was in the morning sun.
Sandy was in the morning sun.
Bing and Sandy sat in the grass.
A little rabbit jumped in the grass.
Sandy jumped up and went after the rabbit.
The rabbit ran away and hid.
The rabbit was lost in the grass.
Bing ran to Sandy.
Bing and Sandy ran up and down the hill.
Bing and Sandy ran to the pond.
Bing and Sandy sat in the morning sun.

Number of words __75__

Student's percentage of word recognition _____

Student's percentage of comprehension _____

Comprehension Questions to Accompany Preprimer 2

Where were Bing and Sandy?
What little animal jumped in the grass?
What did Sandy do when he saw the rabbit?
What did the rabbit do?
Did Bing and Sandy find the rabbit? How do you know?

From *A Happy Morning* by Margaret Early et al. (New York: Harcourt Brace Jovanovich, 1974), pp. 5–7.

Selection 3

**Reading Level—
Preprimer 3**

Little House in the Shadows

Morning was over.
The afternoon sun was on the grass.
A big bee went up and up in the afternoon sun.
The bee went on and was lost in the shadows.
In the shadows was a house.
It was a very, very little house.
The big bee went over the house.
The bee looked down but did not see the little house.
The house in the shadows was Mr. Fig's house.
Mr. Fig was very little.
Little Mr. Fig was happy in the little house.
The little house in the shadows was a magic house.
Mr. Fig was magic.
Mr. Fig had a hat, and the hat was magic.

Number of words ___109___

Student's percentage of word recognition _____

Student's percentage of comprehension _____

**Comprehension Questions
to Accompany Preprimer 3**

What time of day was it?
Why did the bee get lost?
What did the bee see?
Where was the house?
What might be in a magic house?

From *A Magic Afternoon* by Margaret Early et al. (New York: Harcourt Brace Jovanovich, 1974), pp. 5–8.

Selection 4

Reading Level—Primer

Sun Down

Down, down, down went the sun.
The sun went down in the sky.
The sun went down over the pond.
The sun went down over the hill.
The afternoon was over.
Jill was at Stan's house.
Stan and Jill sat on the grass.
They looked up at the sky.
"The sun is down," said Stan.
"It will get dark."
"Yes," said Jill.
"It will get dark fast."
A little star came into the sky.
The star was a little light in the sky.
A light went on in Stan's house.
But Jill's house was still dark.
A car went to Jill's house.
Jill said, "That is Mother!
I see Mother in that car."

Number of words _113_

Student's percentage of word recognition _____

Student's percentage of comprehension _____

Comprehension Questions to Accompany Primer

Where was Jill?
What time of day was it now?
What came out in the sky?
Where did the car go ?
Who was in the car?
Why were the lights out in Jill's house?

From *Sun and Shadow* by Margaret Early et al. (New York: Harcourt Brace Jovanovich, 1974), pp. 7–10.

Selection 5

Reading Level— First Reader

Going to School

The boy with the lunch box is Ben.
Ben lives in a small house.
He lives far away from the city.
It is morning, and Ben is going to school.
He rides to school in the bus that comes up the road.
Ben likes to go to school.
Some days he brings things to school for his friends to see.
Ben's school is small, but the school yard is big.
After lunch, Ben plays in the big yard with his friends.
When school is over for the day, the school bus comes back.
Then Ben rides back to his house.

Number of words _100_

Student's percentage of word recognition _____

Student's percentage of comprehension _____

Comprehension Questions to Accompany First Reader

Who is the boy with the lunch box?
Where does Ben live?
Why does he have to get there that way?
What does Ben do after lunch?
How are Ben's school and house alike?

From *Together We Go* by Margaret Early et al. (New York: Harcourt Brace Jovanovich, 1974), pp. 6–7.

Selection 6

Reading Level—
2¹ Reader

Linda's Smile

Linda was a happy little girl. But this morning Linda did not look happy at all. She did not smile as she walked up the hill to school.

Before long, Linda met Pam. Pam was Linda's very best friend.

When Pam saw Linda, she asked, "Linda, are you mad at me?"

Linda still did not show her smile. "No, I'm not mad," she said. "I just can't smile now. I have a surprise for show-and-tell."

"Oh, good!" cried Pam, who liked surprises. "I'll tell the others."

Pam ran into the school yard to the other children. "Linda said she won't smile," said Pam.

Number of words *105*

Student's percentage of word recognition _____

Student's percentage of comprehension _____

Comprehension Questions
to Accompany 2¹ Reader

Who was Pam?
What did Pam ask Linda when she saw her?
What did Linda tell Pam?
How did Pam feel about the surprise?
What may be Linda's surprise?

From *A World of Surprises* by Margaret Early et al. (New York: Harcourt Brace Jovanovich, 1974), pp. 14–15. Adapted from "Lucy Couldn't Smile." From *Jack and Jill* Magazine, copyright © 1965 by the Curtis Publishing Company.

Selection 7

Reading Level— 2² Reader

The Painted House

The funny little smile on Father's face was something to see. He was having the best time ever, painting his house.

"Yes, that's what I'll paint next," he said to himself. "I'll paint a band of blue for the sky. Then I'll make big splashes of white for the clouds. Then maybe I'll paint silly pictures all over the house."

Before long Mother came into the yard. How she laughed when she saw what Father was doing.

"This will be an odd-looking house," Mother said. "But what a grand idea!"

Mother got some bright yellow paint. She scrunched down on the ground and began to paint flowers on the house.

Number of words _///_

Student's percentage of word recognition _____

Student's percentage of comprehension _____

Comprehension Questions to Accompany 2² Reader

What was Father doing?
What was Father going to paint on the house?
What did Mother do when she saw what Father was doing?
What did Mother paint on the house?
Why do you think Mother and Father might want to paint flowers?

From *Going Places, Seeing People* by Margaret Early et al. (New York: Harcourt Brace Jovanovich, 1974), pp. 8–9.

59

Andy and Mr. Wagner

Andy Brooks sat on the stairs thinking. He was thinking about a dog because he wanted a dog.

Andy had wanted a dog for a long time. And he knew just what kind of dog he wanted. His dog would be a beautiful dog, not too big and not too little. He would have big brown eyes and reddish-brown fur. Best of all, he would have a long, fluffy tail.

Andy even had a name for his dog. He would call the dog Mr. Wagner.

"Mom," Andy called as he jumped up and ran into the house. "When can I have a dog? When can I get Mr. Wagner?"

Mrs. Brooks looked at Andy. "I don't have time to take care of a dog now. When your baby sister is older, I'll have more time. Then maybe you can have your dog."

Number of words   *143*

Student's percentage of word recognition _____

Student's percentage of comprehension _____

**Comprehension Questions
to Accompany 3¹ Reader**

Why was Andy thinking about a dog?
How long had Andy wanted a dog?
What kind of dog did he want?
Where was Andy's Mother?
When did Andy's Mother say he could have a dog?

From *Widening Circles* by Margaret Early et al. (New York: Harcourt Brace Jovanovich, 1974), pp. 8–9. Adapted from *Andy and Mr. Wagner* by Gina Bell. Copyright © 1957 by Abington Press. Used by permission.

The Old Woman and the Tramp

A tramp was once making his way through a forest. He had little hope of finding a place to stay before night set in. But all of a sudden, he saw bright lights shining between the trees. He discovered a cottage with a fire burning in the fireplace. How good it would be, he thought, to warm himself before that blaze, and to find a bite of food! So he went over to the cottage.

An old woman came to the door.

"Good evening, and well met!" said the tramp.

"Good evening," said the woman. "And where do you come from?"

"South of the sun, and east of the moon," said the tramp. "And now I am on the way home again, for I have been all over the world."

Number of words _130_

Student's percentage of word recognition _____

Student's percentage of comprehension _____

Comprehension Questions
to Accompany 3² Reader

Where was the tramp walking?
What did he discover as he was walking?
What was the weather like outside?
Who came to the door?
Where did the tramp say he was from?
Where did the tramp say he had been?
Do you think this may be a made-up story? Why?

From *Ring Around the World* by Margaret Early et al. (New York: Harcourt Brace Jovanovich, 1974), pp. 10–11. Adapted from *Favorite Fairy Tales Told in Sweden* by Virginia Haviland (Boston: Little, Brown, 1966).

Selection 10

Reading Level—
Fourth Reader

Getting to Know the Big Cats

It was six o'clock in the morning and just getting light. I ran into the tent containing the training cage. Mr. Chavan would be waiting there to give me my first lesson in training wild animals.

As I burst into the tent, my eyes traveled quickly to the cage to see which animals were to be my pupils. I stopped so fast I nearly fell down. My high spirits suddenly collapsed and I thought my uncle had arranged with Mr. Chavan to trick me. Mr. Chavan had not yet arrived, but there, in the center of the training cage, were two small lion cubs. They were hardly three months old and the size of big house cats. I was so disappointed I wanted to cry. Only my realization that animal trainers *don't* cry kept me from it.

Number of words __137__

Student's percentage of word recognition _____

Student's percentage of comprehension _____

Comprehension Questions to Accompany Fourth Reader

What time of day does this story begin?
Why was the boy meeting Mr. Chavan?
What was in the cage?
Why was the boy disappointed?
What kept the boy from crying?

From *Goals in Reading* by Margaret Early et al. (New York: Harcourt Brace Jovanovich, 1974), pp. 25–26. From "Getting to Know the Big Cats" adapted from *Wild Animal Man* by Damoo Dhotre and Richard J. Taplinger. Copyright © 1961 by Damoo Dhotre and Richard J. Taplinger. Reprinted by permission of Taplinger Press.

Space Stations

Traffic between Earth and space could be by a shuttle system—vehicles going back and forth between the two. In the design pictured below, the shuttle has a double-decker seating arrangement with the pilot and co-pilot on top and the cargo specialists below. The shuttle would leave Earth and head for the space station, perhaps making stops along the way. It might act as a "flying mechanic," inspecting unmanned satellites to make sure they were in working order. It would deliver its cargo to its destination, pick up new cargo, and then return to Earth.

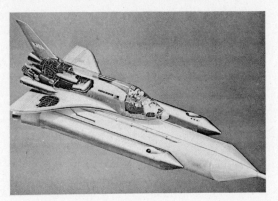

Number of words ___95___

Student's percentage of word recognition _____

Student's percentage of comprehension _____

**Comprehension Questions
to Accompany Fifth Reader**

What is a "shuttle system"?
A space shuttle leaving earth might head for a _____.
What does "flying mechanic" mean?
What might a space shuttle crew do when they come to an unmanned satellite?
What would the space shuttle pick up when it reached its destination?

From *Reading to Learn* by Margaret Early et al. (New York: Harcourt Brace Jovanovich, 1974), pp. 32–33.

This Man Was Mother to a Duck

In Altenberg on the Danube, near Vienna, Austria, there is a man who really lives with animals.

He is Dr. Konrad Lorenz, a world famous doctor and naturalist who has written many charming books about animals and their ways.

Animals are his friends. Sometimes they are his students. At other times they are his children. He has lived and worked with them and studied them closely.

When Dr. Lorenz sits down to tea, he is often joined by his father (who was a great medical doctor in his day), his mother, his wife and child, his twelve associates in research —and also by a large goose, some gray goslings, some very black ravens and their nestlings, a large red dog, a small tame rat, and his own baby ducks!

Number of words ___129___

Student's percentage of word recognition _____

Student's percentage of comprehension _____

Comprehension Questions to Accompany Sixth Reader

Where does Dr. Lorenz live?
What are some of his books written about?
What did Dr. Lorenz's father do?
What does he sometimes call these animal friends of his?
Name four animals that sometimes sat down with Dr. Lorenz for tea.

From *Reading Power* by Margaret Early et al. (New York: Harcourt Brace Jovanovich, 1974), pp. 16–17. Adapted from *How Smart Are Animals?* by Helen Kay (New York: Basic Books, 1962). Reprinted by permission of Frances Schwartz Literary Agency.

A Sample Interpretation of an IRI

It is important to recall that an IRI is not just another exercise in test giving—to be administered, scored, and filed. Rather it is a means to determine an appropriate place to begin reading instruction and a *process* to monitor the continued appropriateness of that choice. We believe that the results of an IRI are neither exacting nor exact, but that they are as accurate a picture as the teacher needs to draw.

In order to demonstrate more clearly how to administer and interpret an IRI, we shall follow the efforts of a teacher as an IRI is administered to Belinda, a second grader.

Recording miscues. As Belinda reads orally from one copy of the story, the teacher marks Belinda's miscues on another copy. To establish a purpose for reading, the teacher says: "Belinda, let's read a story about the first thing you see when you get up in the morning."

Belinda reads (see page 66); the teacher's marks on the selection indicate that as Belinda read the preprimer selection she read *saw* for *was* but repeated the line and self-corrected—indicating that she was looking for the sense of the whole context. "The sun saw up" had no meaning for her, so she reread. After a pause before the word *morning*, she was told the word. Since neither self-corrections nor a single repetition are considered oral-reading miscues, Belinda had only one miscue for this selection of 43 words. The computation of the percentage of word recognition would be as follows:

$$
\begin{array}{r}
.023 \\
\text{(words)}43 \overline{)\ 1.00} \\
\underline{86} \\
140 \\
\underline{129}
\end{array}
\qquad \text{(miscue)} = 2 \text{ percent}
$$

$$
\begin{array}{r}
100 \text{ (percent)} \\
\underline{-\ 2} \\
98 \text{ percent word recognition}
\end{array}
$$

Assuming that Belinda's reading was fairly smooth and fluent, the teacher could safely assume that Belinda was reading near her independent level (as far as word recognition is concerned) while reading this preprimer one material.

To check comprehension, the teacher would ask Belinda the following questions and *note her responses.*

Determining comprehension.   (Belinda's answers are in parentheses)
Who is this story about? (Bing and Sandy.)+
Were Sandy and Bing people? (No, they were animals.)+ How do you know? (I looked at the picture.)+
Where was Bing? (In the sun.)+

Selection 1

**Reading Level—
Preprimer 1**

Sun Up

The sun was up.
Sandy was up.
Bing was up.
The sun was up.
Good morning, sun.
Good morning, Sandy.
Good morning, Bing.
Good morning, Sandy and Bing.
Good morning, Bing and Sandy.
Bing was in the sun.
Sandy was in the sun.

Number of words ___43___

Student's percentage of word recognition ___98%___

Student's percentage of comprehension ___100%___

Where was Sandy: (In the sun.)+

What time of day do you think it was—morning or evening? (Morning.)+

The correct answers given by Belinda and marked by the teacher indicate that Belinda had 100 percent comprehension. Assuming that to be true, the teacher asks Belinda to read the next passage (preprimer two).

From *Sun Up* by Margaret Early et al. (New York: Harcourt Brace Jovanovich, 1974), pp. 5–13.

In the Morning Sun

Bing was in the morning sun.

Sandy was in the morning sun.

Bing and Sandy sat in the grass.

A little rabbit jumped in the grass.

Sandy jumped up and went after the rabbit.

The rabbit ran away and hid.

The rabbit was lost in the grass.

Bing ran to Sandy.

Bing and Sandy ran up and down the hill.

Bing and Sandy ran to the pond.

Bing and Sandy sat in the morning sun.

Number of words ___75___

Student's percentage of word recognition ___95%___

Student's percentage of comprehension ___60%___

Teacher: "That's fine, Belinda. Read the next story to find out what surprised Bing and Sandy." (Note the stated purpose for reading.)

Belinda reads the selection at the top of this page.

Before you read ahead, count the number of miscues that you believe Belinda made on this selection. Then calculate the word-recognition percentage and compare your thinking with our interpretation in Figure 2–9.

   From *A Happy Morning* by Margaret Early et al. (New York: Harcourt Brace Javanovich, 1974), pp. 5–7.

Figure 2–9 Our Interpretation of Belinda's Miscues

Miscues	Interpretation
sit for *sat* (2 times)	The miscue makes sense and, even though it changes the verb tense of the passage, it gramatically fits its sentence context. We didn't count it. (But we will record it—see Figure 2–11, page 70.)
garage for *grass* (3 times)	This substitution fits syntactically, but changes the meaning from the author's intent. We counted it one time. (Again, note the interpretation in Figure 2–11.
hopped for *jumped*	Good miscue; we didn't count it.
want for *went*	We counted it even though we may have heard wrong or mistakenly interpreted a dialect variation. You may have chosen not to count it.
hide for *hid*	We counted it because it changes the syntax of the sentence. You could argue that the meaning was retained and be right.
last for *lost*	We counted it. This substitution changed the meaning of the sentence. (Are you noting some strength and weakness patterns in Belinda's reading?)
pool for *pond*	We didn't count it. It makes sense and fits.

Our total = 4 miscues

Tally

Number of words = 75

Number of miscues = 4

Computing the Word Recognition Percentage

$$\text{(words) } 75 \overline{)\,4.00\,} \text{ (miscues)} \quad \frac{.053}{}$$

375

250

225

= 5 percent

100 (percent)

− 5

95 percent word recognition = instructional level

The following are Belinda's responses to the preprimer two questions:
Where were Bing and Sandy? (In the garage.)−
What little animal jumped in the grass? (A rabbit.)+
What did Sandy do when he saw the rabbit? (Chased it.)+
What did the rabbit do? (Ran into the garage.)−
Did Bing and Sandy find the rabbit? (No.) How do you know? (They went back in the sun.)+

Answering correctly three out of five questions equals a comprehension percentage of 60. This score can roughly translate to an instructional level for reading comprehension for Belinda. The next logical step would be to have Belinda read the next most difficult passage and answer its accompanying questions.

We can assume, however, that Belinda could either:

(1) continue to perform at her instructional level in word recognition and comprehension on the third preprimer
(2) drop to her frustration level in word recognition and comprehension on preprimer three
(3) gain an uneven profile by showing frustration in either word recognition or comprehension—but not both

In any event, we would probably begin instruction at preprimer two and use the information gained from asking Belinda to read one more selection to validate our guesses and to provide additional information. You may remember that often the most appropriate place to begin instruction is the point at which *either* word recognition or comprehension indicates the instructional level.

Figure 2–10 Summary of Belinda's IRI Performance

Name Belinda _____   Bookmark Reading Program

Date 9/17 _____

Book	Selection Grade Level	Word Recognition	Comprehension
Sun Up	pp^1	98% (independent)	100% (independent)
In the Morning Sun	pp^2	95% (instructional)	60% (instructional)
Little House in the Shadows	pp^3		
Sun Down	p		

Analyzing IRI performance. The types and frequency of the miscues a young reader makes can provide additional valuable information for the diagnostic teacher. That is, from the analysis of the miscues that occur in oral reading comes the beginning of their systematic classification, of record-keeping, and of instructional planning. Miscue analysis of a child's reading errors can take place on an individual record sheet; this attention to miscues may indicate patterns of pupil needs. The teacher can plan for those needs in group and/or individual lessons.

From the sample of Belinda's oral reading at the preprimer three level, you can begin to see in Figure 2–11 how the classification of miscues takes place. This sample of classifying miscues is offered to show you that certain miscues can be sorted according to probable causes. Patterns of reader needs should become clearer if teachers take time to get information from miscues. At this point the terminology may be unclear to you. The chapters on word recognition will offer a more detailed guide for miscues. For now, you may want to review the following guidelines:

(1) Miscues at the instructional level provide the teacher with information about what the reader is doing as he or she reads.

(2) When a miscue makes sense in a sentence, it is of lesser importance as a basis for planning word-recognition instruction.

(3) Don't overgeneralize from only one or two miscues. An instructional need should be based on more information.

Figure 2–11

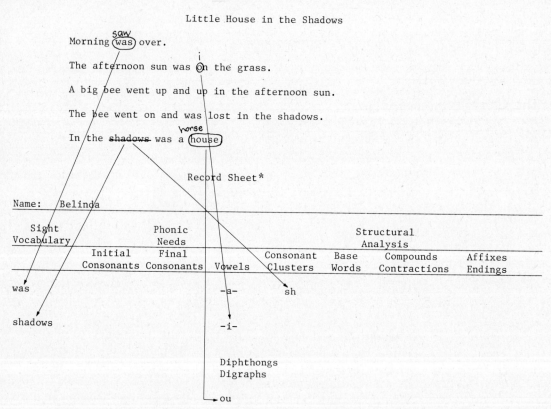

* Frank J. Guszak, *Diagnostic Teaching of Reading in the Elementary School* (New York: Harper and Row, 1972).

From *A Magic Afternoon* by Margaret Early et al. (New York: Harcourt Brace Jovanovich, 1974), pp. 5–8.

Just as the sorting of miscues can be the beginning of planning "tailor-made" instruction, answers offered to questions asked about the reading passages provide diagnostic evidence for comprehension needs.

Classifying comprehension responses will be more meaningful to you after you read Chapter 6. At this point it is sufficient to understand that the results of an IRI can be used to learn more than just the student's independent, instructional, and frustration reading levels.

As with the classification of word-recognition miscues, there are several guidelines that will be useful to you in classifying comprehension:

(1) Don't overgeneralize from one or two responses. You might conclude that a student made an error because of difficulty in following a sequence when the difficulty was due to unusual terminology.

(2) Use as few comprehension categories as are useful and meaningful to you. Breaking reading comprehension into many small parts is difficult and usually not helpful to planning instruction. (Further discussion of this is included in Chapter 7.)

(3) The comprehension errors at the instructional reading level are much more important for determining immediate instructional needs than are those at the frustration level.

The Cloze Procedure for Determining Reading Levels

A second means of determining a child's instructional level is through the use of the *cloze* technique. The term *cloze* was borrowed from the Gestalt principle of clozure and refers to the tendency of an organism to complete that which is incomplete in a predictable direction: "to complete a familiar—but not-quite-finished pattern—to 'see' a broken circle as a whole one, for example, by mentally closing up the gaps" (Taylor, 1953). In reading, a cloze procedure has referred to a procedure in which every nth word (usually the fifth) in a reading selection is eliminated and replaced by a blank to determine if a reader can supply the correct word. The theory is that the reader will attempt to fill the blank by providing the most appropriate word that he or she can think of to complete the author's thought.

The cloze procedure in reading has been applied to judge the appropriateness of materials for a given child by gauging the difficulty or readability levels of the materials. It also has been used as an instructional technique: it forces a reader to rely on the context for clues to the identification of an unknown word. In this section we are primarily interested in its potential as an assessment technique—for determining an instructional reading level.

In the preparation of cloze materials, passages are generally selected from basal readers, and words are systematically deleted at a regular rate (every fifth, tenth, or nth word). The reader's task is to fill in the blank spaces with the correct word, thus indicating an ability to understand the selection and to use the available context to supply the deleted words. (See Figure 2–12.)

It should be noted that research dealing with the validity of the cloze technique has generally studied children at intermediate grades and above. We believe however, that modification of the procedure can make it an effective technique for younger students, too. Certainly the cloze task is in harmony with our definition of reading as a process of comprehension. One advantage of the cloze procedure is its flexibility. Like the IRI, it is an informal test and is usually teacher-constructed. Informal tests offer a great deal of flexibility because they can be devised as needed to supply the information that the teacher decides will be helpful.

Figure 2–12

Sample of a Cloze Passage

WHAT IS THE *PLACEMENT TEST FOR PRIMARY GRADES?*

The *Placement Test for Primary Grades* consists of two selected passages from each basic book in Levels 3 through 10 of THE LAIDLAW READING PROGRAM. The test is designed to be individually administered to pupils in grades 1–3 who enter the program after having worked in some other reading program. In each passage, some words have been deleted and replaced by numbered lines. Taking the test involves reading a passage and suggesting meaningful words for the numbered lines. A part of one of the passages follows.

One night Bobo was playing

with the dog. "Roll over," he said.

But the $\underline{}^{1}$ would not $\underline{}^{2}$ over.

It ran across the floor after a ball.

Then round and $\underline{}^{3}$ it went with the $\underline{}^{4}$

in its mouth. Bobo $\underline{}^{5}$ not far behind.

As established in the numerous tryouts of the test, the pupil who can supply more than half the deleted words or meaningful substitutions for them is likely to read successfully the book from which the passage was taken.

This is an example of how the cloze procedure is used as a placement test for the *Laidlaw Reading Program* (1976). The deletions in this passage are not every *n*th word but are rather deletions that the test authors decided were crucial to determining the student's understanding of the selection.

From Roger Farr and Nancy L. Roser, *Placement Test for Primary Grades: Teacher's Edition* (River Forest, Il., Laidlaw Brothers, 1976), p. 13. By permission of Laidlaw Brothers, A Division of Doubleday & Company, Inc.

Build Your Own Cloze Test

Wilson Taylor (1953) proposed a standard procedure for the construction of a cloze test:

(1) Select a relatively complete passage (one that is not dependent upon preceding information) from portions of books* you intend to use for instruction.

(2) Delete an equal number of words from each passage by simply counting out every *n*th word (every fifth one, for example) without regard for the function or meaning of the deleted words.

(3) Reproduce each passage with a blank in place of the deleted word. When the test is group-administered, the blank must be long enough to permit the student to write in his or her response.

(4) Give copies of all reproduced passages to all children being tested.

(5) Ask the children to try to fill in all the blanks by guessing from the context, or remaining words, what the missing words should be.

(6) Allow as much time as the children need to complete the task.

Score Your Cloze Test

The cloze test is scored by marking as correct those words that are exact duplications of the deleted words. The rationale underlying this strict adherence to the original wording rests with the research that established the criterion percentages for scoring. Therefore, in order to use the percentages of correct clozures for determining independent, instructional, and frustration reading levels, it is important to count as correct only the exact duplications. If you were using the cloze technique to determine a student's understanding of a passage and to determine if he or she were relying on the passage context, it would not be essential to count only exact duplications as being correct. In that case, however, you would not use the percentages to determine the three reading levels.

Earl F. Rankin and Joseph W. Culhane (1969) established interpretations for children's performances on cloze tests by conducting studies in which they compared students' IRI performance with their cloze performance on the same passage. Through these studies, they arrived at the following conclusions:

The child is reading at the independent level when he or she can supply 61 percent or more of the deleted words.

The child is reading at the instructional level when he or she supplies 41 to 60 percent of the deleted words.

The child is reading at the frustration level when he or she correctly replaces 40 percent or less of the deleted words.

* These may be books of progressive difficulty in a basal reader series.

The cloze assessment procedure also has the advantage of being rather straightforward and easily administered by the teacher. It seems to be a fairly rapid data-gathering technique that appears especially useful for upper-level readers; however, its value as an instructional technique is not limited to an age or ability range. Explanations of the cloze procedure for teaching word recognition and for improving comprehension are included in Chapters 5 and 7.

Interpret Your Cloze Test

In order to show you exactly how a cloze test is interpreted, let's assume that instead of constructing the IRI as we suggested, you developed a cloze test with the very same passages. That is, you selected the passages from the various readers and retyped the stories, dropping every fifth word and replacing it with a blank. You then asked Belinda to read the selections aloud and to supply what she thought was the best word to fill each blank as she came to it. On another copy of each selection, you would record Belinda's choices, which are as follows for preprimer one:

The sun was up.

Sandy was up.

Bing was *up* .

The sun was up.

Good morning, sun.

Good morning, *sun* *Sandy* .

Good morning, Bing.

Good *morning*, Sandy and Bing.

Good *morning*, Bing and Sandy.

Bing *saw* in the sun.

Sandy *saw* in the sun.

Number of clozures possible   7

Number of errors   2

Percentage of correct clozures   72%   (Independent level)

From *Sun Up* by Margaret Early et al. (New York: Harcourt Brace Jovanovich, 1974), pp. 5–13.

You would need to record the number of blanks and the number of correct responses Belinda made on each of the passages. By dividing the number of errors by the total number of blanks, then subtracting that quotient from 100 percent, you can determine the percentage of correct clozures. The summary might look like this:

Reading Level of Passage	Story	Number of Clozures	Number of Errors	Percentage of Clozures/Correct	Belinda's Reading Level
pp[1]	Sun Up	7	2	75%	Independent
pp[2]	In the Morning Sun	15	5	66%	Independent
pp[3]	Little House in the Shadows	20	10	50%	Instructional
Primer	Sun Down	22	15	32%	Frustration
First Reader	Going to School	20	14	30%	Frustration

The administration of the cloze test could have stopped with the primer story because Belinda had reached her frustration level with that story. The first-reader passage provided the teacher with an additional check. The cloze procedure by its nature doesn't necessitate the use of comprehension questions after the reading of a selection and is, therefore, somewhat easier to administer. Both the cloze procedure and the informal reading inventory can be used effectively to determine a student's independent, instructional, and frustration reading levels.

Using Standardized Reading Tests for Assessment

Standardized reading tests can be very useful to you in planning reading instruction if they are properly used and understood. Before discussing the uses of standardized tests, we need to clarify what is meant by the term *standardized*, as well as some other terms used in testing reading. The term *standardized* applied to tests means that there is a standard set of procedures for administering the test. Through popular usage *standardized* has also come to mean a test that has been normed.* *Standardized* also means, to some educators, a test that has been published. However, in order for a test to be standardized, it does not need to be published by a publishing company nor does it need to have norms. The test merely has to include a set of specific procedures for administering

---

* A *normed* test is administered to a group of people—such as a sample of fourth graders— to determine their performance. The average score for these fourth graders is then listed as one of the fourth-grade norms for the test.

it. In addition, standardized tests have been called formal tests because there is a standard administration procedure. These standardized tests also appear formal because they are usually administered during a special testing period and are printed either by a school district or a publishing company.

Seemingly, then, one might be confused by the many definitions that can be applied to the term *standardized reading test.* In addition to the multiple meanings for *standardized,* there are many different types of standardized tests; and, to add to the confusion, one standardized test can be categorized in more than one way, as you will see below. One way to straighten out this confusion is to take a very simple test as an example and then use this test to help explain some of the different types of standardized tests.

Our example will be a test to assess students' *letter identification ability.* Each student is given an answer sheet. For every test item there is a row of four letters such as *B G p m* (both upper- and lower-case letters are used). The directions for administering the test read as follows: "Read the following to the students: Draw a circle around the letter *G* in the first row." The test proceeds through many such items. Certainly this is not an unusual test—it is a simple, straightforward test and will serve our purpose to explain different types of standardized tests.

Group tests. If the letter-recognition test described above were administered to a group of children at one time (as it easily could be) it would be called a *group standardized test.*

Individual tests. Suppose that we varied the directions for the letter-recognition test so that the child had to point to the correct letter rather than drawing a circle around it. In that case, the test could be administered to only one child at a time and it would be called an *individual standardized test.*

Criterion-referenced tests. If the letter-recognition test included items for all twenty-six upper- and lower-case letters (a total of fifty-two items), we could describe a child's performance in terms of how many letters (upper and lower case) could be recognized. If we then developed criterion or success levels that said, for example, if the child recognizes 90 percent of the letters, we can assume he or she has mastered recognition of the letters of the alphabet, we would have a *criterion-referenced standardized test.* Of course, the criterion level could be set higher or lower, and 90 percent is an arbitrary example.

Norm-referenced tests. In order to develop a norm-referenced test, the test has to be administered to some norm population. Suppose that the norm group for this letter-recognition test was made up of a representative sample of all the first- and second-grade children in the country. In addition, suppose that the average performance for this norm population on the fifty-two test items (upper- and lower-case letters) was as follows:

Students in the Norm Group	Average Raw Score	Grade Equivalent
Beginning of first grade	12	1.0
Middle of first grade	17	1.5
End of first grade	29	1.9
Beginning of second grade	38	2.0
Middle of second grade	48	2.5
End of second grade	50	2.9

If you administered the test to a first grader, and the student got a score of 38, he or she would have a grade equivalent of 2.0. That is, the score would be roughly equivalent to that of a beginning second grader's in the normative sample. When tests are normed, the test is called a *norm-referenced standardized test*. Notice that the same test can be both norm referenced and criterion referenced. For example, on the letter-recognition test a score of 47 is above the 90 percent criterion mastery level, but it is also a grade equivalent (norm-referenced) of about 2.5.

Survey tests. Our letter-recognition test could be written so that it did not include all fifty-two upper- and lower-case letters but rather just sampled about fifteen of the letters. The purpose of this test would be to survey the children in a class or a school to determine if they were learning to recognize the letters of the alphabet. Such a test would not be used to determine specific instruction on specific letters because the test only sampled from all the letters. The test is a *survey standardized test*.

Diagnostic tests. When our letter-recognition test includes all of the letters of the alphabet and it is used to determine specific instruction on specific letters of the alphabet, it is a *diagnostic standardized test*.

From all of this, it should be apparent that any single test can be described in several different ways. For example, a test can be a group test with both norm-referenced and criterion-referenced scores. The same test could measure just word-recognition skills and be properly labelled a diagnostic test.

What a test is called is not the crucial criterion for selecting a test. What is most important is to determine why you want to test at all. This consideration, as well as what is included on the test, must guide your selection and use of any test.

Why Test? What to Test?

Two things are probably fairly obvious by now: First, testing is a means of obtaining information; and second, testing can take a wide variety of forms, depending on why the information is needed and, of course, what particular information is needed. In previous sections of this chapter, various types of tests have been described. Each type of test has unique strengths and weaknesses; and all tests, whether teacher-made or produced by a publisher, provide only estimates or guesses about a child's performance. For that reason, and because a child's reading ability continues to grow, you need to continue testing (in this case informally diagnosing) while you are teaching.

However, the key to determining what type of test or assessment to use is based on *why* you need the particular information. To use a test with no clear rationale for why it is being used is to misuse testing. And if you know why you are testing, you will certainly be able to answer the question about what to test. There are four major reasons for wanting to test—that is, four reasons that you might need to collect information:

(1) I want to determine a student's reading level.
(2) I want to determine reading subskill needs.
(3) I want to group for instruction.
(4) I want to assess growth.

To use testing effectively to serve these four needs you need to know which tests to use and when to use them—or how to use several types of tests together to provide initial and ongoing assessment. Of course, there are many different types of tests, and you should critically examine any test to see if it will provide the information you need.

As each of the four information needs are discussed in the following sections, standardized and informal testing will be discussed. But this is an oversimplification. Some standardized tests include a complete assessment of all of the word-recognition skills you are teaching. Some provide for continuous assessment. Other standardized tests just sample and test a few reading skills and give you only a general, one-time snapshot of a child's reading ability, similar to your own teacher-made informal test, which may be quite brief because you only want to find out, in general, a child's reading level. On the other hand, you may want to carefully review a child's reading skills over several days because he or she seems to be having considerable difficulty. Therefore, you need to know why you are testing and what you need to know; then you can consider the best assessments to serve your needs.

Testing to Determine Reading Level

Earlier in this chapter we described how an informal test, an IRI, can be used to achieve a student-material match that is conducive to reading growth. Most standardized tests, however, are not developed to provide information regarding the level of reading materials a child should be given for instruction.

Most standardized tests are norm-referenced tests, which rate an individual's performance in relation to others; informal tests can appraise a level of competence on a particular task without reference to the performance of others. In an early study, Betts (1940) compared pupils' performances on standardized reading tests with their performance on an informal reading inventory for assessing reading grade placement. Betts discovered that the standardized tests' scores were inflated estimates of the reading levels for the low achievers. Killgallon (1942) discovered that, on the average, pupils tend to score about one year higher on the standardized reading test than their instructional level as measured by an IRI. Later studies (Sipay, 1961; McCracken, 1963; Glaser, 1964) continued to point up differences between standardized and informal tests in gaining an estimate of the instructional reading level. In reviewing the studies, Farr cited several generalizations:

(1) The purposes of standardized tests and informal inventories differ. Most publishers of standardized tests do not suggest that the grade score norms be used as indicators of the levels at which reading instruction should be provided.

(2) Performance on one informal reading inventory based on only one set of materials or one set of basal readers will in all likelihood differ from performance on another reading inventory based on another set of materials. If an IRI is based on the materials used in classroom instruction, students perform better on that inventory than they would when presented with an inventory based on an unfamiliar set of materials.

(3) Any comparisons between IRI performance and standardized test scores are entirely dependent on: (a) the standardized test used; (b) the materials used to construct the IRI; (c) the criteria used to evaluate performance; and (d) the ability and skill of the examiner in recording errors and judging performance on the inventory (1969), pp. 108–09).

Despite the fact that almost all standardized or norm-referenced tests are not developed to provide information about a child's reading level, there are some exceptions. The *Diagnostic Reading Scales* (Spache, 1963) and the *Standard Reading Inventory* (McCracken, 1966) are both individually administered tests that provide instructional reading levels. The *Metropolitan Achievement Test: Reading* (Farr et al., 1978) is a group-administered test that is developed to provide a child's instructional reading level. These three tests assess a child's ability to read passages of increasing difficulty in a fashion similar to an IRI.

In general, however, most standardized tests do not provide information about a child's instructional reading level. It would seem, then, that one could get a more valid assessment by carefully constructing and interpreting an informal reading inventory built from those selections that the child will actually be using. The validity of such an IRI is greater than the standardized test because the assessment and the instruction are based on the same reading selections.

Testing to Determine Reading Subskill Needs

Informal assessment of a child's reading is the best guide to planning instruction. However, standardized tests can give you initial information as a guide for beginning instruction.

Most standardized reading tests are made up of subtests that attempt to measure such skills as letter recognition, the use of sentence context to determine word meanings, the use of word parts in recognizing words, and many others. The use of subtest scores can be helpful as an initial guide to students' needs. But you must not rely on these scores as an absolute definition of instructional needs—a child's response to instruction is the best basis for determining instructional needs.

If you do decide to use standardized reading subtest scores as one base for determining initial reading needs, you must carefully examine the test to see that it tests those skills that you believe children need to learn in order to be able to read. And in giving this examination, look at the test items themselves, rather than the test names, which can be misleading. One good way to examine a reading test is to take the test yourself. An examination of some of the more common subtest types on standardized reading tests will help you to see how important it is for you to actually examine the test rather than merely relying on the test name.

Word meaning. Often the word meaning subtest is entitled *Vocabulary* and requires the student to mark a word that names a given picture; at higher levels, the student may have to circle a word that fits a particular underlined phrase or definition, select the best synonym from five alternatives, or complete a definition by selecting the best word to fill a blank. The various methods for measuring vocabulary suggest a complex task. Assuming that reading vocabulary is a distinct and measurable skill, the teacher's concerns about testing vocabulary may be somewhat mitigated by choosing a test that matches the instructional goals and procedures of the reading program. For example, a test that presents vocabulary words in isolation by providing a list of words and directs the student to select the best synonym does not represent the teaching of vocabulary from context (Farr, 1969). Thus, a mismatch between the classroom instruction (teaching recognition of vocabulary in context) and

the testing procedure sends up a signal flare for extremely cautious interpretation of the results.

Paragraph meaning. Subtests of paragraph meaning attempt to measure the student's ability to comprehend passages of increasing difficulty. Required tasks often include answering questions covering details, main idea, or sequence. Often they attempt to elicit critical thinking. But the ways in which reading comprehension has been defined and measured are as varied as the number of tests and developers. Because of the variety of ways reading comprehension has been defined, redefined, and examined, you should examine reading comprehension as a totality rather than give undue credence to subtest scores. Of prime importance, again, is the selection of a test that measures comprehension as you have taught it. Whether you believe reading comprehension is as broad as "effective reading" or as narrow as "recalling specific facts" should influence both your selection and interpretation of the testing instrument. Variables that contribute to the difficulty of measuring reading comprehension include whether the test is timed or untimed, whether the student can look back at the material after reading it or must remember it, and whether the child's prior knowledge or background on the particular topic has affected the result. Because of the importance of reading in context, most teachers attach more importance to tests of comprehension than to word meaning or vocabulary.

Reading rate. A subtest of reading rate, or speed, is an attempt to measure the number of words read within a given time period. Rate tests are usually included as part of reading tests at upper elementary, junior high, or higher levels and include reading-comprehension questions as well as measuring reading rate. There is little agreement about the relationship between rate and comprehension or about the way reading rate should be measured or interpreted. McDonald (1966) attempted to measure flexible rates for reading but concluded that there is little evidence to substantiate the assumption that students can adjust their reading rates to suit specific purposes.

try this ▶ Locate a standardized reading test for a grade level that you might be interested in teaching. Take each of the subtests. After you complete a subtest, write down in your own words what you think that subtest is measuring. Compare what you have written with what the test manual says the subtest is supposed to be measuring. Do you think that the intended objective of each subtest is important for a child to learn if he or she is to become an effective reader? This evaluation of the importance of the subtests will perhaps be more interesting to you after you have read the chapters in this book on teaching word recognition and comprehension.

Testing to Group for Instruction

Because we have seen that most standardized tests cannot provide as valid an indicator of instructional reading level as does an effectively administered IRI, nor as complete an assessment of reading needs as the teacher must command, the use of standardized test scores for grouping is limited.

A standardized test can give you an idea of who are the best and the poorest readers in your class. Most standardized reading tests provide scores that rank the students from highest to lowest. This ranking may help you with the initial grouping of students—but most standardized reading tests results do not provide you with as much specific information regarding students' reading levels (independent, instructional, frustration) as an informal reading inventory does.

If you do decide to use a standardized test to determine the ranking of your students to determine initial grouping, what score should you use? Almost any of the total scores from the test will be useful for this purpose. The types of total scores usually provided by a standardized reading test include the following norm-referenced scores:

Percentile ranking is a score that ranges from 1 to 99 and indicates what percentage of students in the norming population scored above or below a particular student. For example, a student who scores at the 65th percentile scored better than 65 percent of the students and poorer than 34 percent of the students in the norming population.

Grade equivalent is a score that is based on the average performance of students in a particular grade in the norming population. For example, a student with a grade equivalent (G.E.) of 5.0 scored about as well as the average score of a beginning fifth grader in the norming population. It is very important that you not confuse a G.E. with the reading levels that are determined by an informal reading inventory.

Stanine is a score that ranges from one to nine and is similar to percentiles except that the scores are divided into nine groups to emphasize that scores are not absolute points but rather represent ranges of performance. For example, a student with a stanine score of three would have scored better than students in the norming population in stanines one and two, the same as others in stanine three, and poorer than those in stanines four through nine.

There are other norm-referenced scores, but these are the most common. All norm-referenced scores are based on comparing a student with some norm group. Norm scores can point out the best readers, the poorest readers, and those in between. You might want to use the scores for initially grouping your students. For example, you could put all stanine one, two, and three students in one group; all stanine four, five, and six students in another group; and all stanine seven, eight, and nine students in a third group. Note, however, that any grouping based on these scores must be very tentative, and your constant informal analysis as a child reads should take over to adjust the instructional grouping as soon as possible.

Grouping based on test scores may mask as many differences within groups as there are differences between groups. Similar total scores on standardized tests are not necessarily indicative of similar needs. Two students with total grade-equivalent scores of 2.0 will likely exhibit as many (or more) specific skill differences as two children chosen at random from the class. For example, one child may be very skilled in using word parts such as prefixes and suffixes to recognize words. Another child with the same total score may be weak in the use of word parts but may be extremely proficient in using context clues to recognize words. In order to plan instruction for each child, you need to examine each child's performance on the individual subtests and even on each test item, and then verify needs in daily observation.

Testing to Assess Growth

We have already noted that standardized norm-referenced tests are reliable for comparing students in terms of general reading achievement. Tests, however, can only provide knowledge of those behaviors that they are designed to sample. A test of vocabulary can provide information about vocabulary, but not much information about reading speed, flexibility, or comprehension. If a teacher wishes to determine the extent of a student's vocabulary before instruction is begun in order to know what vocabulary words to teach, a vocabulary test should be used. If a teacher wishes to know how much vocabulary a student has obtained as a result of instruction, a test of vocabulary should be used that includes those words that have been taught, using the method in which they were taught (for example, context or clozure). A student can scarcely be expected to master vocabulary he or she has *not* been taught. Any test (standardized or informal) that includes material that is not part of the instructional program or its objectives should not be used to assess growth toward those objectives.

For example, a summer reading program was initiated in an urban school system with ecology as the basis for instruction. For six weeks, students from families of poverty-level incomes walked parks, explored creeks, and collected and identified specimens of plant and animal life—and registered general approval of their activities. The purposes of the program included building background and vocabulary to spark rich language, pupil dictation, and subsequent production of their own books. All of *those* events occurred but, after one summer, the program was dropped. The reason? Pupils failed to make significant gains from pre- to post-testing by a selected standardized test. The problem stemmed from a failure to clearly define what was to be measured and why it was to be measured. Did the standardized test reflect the goals of the ecology program? Probably not.

Testing Is Sometimes Imposed on the Classroom

There are administrative purposes for testing that have to do with the overall evaluation of the school reading program, obtaining funding, or comparing students in a particular school with a normative sample.

Misuse of test results can occur in those situations that have little to do with the tests themselves or the teachers who administer them. An example of administrative misuse is when test results are viewed as the sole criterion on which to judge the success of a program. In addition, specific tests that assess a few specific goals are often used to assess the achievement of all goals. It is regrettable, too, that test results are released to news media and the public without accompanying information. Uninterpreted and falsely interpreted data breed fear, anger, and suspicion of all tests.

Finally, test results purportedly collected to aid in classifying children and in planning educational programs have been used to rigorously label and inflexibly track students. In particular, criticisms have been voiced by minority group members who charge that tests "reflect only middle-class values and attitudes and do not reflect . . . linguistic, cognitive and cultural experiences" of all groups (Oakland, 1973).

Based on these concerns, the teacher who is asked to administer a test should:

(1) Know that the information from that test is needed for specific and stated instructional decisions.
(2) View the test as one piece of information for making decisions.
(3) Ask that competent measurement and curriculum specialists be involved in the preparation of assessment reports that are based on the results of standardized tests.
(4) Ask that interpretation of normed scores (grade scores, percentiles, stanines) be under the direction of highly competent measurement specialists (Farr and Roser, 1974).

In addition, the teacher can read reviews of reading tests in Oscar K. Buros, *Reading: Tests and Reviews* (1968). The reviews in the Buros book are written by competent measurement and curriculum specialists. They are particularly useful because they include the name of the test publisher, the authors, the names of the subtests included, and the time needed to administer the tests. Buros's test reviews have been continually updated in a series of books called the *Mental Measurements Yearbook* (1978). You should certainly consult the most recent of these yearbooks if you are looking for information about a particular test.

REFERENCES   Betts, Emmett A. *Foundations of Reading Instruction*. New York: American Book, 1946.
————. "Reading Problems at the Intermediate Grade Level." *Elementary School Journal* 15 (1940): 737–46.
Buros, Oscar K., ed. *Reading Tests and Reviews*. Highland Park, N.J.: The Gryphon Press, 1968.
————, ed. *The Eighth Mental Measurements Yearbook* (2 vols). Highland Park, N.J.: The Gryphon Press, 1978.
Early, Margaret et al., *The Bookmark Reading Program*. 2d ed. New York: Harcourt Brace Jovanovich, 1974.

Farr, Roger. *Reading: What Can Be Measured?* ERIC Reading Review Series. Newark, Del.: International Reading Association, 1969.

———; Prescott, George; Balow, Irving; and Hogan, Thomas. *Metropolitan Achievement Tests: Reading.* 1978.

———and Roser, Nancy. "Issues and Problems Concerning Reading Assessment." *Teacher Education Forum* 2(11), Bloomington, Ind.: Division of Teacher Education, March 1974.

Glaser, Nicholas A. "A Comparison of Specific Reading Skills of Advanced and Retarded Readers of Fifth Grade Reading Achievement." Unpublished doctoral dissertation, University of Oregon, 1964.

Guszak, Frank J. *Diagnostic Teaching of Reading in the Elementary School.* New York: Harper and Row, 1972.

Houghton Mifflin Reading Series. *Informal Reading Inventory*, Teacher's Manual. Boston: Houghton Mifflin, 1976.

Johnson, Marjorie and Kress, Roy. *The Informal Reading Inventory.* Reading Aids Series. Newark, Del.: International Reading Association, 1965.

Killgallon, P. A. "A Study of Relationships among Certain Pupil Adjustments in Language Situations." Unpublished doctoral dissertation, Pennsylvania State College, 1942.

McCracken, Robert A. "The Development and Validation of the Standard Reading Inventory for the Individual Appraisal of Reading Performance in Grades One Through Six." Unpublished doctoral dissertation, Syracuse University, 1963.

———. "The I.R.I. as a Means of Improving Instruction." In *The Evaluation of Children's Reading*, edited by T. Barrett. Newark, Del.: International Reading Assocation, 1967.

———. *Standard Reading Inventory.* Klamath Falls, Ore.: Klamath Printing Co., 1966.

McDonald, Arthur S. "Flexibility in Reading Approaches: Measurement and Development." In *Combining Research Results and Good Practices*, edited by J. Allen Figurel. Proceedings of the International Reading Association 11 (1966): 67–71.

Oakland, Thomas. "Assessing Minority Group Children: Challenges for School Psychologists." *Journal of School Psychology* 11 (December 1973): 294–303.

Powell, William R. "Reappraising the Criteria for Interpreting Informal Inventories." In *Reading Diagnosis and Evaluation*, edited by D. L. DeBoer. Proceedings of the International Reading Association 13 (1970): 100–109.

Rankin, Earl F., and Culhane, Joseph W. "Comparable Cloze and Multiple-choice Comprehension Test Scores." *Journal of Reading* 13 (December 1969): 193–98.

Silvaroli, Nicholas J. *Classroom Reading Inventory.* Dubuque, Iowa: William C. Brown, 1973.

Sipay, Edward R. "A Comparison of Standardized Reading Test Scores and Functional Reading Levels." Unpublished doctoral dissertation, University of Connecticut, 1961.

Spache, George D. *Diagnostic Reading Scales.* Monterey, Cal.: California Test Bureau, 1963.

———.*Investigating the Issues of Reading Disabilities.* Boston: Allyn and Bacon, 1976.

Taylor, Wilson. "Cloze Procedure: A New Tool for Measuring Readability." *Journalism Quarterly* 30 (Fall 1953): 414–38.

FOR FURTHER READING

Blanton, William E.; Farr, Roger; Tuinman, J. Jaap, eds. *Measuring Reading Performance*. Newark, Del.: International Reading Association, 1974.

Burke, Carolyn L., and Goodman, Kenneth S. "When a Child Reads: A Psycholinguistic Analysis. *Elementary English* 17 (January 1970): 121–29.

Farr, Roger, *Measurement and Evaluation of Reading*. New York: Harcourt Brace Jovanovich, 1970.

———. *Reading: What Can Be Measured?* ERIC/CRIER Reading Review Series. Newark, Del.: International Reading Association, 1969.

Goodman, Yetta. "Reading Diagnosis—Qualitative or Quantitative?" *The Reading Teacher* 26 (October 1972): 32–37.

Horrocks, John E., and Schoonover, Thelma I. *Measurement for Teachers*. Columbus, Ohio: Charles E. Merrill, 1968.

Jobe, Frederick W. *Screening Vision in Schools*. Newark, Del.: International Reading Association, 1976.

MacGinitie, Walter H., ed. *Assessment Problems in Reading*. Newark, Del.: International Reading Association, 1973.

McCracken, Robert A. "Informal Reading Inventories: Diagnosis Within the Teacher." *The Reading Teacher* 26 (December 1972): 273–77.

Sheldon, William D. "Specific Principles Essential to Classroom Diagnosis." *The Reading Teacher* 14 (September 1960): 2–8.

Strang, Ruth. *Diagnostic Teaching of Reading*. 2d ed. New York: McGraw-Hill, 1969.

Valmont, William J. "Creating Questions for Informal Reading Inventories." *The Reading Teacher* 25 (March 1972): 509–12.

3 At the Beginning: Reading Readiness

The reading ability of American children is a highly prized skill. For some parents, a child's ability to read before entering school is a status symbol akin to a home in the suburbs, a late-model car, and other trappings of success. Teachers, too, are sometimes caught up in equating children's reading ability with their learning potential. Thus, kindergarten teachers sometimes feel compelled to teach children to read not only to prove their own teaching abilities but also to respond to community values and pressures. The pressure to learn to read is not a universal value in America, but perhaps Americans—in general, an upwardly mobile people—have equated reading with success more than any other nation. And so in many homes parents supply their children with those things they hope will teach the children what they need to learn in order to get a head start in learning to read. There are stacking toys, puzzles, record players, and magnetic letters—supplied with good intentions and in hope that the recipients will be ready to read.

When to Begin: From Controversy to Direction

For over fifty years, controversy as to when children are ready to read has stirred debate. Some experts (Doman, 1964) have contended that even babies can read if their task is structured closely enough, if the teaching is gamelike, and if the learning is reinforced. Other scholars (Dewey, 1896; Huey, 1908) recommended delayed instruction in reading, calling it an "unnatural process" and advocating postponement until the child reached the age of eight. Dewey's opposition to early initiation of reading instruction was primarily an objection to the prevailing methodology of the time. He labelled the instructional practices *mechanical* and *passive,* meaning that the learning tended to be isolated, abstract, and by rote (Durkin, 1968). Since Dewey's time, the controversy (both among professionals and within the public sector) about when children should begin to read has continued. Perhaps the debate has continued for so long and been so widespread and emotional because we as a nation have been relatively schizophrenic in our attitudes. On the one hand, we have been worshippers of childhood and of its joys and pleasures; on the other, we have retained our puritan respect for work, competition, and advancement. Thus, depending on whether the prevailing attitude toward learning to read is as a skill to be acquired or a pleasure to be shared, we have pushed or delayed reading instruction.

This chapter is intended not to continue the debate but rather to offer some background in readiness instruction, interpretations of current research, and the practices of enlightened teachers.

Early Support for Delay

Noted researcher and educator Dolores Durkin (1976) traces the history of the trend to postpone reading instruction. According to Durkin, at least part of the confusion over when to begin reading instruction was underscored by the advent of the scientific testing period in American education—a period spanning the 1920s. With the rapid onslaught of means to measure nearly every behavior, some shocking results were inevitable. One finding with lasting impact was the indication that reading failure was widespread; and then, as now, there was a need to pinpoint blame.

A logical explanation (and one that neatly fit the prevailing philosophy of child development) was that the children had begun to read too soon. Their failure stemmed not from poorly prepared teachers nor from poorly conceived materials but rather from the fact that they had not "ripened" to a stage where they might profit from reading instruction. Research data were heralded if those data appeared to pinpoint a specific mental age for children to attain in order to ensure success with reading (Arthur, 1925; Morphett and Washburn, 1931). The mental age of 6.5 became sacrosanct and was adhered to for succeeding decades as a nearly magical point at which success with beginning reading could virtually be assured. The impact of this requisite mental age took the form of delayed instruction and promoted a near blanket application of reading-readiness workbooks. With these workbooks, which included activities that were often only busy work and were not related to learning to read, some first-grade teachers marked the passage of time from school entrance until most of the children reached the prescribed readiness level of 6.5 years of age.

New Directions

There were, during this time, voices for change. One of the most respected was that of Arthur Gates, who offered the opposition viewpoint that reading readiness may well be the state that occurs when teacher and reading program are most able to adapt to the learner. With common sense that was uncommon for the times, Gates (1937) wrote that readiness may not be a static point to wait for but rather a dynamic state to develop actively. Gates' arguments took the burden of proof off the child and passed it to the teacher and the school. But for many years to come, Gates' thinking was not as popular as the mental age concept of reading readiness.

Several events that followed the launching of the Russian satellite Sputnik in 1957 cut a zigzag path to increased support for Professor Gates' divergent philosophy. First, there was a backlash of critical self-analysis of American education and increased public pressure to teach more in the schools and to teach it earlier (Durkin, 1968). Second, the movement was seeded by such popular psychologists as Jerome Bruner, J. McVicker Hunt, and Benjamin Bloom, who reiterated the importance of the early years and the capacity for learning appropriately sequenced material at any age. Second, these thinkers were received during the 1960s—a period of intense social consciousness, with interest and attention directed toward developing programs that would benefit both poverty-level and culturally different children. A new philosophy reigned—one that assumed that early intervention would help the child achieve his or her full potential.

The current direction underscores the importance of *what* children should be taught and *how* they should be taught, rather than *when*. Readiness is no longer popularly viewed as a matter of waiting until the child can learn to read but rather as finding out what children know, what they need to know, and teaching each so that each can succeed.*

An Operational Definition of Reading Readiness

For all that has been written, researched, and opined, there is still uncertainty about what readiness implies and what skills it assumes. (No wonder the onset of a measurable mental age seemed so attractive as a way to scientifically gauge readiness to read.) To avoid the potential inertia that could result from a more open-ended approach to reading readiness, we will propose an operational definition. An operational definition should help us to avoid abstractions, to describe reality, and to make instructional decisions about real children. That is, we will discuss

* Dolores Durkin, perhaps one of the best known of the recent reading authorities, has emphasized the importance of what children should be taught and how they should be taught.

reading readiness in terms of appropriate ways to help children to get ready to read.

A child's readiness to read is dependent upon how his or her unique set of prereading behaviors can be matched with appropriate instruction.

To formulate the definition, we have leaned heavily upon the works of Arthur Gates (1937), David P. Ausubel (1958), and Dolores Durkin (1976). This definition places the responsibility for reading readiness squarely upon the teacher. Yet, the definition also seems to suggest that there is some absolute set of prereading behaviors that can be taught to children who need it. There is no such set. The description of reading readiness offered by this text reflects the authors' definition of reading, interpretation of existing research, and knowledge of effective practice. The complex of skills, abilities, and knowledge that constitute readiness remains less than fully understood.

" 'B plus' in motivational initiative, 'A' in conceptual visualization . . . so how come you can't read?"

© 1979 Sidney Harris

It has been our contention that all learners are ready to learn something! This means that no matter whether you become involved in teaching infants, four-year-olds, kindergarteners, or fifth graders, each child under your direction—regardless of income, background, intelligence, sex, dominant language—is in a state of readiness for learning. Put that simply, it appears that the term "reading readiness" would be trouble-free. Unfortunately, such is not the case. Since its inception over fifty years ago, the term has been buffeted by the same winds of controversy that we described earlier: for some, reading readiness has meant a *program*—generally a published program, containing either an all-purpose workbook, or various pieces of language, perceptual, or skill-development materials; for others, reading readiness has meant a particular mental or physical age when a child has reached a satisfactory level of development and "real" reading instruction can begin; and for still others, reading readiness has meant a time in a child's education when readiness instruction is supposed to occur—for example, the kindergarten or prekindergarten year devoted to informal learning, socialization, and language development.

Yet, if we could forego the associated program or workbooks, if we could place the readiness age on some back burner, if we could forget the idea that readiness instruction is supposed to occur at some *particular time* in a child's school career, then we would be better able to deal with reading readiness in its least controversial domain—that of meeting the prereader with appropriate instruction. We will begin by taking a look at the general characteristics of the prereader, first in terms of physical development (visual, auditory, and motor), and second in terms of language awareness and its importance in readiness for reading.

Physical Characteristics of the Prereader

To deal effectively with beginners, we should recognize what kinds of behaviors the ready-to-read demonstrate. From that vantage point, it will be easier to identify (and encourage) the not-so-ready. Looking at a beginner in terms of relevant physical characteristics means making judgments about visual acuity and discrimination, auditory acuity and discrimination, and motor development.

Visual acuity. Visual acuity refers to the keenness of vision that a child demonstrates. Not so long ago (Getman, 1962), there was still contention that most five-year-olds hadn't acquired the near-point vision required for reading. Now, more researchers tend to agree that five-year-olds can deal with print successfully and without strain (Eames, 1962). A major breakthrough in screening for visual acuity has occurred in recent years in many districts where children are tested for both far-point and near-point vision. (Previously only far-point vision was assessed if any testing was done at all.) Nonetheless, it is the alert teachers who will still discover many of the cases of visual abnormalities in their classrooms. Common sense dictates that you should refer to a vision specialist any child who persistently complains of blurred vision, moves close to the chart pad, television screen, or chalkboard, rubs or presses the eyes frequently, has reddened eyes or lids, or who squints or scowls a great deal. These are symptoms that might indicate visual problems. An eye-care specialist should be consulted if one or more of these problems persist.

Visual discrimination. Visual discrimination usually refers to the child's ability to perceive differences in shapes and forms. Readiness programs have traditionally given much attention to providing children practice with tasks that force them to identify the squiggle or geometric form that is the same as or different from a model. Most children can discriminate shapes and forms visually from a very early age. It is the perception of letters that is more important to an accurate perception of words, and children who can point out similarities and differences in letters have no need for the more remote exercises.

Auditory acuity.   Auditory acuity refers to the keenness of hearing demonstrated by the child. Hearing is often tested as a prerequisite for school attendance, but when it is not, teachers can make referrals to a hearing specialist on the basis of such symptoms as inattentiveness, confusion with following directions, overly loud speech, distorted speech, rubbing or cupping of the ear, and frequent complaints of earaches. Inability to hear normally affects the child's language input channel and ability to profit fully from oral experiences.

Auditory discrimination.   Auditory discrimination describes the ability to perceive likenesses and differences in sounds. The ability to discriminate auditorially has often been judged by the child's ability to identify differences in highly similar word pairs (differing in one phoneme—for example, *bat-bap*) presented orally.

The belief that ability to discriminate letters auditorially is important for reading success has persisted despite some evidence to the contrary (Hare, 1977). Perhaps it is instruction with intensive phonic programs (sometimes requiring pronunciation of isolated sounds) that has fostered continued attention to auditory discrimination.

In any event, it sometimes appears evident that children have been labelled "poor auditory discriminators" when they are actually confused by what they have been asked to do (that is, isolate word parts). At times the tasks designed to measure auditory discrimination are so abstract that the child fails. Remember that most children do something quite well that is the best indicator of auditory discrimination: they talk.

Motor development.   Motor development has been occurring in the young child since birth. Development of large muscles occurs through kicking, reaching, crawling, walking, running, and jumping. Most kindergarten children are fairly expert in "practicing" the development of these muscles. Experienced teachers try to accommodate the continuing need of the beginner to participate actively in his or her learning. Even as emphasis on fine-motor skills increases, beginners are most involved when both hands are full. In general, however, the relationship of motor development to readiness for reading is unclear. Behaviorally, children who demonstrate readiness can listen (with a minimum number of wiggles) to a story read to them, can do simple copy work, and can turn a page!

Language Awareness

Since reading is a language process, we assume that children with adequate language development should move fairly smoothly into reading. Barring other difficulties, the key word in this assumption is *adequate*. No one, it seems, knows what this adequacy entails. Most six-year-old children have mastery of several thousand *vocabulary* words—if vocabulary is defined as the number of words both understood and spoken (Smith, 1941; Dale, 1965). Best of all, children are language lovers and will trip new words off their tongues just for the musical quality or for the practice.

It sometimes happens that children use vocabulary words correctly but have incomplete or inappropriate referents for the word. For example, a five-year-old told his classmates that he had recently visited an amusement park and "seen bunches of amusements."

"What's an amusement?" he was asked.

He was thoughtful in offering the response: "I don't know, but I think it's a roller coaster."

He was partly right, but he had also provided his teacher with an opportunity to expand both his and his classmates' vocabularies and to clarify a vague concept.

Conversely, children often use vocabulary words that appear difficult, but that represent fully developed concepts. For example, a four-year-old was sharing a picture book with her teacher.

"And this," she said, "is a goose and a gosling."

"Tell me about a gosling," said the teacher.

"A gosling is like a child—only different."

The teacher ensures each child's language awareness by helping to expand vocabulary and by providing experiences

> which will help children develop concepts more fully and accurately; to encourage children to practice using language; and to provide interesting models of language through involvement with people, recordings, films, firsthand experiences, and books. . . . When children are surrounded with interesting language and provided with activities and encouragement for using language, their vocabularies will grow. (Robinson, Strickland, and Cullinan, 1977, p. 24)

Teachers sometimes become concerned with deviations in young children's pronunciations and wonder if speech differences should be "corrected" before reading instruction is begun. It appears that consonant substitution ("The wat wan across the woad.") and inversion ("Let's read this mazagine.") are fairly common and should not be considered defects. Rather, we can assume that with time, appropriate models, experiences, and opportunities to talk, talk, talk, many phonological differences will be self-corrected. In any case, these articulation features are a detriment to reading *only* if a teacher equates reading with correct pronunciation—and we hope by now that you do not.

Finally, teachers alert to children's language recognize differences in the ability to use all the syntactic structures of their language. Acquisition of such structures continues to develop in children until age nine (Chomsky, 1969). So while some teachers hear language like this:

You got scissors?

others hear:

All of the other kids have scissors and there aren't any left for me.

If we adhere to the theory that a child's ability to use more complex grammatical patterns is a learned behavior, we can safely assume that children will acquire the structures of their language (as they will acquire vocabulary and appropriate pronunciation) if their school experience is replete with language. Borrowing from the research of educators and psycholinguists, we can find support for the contention that reading material that approximates the language patterns of the learner will offer the greatest opportunity for successful reading (Strickland, 1962; Ruddell, 1965). Even when dialect differences are acknowledged and accepted, the reading materials that are based upon children's oral language help to ensure success.

But none of this information tells *how much* oral language is requisite for reading. How many words? How much understanding? We know of no data to answer these questions. We do know that a child needs experiences to generate ideas; and he or she needs words and the ability to put words together to express those ideas. But what experiences? How rich and how varied a language? These are some of the unresolved issues. It does appear that the language of successful readers is fairly fluent, has no prerequisite number of vocabulary words, and is intelligible most of the time; and these descriptions hold regardless of dialect differences. Two of the ways a teacher helps to develop language are by providing a language-rich environment and by providing opportunities to read one's own language.

A Language-Rich Environment

Those concerned with developing children's expressive skills attempt to provide both a language-rich environment and the kinds of experiences and activities that evoke reaction—thinking, questioning, and talking. Language growth stems from a child's firsthand experiences. And children need experiences that stimulate all their senses. Teachers travel with them, helping some to see, hear, and touch what they may have never previously experienced, and helping others to appreciate what they may have never fully experienced until their attention was directed by a sensitive adult. Teachers can provide opportunities to see and produce art; to hear and produce music; to take part in creative drama, dance, and movement; to develop projects; to manipulate puppets; to care for pets and plants; and to get involved at "creation stations" about the classroom.

Experiences of a more vicarious nature can also generate talk. *There is no better way to promote reading readiness than to read to a child.* If time to read must be stolen from somewhere else in the daily program, we advocate theft. Anticipation of "Story Time" and the satisfaction gained from sharing vicarious experiences contribute to an enriched language environment. Children can gain experiences vicariously through books, records, tapes, and television. But it is the book that permits a rerun at any speed, or allows a child to ponder over the pictures for a time and then resume reading.

The language-evoking environment, then, is one that allows children to explore existing interests and provides the potential for expanding their interests. It provides the setting for investigation, exploration, and imagination. In short, it provides opportunities.

TO PROVIDE A LANGUAGE-RICH ENVIRONMENT

Opportunities to *produce* (and talk about those productions)

Provide:
art supplies
clay, scissors, paint and brushes, large paper, glue, construction paper, easel, crayons, markers, cloth scraps, cotton balls
building supplies
tool bench, wood, hammer, nails
construction equipment
blocks, tiles, cardboard bricks
garden supplies
seeds, hoes, sprinkling can, pots
musical instruments
bells, cymbals, drum, sticks, tambourine, wood blocks, shakers, triangle

Opportunities to *listen* (and react to it)

Listen to:
tapes
records
read-alouds
flannel board and chalkboard stories
other children
poetry, rhymes
riddles, jokes
sounds of the world

Opportunities to *move* (and describe that movement)

Provide times to:
dance
explore movement

dramatize stories
role play
use wheel toys
play games
manipulate puppets
do finger plays

Opportunities to *become* (and talk about it)

Provide:
dress-up box
housekeeping center
puppets and simple stages

Opportunities to *see* (and discuss those experiences)

Provide:
field experiences
films
filmstrips
televisions
books
resource persons

Opportunities to *read* (even if you can't)

Provide:
books
magazines
pictures

The teacher doesn't attempt to provide *all* these opportunities (at least not every day), but we can tell of a teacher who came fairly close. She entered her room one morning wearing a bright pink apron with a huge pocket—a *poetry pocket*. One child was chosen to pick a poem from the poetry pocket, and the poem was shared with the children as a treasure would be shared. It had a happy, bouncing rhythm and the children chimed in. Before it was replaced in the pocket, several accompanying pictures had been drawn, and it had been "danced" and chorally "read." Now, it "just so happened" that the poem was about an apple—a ripe, red, juicy apple. "What," asked the teacher, "might be in this bag?" The guesses varied, but the consensus was apples. And, indeed, different kinds of apples were inside the bag: Jonathans, Winesaps, Golden Delicious. The children examined, compared, cut, tasted, and exclaimed. In short, they talked, and the teacher wrote what they said. Next she showed the class a film, *Johnny Appleseed*, with the sound turned off:
"What's he doing?"
"Planting seeds!"
"What kind of seeds?"

"Where's he going?"

"Is that his dog?"

"Apple blossoms!"

"I see apple trees!"

"He planted apple trees."

Although turning the sound off is one way to use a film that has a difficult narrative, this teacher had chosen to turn off the sound because she planned to get the children to tape an original narrative, one that would come easily in a few days—after they had listened to *Johnny Appleseed* read aloud. When the film was finished—as if on cue—came additional questions and discussion:

"Could we . . ."

"Did he . . ."

"I bet . . ."

"Have you . . ."

"What I want to know is . . ."

"Well," said the teacher, "Let's make a list of what you'd like to do and to know, and we'll see if the librarian can help."

And of course the librarian did help, for the poem, experience, film and discussion were no secret. Cooperative planning with the librarian was a part of this teacher's success. And you can no doubt point out other leads for further language development in this example. The opportunities are limitless.

try this ▶

Visit a kindergarten classroom and attempt to list:

what the teacher has done to stimulate language
how children react to those stimuli
what the children have initiated as a result of interests
how the teacher reacts to those interests

Review the list of teacher activities. Can you think of some ways the activities might be changed to increase the children's discussion? What other activities would seem appropriate to promote the language activities of these kindergarten children?

One point worth remembering is that all efforts toward enrichment of language are in vain unless the language that is produced and its producer are accepted and appreciated by the teacher.

Reading One's Own Language

Once there was a child who had not yet gone to school, and it happened that the child's father was an amateur photographer. He took many pictures, and the child herself often appeared in these pictures.

When they were developed, the child and her father pasted the pictures into books, and as they pasted, they talked. The child told the father what she saw in the pictures; the father told the child what he saw. Before the child had grown too much older, the father began to write under the pictures the words that the child had said. And they continued to talk. Then the child began to read what she had said. Soon she could read other things, too, and neither the child nor the father knew what had happened.

Given the natural egocentricity of children and the seemingly natural way in which language develops, it follows that seeing one's own experiencies and language translated into print will help to build the logical connections between spoken and written language. The transcribing of children's oral language for the purpose of helping them to read is called the *language experience* approach to reading instruction. Proponents of the language experience approach for beginners describe the value to the child of being an author and of producing a book:

> Instead of reading being presented as a wall of language that has to be penetrated, many teachers encourage children to learn the process of making a book for themselves. This is, if you like, de-mystifying books; they become something you do for others and not only something done to you by others. (Rosen and Rosen, 1973, p. 160)

In addition, the opportunity to experience being an author is another gateway toward development of interest in reading other authors.

Using children's language as a base for reading instruction generally follows one of two patterns: instruction is based on the free flow of language; or instruction is based on a more controlled language. The bias toward one or the other of the emphases usually depends upon the teacher's primary goal, that is, whether he or she defines the program as developing *readiness* to read (experience with language and development of concepts), or whether he or she actually is initiating the *reading* program and teaching mastery of the words dictated by children. The goals need not be exclusive (and often aren't); nevertheless, they provide a better understanding of what is occurring in the following examples of the language experience approach.

Example 1. On a rainy day, the children in Mr. Maxwell's kindergarten class are busily involved at various learning and experience centers when a small, bedraggled kitten on a ledge outside a classroom window is spotted by one of the children.

"Hey, look, there's a cat!"

"That's not a cat. It's a baby tiger."

"Boy, is he crying!"

"That cat looks just like my grandmother's."

"Can we let him in?"

"I think he belongs across the street."

"He's wet, Mr. Maxwell."

"Can I take him home?"

"Man, look at him rub on the window."

"He wants in."

Mr. Maxwell, of course, has the choice of quieting his class and sending them back to the stations or using the experience and the language it has evoked to write a story with his children. He may get a box and rescue the kitten, in which case, the language will surely flow free.

"He saved his life."

"He oughta drive a rescue truck."

"Don't let him scratch you, man."

The teacher tells the class he will check with the neighbors at noon to see if the kitten belongs to anyone. Later that day or the next, when the kitten is calm, the children settle around it, and Mr. Maxwell has materials gathered for the story. He may have chalkboard and chalk or chartpaper and marker; optional (but fun) are manila sentence strips, drawing paper, scissors, and crayons.

"Let's tell a story about our kitten. What shall we call the story?"*

"Let's say 'A Rainy Day Friend'," a child suggests.

"That's a good title!" Mr. Maxwell says as he writes it down.

For the next few minutes, the children recall and discuss the kitten adventure. When talk wanes, Mr. Maxwell prompts it with well-chosen questions (especially ones that tap sensory impressions). He tries to ensure each child's involvement. Often he asks, "What would you like me to write?" He believes that although all children will not be able to recall or reread the full text, there will be some learning for everyone and great interest for all. He prints on the chalkboard and the children watch. Sometimes he stops to point out two words that start alike, a word that has appeared in a previous story, or the reason for a period. But his talk never interrupts the children's.

When the story is finished, Mr. Maxwell reads it back (with flourish and pride); then he invites the children to read along, his voice pulling theirs, if necessary, in order to maintain the sound of "talk written down." When he hears a voice or two pull away from the others or read faster because of increasing familiarity, it is time to ask those children to read alone the parts of the story or even the sentences that they themselves dictated.

Mr. Maxwell next asks the children to illustrate the story. While they are at work, he transfers the story to the chart pad where stories are kept for review. He can also use this time to copy sentences onto sentence strips for later work with matching and sequencing. At this point, the work with the story is far from over. Mr. Maxwell plans to type it and make copies for the children to take home and read. He plans to help the children reread the story the next day, to match the sentence strips

* It's an equally good practice to title a story when it's finished—calling attention to the main idea.

with the chart paper model, to order the sentence strips in a pocket chart as they occurred in the story, and later, to cut the sentences apart and then reconstruct the story.

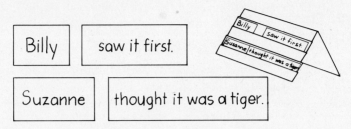

Some of the children's illustrations are cut out and pasted onto the chart.

Example 2. Another way to connect language and print is to have the children first illustrate the experience and then talk about it. As they are drawing, the teacher moves about the room talking to each child and listening to individual accounts. He or she writes what each says at the bottom of the pictures.

A pocket chart is a tool for a teacher. Pocket charts can be made in various ways according to the children's needs and the teaching method used. In other words, it should work for you.

Here are some ideas.

Materials:

Pocket charts may be constructed with almost any type of board. Some possibilities are: folders, posterboard, heavy cardboard (tear up a box).

Size:

The size of your pocket chart will vary with its purpose.

Large pocket charts (24″ × 36″) will be most useful in making presentations to one or more children. It might stand up (but it does not have to).

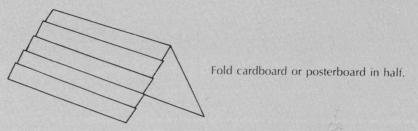

Fold cardboard or posterboard in half.

Small pocket charts might be given to the children to use independently or to follow along with your presentation. Manila folders can serve as individual pocket charts.

Pockets:

The pockets can be made with various materials, also. Be sure to check the depth of the pockets against the size of the phrase or word cards that you will use. The pocket should be about half the size of the cards. (Test this before attaching pockets permanently.)

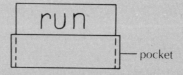

pocket

Materials for pockets:

(a) strips of poster board taped or glued in place.

(b) clear, plastic pockets—take two strips of clear, adhesive paper and stick them together, adhesive to adhesive. These strips may be mounted with tape. The child can see through these pockets and can write on them with wax crayons or water-base markers. Laminate the support board, so that the pocket chart is completely washable.

(c) corrugated bulletin board strips.

Through this language experience activity, the children have developed a story, thought about related experiences, and illustrated their story ideas. They have discussed, listened, read, and illustrated—a complete language experience.

Variation 1. One variation of this method is especially useful to ensure that each child is able to participate and to see his or her language become print. A collection of these drawings can be bound together as a book of personalized stories for rereading. In addition, both of these variations can serve as a realistic and meaningful way to initiate reading instruction. That is, the children who are interested in rereading their own stories will start to retain and recognize words, providing the teacher with the most reliable clue as to who is ready for more opportunities to read.

Variation 2. If language experience is used as a method for beginning reading, some teachers want at times to ensure mastery of the vocabulary of the story. These teachers then limit the length and content of a story. They believe that repetition of the most common service or function words, such as *the, he, go, in,* will provide the preliminary practice necessary to succeed with beginning reading materials. While not a pure language experience approach, in which no constraints are placed on a child's language production, this instruction does grow from the child. In this approach, reading commonly begins with a book authored by the children, who, in effect, dictate a book about themselves.

As much as is possible, without cutting off thought, the dictation is limited and vocabulary is repeated. If children are learning to read using this variation of language experience (that is, controlled presentation of their language), the experiences they have and then talk about are written by the teacher in repetitious patterns. The aim is to provide enough practice so that a body of common words can be recognized on sight. These immediately recognized words will provide the basis for learning sound to symbol relationships and will enable the child to read books with controlled vocabulary.

If the children in Mr. Maxwell's room had been experiencing this variation, their story might look like this:

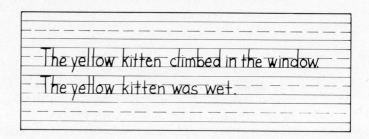

The rationale underlying the use of the child's own language as both the logical tool for developing reading readiness and the initial vehicle of instruction has been stated by R. V. Allen (1976, pp. 51–55), a leading advocate of this approach:

What I can think about, I can talk about.
What I can say I can write—or someone can write for me.
What I can write, I can read.
I can read what I write, and what other people can write for me to read.

The advantages of providing a rich language environment and then capitalizing on that language for reading instruction are many:

High interest and motivation result from sharing and discussing experiences.
Acquiring the necessary "materials" for instruction is easy.
The control of vocabulary is optional but unnecessary.
The reading material is meaningful for each child.
Success is built in.
Reading sounds like speaking, and the relationship between the two is perceived.

Giving children a chance to speak, and then to see that speech become print, helps to develop understanding of what a *word* is and that words are made of *letters*. If the teacher moves his or her hand from left to right as the chart story is read, children have the opportunity to follow the left-to-right direction of print. If frequently repeated words are noted, matched, and made important, a sight vocabulary begins to emerge. Finally, if discoveries are made that two words start alike and sound alike at the beginning, there is basis for work in sound-symbol association. Further description of the language experience approach can be found in Chapter 10 and in the references for that chapter.

Other Aspects of Reading Readiness

While certain degrees of physical development and language awareness seem critical for learning to read, other aspects of learning also have bearing on reading instruction. They include a knowledge of letters and words and the ability to follow directions.

Letters and Words

Even though reading is based on oral language and follows the same grammatical and semantic patterns as oral language, there is logic and evidence to substantiate that reading is cued by letters and by letter sequences. Perhaps it is this information, coupled with research linking knowledge of letter names to success in beginning reading (Durrell, 1958; Lowell, 1971), that has led to the conclusion that letter names should be taught to children before they begin to read. The difficulty with this conclusion is that one cannot necessarily assume that when two measures vary in the same direction (that is, when knowledge of one goes up, success with another goes up) there is a causal relationship between the two. This means that although one might expect knowledge of letter names to affect reading achievement, the ability to remember letter names *and* to succeed in reading are most likely functions of some other common underlying ability. A better rationale for teaching letter names early is simply so that both teacher and learner have common referents when they discuss distinctive features of letters and words; *but reading instruction need not be postponed until letter names are mastered.*

In addition to providing common referents, attention to letters and letter sequences seems to be an ideal way to teach differences in form (visual discrimination)—a method that will have a more direct effect on reading than will great amounts of time spent matching squiggles or geometric shapes.

It is not always necessary to plan isolated drills or separate activities to teach letter names and words. Words and letters can be pointed out as they are used in daily activities: making lists, writing stories or letters, and making labels and namecards. Then the labels, charts, tags, and stories are referred to in order to increase the child's awareness of letters and words.

"Who can find the place for Suzanne's coat?"

"Who is the Lunch Club Chairman today?"

"What word in this story starts like your name, Tim?"

"Look at the calendar. With what letter does this month start?"

The final section of this chapter (pages 134–45) gives some specific activities that can be used to develop awareness of letters and words.

Following Directions

Ask a beginner to point to a word and you may see the finger swoop and land on a picture, a letter, a page number, or simply on blank space. Too often, perhaps, we take for granted that children who have watched others read have made the connection between language and print. There are other concepts peculiar to the language of instruction: school success is, to a large degree, dependent upon the ability to understand those concepts in order to follow directions, both orally and in paper-and-pencil tasks. Like the assumption that children know what a *word* is, so do we also assume that beginners understand such terms as *letter*, *alphabet*, *page*, and *number*. We are sometimes caught lamenting some child's inability to perform a task when we haven't stopped to check whether or not the directions are understood. Determining mastery of the terminology of the instructions is essential before we infer that failure in any task is due to the task itself.

For example, successful performance on one popular reading-readiness test is based not only upon the ability to discriminate symbols and words but also upon the ability to find

"a *row* of pictures at the *top* of the *page*."

"an object *before* a green *line*."

"*another* object that is just *like* it."

The teacher is directed by the test manual to say, "You should have made a mark on the second one of three pictures in the first row." The heavy conceptual load in that sentence is evident. Other tests require an understanding of such terms as *first, under, middle line*, and *bottom line*. Children must also deal with *same, different, above, around, next to, circle*, and *below* as well as with seemingly ambiguous directions: "Go down to the next box."

The risk in assuming that a child understands these frequently used, spatial-conceptual words in oral directions is that both the assessment and the resulting decisions may not be valid. Thus, teachers may flirt with a possibly faulty conclusion that a child can't "visually discriminate," when the difficulty may have been produced by a failure to understand the task.

Teachers who review their beginning-reading curriculum materials and list the most frequently occurring words in the language of assessment and instruction (related to direction-giving, spatial concepts, and similarities and differences) could identify, through preliminary screening, those children who need more practice. Those children who fail to understand key words can be given instruction with real objects in three-dimensional settings, they can learn to manipulate toys (or themselves) on, under, beside, and next to other objects before operating with these same concepts in two dimensions.

Examples of specific activities that can build understanding of these relational concepts are found later in this chapter (pages 138–40). The teacher who uses them is, of course, building much more than just the ability to follow directions: he or she is training thinkers who will not only be able to understand directions but who will, one day, be better able to think for themselves.

Gearing Instruction to Identified Needs

Readiness instruction should provide for each child the set of experiences needed for success in reading. In some beginning reading programs, too much attention is directed toward practices that may qualify for waste-of-time awards. For example, it seems useless to offer a child a complete reading-readiness battery when he or she is already reading. It seems futile to offer a child exercises in matching geometric shapes when he or she can already perceive differences in letters. Any attention given to auditory-discrimination skills should reflect the teacher's intention to emphasize auditory discrimination within the reading program; that is, unless the reading program will put a premium upon discrimination of isolated sounds, there is little need to emphasize auditory discrimination of isolated sounds. And unless the reading program emphasizes "directionality" mazes, there may be no need to teach them. Appropriate instruction, then, should:

> fit the particular child
> be important for success in *reading*

These two guidelines require that a teacher must know the beginner and what the beginner will need to accomplish in order to be successful in the reading program.

One of the tenets of teaching is that learners and programs will vary markedly. Yet each learner can profit from instruction if instruction is geared toward level and need. The next sections of this chapter deal with determining who is ready for what, using both formal and informal checks or measures. We believe that you will find children who are already reading, those who are just beginning to respond to reading instruction, and those who do not respond to reading in almost every class of beginners. We believe that each of these children needs a language-rich environment, further opportunities to read and to be read to, and reading instruction* geared to interests and paced appropriately.

---

* The reading instruction mentioned above *is not* of the formal, group-based, program-prescribed variety, but rather the kind of reading instruction that occurs when children label objects, "write" books, share stories, listen to tapes and records, make charts, visit the library, and are surrounded by books.

Identifying the Beginner with Readiness Tests

Tests of reading readiness flooded the educational market in the aftermath of the First World War, a period in which educational researchers were emphasizing "automatic and unfolding behaviors" and when "early reading" meant perusing the morning newspaper. Results of readiness tests have been used and misused to make decisions relative to placement and grouping for reading, to plan curricular content, and to predict success or failure. Following the readiness-test boom in the early decades of this century came the readiness-research rush of the past forty years (Mortenson, 1968). Characteristically, this research has been concerned with the identification and isolation of variables in an attempt to predict reading success. As early as 1939, however, Gates and his coauthors (1939) concluded from their appraisal of readiness-assessment techniques: "It should be noted that among the tests of little or no predictive value are many tests and ratings widely recommended in books and articles on reading-readiness testing and teachings."

There is little reason to believe that standardized readiness-measuring instruments have improved significantly since this conclusion was drawn. Yet educational judgments regarding placement and programs for preschool and beginning first graders are still commonly based upon readiness-test results (Farr and Anastasiow, 1969; Adelman and Feshbach, 1971).

Once the value of any particular measurement instrument is established, its appropriateness must be determined by a clearly understood instructional need. As we pointed out in Chapter 2, the use of any test (including readiness tests) should be dependent upon what one wants to know. Ask most kindergarten and first-grade teachers why they give readiness tests and they will answer that the tests are part of a dictum handed down from central administration. But why is readiness testing such a universal phenomenon? And of what use are the results? Traditionally, readiness tests have been administered for three purposes:

(1) to determine whether or not the child is indeed ready to read
(2) to reveal—through use of the test as a diagnostic tool—areas of specific strengths and weaknesses
(3) to determine which children to place in which groups for reading or for reading-readiness instruction

The strengths and weaknesses of readiness tests as used to meet each of these three important goals are examined in the following sections.

Can a readiness test predict reading success? A teacher who uses a reading-readiness test to determine whether children are ready to read should decide:

How closely related are the purposes of this readiness test and the purposes of my instructional program?
Is every child ready for the readiness test?

Are there those who don't understand the language of the test?
Are there those who don't need to take a complete battery?

Research results establish a positive correlation (from .40 to .60) between readiness-test results and school achievement (Weintraub, 1967). This means that those children who perform well on readiness tests are more likely to perform well on a reading achievement test than are children who score lower on readiness tests. This also means that a high score on a readiness test is associated with a high score on a reading achievement test taken later in one's schooling. Readiness tests, then, *can* predict which children are more likely to be successful with reading. These tests are most valid if they reflect the subsequent reading program and if the children understand the mechanics and language of test-taking.

Can a readiness test help me group for reading (or readiness) instruction? Since getting ready for reading is a continuous process rather than one composed of discrete phases or skills, and since readiness implies a combination of task characteristics, learner characteristics, and instructional methodology, and since readiness tests are measures of the extent to which a child has achieved the maturity, skills, or information necessary for beginning new learning, the answer is a qualified "no." The diverse viewpoints as to *what* and *how much of it* constitutes reading readiness should make us wary of any single-factor approach to making a grouping decision. According to Durkin:

> Reading readiness *is not one thing*. That is, it is not a single package of certain kinds and amounts of abilities. Consequently, when we talk about readiness for reading, we are referring to different things in different children. We are really talking about readiness*es*—a rather awkward word—not *a* readiness. (1974, p. 228)

Our qualified "no," then, needs explanation. No one factor should prescribe instructional groups; and we have attempted to show this by illustrating both the lack of consistency and the potentially faulty information that could be gleaned from readiness assessments. A better approach is flexible grouping that is based on children's needed skills, learning rates, and individual and overlapping interests in reading.

Flexible grouping means that one child may be a part of several instructional groups depending upon needs and interests. The groups may be short term and have a shifting constituency.

Can I use a readiness test as a diagnostic indicator of specific strengths and weaknesses? A look at several different readiness tests reveals an unsurprising lack of consensus as to what reading-readiness tests should measure—unsurprising because of the difficulties that exist in trying to arrive at a complete definition of reading readiness. Thus, while one commonly used readiness test (the Gates-MacGinitie) measures seven skill areas in seven subtests, another (the Murphy-Durrell)

measures three areas. Robert Rude (1973) examined five different readiness tests and found twelve different subskill areas being tapped:

(1) vocabulary knowledge (the child's ability to store verbal concepts)
(2) listening comprehension (the child's ability to listen and to answer questions or retell based on what has been heard)
(3) letter recognition (the child's ability to match letter names with letter shapes)
(4) numerical concepts and recognition (the child's ability to engage in counting and matching tasks and to recognize numbers)
(5) visual-motor coordination (the child's ability to perform simple manipulative tasks such as copying a figure or tracing through a maze)
(6) rhyming words (the child's ability to match words that rhyme)
(7) phonemic correspondence (the child's ability to match printed letter with letter sounds)
(8) rate of learning (words) (the child's rate of learning a few words)
(9) sound discrimination (the child's ability to identify different letter sounds)
(10) blending sounds (the child's ability to blend letter sounds into words
(11) word reading (the child's ability to identify a word read by the teacher)
(12) visual discrimination (the child's ability to match a stimulus sample with a like pattern from an array of choices)

Given the confusion surrounding the concept of reading readiness, a cursory scan of the list may suggest some value for several of these areas. But for a teacher to sort through subtest scores and then to make diagnostic decisions relative to a child's performance, there must be some understanding of how test, subtest, and item mesh with the teacher's definition of readiness and with the resultant reading program.

Let's assume that you have screened your beginners and determined your readers. Let's also assume that you have located and taught the language of tests and of school. Now, let's take a look at some subtests of reading readiness to see what kinds of information the tests typically yield and of what potential value the information is. We will examine subtests of visual discrimination; visual memory; knowledge of letter names; auditory discrimination; listening comprehension; vocabulary; and motor skills.

We recognize that no test can fully assess the complex skills that are associated with learning to read. None even purports to measure the physical and emotional factors that are so important. Most readiness tests attempt to measure the skills most closely (and obviously) related to reading achievement.

Visual discrimination. Most children are screened for sharpness of vision as part of their school entrance requirement. With such tests as Snellen eye charts and the Keystone Telebinocular, children's visual acuity and accommodation are determined. Deviances from normal vision are re-

"I didn't study for any eye test, did you?"

"The Family Circus" by Bil Keane, March 5, 1975. © 1975 The Register and Tribune Syndicate, Inc.

ferred to an eye care specialist.* Visual discrimination is not visual acuity, however; nor is it dependent upon perfect vision. Visual discrimination, as defined by the task, is the ability to perceive likenesses and differences in forms. A subtest of visual discrimination may require that the child match the first object in a row with another object that is exactly the same. For example:

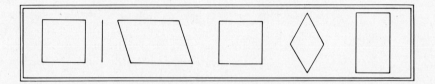

By consistently marking the correct choice, the child is supposedly indicating the presence of visual discrimination and, one hopes, enough of the skill to ensure success with the visual aspects of the reading task.

Some test-makers (and some teachers) forego the assessment of ability to match geometric forms, preferring to measure the more realistic task of matching letters and words, as in the following example:

E					
O		M	O	R	S
1					
H		W	A	H	S
2					
F		P	F	E	D
3					
b		b	d	p	q
4					
at		to	of	it	at

From Lee-Clark Reading Readiness Test devised by J. Murray Lee and Willis W. Clark. Reprinted by permission of the publisher, CTB/McGraw-Hill, Del Monte Research Park, Monterey, Calif. 93940. Copyright © 1960 by McGraw-Hill, Inc. All Rights Reserved. Printed in the U.S.A.

* For a knowledgeable treatment of visual-screening techniques, see Fred Jobe, *Screening Vision in Schools* (Newark, Del.: International Reading Association, 1976).

And, indeed, if a child can successfully discriminate letters and words, there appears to be no reason to assess or to teach discrimination of abstract shapes. However, failure on a visual-discrimination task could mean either:

> that the child did not understand the required task (he didn't know what to do)
>
> or
>
> that he needs instruction that will help to focus on distinguishable characteristics of letters (and words)

A Pooh bear is a Pooh bear regardless as to whether it is right side up, upside down, or backwards. And so is an *l* or an *O*, but a *b* upside down is *p*, and a *b* backwards is *d*. Rotation in space doesn't always work for letters (as it does for Pooh). Some children need instruction before this realization becomes their reality.

At this point, it should be emphasized that poor performance on a readiness subtest does not necessarily mean that reading instruction should be delayed, but rather mandates reading instruction geared to the pattern of strengths and weaknesses the child exhibits.

Visual memory. The majority of readiness tests don't attempt to measure visual memory directly. The element of visual memory is elusive. Defined by task, it is the retention of the visual form in the memory so that it can be recognized when the stimulus form is no longer in view. For example, the teacher may present the word *hat*. When the word is removed from view, the child may be asked to locate and mark *hat* when it appears among a number of choices.

The child who is successful with the task is assumed to have demonstrated yet another characteristic of a potentially successful reader. The child who is unsuccessful (that is, cannot remember and mark the correct word) may need reformulation of the task or more intensive exposure and practice so that he or she will be able to experience success.

Knowledge of letter names. Recognition of letters of the alphabet has long been regarded as an important skill of the prereading period. It appears on nearly all readiness tests. Generally, the children are required to identify the letter from a set of choices or distractors (either in upper or lower case) when the letter name is pronounced by the teacher. The following example is from the Murphy-Durrell test:*

6		N	I	Z	B	L	19		A	Y	C	T	V
7		U	B	O	F	P	20		L	W	F	N	M
8		E	N	S	O	C	21		M	T	W	E	

Reproduced from the Murphy-Durrell Reading Readiness Analysis. Copyright © 1965 by Harcourt Brace Jovanovich, Inc. Reproduced by special permission of the publisher.

While this skill predicts success with reading, knowing letter names is not necessarily the *cause* of later reading achievement. Children who have not yet mastered letter names need not be held back from reading instruction until letter names are mastered. Learning the names of letters can occur simultaneously with learning to read. Ideas for teaching letter names are included on pages 134–36 of this chapter.

Auditory discrimination. Auditory discrimination is most commonly defined as the ability to perceive differences in sounds. By definition, it could be established that all children with oral language (with speech) have indicated ability to discriminate auditorially. Therefore, the method of assessing auditory discrimination adhered to in most readiness tests may be appropriate only when there is a close relationship between the assessment methodology and the instructional program to follow.

For example, an auditory-discrimination subtest frequently calls upon the child to locate the picture of an object that *starts* like a stimulus word or picture; *ends* like a stimulus word or picture; or *rhymes* with a stimulus word or picture.

The teacher says:

"Find a pie, a box, and a pencil. Put your finger on the box so that I can see whether everyone has found it. Now listen carefully as I say the names of the pictures in the box. *Pie—box—pencil*. One of these names sounds like *fox*. Think which one sounds like *fox*. Put a mark on the picture whose name sounds like *fox*.

* Instead of numbers alone to identify the test items, pictures of familiar items are used.

"Move your finger down to the next box, like this. Find a mask, a spoon, and a cap. Listen carefully—*mask, spoon, cap*. Which one sounds like *tap*? Put a mark on the one whose name sounds like *tap*."

From Byron H. Van Roekel et al., *Pre-Reading Test of Scholastic Ability to Determine Reading Readiness,* Teacher's Manual (New York: Harper & Row, 1966), p. 16.

We can assume that children who are successful with auditory-discrimination tasks will experience little difficulty if their initial reading program emphasizes phonics—if, of course, these children understand what they are being asked to do and if the sometimes abstract nature of the phonics approach hasn't confused them. For those who score poorly on auditory-discrimination tests, the teacher *may* first assume that they can't discriminate auditorially. However, it is more likely that the child is confused by the task.

Regardless of whether the child's difficulty on an auditory-discrimination test is due to confusion about the task or to limited auditory-discrimination ability, the difficulty will not hinder initial reading instruction *unless* the reading program is one that emphasizes discrimination tasks. For example, some initial reading programs include exercises in which children are expected to respond to auditory cues: "Here is a word that starts like *ball* and rhymes with *hat*; what is it?" If a child has had difficulty on a auditory-discrimination test, he or she is likely to have difficulty with that kind of instruction.

There are two different strategies that can be used if a child has difficulty with auditory-discrimination tasks. The first is to *avoid* activities that emphasize auditory discrimination. Instead, plan the child's program to build on his or her strengths. For example, perhaps the child has good visual memory or rich language; you might use language experiences and easy-to-read trade books to build on the child's strength.

A second strategy is to determine how the task of listening for word parts confused the child. For example, the child may not understand what is meant by "starts the same as" or "starts alike." The child may be thinking of rhyming words or exact repetitions to meet the criterion of "alike." Carefully sequenced instruction will usually overcome the difficulty.

Teaching suggestions for auditory discrimination can be found on pages 141–43.

Listening comprehension.   It seems reasonable to assume that span of attention is one variable that will directly affect the child's ability to listen and to retain what is heard. Other factors include the extent of the child's language development, emotional and cognitive maturity, and the degree of the match between the required listening task and the child's background experiences. No readiness test tells us much about all these listening behaviors. The *Metropolitan Reading Readiness Test* offers a subtest called *Listening,* which requires the child to mark the appropriate picture after a description of the picture is read. This test is similar to the listening subtests on most readiness tests. The following series of pictures is an item from this test. The teacher reads a sentence, such as "Put your finger on the key. Listen. Ben tried to set a glass of milk on the kitchen table, but something happened. When he saw what had happened, he got a broom. Mark the picture that shows what happened just before he got the broom."

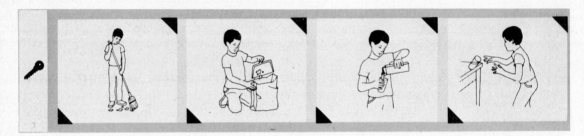

Reproduced from the Metropolitan Readiness Tests. Copyright © 1976 by Harcourt Brace Jovanovich, Inc. Reproduced by special permission of the publisher.

There doesn't seem to be conclusive evidence that *listening,* as measured by MRRT, and by other readiness tests, is a requisite for successful reading. But while no one knows how well or how long a beginning reader should be able to listen, there is no doubt that teachers of beginners use listening behavior as a description of school success.

Vocabulary.   As we discussed earlier, some degree of language awareness and competence appears to be a prerequisite for learning to read. Understanding of certain vocabulary words appears to be essential for effective communication as well as for appropriate responses to school tasks and tests. The teacher should attempt to list the specific terms children need to know for there is little agreement about what such tests measure. A test of vocabulary may sample from an extensive vocabulary list and not be specific to any instructional program. It may be that vocabulary terms are tested as one part of Listening Comprehension or of Following Directions; there may be no vocabulary test on the readiness test. Success with a vocabulary subtest generally indicates that a child has an experiential background similar to the test builders' sample. Lack of success with prescribed vocabulary probably indicates a different set of experiences than those sampled by the test. The crucial vocabulary for a child in your class will, in most cases, be dictated by the instructional program and not by standardized test results.

Motor skills. As measured by readiness tests, requisite motor skills include completing figures and copying figures and letters. Again, it would be dangerous to assume that failure on a motor-skills exercise indicates any deep-rooted problem or that success indicates a bright future with reading. Too little is known about the relationship between motor skills and reading readiness.

All these readiness subtests provide diagnostic information for the discerning teacher *if* they are used to make decisions that are appropriate to the child and for his or her program. Not all subtests appear to be of equal value. For certain programs, teachers could elect not to consider whole subtests or specific items on a subtest. Test information is diagnostic only to the extent that it leads to an instructional decision for a real-life child in a particular program.

The Solution Is Demanding

It is the teacher's responsibility to determine what to test and how to test it. Amid the confusion surrounding reading readiness, that seems a big order. One might argue that it is the test author's job to define what is to be tested. But differences in test content and format would be expected based on legitimate differences in various authors' conceptualizations of what a child needs to learn in order to become a reader. The teacher may choose to accept an author's definitions or may decide what *he* or *she* believes reading readiness to be and select a test accordingly. The latter alternative is preferable, especially if one agrees that a teacher should have the process of reading or reading readiness clearly in mind as materials and procedures are selected throughout a school year.

Eventually, however, the teacher's task in assessing reading readiness will become easier as the all-purpose test is gradually replaced with specific tests for specific purposes. Even after this is done, the teacher must still develop techniques of assessment that are inexorably intertwined with instruction. Teachers should be conscious of their beliefs about the skills of reading readiness and should use these beliefs to select tests or to build informal measures.

Using Informal Assessments

Since readiness tests fall short of providing much of the information needed for instructing a child, a sound alternative is for individual teachers to make individual decisions for individual children continuously and informally.

Although it may sound naive and simplistic, one of the most useful things each teacher of beginners can do is to sit with pencil and pad and write down what constitutes success with reading in his or her own classroom. The more clearheaded we can be about what we are attempting to accomplish with our learners, the more easily it can be accomplished and the more readily we can judge whether it has been accomplished. Formation of clear-cut objectives is also, of course, the first step toward finding out where the learner is in relation to where he or she will be. It is far easier but much less effective to walk into a room and just "start teaching" than it is to think about what you want children to accomplish as a consequence of instruction. Rather than just starting to teach, you need to use your objectives to set about determining what each learner already knows, what each one needs, and how each one can best acquire it.

Because one of your goals is almost certain to be to provide instruction that is aimed toward each child's present level of reading achievement, you will need to first determine if there are children in your classroom who can already read.

"How, then, do I determine a reader?" you may ask. Ask the child if he or she recognizes any of the words on charts and labels around the classroom. This may sound obvious; yet there are many early readers who have gone undetected as they underwent readiness testing and then "relearned" to read.

It follows, then, that the most logical way to determine whether or not a child will be reasonably successful with reading instruction is to offer that instruction using a highly interesting and appropriate method, such as language experience, and then to evaluate the degree of success experienced. (This is opposed to offering a balance beam, a set of mazes, some forms to match, or some dotted lines to trace.)

We can also take another look at the subskills or aspects of reading readiness that were examined by formal measures. This time, the emphasis will be on how to determine the presence or absence of those skills using *informal* means developed by the teacher.

Visual discrimination. A child who can discriminate visually can put the blocks away on the proper shelf, can stack similarly shaped flannelboard objects together, and perhaps can point out to you, "There's a letter that is in my name!" Most children appear to have few problems with visual discrimination. Upper-case letters are sometimes easier for them than are lower-case, since some lower-case letters look very similar and, therefore, cause beginners problems—*p, q, b, d,* for example.

HOW TO ASSESS VISUAL DISCRIMINATION (WITH PAPER AND PENCIL)

Make a letter-matching exercise that is legible and has few items per page. If it will be used individually, make it of heavy oak-tag and laminate it for durability; if it will be used with a group, a ditto master is sufficient. The first item is completed for the child as an example. Children are told to find a letter that is just like the first one. (With a laminated sheet they can correct initial mistakes easily.)

b	d	(b)	p
m	n	w	m
q	q	p	d
c	o	a	c

Note that letters with highly similar visual features are presented together. Children who are unable to match these letters may be offered dissimilar letters or even geometric forms. If they are unable to match dissimilar letters and forms, they may need to stop the paper-and-pencil activity and work with three-dimensional objects such as blocks and beads, until they understand the task.

HOW TO ASSESS VISUAL DISCRIMINATION (WITH MANIPULATIVE MATERIALS)

Make letter wheels. Cut two six-inch circles of posterboard or oak-tag. Laminate, then cut a window in what will be the top circle. Use a marker to write a letter next to the window. Print letters around the perimeter of the bottom circle. Put the circles together with a brad. The child turns the bottom wheel until the matching letter is found. By wiping off the stimulus letter, you can reuse the circle to check another letter. If the stimulus letter is fixed, you will need several wheels.

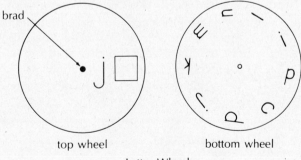

Letter Wheels

Tape words around the room (for example, a child's name, "desk," "chair," and "window"). Give the child a stack of the same words and see if he or she can tape these words up next to the matching words.

Make letter or word pockets. Cut slits that will hold a letter card. The child looks through a stack of letters or words until he or she locates one that matches. That card is slipped into the corner slots.

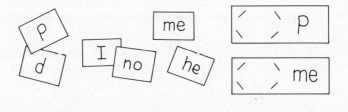

Visual memory. The rationale underlying assessment of visual memory stems from research and experience that links the ability to retain mental images of words with success in reading. There seems to be no clear-cut evidence that the two abilities have a causal relationship. Nevertheless, you may wish to know how your beginners deal with visual tasks that appear related to reading.

HOW TO ASSESS VISUAL MEMORY (WITH PAPER AND PENCIL)

Give the children a sheet of letters, printed or typed on a typewriter that prints in large mansucript letters. (Most elementary schools have such typewriters.) Then show a card with a letter on it to the children. After they have looked at the card for a few seconds, remove it. Ask them to find and mark the letter they saw in the first row on their sheet.

b	d	f
m	n	u
o	c	a
l	f	t

It is important that you make certain the children understand the directions before you assume that any failure on this task was due to poor visual memory.

You can try the same activity with simple words:

cat	bat	man
see	bet	be
he	she	me

If you use the word cards after letter cards, you need to make certain that the children look at all the letters before they mark. Some children (having established a "letter set") will look at the *first letter* in a word and then mark any word on their paper that begins with that letter. A teacher may falsely conclude that the child has faulty visual memory when he or she is, in fact, performing logically.

HOW TO ASSESS VISUAL MEMORY (WITH MANIPULATIVE MATERIALS)

If retaining a letter or words seems too difficult for some children, see if they can construct a three-bead chain in a model you demonstrate and then remove

arrange three to five toys in an order you demonstrate and then shuffle
arrange felt shapes on a flannel board in an order you demonstrate and then remove
locate from three choices and then trace a sandpaper letter after a model is shown and then removed

Knowledge of letter names. Learning the names of letters of the alphabet *need not* occur as a prerequisite to reading. Teachers do teach letter names, however, and they need to know which children know which letter names.

HOW TO ASSESS ALPHABET KNOWLEDGE (WITH PAPER AND PENCIL)

For paper-and-pencil group assessment, you can develop a twenty-six-item test, one item for each lower-case letter. (A second assessment could use upper-case letters.) Tell the children to locate the letter in a row as you call its name. Careful recording of errors will produce a record of which children need experience with letter names.

Make certain that they can follow the directions, keeping their places with a marker.

d	e	m
f	g	k
l	p	r
a	t	j
s	q	p

HOW TO ASSESS ALPHABET KNOWLEDGE (WITH MANIPULATIVE MATERIALS)

When the paper-and-pencil approach to the assessment of letter names is too difficult, not appropriate, or too dull, try

- giving the child a deck (or partial deck) of alphabet cards. Ask the child to locate a letter as you call its name.
- making a clown with no polka dots, or a jar with no cookies, or a tree with no apples. Tell the child to put on as many (dots, cookies, apples) letters as he or she can name.

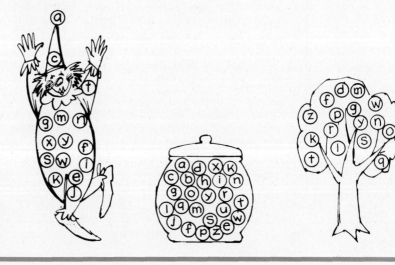

Auditory discrimination. As mentioned earlier, successfully diagnosing a child's auditory-discrimination ability is critically dependent upon the child's understanding of the required task. As you can imagine, the tasks related to auditory discrimination are generally abstract and must appear to the child to be remote from learning to read. If you want the child to listen for words that begin in the same way, you need to make certain he or she knows what "begin with" and "the same" mean. This is no small task. Sometimes, starting with a gamelike activity and very easy discriminations is helpful. Such preparation can be handled in this manner: "Let's play a listening game. I will say two words. If the words are the *same*, clap your hands. If the words are different, do nothing. Ready?"

Try two words that are identical first. If the child claps, you will suspect that he or she knows what "same" means. Next, try two words that are totally different, for example, *penny, tomato.* (If the child doesn't clap, you can try a few more word pairs, which will eventually differ in only *one* phoneme—*bat, pat.*)

HOW TO ASSESS AUDITORY DISCRIMINATION (WITH PAPER AND PENCIL)

For individual or group assessment, word pairs are read. Children mark the two faces that are the same if the words are the same, and two faces that are different if the words are different. In this example, the child marks different faces.

HOW TO ASSESS AUDITORY DISCRIMINATION (WITH MANIPULATIVE MATERIALS)

A continuation of the clapping-silence response that was described above may provide sufficient information about how well individuals discriminate. In addition, another useful exercise is to ask children to finish rhyming couplets:

    I know a bat
    who likes a _____

    I know a mitten
    that fits a _____

Yet another activity is to have the child identify objects (or pictures) from a set of objects or a stack of pictures that a

      hungry horse likes to eat (hay, hotdogs, hamburgers)

                     or that a

      bumbling bear might bring to a party (bananas, babies, Batman)

Children have stimulus pictures with pockets. They place pictures into the pockets that begin like the picture. (They need not see letters or words to play.)

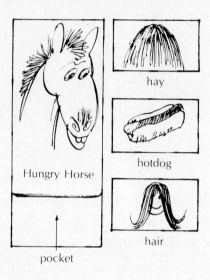

Hungry Horse

pocket

hay

hotdog

hair

Listening comprehension. An important skill for beginners is the ability to listen to stories with understanding.

HOW TO ASSESS LISTENING COMPREHENSION (WITH PAPER AND PENCIL)

A simple group assessment can be constructed by collecting or drawing pictures that fit simple stories. Children can mark pictures in response to questions after listening to the story.

"Find a picture that shows what Sandy liked to eat."

"Find a picture that showed how Sandy felt."

Carefully noting both children's responses to stories and answers to questions about story events and characters provides a great deal of informal information. For example, see if the child can

recall story details
retell the story
give the story a title (main idea)
sequence events
offer reasonable predictions of what may happen
define or give examples of what story words mean

Vocabulary. If a child is to be successful in initial reading instruction, it is important that the child's oral vocabulary include the words he or she is to be taught to recognize in print. If a beginning reader has to learn the meanings of unfamiliar words at the same time he or she is learning to identify those words in print, learning to read has been unnecessarily complicated.

HOW TO ASSESS VOCABULARY (WITH PAPER AND PENCIL)

Important vocabulary words (including the language of instruction) can be gathered from magazine illustrations or drawn by the teacher. Children can select and mark pictures that illustrate objects, ideas, feelings, spatial relations, and so on.

Much can be learned by sharing a book with a child. (*Richard Scarry's ABC Word Book** is good for this.) By asking the child to locate the helicopter, to find the cat next to the worm, to name this object, or to describe how the hippo must feel, you have an excellent opportunity to learn how the child has mastered vocabulary words that will be important for future reading.

Similarly, you can make picture books with illustrations of specific vocabulary. Discussion of those pictures will enable you to discover which children have grasped certain words and ideas and which will need further exposure and experience with the vocabulary.

Instructional Methods to Build Reading Readiness

In the following section we will discuss some specific instructional methods that exemplify the kinds of activities that should prove effective in building reading readiness. And at the same time as you are using the methods described in this section, you can also be assessing the needs of your children. We will describe these ideas as they relate to language awareness, knowledge of letters and words, and understanding of task, as well as various other specific aspects of readiness for children who need special attention in order to strengthen visual discrimination and memory, auditory discrimination, listening comprehension, or motor development.

Promoting Language Development

Language experience activities.   In our discussion of language development, we have stressed the effectiveness of using the language experiences of the child as a way to have each eventually read his or her own language. Sharing such language experiences invites group discussions and paves the way for stories based on common or individual experiences. For example, a child's discovery of a spider spinning its web can lead to a story dictated by the child. When such stories are bound as books, a class library grows proudly.

You may, of course, decide to provoke or plant the experience that generates the language:

(1) Bring a cocoon or other object of general curiosity to class. After the children have watched, touched, and questioned, lead them to dictate their reactions or predictions as a prelude to reading their own words.

(2) Tell a part of a simple but attention-getting story and invite the children to spin a finish.

* *Richard Scarry's ABC Word Book* (New York: Random House, 1971). Or try *Richard Scarry's Best Word Book Ever* (New York: Golden Press, 1978).

(3) Bring a large selection of old magazines to class and arrange for the use of one or more tape recorders. Group the children in teams of twos or threes and encourage them to clip from the magazines pictures they would like to hear stories about. After the pictures have been prepared, each team picks one picture to tell about. They record their stories and listen to the stories of other teams. From the tapes, the teacher can type or print the team stories on chart paper, and the children can paste on the favorite picture.

(4) Give a child a paper bag with a secret object inside. Without letting the child look inside, ask the child to feel, shake, smell, and then to tell a story about the bag's contents.

(5) Let the children use hand puppets or flannel-board figures to retell favorite stories.

(6) With the class, pretend to go to a toy store, to take a wonderful vacation, to meet some exciting person, and so on. In the toy-store experience, for example, a teacher can begin by saying, "I went to the toy store. I bought a scooter." Each child is asked to repeat what other children have previously said and to add a purchase. The account of the imaginary shopping trip is then recorded on a board or in a little book.

(7) Exploit community resources for travel opportunities and in order to bring community-resource people into the school. The children may use what they learn to dictate a story, draw a chart, or make a book.

(8) Introduce pen-pals. Have the children tape record or dictate a letter to their pen-pal, who is right in their own classroom. Children can listen to the dictated or tape-recorded letters that have been sent to them and can then dictate answers.

(9) Animals can visit the class (if they don't already live there). Children almost universally love animals and will talk to them and about them. The resulting stories are always rich in sensory impressions.

(10) Cook in class. Whether it is instant pudding, popcorn, or stone soup, cooking with children provides them with the opportunity to work with printed directions, to engage in an activity that relies on sequence, and to take turns. Best of all, cooking is a language-based activity.

Besides being interesting and fun, language-evoking experiences provide the teacher with natural opportunities to watch children follow directions, demonstrate understanding of what letters and words are, know what reading is, and begin to sense the alphabetic nature of their printed language.

Almost every teacher wants to spend considerable time just promoting communication within the classroom. The language experience activities discussed above are obviously ones that make a child aware of

language. Their distinction is that they are directed to an end result of reading one's own oral language. The potential for language activities is so broad and so rich that we have only touched on a few examples. If you involve children in enjoyable activities, they will talk; if you promote and encourage that talk, their language will be enriched; if you listen and make use of the results, your language-rich environment is achieved.

Music and movement activities.   Music is an experience that children can enjoy all their lives. It is a natural activity to use in early education. The ideas are as simple as teaching songs and movement—and enjoying singing and moving to music. Music lets children experience the sounds of words and their rhythms. They learn that words frame messages, that they relate to feelings and action, and that if they can sing (and everyone can), they can read.

The possibilities of using music are extensive:

(1)   Teach folk songs (for example, "Shoo Fly," "She'll Be Comin' Round the Mountain," "Clementine"), and sing them with children. If you can play an instrument, accompany them. Then, move to the music, talk about the lyrics, and read them from the overhead projector, books, or sheets. Allow each child to illustrate the songs and make his or her personal song book, or combine some of the illustrations in a class song book.

(2) Write songs with children. They can be based on personal experiences, stories you have shared, or just words that sound good together. For example, you might start:

> If I found a dollar,
> I'd run out my door,
> As fast as I can,
> To the _____ store.

A child inserts the missing word; the tune is whatever you like. Later, you could try omitting more than one word, as in the following example:

> I'd buy a _____ ,
> A _____ , too,
> I'd buy a _____ ,
> And a big _____ .

This might come out as:

> I'd buy a *giraffe*,
> A(*n*) *elephant*, too,
> I'd buy a *rhinoceros*,
> And a big *cockatoo*.

The resulting song could be written down by the teacher and taped by the class for future use.

(3) Find books in the library that are songs (for example, "London Bridge" or "Oh, A-Hunting We Will Go"*). Learn to sing the songs, then show the books. Children will pick them up and sing along.

(4) Find simple poems that can be set to music.

> One, two, three, four, five
> Once I caught a hare alive
> Six, seven, eight, nine, ten
> Then I let it go again.
>
> Why did you let it go?
> Because it bit my finger so.
> Which finger did it bite?
> This little finger on the right.
>
> —*Mother Goose* †

Copy the poem onto a chart pad or on a transparency. Using a lively tone, read the poem all the way through to the children.

---

* Peter Spier, illus. *London Bridge Is Falling Down* (New York: Young Readers Press, 1972); John Langstaff, *Oh, A-Hunting We Will Go* (New York: Atheneum, 1974).

† Taken from Elaine H. Wagener, *Poetry for Beginning Readers* (Mimeo).

Then, sing the first line in a tune of your own or one that you have borrowed. Encourage a child to sing the next line. When a tune has been decided upon, everyone can join in to try it out from the beginning. Later (even the next day), children can sing again, then match sentence strips with the lines of the song. Or they can hold up the strips in sequence as the song is sung.

In addition, the strips can be cut into word cards in order to reconstruct the lines of the songs. The chart pad can be used as the model. Pass the word cards to a group of children. As the poem is sung, the teacher can point to a word as a signal to the class not to sing that word when they come to it. The child holding that word on a card must jump up and sing it alone.

Writing the poem on a transparency will also allow matching, pointing, and circling of the words, phrases, and lines.

(5) Have the children make simple musical instruments, such as cigar-box banjos, tin-can drums, or rhythm sticks. Develop oral directions for the children to follow in making the instruments. Let them discuss how they made them; then let children dictate instructions to others.

(6) Have the children listen to music; allow them to move as it tells them, paint as it tell, them, and so on. Afterwards they can talk about what they did.

Art activities. Almost nothing rivals art activities for involving children totally, promoting a child's individual talents, and prompting pride in production. Because children are usually so interested in drawing, coloring, cutting, pasting, and painting, they often want to share and talk about what they have done. In doing so, they may learn how visual and oral communication are related. Words are another way of telling what a picture tells, and they are intrinsic to describing both details in the picture and the method of production. Finger painting is an excellent medium for this type of activity because it encourages expressionistic pictures that may take some explaining. Specific suggestions include:

(1) Try not to use art as a time-filler ("You're all finished? Draw a picture."). That may serve the purpose for some children, but others fall victim to turning their papers over, inserting a sun, two lollipop trees, three v-shaped birds, a grass line, two tulips, and a cloud—finished. No exciting language will stem from an uninspired piece. Try, instead, to offter a motivating purpose for art—even if art will be loosely interpreted here. "Cut from the magazine things that the third little pig might have used to catch the wolf," or "Draw the way the story made you feel—like dancing? like springtime? like clouds?"

(2) Interpret stories that the children have heard with appropriate art techniques. For example, make collages when you have read about the ocean; make sandpaintings when you have read about Indians of the Southwest; make crayon resists for spooky stories; develop murals or television rolls when sequence is important.

(3) Give directions about how to mix paint, pointing out the new colors that can be made. Assign children to take care of the art center and its supplies.

(4) Have the children make string paintings by dipping a string into paint and letting it fall and take shape on one-half of a folded paper. The paper is then folded and blotted. The picture is completed with crayons. The children can take turns describing what they see.

(5) Let the children make stick figures from pipe cleaners, twisting the limbs to represent various actions. Other children can guess what the figures are doing.

Drama activities. Children create exciting situations when they throw themselves into play acting. The idea is to create dialog by allowing children to pretend they are someone else. That's what "Playing House" and "Playing Store" are all about. If some children are too self-conscious when they themselves are the dramatic figures, offer puppets or cut-outs to permit them to get a safe distance from their dialog. The result is almost all language—and language in response to other language. No formal lesson could better teach language and what communication is all about.

The variations of play acting (role playing) are almost unlimited. Here are some sample ideas:

(1) Have the children take turns acting out some occupation they would like to have. Other children can guess what each classmate's occupation is. Or, when some children think they know, they could join the pantomime—as customers of Johnny's grocery or passengers on Betty's plane. The children talk about why they guessed as they did.

(2) Using toy phones, let two children at a time improvise a telephone conversation. It may be necessary to give some a topic with a first line, such as "I have two tickets on a space capsule. Can you go with me?"

(3) Read a story, stopping just before the climax. Divide children into groups and let them dramatize a possible ending.

(4) Have a child act out a favorite book or story character. (You could act out a character too.) The other children will try to guess the book or character.

(5) Have a child act out an everyday event—such as moving through the cafeteria line—and let the others try to guess the action.

The "actors" in all these activites will get firsthand language experience, of course, but the audience can profit, too, by discussing and reacting. The teacher watches to learn more about each child's experiences and needs.

Thinking activities. In all of the activites we have discussed so far, the child is thinking. The demand for thinking when a child is actively involved in doing will be especially apparent in the sample exercises on following directions (pages 138–40). But related to developing language awareness, there are many exercises doubly valuable because, in addition to developing language, they help to develop either the reasoning ability of the child or an awareness of relationships:

(1) Present several objects and ask children to pick one that violates the category established by the others and explain why it isn't related (for example, nail, screw, tack, and paper).

(2) Devise games built around giving words and having the children offer antonyms or synonyms. Such an activity helps to develop understanding of comparison and contrast. For example:

> She is tall, but I am _____ .
> He is big, but she is _____ .
> This is hot, but that is _____ .

(3) Share riddles and jokes. They are a delight to most children, and hearing and solving them involves drawing inferences from language to reveal hidden meaning.

(4) Locate and share pictures that communicate an emotion. Conjecture about that emotion. For example, a picture may include a child with a surprised expression. Let the children discuss the child's expression, conjecture about the causes of the expression, and hypothesize about events that might change the child's expression. Allow children to describe their own emotions in situations similar to the one they have described.

(5) Generalizations about words can be developed by having the children supply as many words as they can that logically complete sentences like these. After all the words have been suggested for a sentence, ask the children to discuss ways in which any of the words are similar.

> The kitten is . . . (soft, warm, furry, fast, and so on)
> The candy is . . . (sweet, gooey, good, and so on)

(6) Size relationships can be emphasized by giving the children numerous objects of different sizes, each with a box to fit it. The teacher encourages the children to discuss their thought processess as they try to find the correct box for each object.

(7) From pictures of items found in department or grocery stores, the children sort out the items by what department they would be found in. Or, more generally, pictures of items that would be found in different kinds of stores (for example, toys, clothing, and food) can be placed inside cardboard representations of toy stores, clothing stores, and grocery stores.

pictures of clothing   pictures of food items   pictures of toys

(made from shoe boxes or milk cartons; the pictures are pasted on sides [or front] or can be shown through a store window)

(8) Bring interesting objects (a thimble, an apple, a piece of cellophane, a small rock) to class in a bag or box. The objects are felt by one child, who describes what he or she feels to the class so that the children can guess what it is.

Projects and creative stations. The effective classroom is marked by the active and creative use of time and space. It should be, as we will discuss in Chapter 9, the scene of many activities. There should be stations where children follow up on interests or develop new ones. There are long-term projects and materials with which to create. Such a classroom gives children much to talk about, many things to learn the names for, a keen interest in being in school, and a natural awareness of language as it relates to activities that are real for them.

Developing Letter and Word Awareness

Developing awareness of letters and of how letters go together to make words is an essential concern in preparing a child to read. It is easy to see how many of the exercises listed in the following sections as examples also relate to visual and auditory discrimination or to listening comprehension. And because of this overlap, the teacher has an excellent opportunity to use activities such as these to observe children who may need special attention with other readiness skills.

Activities that build letter awareness. Usually children first learn to identify the letters in their own names. Help them to do this by calling attention to the letters as you write their names and then the names of important others—Mother, Father, Snoopy, and so on. There are also many other activities:

(1) Have children locate letters on signs and in language experience stories you have written on charts: "Who can find an *E*?"

(2) Read and "play with" colorful alphabet books: "Where's the letter *L* on this page?"

(3) Suggest that children form letters in various ways, including: with "air writing"; with brush and paint or by fingerpainting; with pipecleaners; with glue on paper to be filled with sand, seeds, or cottonballs; with cookie dough (the products can be eaten); with salt dough (the products can be painted); or with clay.

(4) Children can make letters with their bodies for their classmates to guess.

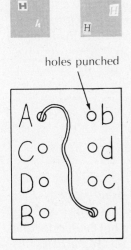

holes punched

(5) Make a big construction-paper letter. Paste it on a sheet of paper. Find and cut the same letter from old magazines and newspapers, arranging and pasting these smaller letters onto the big letter.

(6) Match upper- and lower-case letters by:

Stringing a length of yarn or a shoe lace to connect upper- and lower case letters printed down two sides of a heavy cardstock.

Using pocket cards with slits. Match lower to upper case by inserting the appropriate card into the pocket.

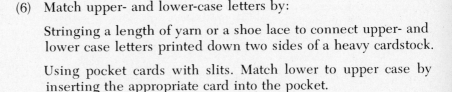

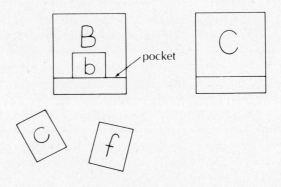

pocket

Using puzzle forms. When appropriately joined, the upper- and lower-case letters should match and the figure should be complete.

Mailing the lower-case "letters" to upper-case "houses."

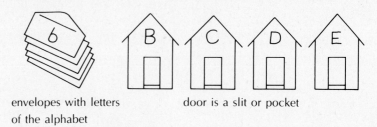

envelopes with letters   door is a slit or pocket
of the alphabet

Activities that emphasize word awareness. Many of the activities we described previously should help to create awareness of words as symbols for things and ideas. As with vocabulary building, an excellent way to help build word awareness is to attach large, readable words to the items in the classroom that are important to children. Later, the labels can be removed, and the teacher can ask the children to take the word cards back to the objects they name, pronouncing them when they are there. Other suggestions are:

(1) Make one set of pictures of animals one would find at a zoo and one set of the words that name those animals. Have the children match them using the rules for the game "concentration." The cards are placed face down and players take turns at attempting to turn up pairs. If a match is made, the player removes both cards and gets another turn. If the picture and word don't match, they must be turned face down again.

(2) Prepare a large menu listing the children's favorite foods. Let each child draw or find illustrations of his or her favorites and mount them on the menu.

(3) Make a funny monster with a slit for a mouth. Put the names of foods on cards and let the children feed the monster if they can say the word.

(4) Put the words *slow, danger, stop,* and *go* on sign-shaped cards. Let the children move or "drive" about the room until the one who is "policeman" holds up a sign. Everyone needs to read the sign in order to know what to do with his or her car, bus, truck, or bicycle.

(5) Play "Simon Says." At first, introduce only one or two action words—for example, *kick* and *jump* taken from a language experience story. The leader says: "Simon says (and holds up the card)." The child responds by doing the action.

(6) Make a book-production center containing pictures, scissors, construction paper, magazines, yarn, and paste. Let children cut out pictures and paste them to construction paper. When the pages are tied together, label the pictures as they dictate.

You will note that many of the *word-awareness* activities are really vocabulary builders because children are learning specific meanings for words at the same time they are learning general word awareness.

Help in Following Directions

As we have noted in our earlier discussion, there are many thinking skills that a child must learn in order to be able to follow directions. The relationship between following directions and thinking skills is important, for it clearly underlines that in teaching a child to follow directions, your aim is not to develop a robot but to help the child to understand relationships and to be a successful learner. There is a distinction between teaching a youngster to be ever more discerning, and thus able to understand and follow directions, and obedience training.

There are as many activities and games to teach the relationships necessary to follow directions as a creative teacher can create. It is possible to develop activities built around high-interest projects—cooking and pet care, to give but a few examples. Having the children follow some simple directions to take an inventory, to order something from a catalog, to pick clothing for a specific occasion, or to make something are simple and useful ways to give children a purpose for following directions.

There are a few general recommendations for teaching how to follow directions. Keep directions simple; three-step instructions ought to be the maximum for awhile. With children who need special attention, the teacher can give one step at a time, thus making the exercise a build-on task. The teacher should let the children discuss what they are doing as freely as possible, remembering that the lesson in following directions can also be used effectively to build language awareness. For this reason, it is also advisable to let children give directions whenever possible. Finally, and as in all reading-readiness activities, the teacher should be observing diagnostically, watching and making notes, if necessary, about children who have problems with specific concepts important to following directions.

Exercises that stress specific relational concepts.   Many children need to learn the distinction between *left* and *right*. One way to teach this is to put a number of chairs in a line and discuss these concepts with the children. Later the children can play a game where one of them, the "leader" or "director," tells the others, who are sitting in the chairs, to move one, two, or three chairs to their left or to their right. In another game that teaches *right* and *left*, the leader tells specific children to hop certain places on specific feet: "Anton, hop to Marcie's seat on your left foot and then hop to me on your right foot." In a similar game, the leader has classmates shake left or right arms or legs (as in the "Hokey Pokey").

To teach words that describe the relation of one thing to another, place a special object somewhere in the room and have the children try to describe where it is. They will need locational words, such as *by, near, on, in,* and so on. Stop occasionally to write some of their sentences on the board, underlining the word that describes the relationship of the object to something else: "Clem, will you tell us where the ruler is?" "It's *on* the floor, and it's also *under* the desk."

To teach other spatial concepts, tape or draw three large circles on the chalkboard and then give each child directions involving them. Tell each child to point to a part (*top, middle, bottom*) of a specific circle (*first, middle, last*). Change words occasionally, using *left, center,* and *right,* for example. Give the children a chance to give the directions.

Activities that help to develop concepts such as *big* and *little, large* and *small,* or *short* and *tall* are just as easy to devise using many common objects (boxes, jars, bottles, buttons, and so on). For example, discuss the comparative size of the objects and then ask a child to line them up according to height or size; or, using several sets at once, you can request objects with similar attributes: "Billy, will you bring the smallest things from each group over here?"

These are just a few examples of activities that build an understanding of some of the concepts important for following directions. In order to decide what to teach, survey the materials you will be asking your children to use—especially any tests they will be taking—to see what concepts they will need to know.

Exercises that mix concepts. It is more than probable, of course, that many activities you will devise will involve a mixture of directions, as those that follow do:

(1) Using three strong paper bags of varying sizes, first you, and then the children, give directions involving these bags: "Alda, please get the middle-sized bag and put it on your left foot."

(2) Give the children paper and crayons or paint and ask them to create a picture containing certain specifics: "Put a sidewalk across the bottom. Now draw a house on the left side. Put two windows in the house, but make one big and one small. Make the house yellow. Put a cloud in the center of the sky."

(3) Pass out paper squares and circles to the children, who should have access to various colors of paint. Ask specific children to paint their squares or circles specific colors. Then put the squares and circles in the center of a large circle and ask children to pick out certain ones. The colored shapes can also be mounted in a collage according to directions.

(4) Tape geometric shapes of various colors close together on the floor and give (or have a child give) directions, such as these: "Put your left hand on the red circle. Now put your right knee on the green triangle. Put your left toe on the yellow square if you can."

General activities. Finally, here are a few examples of some general activities that can involve numerous concepts, depending on what you or the children decide to include:

(1) Give each child three tokens (paper squares, clothespins, and so on). With all the children standing, one child, acting as leader,

gives a direction. Any child who does not follow must turn in one token. All children who still have tokens at the end of the game are winners.

(2) A variation of the game above is to have one child be the "ruler" and give a three-part instruction to a "subject." If the subject follows directions carefully, she or he becomes ruler for the next turn.

(3) Give a child two and then three simple directions to follow at one time, keeping the tasks as amusing and varied as you can. This is both to cover as many concepts as possible and to keep the lesson as entertaining (and thus the children as attentive) as possible. For example, "Put your hand behind your back, stand on one foot, and wiggle your nose."

(4) Have the children make pictures from various geometric shapes, such as lines, boxes, and circles by following directions: "Draw a small circle. Draw a circle that is bigger just under it and touching it. Draw a third and still bigger circle under the second circle but touching it. Draw tiny circles down the center of the two biggest circles. Draw a line out from each side of the center circle.... Who knows what we are drawing a picture of? ... What can we add to finish our snowman?"

During these word-awareness activities, there is a real opportunity for you to note which children have specific problems. You can provide special attention, using activities of the type exemplified in the following sections.

Planning Instruction for Specific Needs

The instructional activities described thus far in this chapter will help children to develop their language and thinking skills, letter and word awareness, and ability to follow directions. Both through these activities and as a natural consequence of maturation, the children will also develop visual discrimination, visual memory, auditory discimination, listening comprehension and motor control.

However, there may be some children who do not develop these skills as a normal course. You can identify the children who need extra instruction in these five skills by using the informal assessment techniques described earlier in this chapter and by observing children as they participate in activities. Your first strategy is to give the children a chance to develop these skills naturally as you provide additional activities to devlop their language and thinking skills. The following instructional activities, however, can be used to specifically develop the five skill areas listed above for the children who need further help.

Activities to develop visual discrimination. The following examples, although drill-type activities, can nonetheless be entertaining if used without pressure:

(1) Some children may profit from exercises in sorting objects either by size and color or by pairing or matching visual shapes. Exercises that urge a child to match visual representations by size, color, and design are useful. Matching beads by color, size, and shape as well as matching small toys are two examples of the many possibilities.

(2) Have each child cut a drawing or magazine picture into five or six pieces and put them in an envelope. Then exchange the envelopes and have the children assemble each other's puzzles.

(3) Cut up ropes or ribbons of various colors, widths, and textures into various lengths. Have the children handle them and ask them to talk about them. Ask them to find pieces of ribbons that are alike in two or more ways.

(4) Print three words in each row, with one repeated twice. Ask the children to circle the two that are the same.

dog   pig   dog

Activities to build visual memory. Visual-memory exercises are similar to visual-discrimination exercises, except that a certain amount of time has elapsed, and the visual stimulus has disappeared.

(1) Put about five to seven objects in front of the children. Have one child turn his or her back and let another child remove one of the objects. See if the child whose back was turned can tell what is missing. If the child misses, let the game continue using fewer objects until there is successful remembering. Then gradually increase the number of objects.

(2) Place a pattern of several *x*'s and *o*'s on the blackboard. Have the children look at it for about five to ten seconds; then erase or cover the pattern and ask each child to reproduce it on paper. A variation of this activitiy would be to write a word on the blackboard and then erase one or two letters and ask the children to copy the word with the missing letter(s) replaced.

(3) Have a child take a simple puzzle (perhaps a picture cut into four pieces) apart and put it back together. Increase the number of pieces in the puzzle according to the child's ability.

(4) Cut out several geometric forms and hold them up in front of the children for three to five seconds. Then ask the children to reproduce the forms on paper.

(5) Hold up several pictures drawn by the children. Ask the children to look at the pictures carefully; then remove them. Ask a child to describe one of the pictures, and let others decide which one was described.

Activities to build auditory discrimination. Activities that develop auditory discrimination can begin as simply as discussing sounds with the children. What sounds do they hear right now? What kind of sounds do they like best? Why? Music they like can be played and discussed. Musical instruments are usually fascinating to children at the age when they begin to read. Bring some instruments to class and let the children produce sounds with them. Encourage them to talk about the sounds. Or you might play two notes on an instrument and ask a child which is higher or louder. What sounds frighten them or make them uneasy? What sounds are comforting?

Rhythm activities depend on auditory discrimination. A common exercise is to knock on a desk or table top in an irregular pattern and have the child who is working on the audio skill try to repeat the pattern. This kind of activity can be done with various rhythm instruments as well. Teach the child the names for the instruments and then hear the sound each makes. Behind the child's back, use one instrument to make a sound and ask the child to identify the source of the sound.

Environmental noises are fun and can also be a source of activities. They can be recorded on tape and played back for the child to identify. (Let them hear their own voices on the recorder, too.) The same activity can be done with the children taking turns behind a screen as the "sound effects person." They can produce noises of their choice—such as pouring water—for their classmates to guess.

Rhyme is a sound phenomenon popular in activities to build auditory discrimination. Some teachers use couplets, omitting the last word in the second line (the second rhyming word) and ask the children to supply it.

> Harry, the horse
> Is big, of _____ .
>
> My friend Fred
> Is sick in _____ .

You can also give the children experience with "real" poetry, too, and allow them to discover rhyme rather than to make its emphasis a formal presentation.

Finally, here are some games that you can have the children play to build auditory discrimination:

(1) Have several children stand with their backs to the class and close their eyes. Then point to another child in the remaining group, who will drop a book or make some other noise. The first of the children whose backs are turned must guess from which direction the noise came and then who might have made the noise.

(2) Have the children stand in a circle and give each a number. Hand one child a large ball. This child will call a number and toss the ball up into the center of the circle. The child whose number is called must try to catch the ball before it bounces two times. If the child does, he or she gets to call the next number.

(3) A child who is "It" thinks of the name of some other child in his class and gives a clue that begins with the same letter: "I am thinking of someone who's name begins with the same letter as *desk*." The class then guesses. The child who guesses correctly becomes "It."

(4) Bring in objects (or pictures of objects) whose names rhyme. Place them together and have the children sort them out, putting all those that rhyme together.

(5) Bring several puppets to class and give them names. Then tell the class that each puppet only likes to eat five things that begin with the sound at the beginning of his or her name.

"Does Peter like pumpkins?"
"Does Peter like eggs?"
"Does Peter like popcorn?"

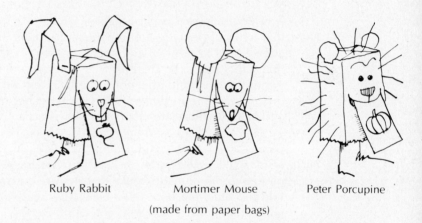

Ruby Rabbit   Mortimer Mouse   Peter Porcupine

(made from paper bags)

The child offers the puppet only the picture that starts with the same letter as the puppet's name. The puppet, of course, "chews" and enjoys the right foods, but the wrong cards drop from its mouth. The child is learning to listen to initial sounds.

While all the children will enjoy these activities, you should give those whose auditory discrimination is limited a greater opportunity to answer and discuss.

Activities to build listening comprehension. Activities that build listening comprehension are varied and of varying degrees of difficulty. Here are some simple exercises:

(1) Display a picture and say two sentences to the class—only one of which describes the picture. Ask a child to repeat the sentence that he or she thinks describes the picture. After a few rounds try having some children select a picture and make up the sentences.

(2) Give a series of directions for a child to follow. Begin with a single task, then two, and then three.

(3) Record a set of silly directions, but preface each with a different child's name in direct address. Then play the tape and let the child addressed follow the direction.

(4) Read a story to a child or a small group and then share pictures, of which only some depict incidents in the story. Have the children decide which pictures belong in the story.

(5) Show a short movie or filmstrip to a group of children and afterwards ask them to tell what they remember of it. Then let them take roles of characters in the film and reenact the story.

(6) Most important, read to the children. Read books and stories that interest you, too, so that your enthusiasm sparks their listening. Let children retell parts of the story and both ask and answer questions.

Activities to develop motor control. There is hardly any physical activity that will not develop motor control. Perhaps the most important task for a teacher is to think of and suggest activities that the child will like and that will stretch physical prowess without creating failure. On the playground, you should give encouraging attention to the children who need this development. Remember, however, not to push too hard, for some children develop later than others.

In the work areas of the classroom, tasks like constructing things from paper—even simple chains, for example—can develop control. Make use of toys that come apart in simple units for reconstruction and of commercial or homemade books that require cutting, punching, pasting, and folding. Stacking boxes can be made creative if the child is helping to make a miniature city. And you can have the child make his or her own simple puzzles. This last exercise stresses visual discrimination, too. It also suggests another general approach that the teacher can use effectively; in teaching other skills or aspects of readiness, individualize your instruction as much as possible so you can gear any motor requirements of the activities to each child's development.

In helping a child control body movements, make frequent use of music. Let each create dance steps to a tune with an easy beat. Encourage each to move expressively. This may instill a sense of timing that will help the child be less awkward and more confident about his or her body.

Summary

The overlap that has resulted between readiness activities and learning-to-read activities throughout this chapter is intentional and believed in. We have attempted to show that reading readiness is a complex and elusive phenomenon. But we have also indicated that practitioners cannot afford to keep real children from learning to read while researchers seek to discover the factors that predict reading success. The operational definition of readiness that has been proposed attempts to place the responsibility for readiness on the teacher and the instruction rather than on the child. We suggest that all beginners be met with a learning environment that stimulates and helps to develop language. Experiences that provoke language form a natural base not only for getting ready to read but also for initial reading instruction. In addition, the teacher is urged to read to children daily because of the experiences with language and print, and because of the model for reading that the adult reader provides. Several factors that are associated with success in beginning reading (visual discrimination, visual memory, knowledge of letter names, auditory discrimination, listening comprehension, vocabulary, and motor skills) have been discussed. Methods have been suggested for informally assessing several of these skills, and suggestions have been offered for strengthening each.

REFERENCES

Adelman, Howard, and Feshbach, Seymour. "Predicting Reading Failure: Beyond the Readiness Model." *Exceptional Children* 37 (1971): 349–54.

Allen, Roach Van. "The Language Experience Approach." In *Perspectives on Elementary Reading: Principles and Strategies*, edited by Robert Karlin. New York: Harcourt Brace Jovanovich, 1973, p. 158.

Arthur, Grace. "A Quantitative Study of the Results of Grouping First Grade Children According to Mental Age. *Journal of Educational Research* 12 (October 1925): 173–85.

Ausubel, David P. "Viewpoints from Related Disciplines: Human Growth and Development." *Teachers College Record* 60 (February 1958): 245–54.

Bloom, Benjamin S. *Stability and Change in Human Characteristics*. New York: John Wiley and Sons, 1964.

Bruner, Jerome S. *Process of Education*. Cambridge, Mass.: Harvard University Press, 1960.

Chomsky, Carol. *The Acquisition of Syntax in Children from 5 to 10*. Cambridge, Mass.: M.I.T. Press, 1969.

Clymer, Theodore, and Barrett, Thomas C. *Clymer-Barrett Prereading Battery*. Princeton, N.J.: Personnel Press, 1966–67.

Dale, Edgar. "Vocabulary Measurement: Techniques and Major Findings." *Elementary English* 42 (December 1965): 895–901, 948.

Dewey, John. "The Primary Education Fetich." *New York Teachers' Monographs* (November 1896).

Doman, Glenn. *How to Teach Your Baby to Read*. New York: Random House, 1964.

Durkin, Dolores. "Confusion and Misconceptions in the Controversy about Kindergarten Reading." In *The Formative Years: Principles of Early Childhood Education*, edited by Stanley Coopersmith and Ronald Feldman. San Francisco: Albion, 1974, pp. 228–35.

———. *Teaching Young Children to Read*. Boston: Allyn and Bacon, 1976.

———. "When Should Children Begin to Read?" In *Innovation and Change in Reading Instruction*, edited by Helen M. Robinson. Sixty-seventh Yearbook of the National Society for the Study of Education. Chicago: University of Chicago Press, 1968.

Durrell, Donald. "First-Grade Reading Success Study: A Summary." *Journal of Education* 140 (February 1958): 2–6.

Eames, Thomas S. "Physical Factors in Reading." *The Reading Teacher* 15 (May 1962): 427–32.

Farr, Roger, and Anastasiow, Nicholas, eds. *Tests of Reading Readiness and Achievement: A Review and Evaluation.* Newark, Del.: International Reading Association, 1969.

Gates, Arthur. "The Necessary Mental Age for Beginning Reading." *Elementary School Journal* 37 (March 1937): 497–508.

————; Bond, Guy; and Russell, David. *Methods of Determining Reading Readiness.* New York: Bureau of Publications, Columbia University, Teachers College, 1939.

————, and MacGinitie, Walter. *Gates-MacGinitie Reading Tests.* New York: Teachers College Press, Columbia University, 1964.

Gesell, Arnold L. *Infancy and Human Growth.* New York: Macmillan, 1928.

Getman, Gerald N. *How to Develop Your Child's Intelligence: More Successful Adulthood by Providing More Adequate Childhood.* 7th ed. Leiverne, Minn.: 1962.

Hare, Betty A. "Perceptual Deficits Are Not a Cue to Reading Problems in Second Grade." *The Reading Teacher* 30 (March 1977): 624–28.

Hilbreth, Gertrude H.; Griffith, Nellie L.; and McGauvran, Mary E. *Metropolitan Readiness Tests.* New York: Harcourt Brace Jovanovich, 1933–66.

Huey, Edmund B. *The Psychology and Pedagogy of Reading.* Cambridge, Mass.: M.I.T. Press, 1908 (1968).

Hunt, J. McVicker. *Intelligence and Experience.* New York: The Ronald Press, 1961.

Jobe, Fred W. *Screening Vision in Schools.* Newark, Del.: International Reading Association, 1976.

Lee, Murray J., and Clark, Willis. *Lee-Clark Reading Readiness Test.* Monterey, Cal.: California Test Bureau, 1967.

Lowell, Robert E. "Reading Readiness Factors as Predictors of Success in First Grade Reading." *Journal of Learning Disabilities* 4 (December 1971): 24–28.

Morphett, Mabel V., and Washburn, Carleton. "When Should Children Begin to Read?" *Elementary School Journal* 31 (March 1931): 496–503.

Mortenson, W. Paul. "Selected Pre-reading Tasks, Socio-economic Status, and Sex." *The Reading Teacher* 22 (October 1968): 45–49, 61.

Murphy, Helen A., and Durrell, Donald D. *Murphy-Durrell Reading Readiness Analysis.* New York: Harcourt Brace Jovanovich, 1964.

Pre-Reading Test of Scholastic Ability to Determine Reading Readiness. New York: Harper and Row, 1966, p. 16.

Robinson, Violet B.; Strickland, Dorothy S.; and Cullinan, Bernice. "The Child: Ready or Not?" In *The Kindergarten Child and Reading,* edited by Lloyd O. Ollila. Newark, Del.: International Reading Association, 1977, pp. 13–37.

Rosen, Connie, and Rosen, Harold. *The Language of Primary School Children.* Middlesex, England: Penguin, 1973.

Ruddell, Robert. "The Effect of Oral and Written Patterns of Language Structure on Reading Comprehension." *The Reading Teacher* 18 (January 1965): 270–75.

Rude, Robert T. "Readiness Tests: Implications for Early Childhood Education." *The Reading Teacher* 26 (March 1973): 572–80.

Smith, Mary Katherine. "Measurement of the Size of General English Vocabulary through the Elementary Grades and High School." *Genetic Psychology Monographs* 24 (1941): 311–45.

Strickland, Ruth. *The Language of Elementary School Children: Its Relationship to the Language of Reading Textbooks and the Quality of Reading of Selected Children.* Bulletin of the School of Education. Bloomington, Ind.: Indiana University, 1962.

Walker, Wanda. "A Readiness Test for Disadvantaged Preschool Children." PREP Report No. 22, U.S. Office of Education, National Center for Education Communication. DHEW Publication OE 72–79, July 27, 1970. Washington, D.C.: Government Printing Office, 1970.

Weintraub, Sam, "What Research Says to the Reading Teacher: Illustrations for Beginning Reading." *The Reading Teacher* 20 (October 1967): 61–67.

FOR FURTHER READING

Allen, Roach Van. *Language Experiences in Communication.* Boston: Houghton Mifflin, 1976.

Ashton-Warner, Sylvia. *Teacher.* New York: Simon and Shuster, 1963.

Carrillo, Lawerence W. *Informal Reading Readiness Experiences.* San Francisco: Chandler Publishing, 1964.

Downing, John. "How Children Think About Reading." *The Reading Teacher* 23 (1969): 217–30.

Durkin, Dolores. *Children Who Read Early.* New York: Teachers College Press, Columbia University, 1969.

Hall, Mary Anne. *The Language Experience Approach for Teaching Reading.* Newark, Del.: International Reading Association, 1978.

———. *Teaching Reading as a Language Experience.* Columbus, Ohio: Charles E. Merrill, 1976.

Martin, Bill, Jr. *Sounds of Language.* New York: Holt, Rinehart and Winston, 1970.

Petty, Walter T. et al. *Experiences in Language.* Boston: Allyn and Bacon, 1973.

Piaget, Jean, and Inhelder, Barbel. *The Psychology of the Child,* translated by Helen Weaver. New York: Basic Books, 1969.

Yardley, Alice *Exploration and Language.* New York: Citation Press, 1973.

2

Recognizing Words

4. Word Recognition

Ideally, word recognition should be equated with the act of reading itself. That is, word recognition is the comprehension of words as they serve to convey the ideas represented by clauses, sentences, paragraphs—the whole expression in which they occur. For this reason, recognition of words should be taught with a focus on reading for meaning. This focus on meaning supports the belief that word-recognition skills, or behaviors, are learned as they are needed to understand a printed message. Thus, children learn to apply word-recognition skills primarily through reading and not through isolated drill. Since word recognition is an interdependent set of behaviors, teaching each behavior separately may not lead to their efficient application in reading; rather, fragmented drill may lead only to the mastery of isolated behaviors that, operating independently, may have only a limited effect on improving reading.

Word recognition is one of the most important aspects of teaching reading. In this chapter, we will examine several teaching methods for developing word-recognition. We will also describe how word recognition behaviors function in efficient and effective readers—and it is the flexible application of these behaviors that ought to be the goal of your instruction. Finally we shall examine the most important aspect of word recognition—context analysis—and how to teach it.

try this ▶

"Cabalistically," he replied, "my underground efforts will continue. If we stick closely together and each does his job with silent dedication, our clandestine effort will succeed before it can be exposed and thwarted."

After reading this short passage, how well do you understand it? That is, did you actually *read* it? What was going on in your attempt to understand? What kinds of behaviors did you call upon? How did you recognize the words? Were all of the words ones you knew immediately? Did you sound out any of them mentally in an effort to call up their meaning? Did you analyze any of the words syntactically—by parts—to see how they operate in the passage? Did you infer the meaning of any word by drawing on your understanding of another? Try to list the behaviors that you used. Do you think that these are the same behaviors that help children to recognize words?

Try to define and explain each of the behaviors that you list. Keep this list to see how it compares with the information in this chapter.

Developing Word Recognition

When you step into the middle of a reading-instruction period in an elementary classroom, you may well be confused by seeing contradictions in teaching word recognition. For example, the teacher encourages a child who is reading part of a story aloud to guess at an unfamiliar word. During silent reading a second child points out an unknown word to the teacher, who may tell the child the word. In another section of the room, a group of children match pictures from newspapers or magazines with a letter or combinations of letters.

Are these contradictions? The teacher appears to be emphasizing a "look and guess" approach with some children, simply telling other children words, and using a phonics approach with still others. Actually, this teacher may well be a very effective reading teacher—knowing when, how, and what word-recognition behaviors to teach and reinforce in order to help students become independent, effective readers.

When the teacher encouraged the child to guess at an unknown word, the teacher was emphasizing the most important word-recognition behavior—reliance on context clues. The silent reader was told the word to make sure that he or she kept practicing word recognition by continuing to read. The teacher was adhering to the following guideline: don't interrupt the thought flow of the absorbed reader unduly; let the reader read—one of the surest, but simplest, ways to build word recognition. And the children who were matching pictures with letters were involved in an exercise that relates spoken sounds to printed symbols, with the emphasis on meaning—the meaning of the pictures. Ideally, this phonics activity would be followed by an opportunity for the children to practice this newly acquired knowledge of sound-symbol relationships by reading meaningful print that is both appropriate and important to them.

While there are several intertwined behaviors involved in word recognition, many new teachers immediately suggest phonics when they are asked how they were taught to recognize words. Indeed, phonics probably reigned supreme in American schools when these new teachers were learning to read. And, at times, phonics has been stressed almost to the point of excluding the development of the other word-recognition behaviors. A heavy phonics emphasis is based on the belief that "sounding out" words is the best—perhaps the only—way to work out the recognition of unknown words. In fact, phonics is only one word-recognition behavior that children learn to depend upon and, therefore, should be taught.

Good readers, in fact, recognize words because the words in print are keys to concepts shared with the author, and in combination they may register with or expand the reader's experiences. Thus, the child who has already learned to read has a mental set that the written symbols, as arranged by an author, will convey ideas. The reader's task is to engage actively in the process of recognizing the words and understanding their relationships. Generally, the reader relies upon certain skills that have developed as he or she learned to read:

> The reader is able to *rely on the context* for clues that a given word fits the pattern of ongoing meaning gleaned from other words, sentences, passages, and illustrations.

Letter Recognition and Word Recognition

There is ample research evidence to conclude that the letter-by-letter sounding out of words is not the way a mature reader reads. As early as 1885, Cattell demonstrated that a word can be read as quickly as a single letter. Since that time, other researchers have shown that a mature reader reads a page of print much faster than he or she could physically see every letter on that page.

More recently, Goodman (1972) has emphasized that reading should not be taught as a set of sounds, letters, and words to be learned. In fact, Goodman has stated that if language (reading) is broken into a set of distinct units, each unit becomes an abstraction. Overemphasis on letter-sound relationships may prevent the child from constantly reflecting on the sense of what is being read by forcing the young reader to focus on abstract and inconsistent sound-symbol relationships.

The reader is able to recognize a word because it is a part of his or her *sight vocabulary*—that is, a member of a growing stock of words that are recognized automatically without conscious application of other word-recognition behaviors.*

The reader may call upon the skill of *phonic analysis* to recognize a word. Provided that the word is already a part of the reader's speaking or listening vocabularies, the reader can relate graphemes to phonemes (symbols to sounds) to translate print into meaningful speech.

The reader may attempt to recognize a word by the skill of *structural analysis,* which involves the ability to recognize roots, prefixes, suffixes, and inflections as clues to the meanings of words. The reader may use meaningful word parts to aid in identification of the whole.

The reader may turn to *outside resources* for help with a word when other word-recognition behaviors are not sufficient. Knowledge of when and how to turn to outside sources (for example, a dictionary) seems only tangentially related to the other behaviors, but is, nevertheless, something the good reader does.

Together, these word-recognition behaviors enable a reader to not just "attack" words but rather to "get sense from" what is read. Without getting meaning for one's effort, that which we call reading hasn't occurred at all.

And that is why the teacher in the earlier example who was working with developing readers was demonstrating purposeful rather than erratic teaching behavior, knowing when, how, and why to encourage a child's dependence upon varying combinations of word-recognition behaviors—just as the mature reader does.

By monitoring children's reading and keeping careful records, the teacher can plan learning activities that build skill in the aspects of word recognition that are least developed and can select materials and stories for practice in those areas.

From this brief description of word-recognition behaviors, you can see that words are recognized in several ways. This is true because word recognition is concerned with a variety of behaviors. The purpose of these chapters is to more fully describe those behaviors and to offer suggestions for teaching word recognition. First, however, let's examine the goal of that instruction in word recognition—developing the mature reader.

---

* Some educators refer to the *sight vocabulary* of a child as all those words that must be taught via a "sight" or "look-say" method, because they are either irregular in their sound-symbol relationships or in their spelling patterns and, therefore, can't be sounded out—for example, *was* or *through.* The definition offered above is broader than this definition, which takes a perspective limited to a specific instructional situation.

Developing Mature Readers

The goal of all reading instruction should be to develop mature reading. Mature reading is the end product of reading instruction. It is fluent reading for ideas without an undue emphasis on any word-recognition behaviors. Mature reading does not denote the age of the reader but rather fluent reading at any age. On the way toward that goal, many good teachers plan opportunities to help children develop the word-recognition behaviors that help to ensure effective and efficient reading. To help you place word recognition in this perspective, let's focus temporarily on the word-recognition behaviors of the mature reader. In so doing, we are not shelving our concern for the developing reader. To the contrary, we are going to compare the mature reader with the beginning reader.

Reading Is an Aspect of Language

As one aspect of language, reading is similar to listening. The act of reading (like listening) is a communication-receiving process. Everyone knows that! But suppose you didn't. Suppose that "the process of reading" was a mystery to you. Suppose that no one had read stories to you, that no one had pointed out that printed words stood for spoken words, or that certain groups of letters made words. If that were the case, the relationship of oral to written language might not seem so obvious to you. Assuming this perspective may help you understand that of many children who do not learn print awareness before they come to school.

In understanding what reading is, then, the reader must be aware that printed language is a system of *sound-symbol relationships* structured into patterns that both originate from and result in meaning. This meaning is arrived at by identifying ideas represented by words and patterns of words that are used to express those ideas. Since ideas are thinking and thinking is reasoning, the mature reader is aware that the inherent logic within language can be used to unlock the meaning represented by print and that this activity requires active, attentive participation by the reader. And since a beginning reader also uses oral language logically, he or she expects oral language to make sense. Thus, the teacher has a natural key to creating an understanding that reading is another communication process by which people share ideas and feelings.

Developing an understanding of reading as a form of language has a circular payoff: the better one understands reading as language, the more quickly he or she develops the word-recognition behaviors of the mature reader; and the more one reads and the more skill one develops, the more capable that person is of understanding what language is. To you, the teacher, this presents the challenge of teaching word recognition as a thinking process—one that strives always for meaning.

Language, Thought, and Reading

The relationships of language, thought, and reading have been the focus of many studies. In reviewing these studies, DiVesta and Palermo noted several important points on which the hypotheses they examined converged:

(1) Language has structure. Words in a sentence operate as a part of a propositional statement, and this implies that there are logical relationships between words.

(2) Developing skill in one's language involves the development of skills in perception. This includes strategies of using what one hears and sees as well as using a growing knowledge about how meaning is conveyed. The latter involves the recognition that words in a sentence or statement intend to say something as a unit—that they have "semantic intentions."

(3) Language develops by interacting with one's experiences and thoughts. (1974, p. 69)

The implied complexities of the relationship of language to thinking and to communication cannot, of course, be taught to beginning readers. Such complexities are probably not often consciously understood by even the most mature readers—although there is evidence that mature readers do use reading strategies based on them. But having a general understanding of how language operates is essential to the young reader. Wardhaugh (1969) makes this point when he lists among his principles for teaching reading: "[Reading instruction] must be based on a thorough understanding of just what children know about their language as this knowledge reveals itself in what they can do in their language rather than in what they can verbalize about their language."

Mature Reading Is Based on Context Analysis

Since mature reading is the ultimate goal, it will be useful for you to consider the word-recognition behaviors that a mature reader uses. In order to demonstrate these, try testing your own skills on the following passage from a novel:*

"We need a bone nose to blow on us," Pierce said.
"You giving the crushers a slum?"

The words are English, but the two lines probably convey little meaning to you, despite the fact that you can, no doubt, pronounce all of the words correctly. Still, you do have a mental set about what reading is, and this knowledge can help you to understand the strange uses of

* Michael Crichton, *The Great Train Robbery* (New York: Alfred A. Knopf, 1975), p. 162.

these words. So you begin using what you know about your language, its grammar and its meaning, trying to come across ideas you may already share with the author.

For example, you could probably answer correctly a number of "comprehension questions" based on the two lines. If you were asked what Pierce wanted to blow on them, you would probably respond, "a bone nose." If the question were, "What might Pierce be planning to give the crushers?" you would probably respond "a slum." You would also guess that there was more than one *crusher*, that a *bone nose* is something or someone that can *blow on*, and that *blowing on* is something that can be done. You, as a mature reader, make reasonable guesses because of what you know about the order of the words and what that order signals about their relation to each other, because of word endings, and because of the way the unknown words relate to words you do know.

Syntactically, you can guess that *bone nose* names something or someone because it is preceded by the article *a* and that it is the object of the verb *need*. Knowing this helps establish the relationship of these words to each other and with other words in the sentence. By seeing how the words relate syntactically, you can make more informed guesses at the meaning of those you don't recognize.

About the *crushers*, Pierce says:

"They must have something to keep them busy.... In five days' time, we'll pull the peters on the train, and I don't want them around to watch."

Since you already know from reading the footnote on page 155 (an outside resource) that the passage is about a train robbery and from previous information in the book that Pierce is a thief, you can draw on your knowledge and assume that Pierce is planning one. Can you guess who the *crushers* are? Is Pierce concerned that the police may be on to his plans? Pierce's cohort asks:

"Where do you want them?"
"I was thinking of Greenwich," Pierce said. "It would be pleasant if they were in Greenwich."
"So you're needing a bone nose to pass them the slang?"
"Yes," Pierce said.

By this time you may have figured out that *giving the crushers a slum* means to send the police on a false alarm so that they don't interfere with Pierce's plans. It is the redundancy of the language that allows you to verify your guess that the *crushers* are police or railroad guards. You can't be positive about what *pulling the peters* on the train entails, but you can be fairly sure that if it does not mean actually holding up the train, it stands for some action involved in doing so. And using what you have already figured out, you can perhaps guess that to *pass the slang* is to inform on someone, that to *give a slum* is to conduct a decoy operation, and that a *bone nose* is an informer.

However, perhaps you were not able to guess what all of those words meant, and, as a result, the communication process was breaking down for you. Let us consider the possible reasons that you might have failed to understand:

You developed different *predictions* about what the selection was all about.
Your *background experiences* were limited in the general topic of the selection.
Instead of *reading for meaning* (trying to make sense of what you were reading), you were just reading (pronouncing) words to yourself.

These three reasons often cause word-recognition breakdown for children, too. However, you can help to prevent such breakdowns; and that is what this chapter and the next two are all about. For the moment, though, you may want to take special notice of the way you read the extracts from *The Great Train Robbery*. You looked for meaning by relying on your understanding of the syntax of the language—that is, your understanding of how words relate to each other as signaled by their positions in sentences and by their form, such as the suffixes they carry. And even though the strange words in this passage somewhat limited your ability to do so, you still relied on the semantics of the language—that is, your knowledge of some of the words (including some strange new words that you figured out) to infer the meaning of other words. In a passage that uses the language more normally, you would be making even more use of context analysis. It would, in fact, be the major word-recognition behavior.

One important point should be very clear: sounding out the words in this passage did not help you comprehend it. Thus, phonic generalizations alone would not be very useful with this passage if meaning were your goal. Sight vocabulary (words you already know) played a role, as in knowing the words *keep busy, want, watch, pleasant, needing,* and *pass*—all important as semantic and syntactic clues to figure out the unfamiliar uses of other words. Finally, other than the footnote that told you the general topic, there were no outside references to turn to. Remember, too, that you were able to use word-recognition behaviors because you began with the mental set that the words were supposed to make sense and that you as a reader were to reconstruct the author's ideas.

The Importance of Phonic Analysis to the Beginning Reader

The difference between word-recognition behaviors in mature and beginning readers is in the priority with which these behaviors are applied. The more proficient with language one becomes, the more clues he or she has for relying upon context as the major aid to word recognition. Thus, the more mature reader relies heavily upon context analysis and resorts to other word-recognition behaviors only when the context fails to supply sufficient clues. But the beginning reader may need to rely heavily on phoneme-grapheme (sound-symbol) relationships until the meanings of enough words in a passage are unlocked to provide context clues. To illustrate this, suppose as a mature reader you were suddenly to encounter new and strange graphemes (symbols) representing the phonemes (sounds) that are familiar to you. In the following passage note how your emphasis shifts to establishing a phoneme-grapheme relationship system. But watch, too, how you use structural and context clues at the same time to find meaning.*

⊥a≡ i∧ ‡e Δ℮∇a≡e over ∇eginning rea∆ing all a∇ou≡? ⊥a≡ are ‡e

variou∧ –ay∧ of ≡ea¢ing ¢il∆ren |o– ≡o rea∆ ‡a≡ paren≡∧, ≡eacer∧,

educa≡or∧, an∆ cri≡ic∧ prai∧e or ∇lame ∧o ve|emen≡ly? ⊥a≡ are

‡e major i∧∧ue∧ in ‡e con≡rover∧y? (Chall, 1967)

---

* We are indebted to Paul McKee for proposing the idea of an artificial alphabet for educating adults about the complexities of learning to read. McKee's system, however, substitutes a new symbol for each letter of the alphabet. See Paul McKee, *Primer for Parents* (Boston: Houghton Mifflin, 1972).

There are only six symbols or letters that have been substituted for the regular letters of the alphabet in the selection above. Perhaps in order to read this material you applied some "discovered" sound-symbol relationships that developed inductively because of what you already know about our writing system.

In attempting to read the selection, some readers might skip to the first immediately recognizable word—*over*. The next word might be difficult to figure out, but after guessing that the word following it is *reading*, the mature reader might employ that as a meaning clue to figure out that the preceeding word is *beginning*. He or she should then be able to establish symbol-sound relationships to figure out the phrase *over beginning reading all about?* deciding that teh word before *reading* is *beginning*, the reader knows that the symbol "∇" stands for *b*. He or she knows, too, that "Δ" stands for the sound at the end of *read*. With the symbol for *b*, the reader can determine that "≡" stands for the *t* in *about*. In addition, the reader knows that this first sentence is a question because of the punctuation. Deciphering the rest of the message should then be easy, because repeated symbols are used in place of the traditional letters. These include "—" for *w*, "l" for *h*, "≡" for *t*, "∧" for *s*, "Δ" for *d*, "∇" for *b*, "+" for *wh*, "‡" for *th*, and "ᗡ" for *ch*. The last three symbols are, however, merely combinations of symbols that have already been deciphered—a useful observation to make in phonic skills.

This exercise with the Chall selection demonstrates the nature of phonics or sound-symbol relationships. The teaching of these relationships is obviously useful and important. They do help a reader, for they constitute one of the intertwined skills that help readers to recognize words. What is most important about the translation—or decoding—you have just attempted is the realization that a beginning reader must learn the principles that you took for granted and applied here. Because you understand these principles, the decoding task you performed really didn't approximate what the beginning reader faces. The principles that guided you may be so second nature that you have difficulty realizing not all beginning readers understand them:

The print represented a meaningful communication.
Graphemes (written symbols) could be translated into phonemes (spoken symbols). This is often referred to as the alphabetic nature of our written language.
The graphemes would more or less consistently translate into the same phonemes.
The result of translating the graphemes into phonemes would be something similar to spoken language.
The graphemes were written in a left to right pattern and when translated into phonemes should be spoken following the left to right pattern.

Imagine how much more difficult it would have been for you if the task did not follow these well-understood principles, and you have a clearer grasp of the difficulty of the task for children.

Did you notice that besides using phonic generalizations to unlock the meaning of this passage, you also relied heavily on context clues? For example, as you decoded the meaning of one word, it suggested context that provided clues for other words. For the mature reader, context is the most used word-recognition behavior. In this passage context aided you to use the words you knew as semantic cues and to use their placement as syntactic cues to make educated guesses at the strange new words.

The other supporting word-recognition behaviors were probably also used. For example, parts of a word, such as the *ing* in *beginning* and *teaching*, provided structural clues that helped you identify the whole word. Clearly, the various aspects of word recognition are interlocked in operation. They can be separated only by focusing on one—for analysis and for instruction—but it is important to recognize that there is no real-life separation between them in operation. With normal symbols, in fact, the mature reader would use word-recognition behaviors in this way: he or she would identify the sight vocabulary words and would employ them contextually in order to unlock the meanings of unknown words; the reader would rely on understanding of the structure of words to support contextual guesses; he or she would attempt to sound out words still alien in the hope that the sound of the word would help in the identification; and if necessary as a final resort, the reader would refer to some reference tool, such as a dictionary.

Because context analysis is the word-recognition behavior that exploits comprehension of the broader context, we strongly emphasize that behavior over the others by developing it separately in Chapter 5. The other behaviors will be treated in a separate chapter. These three chapters will give you some ideas of how to teach each behavior and of its flexibility in helping your children become better readers. Specific examples and the kinds of lessons that you might employ will also be discussed.

General Principles for Teaching Word Recognition

It is important for you to remember that any breakdown of reading into specific subbehaviors is arbitrary at best. Reading is a total process, and when attempts are made to fractionate it into specific subparts, both the teacher and the student may lose sight of the goal—getting meaning from the printed page. Samuels has explained the concern this way:

A major point made by the critics of the subskill approach is that fractionating the reading process interferes with the essential characteristic of reading, which is comprehension. This point is well taken. Many teachers who use the subskill approach have lost sight of the fact that the subskill approach is simply a means to an end. What has happened in many classrooms is that global displacement has occurred and that means have become ends in themselves. In using the subskill approach, care must be taken to prevent the subskills from becoming the focal point of instruction. Once again, perhaps, this point should be made, that it is important for the child to get ample practice reading meaningful and interesting material in context. (1974, p. 22)

Despite this realistic concern, it is important for you to understand word-recognition behaviors and subbehaviors and how to teach them. And there is no more efficient way for ensuring systematic explanation than to deal with each of these separately, still maintaining a holistic philosophy.

Before discussing the teaching of these word-recognition behaviors, however, there are six general principles in teaching word recognition that deserve attention. These principles should guide your instruction in word recognition, for they grow from the same overriding concern for all reading instruction, including word recognition—children's instructional needs must be a primary consideration.

Meaning Is More Important than Pronunciation

We have already stressed the most important of these principles: *meaning should always be the goal of word-recognition instruction—as opposed to stressing merely the pronunciation of words.* This means that a child's pronunciation of words (either in a standard or distinct dialect) is not the key factor. The critical factor is that the child understands what words mean as part of a language context and can relate that word to the material that he or she is reading. If word-recognition instruction focuses on meaning, children will learn to rely on what they already know about their language to provide semantic and syntactic cues. Children are already proficient language users, so it makes sense to capitalize upon this strength when introducing them to printed language. When pronunciation of words is the primary goal, however, the child tends to focus on rules for pronouncing words. Thus, even when the child is successful in applying specific sound-symbol relationships, he or she may lose sight of the fact that the reason for reading is to get meaning. One result of such misfocus is the development of what is often referred to as a word-by-word (or an overly analytical) reader. Such a child may read slowly or haltingly because he or she is intent on trying to sound out each word carefully rather than concentrating on the meaning. On the other hand, the child who has discovered that reading is a way of communicating with a writer has a valuable resource available when a word is unfamiliar. The child's first guess at an unknown word is likely to result in a meaningful substitution. Communication need not be interrupted as it might be if the reader applied other, less well-

"If I have to sit in the corner for *sayin'* it, at least you could tell me what it *MEANS!*"

DENNIS THE MENACE ® and © Field Enterprises Inc.

developed word-recognition behaviors (for example, phonic or structural analysis, or use of an outside resource).

For example, a child who has learned to rely upon language can guess the kind of word that may fit the meaning even when the actual printed word is unknown.

The cat washed her *paws.*

A reader who doesn't recognize the word *paws* may substitute *feet, face, tail,* or *kittens* if he or she is attuned to the fact that reading, like talking, makes sense. That is, the reader will know that the cat washed *something.* The reader who makes a logical substitution knows something about cats, language, and how to use context to recognize words. Some substitutions are based on dialect differences.

Dialect differences. When a child pronounces a word differently from a standard dialect when reading aloud, no attempt to correct the child's pronunciation need be made. For example, suppose that a child read *dat* for *that,* or *gonna* for *going to,* or even *he be* for *he is.* Because the child has demonstrated mature reading behavior by translating the printed symbols into the language that he or she normally uses and that, therefore, makes the most sense, your best response is no response.

There may be times during your day when you will want to specifically model standard pronunciation for your children, but the best time is not when you are attempting to teach a child to read—that is, to make sense of printed symbols. It is important for all of us to understand that communicating through print is not dependent upon standard pronunciation. Ask someone from another part of the country to read a selection orally. Notice the number of dialect variations from your pronunciation of these same words.

Three basic proposals for dealing with dialect differences have been advocated by reading specialists. Briefly, these are:

(1) *Teach the child standard English before beginning reading instruction.* The rationale is that a child's oral language must match the printed language. The problems with this approach are that, first, we all speak a dialect and it is difficult to determine what is standard English. Second, it is not necessary to pronounce words a certain way for them to suggest meaning. Third, if a child comes to believe his or her own way of speaking is not acceptable, all school instruction may suffer because of the child's lowered self-esteem. Finally, it may be impossible to change the dialect of a child (Kochman, 1969).

(2) *Rewrite beginning reading materials so they match the dialect pronunciation of the beginning readers.* The rationale is that books written in a dialect approximating that of the reader will be easier to learn to read. There is no evidence that a story written in a dialect is easier for a speaker of that dialect to learn to read than the same story written in standard English (Sims, 1972; Johnson and Simons, 1973).

(3) *Allow children to pronounce the words in their own dialect while reading.* This approach is based on the rationale that pronouncing words as the reader normally *speaks* the words provides the best insurance that meaning has been gained.

Familiar and Concrete Concepts

A second general principle of teaching word recognition is that you should try to *introduce words that are a part of a child's experience and background.* It is futile to try to teach a child to pronounce a word that prompts no concept or meaning. A reader from warm climes, for example, may have no concrete experience with a *sled*; a rural child may approach

"How do you expect to read when you can't even tell the sun from a mastodon?"

© 1979 Sidney Harris

words like *elevator* or *skyscraper* with the same void. As we stress throughout this text, a teacher can help to build the background to introduce alien concepts, but that preparation needs to be housed within concepts that are already within the child's experience. The same kind of judgment has to be made in teaching abstract words. Concepts like *fear* and *joy*—particularly as broader themes—can be developed, but the teacher needs to first build on the child's experiences with these feelings.

Words representing concepts that are likely to be a part of a child's concrete experience will be easiest to teach and will build his or her recognition vocabulary more quickly. With this larger sight vocabulary, the child's ability to use context clues is increased.

Context Clues and the Instructional Level

A third general principle of teaching word recognition is that the *words that are being taught to a child can be drawn* initially *from his or her instructional reading materials.* After analyzing the results of an informal reading inventory (see Chapter 2), the beginning teacher chooses a text at the child's instructional reading level and often lets that appropriate text help to decide which words to teach. If, for example, the child's instructional level is 2^1 on an informal reading inventory, taken from Houghton Mifflin's basal series, then the words selected to be taught are words that the child will need in order to experience success with those materials. It should be noted that this is underscored as minimal word recognition to be supplemented as additional materials and teaching skill are acquired. The teacher can determine, first of all, if a child will need background material before new words are introduced. The child's mastery of new vocabulary is measured through observation during instruction and by continuous informal assessment.

Flexible Teaching

The fourth principle maintains that, in teaching word-recognition behaviors, *there should be an emphasis on flexibility in the application of the skills.* Word-recognition instruction should emphasize use of *all* necessary word-recognition cues in an attempt to determine what the word is. For example, teaching suggestions should not solely encourage sounding out a word, for that is only one word-recognition behavior. The guidance that teachers provide should also emphasize reliance on the use of context, on the structure, and on outside resources, as well as on phonic analysis. And, through success in recognizing new words, a child begins to understand that all cues (semantic, syntactic, and phonological) work in conjunction with one another to aid in unlocking unfamiliar words. In following this general principle, you can give children opportunities to apply their various word-recognition skills, and you can encourage them to shift flexibly from one behavior to another.

An important consideration relates this general principle to the first principle we discussed—getting meaning preempts any emphasis on striving for correct pronunciation. When a reader flexibly applies the various word-recognition behaviors, he or she must be allowed to read with meaningful substitutions. These substitutions may include dialect variations in the pronunciation of words or phrases, word substitutions when they have the same meanings (such as cat for kitten), and deletions of words when these do not alter the meaning (such as omitting the word *have* in the sentence *I have had dinner.*). These variations can be noted for later interpretation, as Chapter 2 illustrates, but it is usually not wise to interrupt meaningful reading with instructional guns blazing. Achieving word recognition is not always equivalent to achieving exact pronunciation of words or exact replication of the printed text. If meaning is the goal, meaningful alterations of the printed page are often appropriate and indicate strength.

Word-Recognition Behaviors Are Taught as Needed

The fifth general principle is that *word-recognition skills are best taught when they are needed by a child.* That is, it is usually more efficient to teach a child a word-recognition strategy in a situation that requires immediate application. For example, if a child pauses before unknown words and then guesses a word that starts with the same sound as the word in print, regardless of similarity in meaning, you can assume that the reader is attuned to matching letters with sounds and may need guided practice to make use of the meaning and structure of print. Similarly, if a child pauses at a word and then seeks help to identify it, you can develop plans to teach reliance upon meaning, structure, and phonics. The instruction, then, follows the demonstration of need and the instructor offers opportunity to "try out" new skills by offering reading material, appropriate to level, and geared to application of fledgling skills. Teaching a specific behavior need not be dictated by a sequence prescribed in a teacher's manual. By staying in tune with a child's needs and by carefully monitoring word-recognition behaviors as he or she reads orally, you can determine which behavior ought to be taught.

This procedure emphasizes the importance of continuous diagnosis during oral reading so you can return to needed instruction later. An overall concern is that instruction must never lose its focus on meaning—in this case, by letting concern for recognizing an isolated word interrupt reading for too long. It would be better to tell the child the word than to let that happen.

Learning Prerequisite Behaviors

The sixth general principle in teaching word-recognition skills is to *make sure that the child has mastered the necessary prerequisite skills to learning a particular word-recognition behavior.* For example, it is important that children understand the meanings of words before you ask them to try to figure out or to recognize the word in print; it is very difficult for an adult or a child to recognize a word that is not part of his or her oral vocabulary. Other examples of necessary skills are that a child must be able to discriminate letters visually and distinguish sounds aurally before learning sound-symbol relationships; he or she must know the meaning of a word before determining how the addition of a prefix or suffix changes the meaning; and a child must know how to alphabetize before using a dictionary as an outside reference. These prerequisite skills will be considered as we discuss the teaching of word-recognition behaviors in the next two chapters.

In considering these six general principles, it should be reemphasized that the use of context clues is usually the most efficient way to recognize words. Therefore, the emphasis in your teaching should be based on the awareness that the mature reader uses context analysis as the umbrella organizer, with phonic analysis, sight vocabulary, structural analysis, and outside resources to supplement and strengthen the key behavior.

REFERENCES

Cattell, James McKeen. "Ueber die Zeit der Erkennung und Benennung von Schriftzeichen Bildern und Farben." *Philosophische Studien* 2 (1885): 635–50.

Chall, Jeanne S. *Learning to Read: The Great Debate.* New York: McGraw-Hill, 1967.

Crichton, Michael. *The Great Train Robbery.* New York: Alfred A. Knopf, 1975.

DiVesta, Francis J., and Palermo, David S. "Language Development." In *Review of Research Education,* edited by Fred N. Kerlinger and John B. Carroll, pp. 55–107. Itasca, Ill.: F. E. Peacock, 1974.

Goodman, Kenneth S. "Orthography in a Theory of Reading Instruction." *Elementary English* (December 1972): 1254–61.

Johnson, Kenneth R., and Simons, Herbert D. *Black Children's Reading of Dialect and Standard Texts.* Final Report, ERIC No. 076 978. Washington, D.C.: National Institute of Education, 1973.

Kochman, Thomas. "Social Factors in the Consideration of Teaching Standard English." In *Linguistic-cultural Differences and American Education,* edited by Alfred C. Aarons et al. *Florida F L Reporter* 7 (1969): 1–87.

McKee, Paul. *Primer for Parents.* Boston: Houghton Mifflin, 1972.

Rystrom, Richard. "Reading, Language and Nonstandard Dialects." In *Language Differences: Do They Interfere?*, edited by James L. Laffey and Roger Shuy, pp. 86–90. Newark, Del.: International Reading Association, 1973.

Samuels, S. Jay. "Hierarchical Subskills in the Reading Acquisition Process." Address at the Hyman Blumberg Symposium on Research in Early Childhood Education. November 14, 1974.

Sims, Rudine. "A Psycholinguistic Description of Miscues Created by Selected Young Readers During Oral Reading of Texts in Black Dialect and Standard English." Unpublished doctoral dissertation, Wayne State University, 1972.

Smith, Frank. *Understanding Reading*. New York: Holt, Rinehart and Winston, 1971.

Venezky, Richard L., and Chapman, Robin S. "Is Learning to Read Dialect Bound?" In *Language Differences: Do They Interfere?*, edited by James L. Laffey and Roger Shuy, pp. 62–69. Newark, Del.: International Reading Association, 1973.

Wardhaugh, Ronald. "The Teaching of Phonics and Comprehension: A Linguistic Evaluation." In *Psycholinguistics and the Teaching of Reading*, edited by Kenneth S. Goodman and James T. Fleming, pp. 79–90. Newark, Del.: International Reading Association, 1969.

5

Context Analysis

Context Is the Key

A teacher we know was concerned about the way some children in his class were reading. He asked us to sit in on his class and watch while he prepared a child to read a story. This is what we saw:

Step one. The teacher identified the "new" vocabulary words for a story by checking the teacher's edition for new words.

Step two. The teacher wrote the words onto cards.

Step three. He showed the cards to the child, pronouncing each word carefully, and asked the child to repeat the word.

Step four. The teacher asked the child to read the story.

While we watched, the child (we'll call her Sandy) began to read.

Sandy: "Tommy Sherman didn't believe there was such a thing as a flying . . . (pause), as a flying . . ." What's that word?

Teacher: Remember? We just learned that word. It's your *new* word. (The teacher searched the word cards, located *saucer*, and held it up.) Remember this word?

Sandy: (nodding her head) Uh-huh.

Teacher: The word is *saucer*. Now, read on.

Sandy: "He thought . . ." (pause)

Teacher: New word. We just had it. Remember?

Sandy: Saucer?

Teacher: Right.

Sandy: "He thought a *saucer* belonged under a cup."

Just this much of a peek at the teacher-student interaction provided us with a few clues as to what might be happening to some readers in this classroom.

The teacher thought he had prepared the child. In an attempt to make the new words a part of the sight vocabulary of the child, he had made cards for the words. (To be fair, we should note that in some cases, he made a picture or offered a definition on the back of the card). The child had successfully identified the words on the cards, but seemed unable to recognize the same words in the story—pausing before each, seemingly with no retention from the preliminary introduction.

The teacher was tempted to return to a drill on the new words. He was also tempted to adjust the reading material and to offer a less difficult level. However, all other indicators (total word recognition, comprehension, and fluency) spoke to the appropriateness of the instructional placement. As we talked later, we agreed on two significant points:

(1) Sandy had initially met the new word in a rather unlikely situation, that is, in isolation. She had been presented the rather frustrating task of trying to memorize words divorced from any context.

(2) By isolating the word from its natural setting—language—it was partially robbed both of its meaning and the clues to its meaning that language provides. In short, Sandy probably wasn't learning any strategies for identifying new words—other than remembering them—and she had become heavily dependent on an outside resource (teacher) when her memory failed. At the same time, Sandy's teacher had had an opportunity to extend an understanding Sandy needed in order for her to read for meaning. While Sandy later indicated she knew what a saucer was (of the cup-and-saucer variety), she didn't know what a flying saucer was. This one word, then, could interfere with Sandy's comprehension of the entire story.

Sandy's teacher decided to try a different procedure, one that emphasized the context of the story and helped Sandy begin to develop a strategy for identifying words by relying on that context.

A Practical Definition of Context Analysis

Context analysis in word recognition is the skill of using information surrounding a word to help recognize that word as one that has been experienced aurally but perhaps not visually. Put another way, use of context is the reader's use of syntax and semantics to arrive at the most probable meaning of a linguistic unit.

Generally, there are three kinds of information that give clues to the reader using context analysis: semantic, syntactic, and pictorial. Semantic clues involve the use of the *meaning* of the other words in the sentence—and in surrounding sentences—to identify the new word. Semantic clues also allow the reader to use prior knowledge and experience to establish meaning and predict a word. Syntactic clues involve an analysis of the function of the unrecognized word by looking at its *grammatical relationship* with other words. All children have syntactic expectations for their oral language. When they hear a noun at the beginning of an expression, they come to expect a verb to follow. They also develop the very accurate expectation that a noun—a naming word—will follow the word *the*. It is this syntactic expectation of the predictability of our language that can be used as the basis for helping children use context clues in reading. Pictorial clues come from illustrations accompanying the text and provide a *graphic extension* and interpretation of the print.

By relying upon the context, the child draws information from the rest of the sentence, from other sentences in the context, and from his or her own experience with related ideas to make an informed guess of the unknown word. In many children's beginning texts, most words are not new aurally; the child has heard them used many times—often in phrases like the one encountered in print. That is, the whole context in which the word appears is not unfamiliar to the child as a listener; and when reading, one or several familiar words may trigger comprehension.

Before we take a more detailed and analytic look at the three types of context clues, let us examine some strategies that Sandy's teacher finally decided to use.

Step one. The teacher reread the story and identified words that were likely to be new or difficult for Sandy. (He continued to rely on the teacher's edition.) The difference in the approach was that now the teacher recognized Sandy's need both to identify and to supply meaning for words.

Step two. The teacher then pulled sentences directly from the story, which contained new vocabulary words. He typed the sentences onto paper, leaving out the new words, and inserted a blank in the place of each word. The new words were placed at the bottom of the paper. Then he slipped the paper into a plastic sleeve to preserve his effort.

(1) Tommy Sherman didn't believe there was such a thing as a flying _____ .
(2) He thought a _____ belonged under a cup.
(3) First his father talked about it one morning while eating _____ . Later some people saw things right in his town.
(4) Then one night, some _____ thought they saw it.

neighbors   saucer   breakfast

Step three. This time, Sandy's teacher helped Sandy to get ready to read. He put a cup and saucer next to a drawing of someone's concept of a flying saucer. The conversation sounded like this:

Teacher: What do you think this story is about? Here are some clues for you.

Sandy: Well, that's a cup and saucer and this is a picture of a spaceship, I think.

Teacher: Surely. Do you see any similarity between the spaceship and this saucer? (pause) Another name for this saucer-shaped ship is a flying _____ ?

Sandy: Saucer!

Teacher: Right! Have *you* ever seen a flying saucer?

Sandy: I don't even think there *is* such a thing as a flying saucer.

Teacher: Some people in this story thought that they saw one. Tommy Sherman was sure of it.

Sandy: Maybe it's a make-believe story.

Teacher: Soon you'll read and find out, but first try to guess what words have been left out of the sentences on this page.

Step four. As Sandy read, the teacher encouraged her to use the sense of the sentence to make a guess. When she paused, the teacher encouraged her to guess, and the teacher reinforced "good" guesses—ones that fit the meaning and grammar of the sentence—by rereading the completed sentence aloud. Additional meaning clues helped Sandy to narrow the range of alternatives and eventually to produce the expected response.

Sandy: "First his father talked about it one morning while eating bah . . . bah . . ."

Teacher: What is Tommy's father doing with this word?

Sandy: He's eating it.

Teacher: When is he eating it?

Sandy: (reexamining the sentence) One morning.

Teacher: What do you eat in the morning?

Sandy: Cereal!

Sandy's teacher might have settled for *cereal* and made a note to attack *breakfast* another time. Or, hoping Sandy would draw *breakfast* from the clue, the teacher might have tried one more question: What do we call things like eggs and cereal that we eat in the morning? The illustration emphasizes that while the three types of context clues can be separated for analysis and teaching, they usually operate together.

The teacher was concerned about the double use of the word *saucer*, and so helped Sandy recognize it both as a plate that goes under a cup and as the object that people in the story thought they saw in the sky. The latter, more difficult use, appeared first in the story. If *saucer* still went unrecognized, the teacher was prepared to tell the word, but he had come to believe that helping Sandy rely on context clues to make guesses was a strategy that would expedite all her reading.

The clues had piled up and worked for Sandy. She was able to connect the saucer that she knew with another name for the spaceship in her experience. The teacher wasn't sure which clue had helped the most, but he suspected that the semantic, syntactic, and pictorial clues in combination had prompted the word. The teacher successfully helped the child to make use of the sentence sense—context—to recognize the word and to prepare her to read a story successfully.

One of the most effective procedures to teach use of context clues is to ask questions that lead children to focus on the "sense" of what they are reading. A teacher-questioning strategy should eventually result in getting children to form their own questions as they read. When children stay alert to the sense of a passage, when they question, make good guesses, and check the selection for answers, they are becoming mature readers—i.e., expert users of context clues. Remember, however, that it is important to transfer the questioning attitude to your students as soon as possible. To use context clues as the mature reader does, *they* need to ask the questions that establish purposeful reading.

Semantic Clues Aid in the Recognition of New Words

Any attempt to describe semantic clues apart from syntactic clues serves to emphasize how interrelated they are. The illustrations of semantic clues discussed on pages 172–78, for example, could also appear in the subsection on syntactic clues (pages 178–82). Conversely, syntactic clues are aids to using semantic clues because the meanings of the words that syntactic clues reveal can be used to unlock still other words. For example, understanding that *flying* belongs with *saucer* is

a syntactic clue. Knowing that allows the reader to apply the meaning of *flying* to *saucer* as a semantic clue.

This is an excellent example of the redundancy in language (the tendency of our language to offer multiple clues to meaning) and of how that redundancy allows readers to exploit the context surrounding a new word to help unlock its meaning. In the following focus on narrow aspects of semantic analysis, keep in mind its broader applications, in which the reader draws clues to meaning from surrounding sentences and the whole text. Children should be led to ask themselves such questions as: "Does my guess at this word fit the overall meaning of the sentence?" "Does it coincide with the meaning of the story?" "Do my guesses agree with clues drawn from the pictures?"

Synonyms. One example of the redundancy of language is its use of synonyms. Synonyms operate as semantic clues to help a reader recognize the word they rename.

> The *vessel* tossed on the high waves for days without passing another *ship*.

A child who cannot recognize *vessel* ought to be encouraged to read on to the synonym *ship* to see if it helps with *vessel*. Another significant clue in this example supports the synonym—namely, the sea setting, which may help some readers identify *vessel* as a word they may have connected with discussions about the sea. Even if the child mispronounces *vessel* but understands that it is a ship, he or she has *read* the sentence adequately, that is, gaining meaning. The habit of reading on to the end of a meaning unit is a good one to build within young readers, although it sometimes seems much easier for teachers to dispense words than to help children build detectivelike habits of searching for clues to meaning.

It is the teacher's task to encourage the reader to look for the synonym as a potential clue to the word not recognized, but it is not the teacher's task tediously to question until loss of meaning results. The teacher might simply say, "This says *another* ship. Where is the first ship mentioned in this story?" Interruptions should be characterized by their brevity and their attention to preserving meaning.

Definitions. Sometimes the surrounding context offers a direct definition of an unrecognized word.

> Mr. Parker owned a grocery, where people came to buy fruit, vegetables, meats, and other foods. He sold soap, pet food, and lots of other things, too.

The child who fails to recognize *grocery* should be encouraged to read on to see if the information following enables him or her to guess the meaning of the unknown word. (Even if the child doesn't supply the expected response, if he or she recognizes that the word means a place where all these items are sold, the child has *communicated* with the author.) The teacher's objective should be to encourage children to look for definition clues in the context. In this example, the teacher's approach might be as simple as saying, "Maybe the story will help you to discover what that word is. Read to the end of the sentence and see."

Teachers can create practice activities that use the same new word in various contexts to aid in recognizing the word.

Tina thought the zebra looked like a striped horse with short legs.
Zebras are very strong four-footed animals.
The zebra is related to both the horse and the donkey.
When the zebra moved, its black and white stripes made Oscar dizzy.

After reading these clues, the child is encouraged to identify the word *zebra*.

Accruing semantic clues.   In some passages, a kind of definition of a new word, or package of clues to its meaning, accrues in ideas preceding or following the unrecognized word. The child needs to be taught that it is possible to use this kind of information. For example:

It seemed to come in the window. It looked like a faint cloud. It wasn't really like a person, but it seemed to stand. And it floated—it didn't walk. It reached out slowly with something like arms under a cape. It was a fearful apparition all right!

Perhaps you might not expect a given child to know what an *apparition* is, but he or she might understand that it is all the things described before that word. If you asked the child to describe it, the answer might be, "It's a ghost!" That is probably the time to respond, "Another word for *ghost* is *apparition*." Once a child can use clues that effectively, it is not absolutely essential that *apparition* be pronounced. When the teacher pronounces and writes "A ghost is an *apparition*," the reliance on context is reinforced. Knowing that one can look for clues throughout a passage to aid in recognizing a word is an important understanding to achieve. In the following example, the explanation of a new word follows, almost as a direct definition.

Oscar was afraid he would be sued for libel. As editor of the newspaper he had allowed the story to get into print. And now it was on everyone's doorstep, calling Mr. Jacobs a thief. There weren't many facts in the story to back that up. Mr. Jacobs would say it was a lie and that it would hurt him as a businessman. He would call it libel, and libel is against the law.

The reader who doesn't recognize the word *libel* won't learn to distinguish it from *slander* by reading the whole passage; but if he or she has learned to depend upon the accrual of semantic clues, it should be clear enough why Oscar is worried and why Mr. Jacobs may sue. What a developing reader needs to learn is that there is no need to let an unknown word cause a "hang up." Instead, the reader should look for clues to the meaning in the context.

The word *moor* is not likely to be familiar to many third graders, but this passage may enable the third-grade level reader to describe one adequately.

> Emily Brontë grew up on the English moors. There were rolling hills covered with little shrubs and clumps of long grass. The ground was soggy and the air was damp.

A follow-up conversation with the teacher about a moor provides opportunity for the pronunciation to occur naturally. In any case, the word is more likely to be remembered than if a child is asked to memorize it and its definition from a list.

Inferences. The clues that can be pieced together in a passage to help define a new word are not always literal. Often a definition must be inferred. The following example shows how the mood set by information in the passage can help to identify a new word.

> Peter got up early, and what he saw through his window made him whistle. Sunlight played on the lawn and sparkled off the lake. White clouds puffed by. The birds were singing like crazy. He just knew that this day would be glorious.

Since it is not defined directly, the meaning of *glorious* must be inferred from the rest of the passage. To that goal, the teacher could direct the reader's attention to those clues. Did Peter expect it to be a good day? What made him think so? Is there a word in the story to describe Peter's day?

How might you get an intermediate-grade child to understand the word *intimidate* in the following passage?

> Mary was always afraid she would make a mistake. She wanted to be fair to everyone, but she always had to apologize no matter how things turned out. She felt she wasn't smart enough to do her job well, and she was sure almost anyone could do it better. Alan knew he could get her to quit by intimidating her.

The word-recognition skill taught in such an exercise is contextual inference, and teaching a child to infer meaning is much more difficult than teaching the child to remember a specific word. As a teacher, you should examine materials that your children will read to discover opportunities for helping them to infer meanings.

Comparisons. Another useful semantic tool to aid in recognition of words is comparison. In a comparison, either the similarity or the difference of two things is pointed up. If the reader knows the words in one half of this equivalency, he or she can make an informed guess on unknown words in the other half. Watch for the use of comparison or contrast in passages and use both when possible to facilitate word recognition. Suppose a child failed to recognize evening in the following passage:

In the bright morning light, Sue could always see who was coming over the hill. But in the gray evening, it was not so easy to tell.

For some readers, the contrast between a bright beginning of day and a gray time (opposite signaled by *but*) might lead to hypothesizing that the printed word is *evening,* a word probably aurally familiar to many. But sometimes comparisons need to be pointed up. The teacher might ask, "What time of day do things get gray?" Since the contrast is not as familiar as is *day* to *night*—the teacher's probe question might prompt the word *night,* which is not an appropriate synonym here. If that happened, the teacher must prompt the reader to look for additional clues or tell the word.

Figures of speech. Figures of speech are often comparisons, and the reader can use the familiar part as an aid in recognizing the less familiar. When the familiar part of a figure of speech gives clues to a new word, context is being used for word recognition.

The figures of speech that young readers encounter are usually fairly easy to understand; similes are most common. Suppose a young reader didn't know the word *puppet* in the following sentence:

The puppet moved like a tiny man, old and bent.

From brief discussion as to what the second half of the simile reveals about *puppet,* a child could be led to discover that it is something that has some characteristics of a real person but may differ from a real person, too. It is much smaller, for one thing. This does not mean that you try to explain to the child what a simile is; but only that you encourage the child through discussion to exploit the context of the simile to help identify a new word.

Figures of speech—even the humble simile—are not always obvious or easy to use; but even when they are complex or ambiguous, a reader can still infer from one part to another to help recognize a word. Suppose the unfamiliar *puppet* were in this sentence:

Martha jerked around like a puppet.

Although *jerked around* doesn't define a puppet, it does describe an important aspect of a puppet—its movement—that can, with other clues, help in recognizing the word.

Like the second simile above, metaphors can provide contextual clues to identify words if the reader infers from one part of the implied comparison to the other. This inferential behavior—known as explication—is a high order of contextual analysis; but that is not to say that metaphors do not appear in materials for beginners and that they can't provide good opportunities to devlop context analysis. Take a descriptive sentence such as this:

The brawny farmer was a bear of a man.

The redundancy (two descriptions of the farmer—*brawny* and a *bear*) in this sentence is intentional to encourage the young reader to infer from the second part of the metaphor (*a bear of a man*) to the first (*the brawny farmer*). If the teacher encourages the child who is stumped by *brawny* to discuss what *a bear of a man* might look like, the child will be inferring a meaning for *brawny*. The practice will lead the child to use metaphoric language even when it is not a clue for new words, so that the descriptive power the author intended will work when he or she reads:

Mr. Turner was a bear of a man.

The power of figures of speech to invite contextual analysis is unlimited. And when the reading material introduces new words in a figure of speech, the opportunity exists to teach reliance upon context analysis as a word-recognition behavior. The very nature of figures of speech demands that the reader draw inferences from the context.

Idioms. One definition of idioms describes them as words or phrases that do not mean what they say on the surface; that is, they cannot be literally translated. Originally they were metaphors, but through repeated usage, they have lost their metaphorical quality and figurative meanings. Understandably, beginning readers can be misled by phrases like "beat a dead horse," "kick the bucket," "hit the sack," "come up smelling like a rose," "stick to the straight and narrow," "sing a different tune," and so on. Such idioms may contain recognizable words, but the words no longer mean what they say. "On the other hand," the idioms are in such frequent usage that the child may have them "on the tip of that do not mean what they say on the surface; that is, they cannot be child's aural experience. When they cause trouble, the teacher can present them as a unit by copying the sentence they appear in on the board and boxing them as though they were one word:

The neighbors had fought for years over small things. One day they

talked it over and decided to | bury the hatchet. |

Recognizing the idiom as a unit may trigger immediate recognition of the whole phrase if the child has heard it many times and if there are sufficient context clues. The teacher can provide additional clues that may be added to the context where necessary. In the example above, the teacher could discuss with the child what it would mean if one of the warring parties were to bury its weapons.

Cause and effect. The operation of cause-and-effect clues is similar to question-and-answer clues. If the reader has experienced the cause presented in the text, he or she may anticipate the effect and thus more readily identify new words used in describing the effect. Or this could work in reverse; having experienced the effect he or she reads about, the reader may be able to backtrack in order to make sense of problem words used in describing the cause. Here is an example of how cause-and-effect clues operate at an elementary level:

> Billy was late getting home for dinner again. He knew he might be punished.

If *punished* in print were new to the reader, his or her own experience with the effect of being late might help in recognizing the word. And, of course, the teacher can prompt the clue, "Does someone tell you not to be late for dinner? What might happen if you are always late?"

Other semantic context clues. A more complete list of types of semantic context aids has been compiled by Wilbur S. Ames;* he bases them on the reading behaviors of a number of adult readers and suggests that in using semantic clues, the reader is relying on:

(1) experience with language and familiar expressions
(2) modifying phrases and clauses
(3) definition or description
(4) words connected in a series
(5) comparison or contrast
(6) synonym clues
(7) time, setting, and mood
(8) referents or antecedents
(9) association clues
(10) main idea and supporting details
(11) question-answer pattern of paragraph
(12) preposition clues
(13) nonrestrictive clauses or appositive phrases
(14) cause-and-effect patterns

All of these examples of context clues involve the use of inference by the mature reader and emphasize the relationship between thinking and reading. In effect, what happens in semantic context analysis is that words and ideas that the reader *knows and has* spark thought that allows the meaning of unknown words to be inferred. This is a natural language behavior that children should be encouraged to rely on in reading.

Syntactic Clues Trigger Semantic Clues

As with semantic clues, the object in teaching the use of syntactic context clues is to help children make logical hypotheses about print. The examples of syntactic clues that follow are not intended to represent grammatical structures that should be taught directly to children; they are merely instances in which a teacher can help a child focus on what he or she already knows about language.

* Wilbur S. Ames, "The Development of a Classification Scheme of Contextual Aids," *Reading Research Quarterly* 2 (Fall 1966): 57–82.

A syntactic clue is derived from a grammatical relationship that exists between elements of a sentence. Sometimes knowing the function of a word is enough of a clue to prompt recognition of it. More often, the syntactic clue enables a reader to exploit semantic clues within the grammatical structure. For example, a child intuitively knows that modifiers describe or limit the nouns they modify and so can be taught to use the information in the modifier to help in recognizing the noun. As you will see in some of the examples that follow, *the teacher can phrase questions that prompt the use of syntax for word recognition without stopping to teach a grammar lesson.*

Since use of syntax is often just a trigger to semantic analysis, the emphasis in this discussion may appear to fall heavily on semantic analysis after an initial syntactic identification.

Nouns follow articles.   We have previously alluded to how the articles *a, an,* and *the* can cue the reader to expect a noun form to follow. This awareness provides the reader with a syntactic cue. A good way to illustrate this expectancy is to provide children with sentences that leave a blank for the noun (or remainder of the noun phrase) following an article.

The _____ was standing at the corner waving his arms and telling the cars when to stop and go.

Repeated experience with guessing new words that follow articles can help a child to understand that the words will name persons, places, or things. Note in the example above how the details in the rest of the sentence help the reader respond successfully to the cue word *the.*

Appositives pause to rename.   The appositive, in which a noun or noun phrase is placed with another to serve as explanation, is another example of how syntactic cues work with semantic clues. The appositive can be pointed out as a phrase to be interpreted as a unit. Boxing the appositive within the whole sentence can be an effective visual technique that gives the teacher a chance to help readers discover what the writer has really done within the commas.

A giraffe, |an animal with a very long neck,| was Maxine's favorite.

For the example given, the teacher may indicate that the writer wanted to be very clear, thus the pause within these commas to explain or cue the word.

Subjects signal verbs. Because sentences in children's reading material often begin by naming something and then usually tell what that something *does* or *is*, the child can call upon his or her normal language patterns to give clues for recognition of verbs.

The worm wiggled across the sidewalk.

Many young readers might fail to recognize *wiggled*, but they can guess that the word tells what the worm did. In this case, the teacher might ask, "What do you think the worm did?" Or, the teacher may ask, "How do worms usually get across the sidewalks?"—relying on a semantic clue based on the rest of the sentence.

Some verbs demand completion. When a sentence tells us that something *is, was,* or *will be,* we can expect the rest of the sentence to then tell *what*—completing the thought.

The losers were unhappy.

This same kind of expectancy is developed in sentences that contain action verbs in need of completion. The subject and verb tell that someone (or something) did something and beg the question "to what (or whom)?" The teacher can help a child to rely on this expectancy. For example, after the following sentence:

The salesman carried his briefcase.

the teacher can ask, "What do salesmen usually carry?"

Adjectives and nouns tell on each other. The oral language of children also reflects grammatically significant modifiers. Again, this language awareness allows the reader to exploit many semantic clues. Adjective forms preceding the word they modify can serve as clues to that word; understanding the adjectival relationship can also help readers to recognize the adjective itself.

Here is an example of how knowing the adjective's function aids in recognizing the noun:

The strong athlete won the gold medal.

The teacher can help the reader who does not recognize *athlete* even after completing the sentence by asking, "What do we call strong people who compete for medals?" You could easily argue that the clue is more semantic than syntactic, but the illustration is intended to show the relationship of the adjective to the noun; it further illustrates how the syntactic clue usually sets up the semantic one.

In the following example, the reader needs to understand that the adjective describes the noun and can be coupled with a semantic clue from the surrounding words to unlock the adjective itself:

Her glistening eyes told me she had been crying.

As the child experiences this kind of clue-gathering, he or she generalizes to the relationship between nouns and adjectives as a tool for guessing the meanings of new words in print.

The relationship of adverbs to verbs works just as adjectives to nouns; and the brief kinds of prodding cues the teacher provides to provoke recognition can often exploit the function relationship while the child is searching for the semantic clue.

Clozure can help teach syntactic clues. An effective method for practicing reliance upon syntactic clues is to tape small paper flaps over some of the words in a book at the child's reading level. Choose such function words as: a noun following an article, a noun preceding an appositive, a noun following a preposition, a verb following its subject (or a subject noun preceding a verb), or a noun modified by an adjective (or the adjective that modifies a noun). The child is then asked to read the text, to guess at the covered words, and then to lift the flaps to check the guesses.

Rudy's turtle lives in[⎽⎽⎽].
It is called a red-eared turtle.
See if you can[⎺⎺]why.

A red-eared turtle will eat meat
when it is[⎽⎽⎽].
It will eat[⎺⎺⎺]when it gets big.

[⎺⎺⎺]turtles eat meat
and plants.
Some turtles eat fish.
Some[⎺⎺]big turtles
will eat birds.

121

From *Blue-Tailed Horse* by William Eller et al. (River Forest, Ill.: Laidlaw Brothers, 1976), p. 121. Reproduced by permission of Laidlaw Brothers, a Division of Doubleday and Company, Inc.

Syntactic clues relate to meaning. The fact that reliance on syntactic context clues usually triggers the use of semantic ones underlines once again the basic theme of this text: the whole purpose of reading is to bring meaning to and get meaning from written language; thus the teacher of reading should capitalize on every opportunity to stress meaning in developing skilled readers. It is a happy phenomenon that, rather than stressing a grammatical analysis of written language, the exploitation of syntactic clues slides automatically into an analysis of semantics—what the words being used in certain ways mean in relation to each other. And this should happen solely because the child is eager to understand and enjoy the written ideas he or she is encountering.

Pictures as Context Clues

Illustrations that accompany print can offer graphic clues to meaning, and children should be guided to use them. Suppose, for example, that a young reader had difficulty with the two words italicized in the following sentence, which appeared on a page opposite a drawing of a girl racing a tricycle ahead of a smaller boy:

Jenny was able to ride her *tricycle* much *faster* than her little brother Jack.

The picture might help the reader identify the word *tricycle*. Even if the child were sounding out the words, the picture might prompt a quicker identification. And the relative position of the two children in the picture might help with the word *faster*. Note in this example how

semantic and syntactic clues can work with the picture clues. For example, if the child knows that Jenny is riding something, he or she may realize that *tricycle* is a thing ridden (a syntatic clue).

Using Pictures as Context Clues

Research findings concerning the value of encouraging and developing picture context clues are ambiguous. Samuels (1967) found that pictures associated with words hindered word recognition under some conditions for poor readers, but Hartley (1970) found that pictures appeared to facilitate word recognition. Although the conditions in these studies differed, little conclusive evidence on the use of pictures to teach word recognition is available. Many beginning reading texts and teaching techniques rely on pictures to carry meaning. When related to the context, illustrations *can* be useful tools, but in isolation, in exercises or on devices such as word cards, their use is questionable. Most sources claim they are useful in the initial stages of learning as a bridge from concrete to symbolic learning, but others suggest that if they are not phased out as a learning aid they may foster overdependence. In preprimers, where the vocabulary that is used to convey a story is very limited, pictures are often used to carry the interest and message—even within sentences—where they are substituted for words.

There are some types of reading where relating picture context to accompanying writing is an essential skill if the meaning is to be fully understood. This is especially apparent in comic strips. In the Snuffy Smith cartoon below, the humor is evident only from the last picture. After all, "getting a break" can have two meanings—one literal and one figurative. Picture context in cartoons is often imperative for complete comprehension and appreciation.

© King Features Syndicate Inc., 1975.

In this age of near video addiction, relating picture content to oral vocabulary is an essential skill; thus, developing skills in using picture clues is a valid goal, for it relates to alert television watching. No teacher can be faulted for encouraging the use of picture clues that accompany a text in developing word recognition. Such a teacher is not only exploiting an additional word-recognition clue to build children's sight vocabularies but he or she is also grooming a very practical skill. Any valid challenge of this position appears to stem from teachers' use of pictures as the *only* means to word recognition.

Most basal reader programs make extensive use of picture clues to help children increase their word recognition. The following page from a teacher's workbook for first graders is an example. The pictures play a very definite part in helping the children to read the sentences. Notice that in this exercise the emphasis is on meaning. The children are to decide which two of the three statements are correct.

From *Skills Book* for *Blue-Tailed Horse,* by William Eller et al. (River Forest, Ill.: Laidlaw Brothers, 1976), p. 17. Reproduced by permission of Laidlaw Brothers, a Division of Doubleday and Company, Inc.

When to Teach Context Analysis

Use of context to identify unknown words is perhaps the primary word-recognition technique used by the proficient reader. Think of your own reading behavior. What do you do when you come to an unknown word? Do you use the context of the sentence, surrounding sentences, or the whole selection to comprehend the unknown word even though you may not be sure of its pronunciation? Very likely you do. Keep this in mind, then, as you evaluate your students to determine those who are progressing satisfactorily and using context as an aid to identify strange words, and to single out those who are in need of more direct instruction.

As individuals read aloud to you at various times during the week, notice what they do when they come to difficult words. Do they call words that are synonyms for those actually appearing in the written text? If so, they are using context. Do they correct their own miscues? Then they are reading for meaning. However, readers who consistently seek help for unknown words or ponderously try to sound them out may need help in developing skills in context analysis. They need to discover that reading is relevant and meaningful. You can help children to develop the important skills of context analysis by encouraging the practices of reading on to the end of a phrase or sentence, making good guesses, and self-questioning. By listening to and evaluating children's reading, you can determine how much emphasis to place on context analysis and which pupils need increased attention to better develop the skill.

Some Suggestions about Context Analysis Activities

In discussing context clues, we have tried to intersperse various examples of methods you can use to help to develop the skill in young readers. Many teacher's manuals provide suggestions for activities, too; you need to evaluate any you use—to modify if necessary, and to reject those activities that don't focus on reading for meaning. Children cannot learn to use context analysis in word recognition when they are drilled on words that are stripped of surrounding and meaningful context.

A concerned teacher can develop many types of meaningful activities that allow a student practice in using context. Here are some examples:

(1) Short stories can be composed in which there is a "mystery word." The students read the story and try to figure out the mystery word. A blank is used in place of the mystery word. When a student has given some ideas as to what the word could be, he or she should be helped to identify clues that led to the conclusion. A sample of such a story follows:

Let's Go Fishing

One Day Billy and Tom decided to go fishing. They got all their fishing equipment together. They got their rods and reels and their tackle boxes. They checked their tackle boxes to make sure everything was there.

In Billy's tackle box, he had two purple artificial worms to use as _____ . He had a yellow and purple lure with two big hooks to also use as _____ .

Tom thought they should stop at the _____ shop and buy some night crawlers. Tom had used shrimp for _____ in

Florida, but he knew he could use worms at Lake Monroe.

The boys stopped at Bob's _____ Shop, and Bob sold them twelve night crawlers for _____ . They went to Lake Monroe and used their _____ to catch some fish.

(2) Collect pictures to connect with the function words *the* and *and*. This approach also provides a child with practice in the intuitive learning of function words.

(3) Answering riddles depends on context clues. They can be culled from commercial books or created. They can be rewritten, if necessary, on index cards, so that the answer appears on the back.

> I am very huge and heavy.
> I am an animal.
> I have four legs.
> I have a trunk.
> I am an _____ . (elephant)

Children can be encouraged to write riddles for classmates. These can be kept in a special "riddle center."

(4) Poetry (especially couplets) is useful for teaching context analysis because the students can use rhyme as an additional clue.

> One, two
> Buckle my _____ .
> Three, four
> Shut the _____ .
> Five, six
> Pick up _____ .
> and so on.

(5) Students can be asked to match sentences with appropriate pictures. For example:

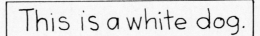

This is a white dog.

This is a blue house.

The kite is flying in the sky.

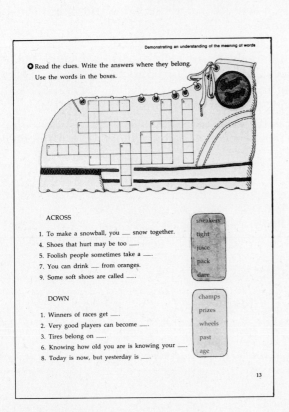

Demonstrating an understanding of the meaning of words

❍ Read the clues. Write the answers where they belong. Use the words in the boxes.

ACROSS

1. To make a snowball, you ___ snow together.
4. Shoes that hurt may be too ___.
5. Foolish people sometimes take a ___.
7. You can drink ___ from oranges.
9. Some soft shoes are called ___.

sneakers
tight
juice
pack
dare

DOWN

1. Winners of races get ___.
2. Very good players can become ___.
3. Tires belong on ___.
6. Knowing how old you are is knowing your ___.
8. Today is now, but yesterday is ___.

champs
prizes
wheels
past
age

13

(6) Specially designed crossword puzzles can be good exercises to use to improve the use of context clues. In the example at the left, from a basal reader workbook, notice how the emphasis is on identifying words using context. Even though choices are given, the child has to select the word with the best meaning for each blank.

From *Skills Book* for *Wide-Eyed Detectives* by William Eller et al. (River Forest, Ill.: Laidlaw Brothers, 1976), p. 13. Reproduced by permission of Laidlaw Brothers, a Division of Doubleday and Company, Inc.

(7)   The very best way to encourage use of context is to encourage reading. Children who are reading are—by definition—using the context. The more they read, the better they get. Reading *to* children is equally important. Hearing the language of an author prepares children to seek sense from print.

Context Analysis and Other Word-Recognition Behaviors

The emphasis on context analysis as the key word-recognition behavior stems from the firm belief that a child should be taught to read for meaning. This commitment guarantees that the purposes of reading—to enjoy, to relate, to learn, and to feed one's own creativity—always determine the attention given to the process. That is, we should directly teach specific reading skills and behaviors only as they develop the child's ability to get meaning from written material. Since using context analysis is using meaning to get more meaning, the reason for its priority should be obvious.

This emphasis, however, is not an argument that other word-recognition behaviors are unimportant. In the beginning of this chapter, we attempted to show how an understanding of grapheme-phoneme relationships is a basic behavior—especially to beginning readers. And phonics skill works in conjunction with context analysis, and structural analysis, and use of outside resources. All these behaviors help to increase a child's sight vocabulary.

The point here is that the word-recognition behaviors discussed in the next chapter are also important to develop in young readers; and that while using context analysis to unlock a word is the behavior most in tune with the purpose of reading, other behaviors facilitate its use. The high priority given context in your instruction should instill a similar priority in the children you teach; but, at the same time, you should help them develop the other word-recognition behaviors that work along with context analysis.

REFERENCES   Hartley, Ruth N. "Effects of List Types and Cues on the Learning of Word Lists." *Reading Research Quarterly* 6 (Fall 1970): 97–121.

Samuels, S. Jay. "Attentional Processes in Reading: The Effect of Pictures on the Acquisition of Reading Responses." *Journal of Educational Psychology* 58 (1967): 337–42.

FOR FURTHER READING   Durkin, Dolores. *Strategies for Identifying Words*. Boston: Allyn and Bacon, 1976.

———. *Teaching Young Children to Read*. 2d ed. Boston: Allyn and Bacon, 1974.

Goodman, Kenneth S., and Fleming, James T., eds. *Psycholinguistics and the Teaching of Reading*. Newark, Del.: International Reading Association, 1969.

Jongsma, Eugene. *The Cloze Procedure as a Teaching Technique.* Newark, Del.: International Reading Association, 1971.

Schell, Leo M. *Fundamentals of Decoding for Teachers.* Chicago: Rand McNally, 1975.

Spache, George G., and Spache, Evelyn B. *Reading in the Elementary School.* 4th ed. Boston: Allyn and Bacon, 1977. Chaps. 12 and 13.

Weintraub, Samuel. "Vocabulary Control." *The Reading Teacher* 20 (May 1969): 769–75.

Teaching the Basic Skills

Context analysis, as we noted in the previous chapter, is the key to word recognition; but there are other skills that can not only be taught but when used in conjunction with context clues help the reader to recognize words and to make sense from reading. These skills include the development of a sight vocabulary, the use of phonic analysis, the use of structural analysis, and the use of the dictionary as a resource in word recognition.

The principles of teaching word recognition apply to these skills as well as to context analysis. Briefly, the principles are:

Meaning is more important than pronunciation.
The more familiar and concrete concept is easier to teach.
Adhering to instructional levels can avoid frustration.
Flexible teaching allows the word-recognition behaviors to operate together.
Word-recognition behaviors should be taught as they are needed.
Learning word-recognition behaviors necessitates learning prerequisite behaviors.

Building a Sight Vocabulary

Mature reading is characterized by the instant recognition of a great many words. The content of most basal readers is developed by gradually increasing the sight vocabulary, so that the difficulty of each succeeding level in the series is judged primarily by the extensiveness of the cumulative vocabulary list. If the vocabulary words of one basal overlap with other series or with trade books, children will be able to read the similar materials with relative ease. Because one basal publisher may use one particular vocabulary list in writing and selecting stories and another publisher may use a different vocabulary list (or set of lists), there are differences in the amount of overlap from one basal series to another. These differences increase as the level of difficulty of the reading materials increases; this means that the decision about which words need to be sight words should be based on the particular books and stories the child will be reading, as well as on the child's knowledge of the words in those materials.

Words a Child Needs

Sight words are those words the reader recognizes immediately without having to apply any of the other word-recognition behaviors—such as the use of phonic generalizations or word-part clues like prefixes and suffixes. Words can become sight words even though the reader applied other word-recognition behaviors on the first exposure, but it is important to recognize that some sight words can be taught by provoking immediate recognition that does not rely on any of the other word-recognition behaviors. This phenomenon is particularly significant for the beginning reader, who needs a quickly developing vocabulary in order to have a base for practice of the other word-recognition behaviors.

In the classroom example that follows, the teacher builds activities that are guided by several important principles for teaching sight words. As you follow the example, note how Ms. Jones teaches the words a child will need to know in specific materials, bases decisions on what words to teach by diagnosing the child's reading, uses words that the child already knows as part of his or her oral language, urges children to rely on context for recognition clues (yet keeps the focus on the new word), and, finally, gives the child multiple opportunities to use and see the word.

Ms. Jones read through several pirate stories she was planning to offer the children to read; she listed words that she suspected were not sight-vocabulary words for most of her children. Some basal readers contain lists of new vocabulary, but the books and stories that she would offer the children did not. After previewing the material and making the tentative list of new vocabulary, she consulted each child's informal reading record to determine if the record indicated that some children had already been taught some of the words. As part of her continuous assessment, Ms. Jones kept both a list of the new vocabulary words she had taught each child and also a record of miscues from children's oral reading. She compared the vocabulary list from the pirate stories with the children's growth and need records. Finding none of the words on the cumulative lists, she prepared a set of word cards with one of the vocabulary words on each card. She recognized that while word cards with isolated words were not a particularly effective way to *teach* the vocabulary of the upcoming reading, she could use the cards as a rapid initial check (or preassessment) of each child's needs. She would simply ask that each child in the "pirate stories group" sort the cards into two stacks: "Words I know" and "Words I'd Like to Know." She accomplished this individual assessment at opportune times—when the children were working on independent activities. When the sorting was completed, she asked the child to read the "Words I Know" stack. She knew that the other stack might also contain vocabulary the child knew, but his or her own insecurity with the word (attested to by the sorting) was enough reason to teach it. She asked for brief definitions or explanations when the definition might be difficult. She kept a pencil handy to record responses; and when finished, she had a list of sight words for each child. Armed with this diagnostic information, she got ready to teach words that children actually needed for meaningful reading. The assessment had taken some planning time, but Ms. Jones was satisfied that she would not be wasting time teaching sight vocabulary to children who already knew the words.

The new vocabulary words that had stumped one or more children included: *minute, neighbor, climbed, quiet, pirate* and *excited*. One girl, Tina, needed to learn only *excited*. Brian had recognized none of the words. Instruction with the vocabulary began with some pictures of pirates that the teacher found and used to initiate discussion about the upcoming story. When possible, she attempted to include the vocabulary she was going to teach in the discussion. She did this to be sure the children had heard, understood, and used the six words as part of their speaking and listening vocabularies. She was also attempting to heighten the students' interest in reading about pirates.

Before the group met, Ms. Jones had written sentences on strips of paper that gave a meaning clue for each word, but which left blanks where the word to be learned should go. The rest of the words in the sentences were already part of the children's sight vocabularies. Some of the sentences she wrote were copied directly from the pirate stories the children would be reading later. Some of these sentences included:

It took the men less than a _____ to load the cannon.
As Billy _____ the steps, he saw a lame man slip into his cabin.
The most famous _____ was never caught.

She handed each child an envelope of his or her "new" words. Tina had one word in her envelope; Brian had all six.

Then Ms. Jones set the first sentence strip up in the pocket chart and ran her hand under the sentence as the children read, "It took the men less than a *blank* to load the cannon."

"What words can you think of that would make sense in this sentence?" asked the teacher.

"Second."

"Hour."

"Year."

"Wink."

"Minute."

The teacher wrote each of the responses on the chalkboard. She wanted the children to begin to recognize in print the words that they used in their oral language. Then she suggested that the children try out some of their guesses by reading them into the sentence. All of the words made sense in the blank, so Ms. Jones made the letter *m* at the beginning of the blank and asked the children to open their envelopes to check for a word that made sense and began with an *m*.

When three children found *minute,* they took turns dropping the word into the blank in the pocket chart and reading the sentence. The child who didn't find the *minute* card in her envelope was offered the story and was told that she had one minute to find the word *minute.* She succeeded.

When all six sentences had been presented, Ms. Jones handed all five children a mimeographed story she had written. The story included the six new vocabulary words. She told the children: "This is a story without an ending. When you have all read the story to yourself, maybe we can think of some ways the story could end:

Billy and Mr. Jayson were good neighbors. They didn't bother each other. Billy wasn't a noisy boy. That was important to Mr. Jayson. He liked things to be quiet around his house. Billy wanted Mr. Jayson to treat him like a man. And Mr. Jayson was always ready to do that.

Mr. Jayson liked to tell Billy about his youth. He told about the times he climbed mountains. Stories like that excited Billy. Then one day Mr. Jayson said, "Billy, do you want to see something really different?"

"Oh yes," said Billy, leaning toward his friend. Mr. Jayson reached in his back pocket.

Mr. Jayson pulled an old gold key from his pocket and told a story about a noisy friend he once knew as a sailor. They had found a chest of pirate treasure, but before they could get off by themselves and open it, the friend had talked about it really loudly in a crowd. When they went to where they had hidden the chest, it was gone and they were left with just the key to the chest.

"Wait a minute," Billy said suddenly. "Are you saying that this is the key to that chest?"

"I think this is the one," Mr. Jayson smiled. "I have so many old keys around the house."

Ms. Jones asked the students to read the story silently and then asked different students to read various parts of the story aloud. She asked children to read sentences containing their new words. Next, she asked students to underline, circle, or box certain words. Naturally, she asked Tina to underline *excited*. When a child was reading part of the story aloud and had trouble with any word other than the sight word, Ms. Jones read the sentence smoothly, pausing for the new word to be inserted by the child. Again, all sensible insertions for the blank were accepted and written on the board.

After reading the story through a second time, the children were each asked to tell some different ending for the story Ms. Jones had written. She quickly copied the ideas for a chart story, especially drawing upon those that contained the new vocabulary words.

Finally, she gave the children time to examine a collection of library books at appropriate reading levels on pirate adventures. She talked briefly about each book, introducing each story with an exciting tidbit from the complete book. The children were encouraged to "help themselves" to extra reading.

Ms. Jones used an effective method for introducing new vocabulary, and it was carefully guided by the principles we discussed at the beginning of this teaching incident.

Principles of Teaching Sight Vocabulary

Ms. Jones had carefully thought through the activities she planned in order to teach the new vocabulary, and she taught those words the children needed to know in order to read specific stories. But there were six other principles she also followed.

Diagnosis. One way a teacher can learn which vocabulary words need to be taught is to keep a record of the words a child at the beginning stages of reading already knows. At upper-grade levels, where the cumulative list would be too long, the record contains either the words that a child has missed in oral reading or the words that the child will need to be successful with future reading assignments. Determining what words need to be taught for beginners is a matter of comparing the vocabulary of a story against that beginner's cumulative word list. For upper-grade students, the miscues signal which words may need to be directly taught.

Keeping track of a child's sight vocabulary can be accomplished by using the process of informal diagnosis. Ideally, you would listen to each child read aloud as often as possible (but at least twice each week) and note the basic words he or she does not recognize. If the child makes long pauses before a word, mispronounces it, or stumbles over it, the word is not yet a part of the sight vocabulary. This careful monitoring for word recognition provides the individual attention every teacher would like to give to each child. When possible, children can be rapidly assessed for recognition of vocabulary that is potentially new. This is what Ms. Jones did in our example.

Listening and speaking vocabularies first.   Once the teacher knows which children need to be taught which words, he or she needs to be sure that the child who is going to be taught a specific word knows the word upon hearing it and can use the word in speaking. The difficulty in teaching new sight words is much greater if a child does not recognize the word when he or she hears it. In our example, Ms. Jones had the children discuss pictures, tell stories about pirates, and discuss those stories. She made sure that the children's speaking and listening vocabularies included the six words she wanted to teach.

Context.   A child often recognizes a word in print that he or she has heard because the child recalls hearing not only the word but also the context in which it was used. In effect, the new word in print "fills the blank" in the aurally remembered phrase, clause, or sentence. Therefore, immediate word-recognition behavior *requires* context to operate. In effect, context analysis is in operation as sight words are developed.

The introduction of words in context offers aid to the word-recognition process by providing the syntactic and semantic constraints that narrow the range of possible word choices for the reader. That is, when Ms. Jones provided her pirate group with sentences, the children had a good opportunity to guess the kind of word that would fit the blank and a feeling for the sense of the sentence with that kind of word inserted. She further limited the range of possible insertions by providing the initial consonant. When teachers rely on techniques of teaching words in isolation or from cards or lists, they divorce those words from meaning and forego opportunities to encourage development of other word-recognition behaviors in readers.

Focus on the word.   If a child is to learn a new word, he or she must focus on the relationship between the spoken word that is already known and the written word that represents it. Therefore, the context surrounding the new word must suggest the word while not being so difficult as to pull the child's attention away from the new word. By exposing the child to a new word in material that can be otherwise read easily (or that is read by the teacher), the teacher leads the reader to focus on the new word. If the context is helpful rather than distracting, the child can make an immediate good guess. A few of Ms. Jones' sentences might have offered a more meaningful clue, but she did use only one focus word per sentence and readily aided the readers with any other words that they failed to recognize.

Multiple exposure and application.   A child should be given many opportunities to read and to use the new word in contexts that are meaningful. Ms. Jones provided multiple exposure to new words on the pocket chart,

in the children's own stories, and in books. She encouraged application by having the children dictate their own stories for later rereading. Further reading was an experience that provided more exposure in context.

Teach Vocabulary as Need Arises

In the example above, Ms. Jones attempted to decide what words in a particular story may be unknown to her children and then tried out the word on each child. She also checked the ongoing record she kept for each child. This assessment then led to the introduction of certain words as children indicated need. However, this is not the only way to determine what words to teach. Here is an example using another approach.

Mr. Burns, a fifth-grade teacher, had his children keep track of words that they were not sure of as they were reading silently. When a child encountered a word that presented some difficulty, the child lightly underlined the word with a pencil, then guessed the word from the context and continued reading. When the child was finished reading, he or she copied the underlined word on a three-by-five card that became part of the child's file box of words. If the child couldn't make a reasonable guess at the word, Mr. Burns would come to the child, offer clues, help with analysis, or turn the card over and teach the word in a sentence.

In order for this procedure to be effective, it is very important that the teacher have each child reading at the instructional level. If the child were reading stories at a frustration level, there would be far too many words that the child would be unsure of. Aside from the frustrating experience of trying to read a story in which so many words had to be guessed, the reader would be spending too much time keeping track of unknown words and would fail to comprehend the story itself.

Mr. Burns used the student's sight-vocabulary cards to plan various kinds of locating and writing assignments so that the children could learn and practice the unknown words. He used many of the techniques that Ms. Jones used and followed the same principles. The difference between methods used by Ms. Jones and Mr. Burns was that Mr. Burns didn't preteach the vocabulary; instead, he taught the words as they were needed after reading a story. In your classoom instruction, you will probably be able to make use of both methods.

Activities to Learn and Practice Sight Vocabulary

In the classroom examples with Ms. Jones and Mr. Burns, the emphasis was on determining what words to teach to what children and how to introduce those words. However, one of the most important concerns in teaching sight vocabulary is to provide each child with interesting activities to practice the new vocabulary. In the following sections, we shall discuss five types of activities that you can use to give children practice with words. These include reading stories and books, dictating language experience stories, using cloze materials, practicing with games, and labelling. Each of these activities is not, of course, discrete and the use of each depends on the interest of students.

Reading.   All too often the teaching of reading happens without books. This is especially true with the teaching of vocabulary. Teachers use drill sheets, games, the chalkboard—almost everything except books— to teach vocabulary. Reading is the best way to learn and practice sight vocabulary. Sight words are acquired quite naturally and automatically just by reading. Thus, the final part of Ms. Jones' lesson was bound to build the sight vocabulary of some of her pupils beyond the list she was attempting to teach.

This natural expansion of sight vocabulary is supported by Goodman's research (1972). He pointed out that readers can identify words without sounding them out. Contextual constraints play an important role in learning sight words by supplying vital clues for unlocking the words. Goodman's contention is reinforced by the experience of good teachers everywhere, who encourage their pupils to expand their sight vocabularies by reading as much as possible. Voluntary reading is more creative, meaningful, and effective than mere assignments of required reading. Encouraging voluntary reading involves the introduction in class of provocative topics, the careful fostering of class discussion that leads to interesting questions that can be answered by turning to books, the encouragement to share what is learned from the books in order to generate more specific questions, and the direction of ensuing special interests into projects that encourage further reading.

Language experience libraries.   Closely related to the idea of encouraging independent reading is the development of language experience libraries. In Chapter 3 (pages 98–105) we described how to develop language experience stories with children and suggested binding children's stories into books.

Language experience stories are child-authored or dictated and then transcribed and turned into books that are illustrated by the children. After the books are bound, they can be shared through the classroom library. Language experience stories can also be transcribed onto large cards or onto newsprint for the children to read together in class.

Language experience stories are especially effective in increasing a child's sight vocabulary because the stories are based on words the child already knows—the words that were used to tell the story. Those words are translated into print by the teacher. The context is meaningful and interesting to the child because it is his or her story. And, of course, visual recognition is reinforced as the child reads his or her own story.

Cloze.   The cloze technique can be useful to help readers at all levels develop sight vocabularies.* In the cloze procedure, a word or words in a sentence are deleted and the reader must guess the word that fits in the blank. We described this technique in the previous chapter (pages 181–82) and gave an example there of how it could be used to emphasize the use of context analysis. However, by deleting the vocabulary a teacher wants to emphasize, the cloze technique can also be an aid in developing sight vocabulary.

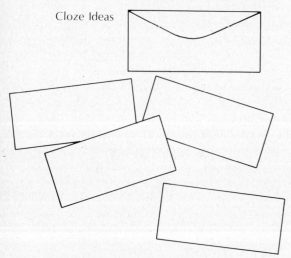

Cloze Ideas

A red-eared turtle will eat ▭ when it is ▭. It will eat ▭ when it gets big.

familiar stories with flaps pasted over certain words

Today's Schedule includes several _____ games _____

classroom directions or announcements with certain words deleted

story envelope with scrambled cloze sentence cards

* In a review of the literature on the use of cloze as a teaching method, Jongsma (1971) concluded that little was known about the use of cloze as a teaching technique.

The teacher can develop a number of different cloze-type materials that can be used as either independent or group activities. For example, the teacher might develop a set of envelopes that include a set of cards with a story sentence on each card. The child's task is to put the cards in the proper order so that they make a story. Each sentence, however, will have one or more blanks that need to be completed before the sentences will make sense. Children enjoy developing variations of stories and sharing them with classmates.

In the previous chapter, we also described how to take stories from basal readers no longer in use and paste small flaps over selected words (pages 181–82). The same thing can be done with the children's language experience stories that we discussed on page 198 of this chapter. Another way to use the cloze technique is with classroom directions. For example, the teacher might post the class schedule or the lunch menu or the directions for playing a game on a bulletin board. The words that the children are supposed to learn are covered and the children must guess the covered words.

Practice games.   Word games can be used to practice new words after the words have been introduced, particularly if they focus on target words that are plugged into blanks in sentences. Creating an original vocabulary game that is worth the trouble and class time it requires to play means the teacher must choose the idea with care and select the new words from children's recorded needs. The following game ideas can be used to create other classroom games based on the reading needs of your students.

One of the simplest and easiest games to develop is one in which pictures are matched with words. To build the game, cut out magazine pictures that represent sight words you want to teach or have children cut out pictures for a book of words they want to learn. Mount the pictures on cards, and on other cards print a sight-vocabulary word that corresponds to each picture card. Put both sets of cards in an envelope. Children can work on the game by themselves or in pairs. Or you might have one child select a picture and challenge another child to find the word card that matches it. If the pictures are pasted in a book, let the child copy from your written model the caption for each picture.

Another game that many teachers have used and which children seem to enjoy is "canned words." In this game you need a can with a plastic cover (an old coffee can, perhaps). If you wish, you may cover the can with construction paper or paint it to make it more decorative. Cut a slot in the plastic top of the can so a rolled list of words can be pulled out. Write a list of sight words on a strip of paper and then roll up the list and put it in the can so that one end protrudes from the slot (taping a stick to the end of the paper strip will prevent it from slipping back into the can). The child pulls the list of words out of the slot, pronouncing the words as he or she pulls; or, as each word comes into

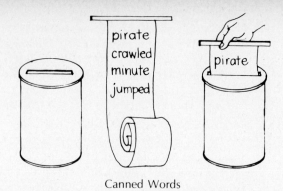

Canned Words

view, the child can use it in a sentence. And of course, you can use on the list the vocabulary words each child has been taught.

Two or more children can play "Guess the Mystery Word." All that is needed for this game is a set of sight-word or phrase cards that are based on the words particular children need to learn. Ten word or phrase cards are placed on a desk. One child covers his or her eyes while another writes one of the words or phrases on a slip of paper. The child then uncovers his or her eyes and tries to guess which word is the "mystery" word or phrase. If a child guesses correctly on the first guess, score three points, score two points for a correct answer on the second guess, one pont on the third, and no points after that.

A game that can be played by one child, or that can be modified so several children can play, is "Word Lotto." For this game you must make a set of large cards with different headings. Next, make a number of word cards. Each card should have a word on it that fits one of the categories. In playing the game, each child is given a large card with subject headings. The word cards are turned face down, and a player draws one and places it on the page card in the proper category. If one child plays, the goal can be to fill all the classifications, and the game should be made self-checking by numbering the categories and listing

Word Lotto

Animals	Sports	Flowers

Minerals	Dogs	Places

the words on the back of the playing card. If more than one child plays, the children can take turns to see who can fill the large card first.

Children are also easily motivated to build their own sight-word games. Show your children some examples of word games and then provide them with the materials and the opportunities to develop their own. For example, on a table in some corner of the room you might put old game boards or stiff cardboard, spinners, dice, and the moveable pieces needed to play games. Add scissors, paste, colored paper, magazines (for pictures and words), and crayons and you have a very interesting and active "game-building center." Children would certainly enjoy exchanging game boards even though their playing deck (words and sentences) differ. Most important, the children are practicing the words not just from playing the games but by making their card decks as well. In addition, they may be developing other reading behaviors, like learning to follow written directions and reading for details in the game-building center itself.

Many of the games that can be developed to give children practice in learning sight words use word cards. Yet these cards can be ineffective if not used properly. For example, if such cards offer only the word on one side and a brief definition on the other, they are not providing any real help for word recognition should a particular word not be recalled. There are, however, several ways of using cards that involve practicing the word in context. Some cards present the word underlined in a sentence, with the definition on the reverse side. Another design gives the sentence and leaves a blank where the word goes; the complete sentence is on the reverse side.

The _____ galloped away. (front)

The horse galloped away. (back)

Another card offers three choices on the first side, and only the word to be learned in the sentence is on the reverse side.

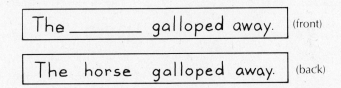

We set off to climb the { river. / mountain. / highway. (front)

We set off to climb the mountain. (back)

The pancake _____ right off the table. Before they could yell "Stop!" he went out the open door.

They _____ him down the busy street. Horns were _____; people were _____ to watch.

rolled	chased	honking	turning
saved	raced	hurrying	seeing
ate	cane	helping	timing

Alex lives in a big _____ in New York City.

He sleeps in a room with two of his _____.

Alex has four brothers and three _____.

Sometimes Alex takes a book up on the roof to be by _____.

Something is _____ in our room today. Can you find it? Take 15 _____ and look all _____ you. Is it under your desk? Have you looked under the _____ table? There are some good _____ on the blackboard. They can tell you _____ to look.

Still another way is to use a picture on the first side and the word on the back.

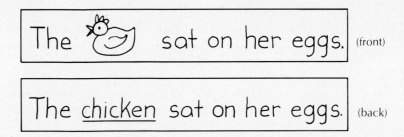

Some games can be developed by supplying each child with noun and pronoun cards, adjective cards, verb cards, function-word cards, and punctuation cards. The child is then asked to put them into an order that makes a sentence. For example:

A pocket chart to hold words in horizontal slots can be provided, but the desk top or the floor will do.

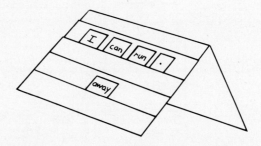

Finally, as skills increase, so can the number of words.

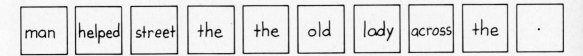

Practice games like these can use sentences drawn from the reading materials used in class. It is important to remember that all the words but the word on the new-word card already be in the reader's sight-word vocabulary. In that way, the reader can focus on the new word.

Labelling. Objects in the classroom can be labelled, often with sentences instead of with isolated words. Taped to a chair, a label might read, "This is a chair" or "This is Betty's chair." On the door, a sign announces, "You can open this door" or "The door is closed." A window's sign could read, "Don't forget to close the window." The use of complete sentences, instead of nouns only, also introduces the area of function words, which, without the surrounding context, are difficult to teach.

You can also use labels to remind children of daily routines and assignments. Like an adult's attachment to the morning newspaper, children can develop an addiction for reading necessary daily school information. Children love to be assigned daily tasks that are fun to carry out, and you can use this to introduce new words:

This type of chart can be adapted to exploit daily happenings in the classroom or school, to plan trips or explain visits, and to help the children participate in special days.

Facts from history or news, jokes, cartoons, or riddles posted each day in the same place on the board can introduce new words and will intrigue readers. The board should be changed often to maintain interest. In the third or fourth grades, students can produce their own newspaper on the bulletin board. Such a newspaper bulletin board might look like this:

try this ▶

If you have an elementary school child available to you, try to teach the child three or four sight-vocabulary words. After instruction, try out an original game or other activity with the child to allow practice with those words. Let the child continue with the activity on his or her own. Check back later to find out if the child has mastered the words. Were you successful? Did the follow-up game or activity follow the general principles that Ms. Jones followed in teaching sight vocabulary? How could you improve the procedure next time?

If no child is available, devise an experience to introduce new words to a hypothetical child. Review the plan or have a colleague review it to see if it follows the principles of teaching word recognition that were introduced earlier in this chapter.

All of these examples suggest ways of introducing new words into a child's daily classroom activities. The context in which they are introduced and practiced is based on the child's spoken and aural experience with the words in order to reinforce sight recognition.

Instruction in Phonics

"Who knows a riddle?" asked the teacher.

Several hands shot up in the group of four children seated around the teacher.

"Will you tell me one you know," the teacher asked Susan.

After Susan told her riddle, the children tried to guess the answer, and then other children recalled and told riddles. The teacher then announced, "Now that you've been able to tell riddles and guess the answers, you can join our 'riddlers' club.' As members of the riddlers' club you can try to guess the answer to one of the riddles in the riddle grab bag." The teacher produced a paper bag with the words *Riddle Grab Bag* printed on the side.

"Who wants to pick the first riddle?" asked the teacher.

"I do," Tommy quickly responded and picked a riddle from the bag.

Tommy read his riddle aloud, and the teacher helped with a word he didn't know. This was Tommy's riddle:

I can open.
I can close.
I am in a room.
What am I?

Tommy said, "A door!"

The teacher wrote *door* on the board. "Does anyone else think the answer may be another word?" the teacher asked the other children. No one disagreed with Tommy's choice.

The second riddle was picked by Susan:

I have four legs.
I am not a table.
I have a bark, but I am not a tree.

Susan said that the answer was *dog*, and the teacher wrote that word. The answers to the next two riddles were *doughnut* and *dish*. As each riddle was answered, the correct word was written on the board.

When all four words were on the board (or on the pocket chart), the teacher asked that the children look at the four words and try to think of a way in which the words were alike.

"They all have *d*," was one response.

"They all have *d* at the beginning," was another.

"They do have *d*," said the teacher. "Now, let's play with these words. Here are pictures of a doughnut, a door, a dog, and a dish. I would like each of you to pick a picture and match it to the word on the board."

When that was done, the children traded pictures and matched again. They traded until the teacher was sure that they could recognize the four words. The teacher then gave each child four small cards and a

(front of card)

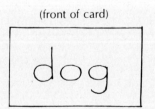

(back of card)

marking pen. She asked that each child copy the four words, one to a card, and make a small picture of the word on the back of the card.

When they had finished their cards and put them on the floor in front of them, each child was given a deck of picture cards. They were asked to find the pictures in the deck that started like *dog, doughnut, dish,* and *door* and to put those pictures by their word cards. Other pictures (not starting with *d*) were to be discarded into a box called the Dump. When necessary, the teacher helped the children with identification of the pictures and also with making the sorting decision. For example, she cued by saying, "Donkey. Does *donkey* begin like *dog* and *door*? Donkey. Dog. Door."

(deer) (duck) (doll) (diamond)

(table) (donkey) (cane)

When the sorting was completed, the children checked their decisions: They turned over the picture cards to discover that each *d* card had a yellow circle on the back. The teacher told them that a yellow circle meant that they had picked a picture that started like *dog, doughnut,* and so on.

These children had been brought together for instruction because the teacher had previously determined that they had sometimes failed to attack words using the initial consonant *d*. After the initial phases of instruction, the teacher felt confident that the children heard the sound /d/ at the beginning of words and associated that phoneme with the grapheme *d* (evidenced by the successful picture sorting).

To determine application, the teacher offered some sentence strips, for example:

I like to d_____.

"This sentence says, 'I like to *blank*,' the teacher read; but all four children chimed in immediately.

"The missing word starts like *dog* and rhymes with *lance*," added the teacher.

"Dance," said Bonnie, and was then offered the word card *dance* by the teacher. Bonnie slipped it into the blank in the sentence. Other sentences followed, each with a missing *d* word, and each time the teacher cued the word.

This teacher was obviously involved in helping children to recognize and use a sound-symbol association. This lesson is one that will be followed on successive days. The teacher will next want to provde these children with stories that include words that begin with *d* so they can practice their developing skill in real reading situations, especially since there is solid evidence that these children understand the use of initial letters in recognizing words and that they can associate the /d/ sound (phoneme) with the letter *d* (grapheme) when it appears at the beginning of a word.

Principles in Teaching Phonics

There are four important principles that the teacher in the preceding classroom scene followed in teaching phonic analysis:

The first principle is to teach the relationship of phonemes to graphemes within the context of a word rather than as isolated letters and sounds. When words are divided into separate sounds and each sound-letter match is taught in isolation, the sounds become very artificial, even distorted. The sound that we hear at the beginning of words like *dog, door,* and *do* is different from the "duh" sound spoken in isolation. Never did this teacher ask for the match of the "duh" sound with the letter that makes that sound. Isolating sounds makes the phonic generalization* more abstract than it needs to be for the beginning reader. It

---

* A phonic generalization is a generalization about the relation between spoken sounds (phonemes) and the letters (graphemes) that usually represent those sounds. For example, the phoneme that we hear at the beginning of *dog, door,* and *do* is represented by the grapheme *d*.

seems easier to learn sound-symbol associations within words; and more important, it is within the context of words that a child not only produces sounds but also reads.

The second principle is to emphasize meaningful, rather than abstract, letter-sound drill. In this lesson, the teacher focused on comprehension by asking the children to answer riddles. In fact, each time the teacher asked a child to identify a certain word, the purpose for identifying the word was related to the meaning of the word.

The third principle is to plan the instruction so that the children can develop their own phonic generalizations after they analyze several examples.

The fourth principle stresses the importance of teaching phonics (letter-sound relationships) as one of several word-recognition behaviors that, used together, support each other.

Although the above classroom example was brief and phonics instruction can take many different forms, these four principles that the teacher relied upon may be useful guides.

Terms that Define the Content of Phonics

You are already familiar with the terms *phonemes* and *graphemes*. However, there are a number of other terms that are used quite frequently to describe various aspects of phonics and phonics instruction. We will define those terms briefly here. While these terms are useful to you in understanding phonics instruction and the content of phonics, there is no need for you to teach them to children. Young readers need to learn to apply phonic generalizations in reading, but they do *not* need to define the terminology of what they are using.

First, there are two terms that have to do with speech sounds.

Phonetics is the analysis of *all* the different spoken sounds a human being can utter. The study of phonetics is not especially useful in reading instruction because in teaching reading you are only interested in those speech sounds that make a difference in the meaning of words.

*Phonemics** is the analysis of those speech sounds (phonemes) that make a difference in the meaning of words.

The definition of phonemics or of phonemes leads naturally to the topic of this section—phonics.

Phonics is a set of generalizations about the relationship of phonemes (sounds) to graphemes (letters). These relationships are sometimes taught to children as one dimension of reading, and sometimes readers discover the relationships for themselves.

* We will discuss the importance of phonemes more fully in the next section of this chapter (pages 210–13) as we describe the language base for phonics instruction.

The content of phonics includes the following:

Consonants are graphic or written symbols representing speech sounds characterized by complete or partial stoppage of the air stream. They may be voiced* (*b,l*) or unvoiced (*p,f*).

Consonant blends are combinations of two or three consonants (such as *br, gr*, and *sr*) blended in such a way that each speech sound in the blend retains its own identity, contributing to the blend of two or three sounds.

Consonant clusters is a term applied to those letters that appear frequently together in our spelling system. Decoding may be facilitated if the reader considers the two or three letters together.

Consonant diagraphs (such as *sh, th*, and *ch*) consist of adjacent letters which represent one sound.

Vowels are graphic symbols representing speech sounds characterized by the use of the vocal chord and no obstruction in the air passage. There are five symbols (*a,e,i,o,u*, and sometimes *w* and *y*) used to represent these sounds. Hence, the same symbols that are used to designate long vowel sounds (*a*cre) also designate short vowel sounds (b*a*t).

Vowel clusters (vowel digraphs and diphthongs). Vowel digraphs are combinations of two graphemes representing one phoneme such as the *oo* in *look* and the *ea* in *real*; diphthongs are graphic symbols representing two vowel sounds blended so that they almost pronounce a single speech sound (*ow, ou, oi*, and *oy* as in words like *owl, out, oil*, and *boy*.)

The Base for Phonics Instruction

Effective phonics instruction is based on the teacher's knowledge of the linguistic competence that a child brings to school. The available research suggests that by the time a child is about four years of age, he or she has mastered the great majority of English sounds (Tripp and Miller, 1963). Furthermore, by the time a child reaches school age, he or she has progressed well beyond the stage of short "telegraphic" sentences. Indeed, the child possesses a high degree of sophistication in his or her ability to communicate orally and seldom produces sentences that fail to convey meaning, even though these sentences may not always be grammatically acceptable by adult standards. When a three-year-old says, "I don't have none," or a two-year-old says, "I rided my bicycle," adults have no difficulty understanding. The speaking vocabulary of the child entering school is extensive.† The child at this age is also in control

---

* Voiced and unvoiced refer to whether or not the vocal chords vibrate. While of interest to linguists, the differences are not important in teaching phonics.

† James Smith (1972) says about a child's vocabulary: "Studies of school beginners indicate that these children have a speaking vocabulary of at least 8,000 words, and that they may know and understand over 20,000 words" (p. 13).

of other components of oral language, including *pitch* (the relative height of frequency of the voice), *stress* (the degree of the loudness of a syllable in a sentence), and *juncture* (the length or degree of pause between one segment of speech and the next). Even children who are linguistically distinct* have this control; they just have a slightly different oral system from children who speak a more standard dialect.

The point is that the child typically enters school already a competent user of language. With this important base, the child is ready to develop the awareness that the various phonemes of spoken language are represented by certain graphic symbols. We want to emphasize here that the beginning reader is not devoid of phonemic generalizations. Rather, existing language competence permits the child to be an active participant in the instruction, one who can use the knowledge he or she already possesses about the sound system of the language to comprehend the correspondence between oral language and written language.

* A number of different terms have been used to describe those who use a spoken dialect different from the current standard dialect, including *nonstandard, language different,* and—the most recent term—*linguistically distinct.*

Linguists* (those who study language) have provided educators with much useful knowledge about reading. As linguists have studied various languages, they have discovered that speakers of a language select (through tradition and over many hundreds of years) speech sounds, or phonemes, that make a difference in that language. For example, a native speaker of Japanese hears the difference between the sounds in the middle of the English words *pilot* /l/† and *pirate* /r/, but will tell you that they are only slightly different ways of saying the same word. The

Figure 6–1 The Basic List of Phonemes

Consonant Phonemes

1.	/p/ pin	9.	/t/ top	17.	/ǰ/ jump
2.	/b/ bin	10.	/d/ dot	18.	/š/ shine
3.	/m/ mat	11.	/s/ sun	19.	/ž/ measure
4.	/w/ wet	12.	/z/ zoo	20.	/y/ yes
5.	/f/ fun	13.	/l/ led	21.	/k/ kind
6.	/v/ vat	14.	/n/ not	22.	/g/ go
7.	/θ/ think	15.	/r/ rat	23.	/ɚ/ sing
8.	/ǫ/ then	16.	/č/ chew	24.	/h/ he

Vowel Phonemes

25.	/i/ in	28.	/ə/ up	31.	/o/ (usually doesn't appear in English except in the word *home* as spoken by some New Englanders)
26.	/e/ men	29.	/a/ father	32.	/ɔ/ law
27.	/æ/ at	30.	/u/ put	33.	/ɨ/ fur

*Vowel Diphthongs**

34.	/iy/ he	36.	/ay/ ride	38.	/aw/ out
35.	/ey/ way	37.	/ɔy/ boy	39.	/ow/ rode
				40.	/uw/ few

Only thirty-three phonemes are listed, twenty-four consonant phonemes and nine vowels. The other twelve phonemes are intonation phonemes—stress, pitch, and juncture—and are not specifically pertinent to the study of phonics. Also listed are the seven vowel diphthongs. The vowel diphthong phonemes have the least consistency in relation to the graphemes used to represent these phonemes.

* These are the most common vowel diphthongs; others occur in the various dialects of English.

* Linguistics, the study of language, was originally investigated by anthropologists who discovered that one of the most revealing dimensions of a culture was the language of the people of that culture.

†Phonemes are always written between slash marks to indicate that they are spoken sounds and are representative of sounds in context as opposed to sounds in isolation.

/l/ and /r/ are, therefore, not phonemes in Japanese as they are in English. Similarly, each language evolves a set of phonemes that native speakers come to identify and understand as being important. Most linguists agree that mastery of these phonemes is complete by the age of four. In English, there are about forty-five different phonemes* (see Figure 6–1). However, various linguists argue about the exact number and sometimes list forty-three, forty-four, or forty-six. For our purposes, these fine distinctions are not relevant.

In Figure 6–1, it is important to recognize that certain phonemes may not be represented by the same grapheme in each spelling. For example, the /iy/ phoneme can be represented by the following graphemes: h*e*, r*ea*d, n*ee*d, and rec*ei*ve. Other phonemes are always represented by the same grapheme; for example, /d/ is only represented by *d*. Being aware that such differences may exist will help you in teaching word recognition. First, you will find it easier to help children develop phonic generalizations if you begin with those cases in which there is only one grapheme for a particular phoneme. Second, in some instances there are so many graphemic representations for particular phonemes that trying to help children to develop generalizations about them is very difficult; indeed, some of these generalizations are not useful to a child.

Where does this leave you? Which phonic generalizations should you teach? How should they be taught? The next section provides the overall guidelines for determining the phonic generalizations to be taught, and in the section following that we shall present some procedures for teaching phonics.

Determine the Child's Phonic Needs

How does a teacher go about matching a child with the necessary phonic elements that need to be learned? One good way is to listen to a child read orally at regular intervals, making notes (by recording and analyzing miscues) of which elements are applied as well as of those there are difficulties with. It is important to know what a child can apply and use effectively, because it is senseless to teach a skill that is already known. In addition, those elements already mastered form a foundation upon which others can be developed. Records should be kept by the teacher of the generalizations the child has mastered and the ones that need to be learned. (See the record-keeping suggestions as well as the suggestions for assessing and recording word-recognition information in Chapter 2, pages 68–71.)

Suppose that the child is reading to the teacher and says, "There was a ch . . . chu . . . chuch [church] in the town." He has displayed a similar

*Italian has twenty-seven phonemes, French thirty-five, and Japanese twenty. Of those languages that have been studied by linguists, Abkhas, a language spoken by a group of people who live in the Caucasus Mountains, has the most phonemes (seventy-one) and Hawaiian has the least (thirteen) (Thomson, 1975, p. 45).

problem with other words he has encountered containing the *ur* grapheme. The teacher now knows that the child needs instruction in this generalization.

Instruction may be individual or in small groups; this is dependent upon whether other children in the class manifest the same need. However, be careful that one similar need does not lead you to create inflexible groups. Just because five children can validly be grouped for instruction on one day does not necessarily mean that they will all need the same instruction on subsequent days.

Getting started. Beginning readers need to develop an understanding of phoneme-grapheme relationships as they learn to comprehend written material. Remember that each enters school with the ability to express himself or herself orally. The child will learn that what he or she pronounces as "cause," "dija," and "gonna" will appear in written language as "because," "did you," and "going to." One major objective of the teacher is to guide the child to the recognition of the predictable nature of his spelling system. To achieve this the teacher must first assist the child to identify phonemes in spoken words, to recognize graphemes, to match these phonemes with graphemes, and finally to apply these knowns to new words. These will free the child to be an independent reader, secure in the use of phoneme-grapheme cues.

The teachers in the following illustrations are providing instruction about specific elements, which can be adapted to lessons for other elements.

A sample lesson. Our teacher is seated with three children; with her she has a grocery bag and a pocket chart.

"Today I have some surprises in our grab bag. Sally, why don't you grab first?"

Sally pulls out a rubber ball. "It's a baseball!" she says.

"Hold on to it. Now it's Jimmy's turn."

Jimmy grabs a toy boat, and Allen pulls out a small bell. The children keep taking objects from the bag until it is empty. As each is pulled from the bag, it is named. There is a ball, a boat, a bell, a picture of a bird, a book, a bottle, and a balloon.

"There is something the same about all of the things in our laps. Say their names again. What did you hear when you said their names?"

Sally pipes up, "They all sound the same when you first start them."

"Let's see if Sally is right. We'll put some words on the pocket chart and check."

The children verify Sally's hypothesis with the word cards. The teacher then writes the following sentence on the board:

Tommy rode his new b_____.

Because the teacher wants the children to focus on the missing word, the sentence is read by the teacher. "What word could we use to complete the sentence?" asks the teacher.

"*Horse*," answers one child.

"Good try," says the teacher, "but look at *horse*." (She writes *horse* on the chalkboard.) "Does horse begin like *bell, book,* and *ball*?"

"How about *bike*?" offers Allen.

The teacher writes the word *bike* on the board and the children again verify the choice. Then the teacher follows the same procedure with different sentences.

Allen got a b_____ for his birthday.

Sally saw a b_____ in a boat.

Can a b_____ read a book?

As a follow-up to this lesson, the children cut out pictures that begin with *b* from magazines. These pictures are pasted on construction paper, labelled with upper- and lower-case *b*'s, and the name of each is printed below the picture by either the teacher or the child.

The opportunity to apply the developing sound-symbol association—that is, the opportunity to read—is the essential test of the child's mastery of the skill. The teacher may provide practice reading, slanted toward the phoneme-grapheme relationship being taught (Baby Bat bit his bird book), or simply monitor reading in ongoing materials to watch for application of the skill.

The preceding instruction is one in which the teacher made sure that certain things happened:

(1) The concept was presented so that learning was inductive. That is, the children were given a number of examples, and discovered for themselves the idea that the objects and words began alike. Having children discover such relationships, as opposed to telling them, encourages them to seek other such relationships on their own.

(2) The children were *actively* involved in the instruction. Not only were they choosing articles from a bag, they were also helping with the pocket chart, as well as being mentally and verbally

involved. Involving the children in the lesson ensures both that the children attend to the task and that they are motivated.

(3) The teacher didn't present too many elements at once. The teacher knew that one element at a time was enough for these students to grasp. With other students she may teach two elements. That depends on the student. But there are limits; to attempt to teach the phoneme-grapheme relationships of too many consonant sounds would result in superficial learning—if any learning at all.

(4) The teacher created activities that helped the children to learn the element and then to give them practice with it. None of her materials or activities were expensive.

(5) Follow-up reading should be provided by the teacher, especially reading material in which the children can apply their new sound-symbol association in reading a story. Other follow-up can be provided through practice games and exercises.

During a follow-up activity, the teacher has a good opportunity to observe and evaluate each child's performance to see if each is able to apply the new learning. When the child reads aloud, notice how he or she fares in applying the new knowledge of the *b* sound-symbol relationship. Watch a child play a game in which the use of this knowledge is important. Check a child's practice activity. And record your observations in the child's ongoing reading record.

Phonics as needed. Let's observe a teacher who teaches phonics and knows when to teach what. His instructional plan allows him the opportunity to diagnose the child's specific phonic needs so that he can teach to them. This teacher has provided his students with a free-reading period and the chance to choose their own books and activities. He is using this time to have a few children read individually to him from books they have chosen themselves. Jimmy, presently seated next to him, has brought a picture book about a knight.

"A long time ago there was a large castle on the top of a hill. In this castle lived a rich king who owned the land for miles around him. Other people lived and worked in the castle. Some of them were k . . . kn . . . kun. . . ."

The word causing Jimmy difficulty is *knight*. He studies the picture on the page and presently says, "It looks like some kind of soldier, but this word begins with a *k*."

"That word is *knight*. Have you ever heard of knights?"

"Sure, they were soldiers years ago. But I always thought they started with an *n*."

"Well, sometimes *k* is silent. We'll talk about that, but right now let's continue reading."

Jimmy does so. The teacher records on Jimmy's record sheet the silent sound of *k*, which he will teach within the next few days.

While the teacher in this example is not precisely teaching phonics, he has done something that must precede teaching: diagnosing. There are several comments to be made about such informal assessment:

(1) This teacher does the diagnosis in an informal way. There is no need to administer a phonics test or have the student read a long list of words. Rather, the teacher listens to the oral reading of this child, recording those elements that are causing difficulty. It is not a time consuming process nor is it difficult. All that is required is an observant teacher, one who knows what to watch and listen for.

(2) It's not necessary to teach phonics during an oral reading period. Sometimes it is better to just tell the child the unknown word rather than interrupt the reading with an impromptu lesson about some element. Since teaching phonics is not the prime objective of the above lesson, the teacher chooses to merely identify the word and make a note to teach the child that element in the near future.

(3) The child evidenced a need for knowledge about this particular element. This is an important point to remember. Phonic elements should be taught to children when they are needed—not before and not later. This provides the basis for instruction that the child can see is important to reading.

(4) Finally, it is important to note that ongoing diagnosis leads to instruction that is specifically planned for the needs of each child. Therefore, a teacher should have available a wide variety of materials. No teacher's edition of a reading program, no work-wook, and no producer of instructional materials can anticipate the varied reading development of each child. Some of the materials you may gather to help you teach sound-symbol associations are suggested in a later section.

This teacher will plan a mini-lesson on words that are spelled with a silent *k*. This lesson may be for Jimmy alone, or for other members in the class who have the same need.

Determining Which Phonic Generalizations to Teach

A wealth of books, articles, and materials have been published concerning the specific content that should be included when a teacher teaches a phonics curriculum. The content of phonics instruction suggested in these materials differs in the amount of phonics instruction, the particular method, and the sequence in which certain elements are to be taught. In general, there are three major guidelines to keep in mind as you try to decide which phonic elements to teach. While we will examine these guidelines separately and in some detail, they are all closely related.

First, only the most useful phonic elements should be taught. Contrary to expectation, not all sound-symbol correspondences are of great utility. Since some are not widely applicable, it is in the student's best interest to discover those that have the most applicability for recognizing unknown words independently. You are probably very familiar with the phonic generalization "When two vowels go walking, the first one does the talking"—as in *bead* and *eat*, for example. However, the results of a number of different research studies that looked at this and other phonic generalizations (Clymer, 1963; Emans, 1967; Bailey, 1967) indicated that many of them did not hold up when applied to the words found in the reading selections of books in the primary grades. In fact, many of the generalizations, including this example, were found to be useful with fewer than 50 percent of the words.

Nevertheless, reliance on phonic generalizations is an essential part of word recognition. How do you know which generalizations should be taught? The answers to the following two basic questions provide the answer to that general query: Will the phonic generalization contribute to the learning-to-read process? Does the phonic generalization apply to enough words that the child will meet in daily reading in order to justify its being taught now?

Which phonic generalizations contribute to the learning-to-read process? Those that the child needs now, those that are applicable, and those that are used frequently in the words from the stories the child will be reading. Research by Marshbanks and Levin (1965) found that children tend to use a definite pattern in applying phonic generalizations in recognizing words. They first examine the initial letter or letters, then the final letter or letters, and finally the middle letters. A valid conclusion would be that those phonic generalizations relating to initial and final sound-symbol correspondences would be of great benefit for the learner, since these are the ones used first and most often.

While both consonant and vowel sound-symbol correspondences are important, it is obvious that consonants in and of themselves provide more clues to the identity of a given word. Consider the following sentence in which all the vowels have been deleted:

M__ gr__ndm__th__r __s b__k__ng __ c__k__ f__r m__.

Chances are you had no problem reading it. Now look at another sentence in which only the vowels have been given:

__y __a__ __o__e__ i __a_i__ __ __a_e __o__ __e.

Knowing consonant sound-symbol relationships helps to achieve independence in reading. Approximately 80 percent of the words typically met by beginning readers begin with consonants (Heilman, 1964).

Second, the sequence for the presentation of phonic elements should follow from simple to complex. Determining a sequence for introducing phonic elements is one aspect of effective phonics instruction. Logically, the sequence should progress from the easier generalizations to those that are more difficult. To understand the basis for systematic phonics instruction, examine the following tasks involved in learning phonics.

Effective phonics instruction is based on a child's oral langauge and the child's ability to use phonemes as part of everyday language. The child is then taught to match sounds (phonemes) in different spoken words, to match the spoken sounds in words with the corresponding letters and words in print, and, ultimately, to apply the sounds by reading.

But beginning readers do not learn phonic generalizations in a specific sequence. Rather, each learner seems to learn some before others. *No single sequence is adequate for all learners.* Nevertheless, some generalizations are easier to learn than others. The phonic generalizations below are arranged in the general order of learning difficulty.*

Consonant sounds

> Single consonants in initial position (b, d, f, h, j, k, l, m, n, p, r, s, t, v, w, y, z)
> Single consonants in final position (b, d, f, j, k l, m, n, p, s, t, v, z)
> Consonant blends and diagraphs (bl, br, cl, cr, dr, dw, fl, fr, gr, gl, pl, pr, str, sc, sk, sl, sm, sn, sp, st, sw, tr, scr, spl, th, ph, gh, sh, ch, ng, ck)

Vowel sounds

> Single vowel sounds that are short (bat, set, sit, pot, but)
> Single vowel sounds that are long (we, so sight, babe, cute)
> Vowels as modified when followed by *r*, *l*, or *w* (art, all, crawl, drew)
> Vowel clusters (diagraphs and dipthongs) (ai, ay, ee, ea, ie, oa, oe, oi, ou, ow)

Consonant irregularities

> Graphemes *c* and *g* represent two sounds each (city, cut, go, giant)
> Silent letters (*k*now, *g*nu, nig*h*t)

Most reading authorities agree that some consonants are usually learned before vowels. For example, Heilman (1964) states that consonants are easier than vowels because consonants tend to be much more consistent in their sound representations. There are eleven consonants (j, k, l, m, n, p, b, h, r, v, w) that generally represent only one phoneme each. Other consonants that represent different phonemes may cause little difficulty, since one of the sounds can be taught (if necessary) at

---

* Other sources of specific sequences of phonic concepts can be found in the teacher's manuals accompanying basal reading series. Any teacher using these in the classroom should be familiar with the total phonics program outlined in the manual but should also be aware that the sequence should be based on the individual needs of the learner.

a later date—for example, the grapheme *d* represents both the phonemes in *don't* and in individ*ual*. However, the first of these phonemes occurs with greater frequency in beginning reading material. In contrast, the five vowel graphemes (*a, e, i, o, u*—six if *y* is included) each represent numerous phonemes as *a* does in *arch, acre, bat, read, about,* and *care.*

Third, the phonic generalizations that are taught should be those that appear in the child's reading material. A child needs to learn phonic generalizations that will help to identify new words that he or she encounters when reading. Such generalizations are the ones that are both critical to the reading task and will give needed independence. Teaching those that appear in the reading material and those that are needed ensures that the child has the opportunity to apply them meaningfully.

Because the reading ability of children in the same grade varies, grade-level material is an undesirable criterion for determining the phonic generalizations that are taught to each child. The teacher needs to examine children's materials and to listen for each child's reading behaviors to determine which phonic generalizations are necessary. The same process that is used to match a child with a book should be used to match a child with needed phonics instruction.

Phonics in Perspective

Phonics is one facet of reading instruction that has stimulated many controversies. It is as apt to be discussed by two parents ("If they would just go back to teaching phonics, Jenny wouldn't be having so much difficulty with her reading.") as it is by two teachers ("Eddie is really having a lot of trouble with phonics. Do you have any ideas I can try?"). Further, phonics has long been a popular topic, generating countless education publications, books, and magazine and newspaper articles.

Value of phonics. It seems quite obvious that in order to learn to read, a child must somehow became aware of the connection between the sounds of human voices and marks made by human beings on paper to represent those sounds. However, a great deal of confusion and controversy have historically surrounded phonics instruction in the reading curriculum. The direct effect of this has been the tendency to discard phonics instruction only to reintroduce it again later. Wardhaugh (1971) suggests that much of this controversy has waned, since surveys (Spache, 1963; Russell, 1955; Austin and Morrison, 1963) indicate that phonics of some type is taught in most schools today.

A lot of confusion has emanated from the absence of a one-to-one correspondence between the sounds of the English language and the alphabet used to represent it graphically. The problem is that there are approximately forty-five phonemes in English, but only twenty-six letters in the alphabet. Consequently some letters represent a number of different phonemes.

At other times, letters appear in the spelling but represent no sound, as, for example, the *h* in *honest* and the *gh* in *night*. How did this happen? Such spelling patterns sometimes reflect the original pronunciation of words. The *gh* in *night* was actually pronounced at one time. But spoken language changes over time. Dialects drift apart so that frequently letters appear in the written word that have no oral counterpart, as in *honest* and *night*. Thus, phonic analysis cannot be the simple matching game that some proponents imply.

Then is phonics instruction helpful? Yes. Phonic analysis is not the random guessing game suggested by some critics, because patterns of letters do tend to represent the patterns of sounds of the spoken language. There is an especially high degree of consistency between consonant phonemes, and the developers of beginning-reading programs include words with the most consistent patterns.

Historical perspective.   Interestingly enough, it was for the expressed purpose of developing a uniform American dialect that the phonic method of teaching reading was first adopted. Reading was originally taught by an alphabet-spelling approach as it first appeared in the *New England Primer* of 1690. Children taught by this approach first learned the names of the letters of the alphabet. They were then taught how to spell each new word. The limitations of this procedure should be clear.

Although there is enough consistency between letters and letter combinations as *symbols* for sounds, there is little likeness between the spoken *names* of the letters and the phonemes they represent. Try, for example, to get the pronunciation for the word *band* by blending the oral names of the four letters: Bee-*a*-en-dee.

It was Noah Webster who developed a scheme of phonics in his *American Spelling Book* (1798) as a means of establishing a standardized American speech. He felt that this would reflect the nation's concern for communication in a new democracy (Emans, 1968). Webster failed to achieve his original goal, but his scheme of phonics was adopted as a method of teaching reading.

Meaning and phonics.   This is the issue that has usually caused phonics to lose favor in the reading curriculum at times. The purpose of reading should be to gain meaning and not just to pronounce words. Sound familiar? We, too, have reiterated the importance of reading for meaning. But the teaching of phonics can, and should, include meaning. Properly taught, phonics serves reading, and reading is meaning.

Oral language is a code. When the listener receives a stream of sounds from a speaker, he or she organizes them according to certain perceptual categories. By processing the oral coded input (language), the listener analyzes it, decodes it, and derives meaning. Only when this is done does the listener understand what was said. By the time a child enters school, he or she has already become such a competent decoder of the oral language that the transition from oral code to meaning is efficient and rapid.

Similarly, written language is also a code. To be a decoder of written language, one cannot merely say the word or recognize the word. The reader must get the meaning. The mere translating of written to oral language without obtaining meaning is not decoding, but recoding. In other words, the person has merely moved from one code that is graphic to another code that is oral.

The issue cannot be one of phonics versus meaning because they should be one and the same. Unfortunately, it is sometimes the case that a child is taught to pronounce words rather than understand written material. This happens when the teacher overemphasizes pronunciation; when the child is encouraged to go through a new book and "name the words you know"; or when the child sounds out each word, eventually coming up with a very close correspondence to the written word in oral reading.

Phonics in schools. Parents often find it hard to believe that phonics is being taught, because the teaching of phonics is not always labelled as such. In addition, methods of teaching phonics have changed. But the end result of the change has not been one uniform way of teaching phonics but numerous ways. For example, Spache (1963) notes that only about 15 percent of the elementary teachers he surveyed taught phonics isolated from actual reading. And the 85 percent who combine phonics instruction with reading instruction do not have identical procedures for doing so. One extensive national survey found that all basal reading series currently in use in schools included some provision for phonic principles and their application (Austin and Morrison, 1963).

Austin and Morrison summarized the state of phonics in the early sixties, a state that continues today:

> The question, then, as to the importance of phonics or to its utilization in the classroom cannot be considered controversial. Reading authorities agree on its importance, and school officials attend its universal adoption. Any bona fide controversy must be elsewhere, and in this instance it is to be found in the approaches used to teach phonics and in the program of instruction which accompanies each approach. (1963, p. 28)

Gathering Materials for Phonic Instruction

Pictures. Some of the materials that you will useful for instruction in sound-symbol associations are pictures—large ones for discussion and small ones for sorting, matching, and playing practice games. Pictures from magazines, catalogs, calendars, or advertising brochures should be selected because of their size, appeal, and familiarity to children. Cut and mount them on sturdy cards; if possible, laminate them for dura-

bility. You may choose to file them by their initial sounds, by their medial vowel, and so on. In any event, having the pictures readily available will help children to participate in some of the games that have been suggested: matching pictures that begin alike; feeding pictures to a puppet that start like the puppet's name; making books by labelling the pictures; or playing games like *Go Fish*, in which players ask others for cards that begin like ones already in their hands in an attempt to make a pair.

Letter and word cards. You will also find it helpful to have several sets of upper- and lower-case letters so that children can match pictures with their initial sounds, their final sounds, and so on. Sometimes the letters can be written on cards and punched at the top so that they can be hung on a pegboard and matched with pictures that have also been punched.

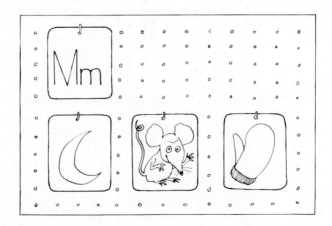

The letters can also be written on envelopes so that small pictures can be "mailed" to the appropriate letter by children who are sorting by initial sounds. For example:

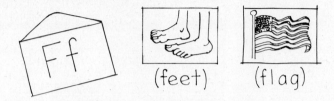

(feet)   (flag)

The letters can also be for individuals to hold so that when you (or a child) hold up a picture of a hat, the children can search for their own H h and hold it up in response.

Word cards are helpful when children begin to suggest words that begin alike or end alike. Since you want these words to come from children, to represent their oral-language backgrounds, the word cards will be prepared on the spot. Therefore, you may want to make a set of blank laminated word cards, so that they may be wiped off and used again and again.

For example, two children working on the blend /bl/ are sitting near you. As they think of a word that begins with /bl/, they name it and you write it: *black, blot, blank, blue*. When they are each holding a number of words, you write on the board (or on a blank laminated sentence strip) a sentence that needs one of the children's words to finish it. The children read the sentence, search their decks, and the child who finds the appropriate word tapes it to the board or drops it into the pocketchart.

Objects.   Teachers of beginners often collect small objects or toys, keeping them together by initial or final sound in tins, small boxes, or margarine tubs. They find that objects make for more manipulation (involvement) than do pictures, increase students' motivation, and can be used in a variety of ways.

Magazines.   Finding and collecting old magazines with good pictures will provide your students with a good resource for making some of their own materials, such as books and practice games for phonic analysis.

Gameboards.   If you make trail games like the following simple example and leave them blank (as far as the sound-symbol association to be practiced is concerned), you can use them for a variety of practice activities: for example, place a deck of picture cards beginning with *h* face down; insert a few other picture cards beginning with other sounds. Each player rolls a die, turns up a picture card, decides if it starts like *H*aunted *H*ouse, then moves ahead the number of spaces indicated by the die if the guess is correct.

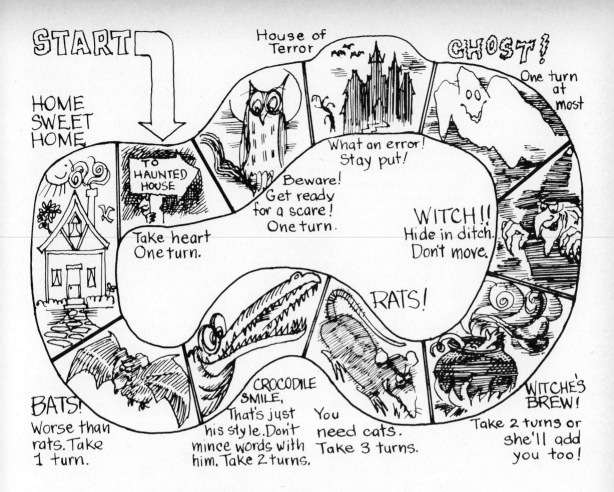

Published material. It is a good idea to collect, classify, and modify a variety of published and printed materials so that practice activities are available when you need them. Cutting apart skills books and filing the parts by the skills they teach is a sound practice. Some teachers like to cut apart colorful skills books and make study games from the pieces.

Teaching Structural Analysis

Analysis of the structure of words is a useful clue in determining meaning. The following sentences and questions serve to illustrate the importance of the structure of language:

(1) The *boys* went swimming.
    Question: Did more than one boy go swimming?
(2) Anna *didn't* finish the race.
    Question: Did Anna finish the race?
(3) The *racehorse* was sold to the farmer.
    Question: What kind of horse was sold to the farmer?

(4) Jerry *climbed* to the top of the mountain.
Question: Did Jerry get to the top?

The answer to each of the questions is based, in part, on the reader's ability to use structural word clues. In the first sentence, you knew more than one boy went swimming because of the plural ending; in the second sentence, you knew that *didn't* was a contraction that means *did not*; in the third sentence, you knew that *race* and *horse* were put together to form a new word that described a special kind of horse; and in the fourth sentence, you knew that *ed* added to the word *climb* meant that climbing was something that happened in the past. Each time you used structural analysis, however, you checked the meaning of the word to see whether it made sense in the context of the sentence you were reading.

The key to the role of structural analysis in word recognition is the word *analysis*. To recognize a word by analyzing its structure, the need to analyze has to be motivated by the desire to understand a context. The analysis is frequently one within the word; but, more often that not, it also involves relating the word to surrounding words. Thus, structural analysis is almost always used in conjunction with one or more of the other word-recognition skills. Although there is never an excuse to memorize highly questionable rules about syllabication and accent in pronunciation, a reader who can sort out a word's parts—as a root with additions or as two words in one—may be able to apply sight-recognition or phonic skills so the word can be recognized from aural memory.

Affixes

Affixes are combinations of letters that are added to words that change the meaning of words. The word to which the affix is added is called the *base*. (Linguists call the units that act as affixes *morphemes*— a separate unit of language that has a specific meaning.) Each affix, therefore, is a combination of letters that adds meaning to a base word. *Affixes* is the general term that includes *prefixes* and *suffixes*. A prefix is added to the front of the base, and the suffix is added after the base word.

Many prefixes and suffixes have multiple meanings. For example, *con-* can mean *together, with,* or *very; ex-* can mean *out of, from, beyond,* or *without.* Usually the addition of a suffix or prefix doesn't merely add meaning to a base word but can entirely change the meaning of the word. Thus, even if an elementary child could enthusiastically learn a long list of affixes, the information would provide only an erratic key for an analysis of words. Often through usage, the base to which a morpheme is affixed loses its discreteness as a word; that is, the base is only meaningful and only used as a word when affixes are attached to it. However, one definition of prefixes and suffixes (Marchand, 1969)

Figure 6–2 Selected Common Affixes

Prefix	Meaning	Suffix	Meaning
bi-	two, twice	-able	capable of being
con- (com-)	with, together, very	-ful	full of
dis-	apart from, reversal of	-less	without
ex-	out of, from, beyond	-ous	full of
in-	in (or) not	-ward	in the direction of
multi-	many		
non-	not		
post-	after		
pre-	before		
re-	again		
semi-	partly		
sub-	under		
super-	over		
trans-	across		
tri-	three		
un-	not		

states that the base word must be able to stand alone as a word after the prefix or suffix has been removed. Thus, using this definition, *pre-* is a prefix in *preapplication* but not in *prefer* or *predict*.

One ideal time to teach a prefix or suffix is when a child encounters an unknown word with an affix. While the whole word is unknown, its base may be a part of the child's recognition vocabulary. Such an opportunity often arises when the teacher is listening to a child read individually. A word of caution, however; no timely teaching of structural analysis is worth interrupting a child who is excitedly fulfilling his or her purpose for reading. If a young reader is eagerly involved in an activity that is meeting some need, stopping for analysis could destroy the impetus that a valid purpose has set in motion. In such a case—if other, more rapid or already acquired skills don't unlock the word—the teacher may want to just supply it, noting it (in writing) as an opportunity for a planned later encounter that focuses on that affix.

In addition, the teaching of affixes can be overemphasized as a word-recognition strategy. For example, the memorizing of lists of affixes is not a useful strategy.

Teaching prefixes. Suppose a child attempted to read the following sentence: "The teams decided to replay the game." The child is stymied by the word *replay*. The teacher may initially ask questions to unlock the word through context analysis: "What do you suppose they decided to do with the game?" "What would you do if your game came out like that?" By doing this, the teacher hopes the child can draw *replay* out of his or her aural memory or even come up with "play it over." But suppose this is not the case? It is often easier to try drawing attention to the structure of the word first—rather than prodding phonic analysis both because it is more closely related to context and because, should a phonic attack be used subsequently, the structural analysis would aid the approach. The process of trying to get the reader to focus on the structure of a word should always focus on meaning. It is unwise to merely have a child search for "a little word in a big word" because often the little word does not contribute to the meaning of the longer word, such as the word *lay* in the word *replay*.

If the child has stated that they are going to "play it over," the teacher might ask if the child knows the meaning of several words in sentences that are made up on the spot. For example,

> Teacher: What does *redo* mean in this sentence: "Sam has to *redo* his homework."
> Student: He has to do it again.
> Teacher: And *rewind* in this sentence: "We have to *rewind* our clock every day."
> Student: Everyday we have to wind our clock again.
> Teacher: How about *rebuild*: "The men started to *rebuild* the bridge."
> Student: Build it again.
> Teacher: So if the teams are going to play the game again, you might say they are going to _____ the game.
> Student: Replay.

Now the student can move back to reading and will have no difficulty recognizing the word *replay* in context. In this example, the student discovered the meaning of the prefix *re-* because it was part of an aural vocabulary. The teacher focused on the meaning of the prefix and helped the child associate existing knowledge with the printed word.

It is worth restressing here, however, that for discovery of the meaning of a base plus affix to be effective, the base should be a recognizable word and the addition of the meaning of the prefix to that root ought to translate literally to the meaning of the word. For example, in the sentence "The funny face seemed to *transform* Betty. She began to act like a clown," it seems improbable that pointing out that *trans-* means *across* would help many elementary children understand the meaning of *transform*. It would be a fruitless and forgotten fact. Breaking the word into its prefix and base, though, might facilitate pronunciation and thus lead indirectly to meaning. There are times, of course, when *trans-* lends itself effectively to structural analysis, as in words like *transplant*, *transatlantic*, and *transport*.

Teaching suffixes.   A student is stumped by the last word in the following sentences:

Arthur couldn't hit the ball very hard. They laughed at his *weakness*.

After attempts to prompt recognition through context analysis, the teacher might cover the ending and ask the child to pronounce the base. Once the suffix is separated from the familiar word *weak*, the reader is able to add *ness* to the base word called up by aural memory—the word has been heard and understood, and the child has used the word in discussions. The teacher could then point out how adding *ness* changed *weak* from a word that tells about something (an adjective) to one that names something (a noun). Such a grammar lesson would allow each child to discover the proper generalization.

To follow up, the teacher might write several sentences in which the -*ness* suffix has been left off of a word in the sentence. Preferably, the words would come from stories the children will soon be reading. At the same time, the teacher should plan a lesson for those children who have difficulty with suffixes, particularly the -*ness* suffix. Examples of sentences might include:

> The bright_____ of the fire could be seen for miles.
> His short_____ seldom got him in trouble.

The teacher should read aloud any parts of the sentences that the students couldn't read. The students would be asked for an ending that could be added to make sense in the sentence. The teacher could also ask the children to think of other words that end in -*ness* and determine what each word means.

---

try this ▶ Outline a sequence for teaching one of the following words to a reader who fails to recognize the italicized word. Note what skill(s) you would try to prompt, the materials you would use, and the generalization you would like the child to discover.

> Tim was *unable* to get there on time.
> Tops, the kitten, was very *lovable.*
> The cart rolled *backward* down the hill.
> Mrs. Trombal was *fearful.* She was sure the children were lost.
> The band played for the *pregame* show.
> The *tension* was more than Helen could stand.
> The radio was broken and wouldn't *transmit.*

The meanings for the affixes are: *un-* = not; -*able* = capable of being; -*ward* = in the direction of; -*ful* = full of; *pre-* = before; -*sion* = state of being; *trans-* = across.

In teaching structural analysis it is important to keep in mind that adding suffixes usually changes the grammatical usage of the word. Such grammatical distinctions are generally too abstract for beginning readers and may actually hinder comprehension. There may be valid reasons for teaching suffixes and their effects on the grammatical functions of words, but not at the expense of reading comprehension. Usually, there are more efficient and effective ways to recognize an unknown word.

Inflectional endings. Inflectional endings are added to several different parts of speech in order to denote grammatical changes. If a reader can recognize known words, then the inflectional ending can be separated from the known word—shortening it to a form that may likely be in the reader's sight vocabulary. Soon, of course, many of these forms of the words become a part of the sight vocabulary as well.

Inflectional endings are added to nouns to show number, gender, and case. They are added to verbs to make participles, and to show tense, third-person singular, and the progressive form of the verb. They are added to adverbs to show degree and to adjectives for comparison.

Inflectional endings are, of course, used quite naturally by children as part of their oral language, and they learn them quite as naturally in reading. For example, if a child (or teacher) were reading a story that was easy to read and there was a typographical error in which an inflectional ending was omitted, the reader would most likely add the ending while reading and usually not even note that it was missing.

With the exception of nouns that change to form plurals (mouse/mice, woman/women) most words are made plural by adding *s* or *es*. The task is not how to teach children to form plurals but how to get the children to recognize the plural forms when they see them. Most reading texts begin inserting plurals at very early levels without any special pedagogical attention to them. Usually, this natural recognition and comprehension of plurals happens without any teaching. Whether recognizing the difference between *girl* and *girls* occurs as the assimilation of two separate sight words or as an inflection of a single word is not clear, but when such inflections cause no problem, it is counterproductive to stop the communication between author and reader to make the generalization in words.

Occasionally, however, a young reader will falter on a word because the inflectional ending has made the word strange. Then is the time to ask if, by removing that *s*, the reader recognizes the word. If the answer is "yes," follow up, for example, with "How many _____ does it say were in that tree?" Or if the number is not indicated in the sentence, the teacher might ask, "Does this mean there was more than one _____?" Activities for reinforcing inflectional endings can be the same as those used for reinforcing prefixes or suffices.

Activities to reinforce learning. Because comprehension should always be the goal, the ideal way to teach word recognition using affixes is to direct the analysis when an unrecognized word is encountered in context. Here are three types of practice activities that can be used for reinforcing prefixes, suffixes, or inflectional endings.

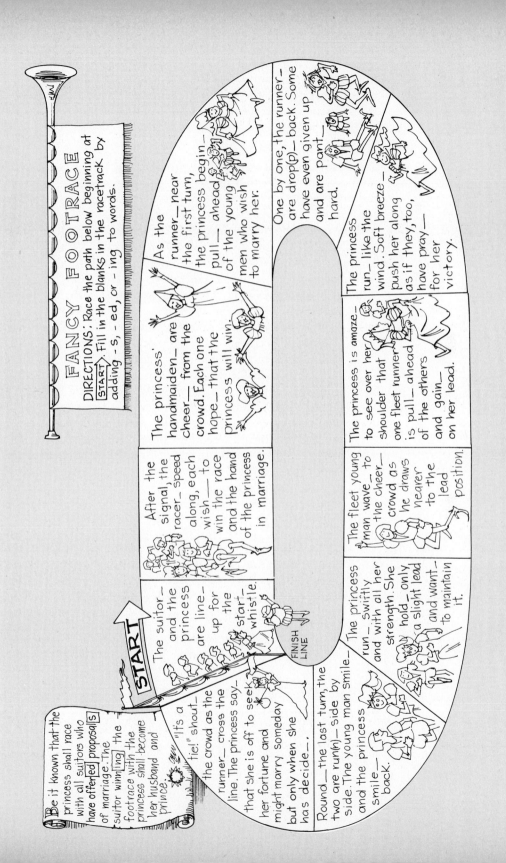

FANCY FOOTRACE

DIRECTIONS: Race the path below beginning at **START**. Fill in the blanks in the racetrack by adding -s, -ed, or -ing to words.

Be it known that the princess shall race with all suitors who have offered proposal[s] of marriage. The suitor winn[ing] the footrace with the princess shall become her husband and prince.

The suitor_ and the princess are line_ up for the start_ whistle.

the crowd as the runner_ cross the line. The princess say_ that she is off to seek her fortune and might marry someday but only when she has decide_.

After the signal, the racer_ speed_ along, each wish_ to win the race and the hand of the princess in marriage.

The princess' handmaiden_ are cheer_ from the crowd. Each one hope_ that the princess will win.

"It's a tie!" shout_

As the runner_ near_ the first turn, the princess begin_ to pull_ ahead of the young men who wish to marry her.

One by one, the runner_ are drop(p)_ back. Some have even given up and are pant_ hard.

The princess run_ like the wind. Soft breeze_ push her along as if they, too, have pray_ for her victory.

The princess is amaze_ to see over her shoulder that one fleet runner_ is pull_ ahead of the others and gain_ on her lead.

The fleet young man wave_ to the cheer_ crowd as he draws nearer to the lead position.

The princess run_ swiftly and with all her strength. She only hold_ only a slight lead and want_ to maintain it.

Round_ the last turn, the two are run(n)_ side by side. The young man smile_. The princess and the princess smile_ back.

START

FINISH LINE

In the first activity, the children need to add three inflectional endings to words in a story. By adding the correct ending, the children can understand the story. This gamelike activity usually creates greater motivation.

In another activity the teacher has mimeographed the following letter and asks the children to help in adding the correct endings to certain words in the sentences so the letter will make sense.

Dear Sir:

I recognize that you are the president of Bloopy Cola while I am a nobody and ____important to you. But I am a reason_____ person and not like____ to be a complain____ without good cause. My family has bought delicious Bloopy Cola ____hesitating____ for years.

However, recent____I became ____satisfied. Let me tell you about it. We were all give__ tickets for Saturday's big game between the Bats and the Belfries. Our seats were right beside the ____field. While sitting comfortab____ and enjoying the game, I open____ my cold bottle of Bloopy Cola. Or, more precise____, the bottle of Bloopy open____ itself. The cap went fly____ across the ____field, mak____ a dizzy arch and strik____ the ____field wall. The batt__ looked puzzle____ for one moment before mak____ a dash for first. The guy on second start____ for third. Since the bases were load____, the guy on third crossed home plate. The ____field____ headed for the bottle cap. The crowd was cheering wild____. Everyone seemed to think that our team had just success_____ scored four runs. The fans were ____controll_____.

When the excite_____ died down, people tried to figure out who had ____rupt____ the game with a fly____ bottlecap.

Now, sir, I didn't tell. And my advice to you is: ____takes like that shouldn't happen twice.

Yours sincere____,

Peter Floogle

Yet another activity is to make up advertisements with blanks to be completed by adding a missing word plus an ending. For example:

Directions: Add the suffix -ic or -ish to the words below and see if you can complete the newspaper advertisements below.

majesty	photograph	red
fool	England	class

(1) Our _____ studio will take your individual or family portrait. Our photographer is a specialist in color work.
(2) Plan your next trip to our resort in the _____ Rocky Mountains. The scenery is outstanding and the outdoor fun is stupendous.

(3) You'd be _____ not to take advantage of our sale on winter coats. Be wise and come early—the sale starts tomorrow at 9:00 A.M.

(4) If you want to own a perfect ruby, shop at Smith's Jewelers. The _____ glow of our rubies assures you of fine quality.

(5) The design of our antique autos makes them something to be proud of. If you want to own one of these _____ cars visit our showrooms at 186 Main Street.

(6) You'd love the taste of our _____ muffins. They practically melt in your mouth.

Children also enjoy making up their own ads.

Contractions and Compound Words

Children use contractions and compound words easily and naturally in their oral language. This phenomenon should be capitalized on in teaching the recognition of these forms.

Contractions.   When a child is stumped by a contraction, the teacher can cue recognition by using the child's language. For example, suppose a child didn't recognize the word *shouldn't* in a story.

Teacher: If John can not do something we say he _____ .
Student: Can't do it.
Teacher: And if John did not do something we say he _____ do it.
Student: Didn't.
Teacher: And if John should not do something we say he _____ do it.
Student: Shouldn't.

Through such an activity the teacher has determined that the child understands the contracted form—including the contraction *shouldn't*. The teacher has also discovered that the child can use contractions by correctly completing oral sentences. And if the timing is appropriate in the particular lesson being taught—that is, if the child's reading and enjoyment of a story won't be interrupted—the teacher may also write the contractions used in the oral sentences. In that way the child would have heard, used orally, and seen the contractions.

If, however, a child still seems to be unsure of the contraction, the teacher should tell the child the word and make a note in the child's reading record; and, at a later time, additional instruction should be provided. An activity that sparks awareness of contractions in children's language is to tape record an impromptu conversation between several students. The teacher transcribes the conversation—but spells out all the contractions the children used. Then the recording is played back,

and the children follow on the transcript. "Did I get it right?" asks the teacher. But the children notice that something is wrong. Another replay and a close look will show that Jan wasn't saying *cannot* and *should not*, for example; she said *can't* and *shouldn't*. Betty didn't say *I will*; she said *I'll*. "Same thing, isn't it?" asks the teacher. "It doesn't sound right!" the children object. So the teacher asks them to go through the script and put in the contractions until it matches their tape.

Compound words.   Perhaps no language phenomenon lends itself more efficiently to structural analysis than compound words, which consist of two or three words run together as one. The combined word has the combined meaning of all the elements. Children are often stymied by the complex appearance of compound words such as *drawbridge, nonetheless, snowman, classroom,* and *cowboy.* Our language is surprisingly full of them; but recognition is vastly simplified for the reader by dividing the word into the words that make up the compound word. The reader can then recognize the two sight words that make up the compound. He or she can pronounce each easily, and combining their meaning can be great fun. The teacher's technique is merely to guide the child through this process.

Some compound words are easy for children. Compounds like *someplace* and *everywhere* are a bit more difficult. Beginning readers who seem to have some difficulty recognizing compounds can be given activities like those at the left, which are two-piece puzzles that the child puts together to form compound words.

For more advanced readers, activities such as the following may be useful:

> Here are some sentences with new words made up of two words you already know. See if you can fill in the blanks after reading the hint below each sentence.
>
> (1)   I've always wanted to sleep on a _____ .
>   (A *bed* that has a mattress stuffed with *feathers*)
> (2)   We couldn't swim because the tide was creating a strong
>
>   _____ .
>   (A force created by waves rolling away from shore. It can pull [*tow*] you *under*.)
> (3)   We spent our vacation on a big lake living in a _____ .
>   (A large *boat* with rooms in it just like a *house*)
> (4)   The new _____ rang so loud it made me jump.
>   (A *bell* that rings when someone pushes a button just outside the *door*)
> (5)   Bill started to slip off the dock, but Cathy had a _____ .
>   (A grip using the *foot* to try to get a *hold* or footing on something)

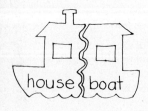

People have always made new words by putting two words together. These are called *compound words*. Here are some sentences with blanks for words that are made up of two words. See if you can put the compound word in the blank. Use the clue below each sentence to help you.

(1) I always start the day with a healthy b_____t.
   (The first meal you eat after not eating [fasting] all night)
(2) Mother grows violets on the w_____l.
   (A piece of wood across the bottom of a window)
(3) The boat we rented didn't look very s_____y.
   (Worthy of trusting on the sea)
(4) They wouldn't let the b_____t girl come in the restaurant because she might hurt her feet.
   (Not wearing anything on your feet)
(5) Tom practiced his arithmetic at home on the c_____d.
   (A dark board to mark on with chalk)

The names of many products are compound words that people make up to describe what they are selling. Pretend that you are going to sell the products described below. Make up names for them by combining two of the words in the lists on the sides of the page. Use one word from each side of the page for each product. Don't forget to begin the name of your product with a capital letter.

color	(1)	A comb that colors your hair as you comb it.	sponge
funny		The Colorcomb	fingers
tall	(2)	A coat that has stars and a comet on the back.	comb
		The _____	
night	(3)	A game where you try to scare each other by making noises you hear at night.	feet
comet		_____	noise
	(4)	A soft sponge that you soak in water and throw.	
fleet		The _____	talk
splash	(5)	Silly little faces that you wear over your fingers so that they look like clowns.	coat
		_____	
	(6)	A game where you make up tall tales to tell each other.	
		_____	
	(7)	Rollerskates with wheels that help you go very fast.	
		_____	

Make up names for some make-believe products by combining words you already know. See if your friends can guess what your product is.

Principles for Teaching Structural Analysis

The end result of all instruction with structural analysis should be meaning in context. Ideally, the instruction should grow out of an unrecognized word encountered in context—and one in which structural analysis speeds its recognition. If prefixes are being taught, instruction should include the use of prefixes in context so that children can see how the meaning is affected by the use of prefixes.

Structural-analysis clues should only be taught with words that a child can already partly recognize. For example, if a child does not know the meaning of a base word, he or she should not be taught the use of affixes, compound words, or contractions with those base words.

The structural-analysis clues that are taught to a child should be those that will be encountered as part of his or her reading. The teaching of uncommon or little-used affixes will not expand a student's reading ability.

Structural-analysis skills should be taught in conjunction with other word-recognition clues. Isolated drill on word parts should be avoided. If students are given practice exercises for any of these skills, the practice materials should be interesting and motivating to children. It is important that the children should understand the skill they are practicing.

Throughout our discussion of the usefulness of structural analysis, we have noted its limitations at the same time. For several valid reasons, the extent to which structural analysis should be emphasized is being challenged today. For example, the meanings of specific affixes are frequently multiple and vary from word to word, and the combination of affixes with different base words has created varied spellings of the additions—and, in effect, new affixes. Furthermore, too often the classroom procedure is to teach affixes as lists to be memorized with their meanings. Teaching word recognition divorced from context ignores what reading is all about—getting meaning from words in combination. Thus, helping children to recognize isolated or even syllables within isolated words in the hope that this skill will transfer to reading in context is less efficient than teaching children to use structural analysis by identifying the base word and relying on both context and the meanings of similarly structured words to recognize a word that is new to them.

Using the Dictionary

Use of a dictionary to expedite word recognition is the "court of last resort" for most young learners. There are valid reasons for this: first, if reading is best defined as a communication act or a meaning-getting process, the interruptive nature of looking up an unknown word may detract more than it adds to ongoing communication. Second, the reader must have many skills in order to use a dictionary efficiently—including an understanding of its nature, organization, and format. As a result, dictionary use has been relegated to a "when-all-else-fails-try-to-look-it-up" status. "All else," in this case, is use of context analysis, sight vocabulary, phonics, and structural analysis.

Perhaps the when-all-else-fails syndrome is not wrong for the young reader. There is so much else to grasp, so many aspects of reading that are not automatic, so great a need to focus on meaning that, perhaps, the use of the dictionary or glossary deserves low status at the beginning stages of learning to read. But low status does not mean no status. Experts tend to agree that proficient and prolific readers have a "dictionary habit." This habit is started early by providing children with the keys to unlock this useful tool.

Dictionaries Should Be Introduced to Beginning Readers

At the earliest stages, a child's preparation for using a dictionary can occur by discovering picture dictionaries that are a part of the classroom book collection. Some picture dictionaries and A-B-C books are as appealing as other picture books and will be readily perused by young

From *My First Golden Dictionary* by Mary Reed and Edith Osswald. © 1957, 1949 by Western Publishing Company, Inc. Used by permission of the publisher.

barber *barbers*

A *barber* is someone who cuts hair and shaves men's faces. Jerry likes to talk to his friend the *barber* when he has his hair cut.

From *The Golden Picture Dictionary* by Lilian Moore. © Copyright 1954, 1951 by Western Publishing Company, Inc. Used by permission of the publisher.

book browsers. Another advantage of having picture dictionaries readily available for children is that the teacher can capitalize on opportunities that occur in the children's experiences that will serve well to demonstrate dictionary use and an adult's reliance upon dictionaries. For example, "Sandy says her brother is bringing a *reptile* to school today. I'm going to use this dictionary so that we can make some good guesses about what he will bring." Or "This story is about a funny barber. I can show you a picture of a barber in our word book—the dictionary. We can find out what a barber does." Or "The principal told me that you are considerate in the lunch room. I'm going to look that word up in my dictionary to find out what she meant."

There are two guiding principles for introduction to dictionaries: dictionaries should be available, at appropriate levels, and appealing; and dictionaries should be used (or their use demonstrated) in incidental, natural ways. These principles do not deviate from the way in which any reading instruction is offered. And, as with other books, some children will eventually begin to seek out dictionaries on their own in order to verify a word or its meaning. It seems naïve, however, to imply that offering a child direct help with specific dictionary skills should occur only after an interest in the dictionary is demonstrated. The rudiments of dictionary usage can be taught along with (and as a part of) any program because, contrary to the appearance of king-sized lists of dictionary skills, learning to use the dictionary can be fun.

After dictionaries have been discovered and dealt with incidentally, children can be offered a sequence of instructional steps in dictionary usage. Specific skills vary from source to source, but all obviously include locating words, acquiring meanings, and becoming aware of pronunciation keys.

In order to use a dictionary to *locate* words, a child must first (1) recognize letters by name; (2) be aware of a sequence of letters (alphabetical order);* (3) be able to alphabetize by the first letter of a word; and (4) be able to locate a word in a picture dictionary without turning every page.

When these initial skills are mastered, the child will be ready to (5) open a dictionary to the section where a given word is located; (6) alphabetize by the second or third letter; (7) use guide words to identify the page on which a word is located; and (8) learn to locate inflected and derived forms of words.

In order to use a dictionary to *obtain meaning* a child must be able to (1) use a picture dictionary to associate word and meaning; (2) use a (picture) dictionary to locate synonyms; (3) use a (picture) dictionary to find more than one meaning for a word; and (4) use a dictionary to select one meaning from alternatives for a given word in context.

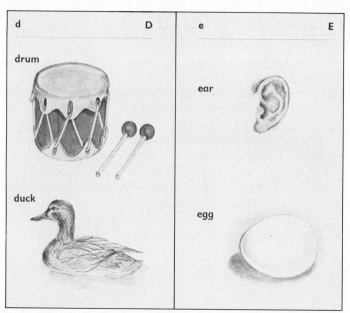

From *Dictionary I: Pyramid Primary Dictionary Series* by Ann Brown, John Downing, and John Sceats, copyright 1971 by Jove Publications, Inc. Reprinted by permission of Jove Publications, Inc. and W. & R. Chambers, Ltd.

* As Robert Karlin wisely notes, "Teachers should not assume that children can use alphabetical order just because they say or sing the letters of the alphabet in sequence" (p. 202).

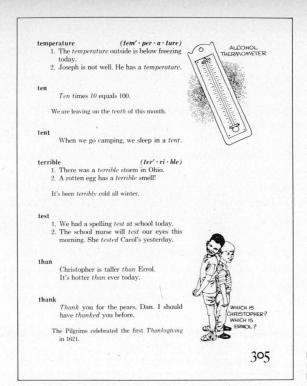

Pronunciation

A child may be able to locate a word in a dictionary, select a definition, successfully apply that definition in his or her reading, and still not be able to pronounce the word. Although reading, as we have said many times, is not "pronouncing correctly," the skills for using pronunciation keys can lead to an increased oral-aural vocabulary. Pronunciation skills can be useful and important ones. Thus, learning how to pronounce is one (deceptively narrow) aspect of dictionary skills.

In order to use the dictionary to learn to *pronounce* a word, the child must (1) be able to use dictionary phonetic respellings; (2) be able to identify syllables; and (3) be able to use accent marks.

Teaching Children Dictionary Skills

Unlike other aspects of word recognition, the use of outside sources (dictionary and glossary, for example,) isn't relied upon heavily at the beginning stages of learning to read. Yet most teachers neither want to withhold these rich resources nor force their use through set exercises and drills. It is important that young readers learn the purpose and organization of the dictionary. Older readers can expand their dictionary skills to learn synonyms, antonyms, the origins of words important to them, and how to further exploit a dictionary's information.

Teaching Children to Locate

When children can identify letters by name with ease and have a posted model of the alphabet available, they can learn something about A-B-C order. There are many activities that can be used to teach alphabetical order. For example, objects on a table are labelled and children rearrange them alphabetically. The accuracy of the rearrangement is then tested with a picture dictionary.

Other activities might have a small group of children, all of whom are wearing namecards, try to put themselves in alphabetical order. Or the children can make a telephone directory of their class. Also individual word boxes with either favorite words or words used for creative writing can be kept in alphabetical order. In addition, when using a dictionary, glossary, encyclopedia, or card catalog, the teacher should emphasize that he or she is relying upon the order of the alphabet to help in the search.

Any teacher who is unsure about where to start or what to teach a child about locating words in a dictionary can simply invite the child to locate a given word while the teacher watches. Much can be learned about a child's locational skills through simply observing the process the child uses to locate the word. Does the child turn each page and look for the word? Does the child estimate the section and open the dictionary to that spot? Does the child use guide words to arrive at the correct page? Does the child read every word on the page or merely move rapidly, examining the second, third, or subsequent letters?

Depending on the skills exhibited, the teacher can attempt to provide meaningful practice. One exercise for this is to tape four different colored tabs of paper on the edges of the dictionary's sections.

A – F	G – M	N – S	T – Z

The child then thinks of a list of favorite words. The teacher helps the child to guess which tab to lift so that the word in question will be found.

Another useful exercise is to encourage the children to collect words. Small, spiral-bound notebooks are good word collectors. If each child has a tabbed page for each letter of the alphabet, he or she can enter new words (or used words) as desired. More proficient (or older) readers can enter definitions as they find time to look up the words. (We know one fifth grader who watches William Buckley's television program, *Firing Line,* in order to fill up her notebook! Needless to say, it is vocabulary she's developing, more than locational skills.) Most beginners select words they have read in stories or have heard from their experiences. Upper-level elementary students build their pocket-sized dictionary not only from classroom reading but also from outside reading and from newspapers, television, and magazines. When a child builds the notebook to the point where several words have been collected that begin with the same letter, the teacher might ask that the child figure out a way to order those words systematically for easier retrieval. Several schemes might be tried. Then the two of them can check a dictionary to determine how a dictionary author solves the problem of ordering words that begin alike. Thus, alphabetizing by the second letter is introduced. The transfer and application of this skill must be judged by again observing the child the next time he or she uses the dictionary to locate a word.

Other practice exercises that may help a child to alphabetize to the second and third letters include using a telephone book to find a child's family name or the name of a friend ("Here's Silvan. Should we go forward or backwards to find Seibert?"), making an alphabetic guest list for a real upcoming event, ordering the classroom book collection by the author's last name, and producing an author or title card catalog for classroom books. Although there are many published materials that are designed to help children practice alphabetization skills, it is more useful and appealing to design activities that are closely related to the child and his or her interests.

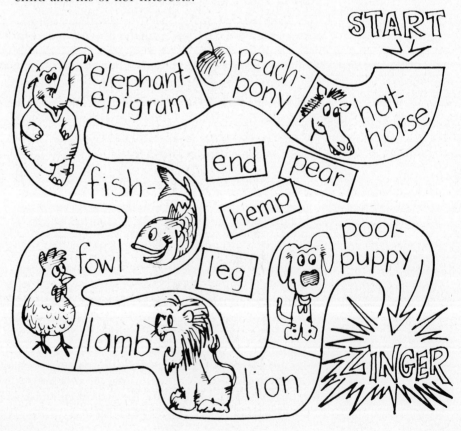

Using guide words can be taught when the children have dictionaries available that use them. There are many activities that teach this skill. For example, the children can locate pizza places and grocery stores in the Yellow Pages of old phone books. The guide words are clear, change infrequently, and are easy to find. The teacher can point out that these words speed the search when one is in a hurry for pizza! The teacher can also reproduce a dictionary or telephone-book page, obliterating guide words. The children "guess" what the guide words might be. Or the teacher asks a child to pretend that his or her name is in the dictionary. The children must say what the guide words are on his or her page. Another activity is to have the children think of words that are of one category (for example, animals); the teacher locates the word in a dictionary, copies the guide words from that page onto a card, and says, "I'm thinking of an animal and its guide words are cousin and coward." Make a "guide word" game—a trail game in which pieces are moved forward or backwards as word cards which are drawn "fit" between the guide words offered in the board's spaces. For example, if a player draws the word *hemp*, he or she must then move the playing piece to the square on the gameboard where the appropriate guide words are printed, *hat-horse*.

Teaching Children to Find Meanings

Again, at beginning stages, children actually know many of the words they look up in the dictionary, when knowing is defined as having an understanding of what the print represents. They look up words to check their form or spelling and to verify meanings by checking print against pictured representations. As in teaching other dictionary skills, here, too, there are many activities that may help children to connect words and their meanings. The children can make picture dictionaries by pasting small pictures onto cards; the pictures can be labelled, sorted, and bound. Personal glossaries can be developed with words that can be categorized together: for example, words from science units, social studies investigations, or mathematics. Or, when the teacher reads a story, the listeners may guess at the meaning of new words from context or picture clues; later, the teacher can offer to help children check their meanings with the dictionary. For example, these are sentences from Bill Peet's *Cyrus the Unsinkable Sea Serpent** that are appropriate for reading to primary-aged chldren:

The serpent slipped under a pier to hide in the *pilings*.
    "You're in for trouble!" he bellowed. "You'll never make it! You'll run into the *doldrums* and be stranded forever!"
    "The old *scoundrel*," muttered Cyrus. "How could he be so *mean*!"

---

* Bill Peet, *Cyrus the Unsinkable Sea Serpent* (Boston: Houghton Mifflin, 1975).

The teacher may say, "You made some good guesses about these new words. Let's check to see how close your meanings match those in a dictionary."

The teacher can also attempt to capitalize on those situations in which words that a child already knows can be discovered to have more than one meaning. For example:

I *can* go.
A *can* of pears

The tree's *branches* were bare.
The library *branch* opens at 9:00.

When children contact words in language or print that offer alternative definitions to more common usages, the teacher should provide the challenge to compare definitions. Locating synonyms usually begins with known words, too. The teacher might say, for instance, "The author said it in this way. What's another way to say the same thing?" Another activity is to have children produce synonym games, such as "Password," in which one player reads a word silently from a card and offers synonyms to his or her partner until the original word is guessed. If children prepare the game, they can also prepare the lists of synonyms (using the dictionary). A similar game is "Webster," in which one player reads a definition or synonym from the dictionary and the others must try to guess the word. If only one synonym is read, and the word is guessed, the guesser gets one point; if two synonyms are read before someone guesses correctly, two points are awarded. The person with the fewest points wins. Solving crossword puzzles is also a useful way to locate synonyms. Laminated board games and wipe-off word cards will allow the teacher and students to make interchangeable synonym games, using vocabulary from texts, free reading, and other experiences. For all synonym games, the classroom dictionary is the referee.

One last activity is for the teacher to create a "Look-It-Up Club." In this club the members are challenged to find and write an answer to riddle cards that the teacher has placed next to resource materials.

Does a praying *mantis* go to church?
Is a *harrier* bald?
Could you weigh an *epigram*?

Teaching Children to Use the Pronunciation Key

Once a child hears a word pronounced, he or she may quickly associate the sound with the meaning. But to "hear" from a dictionary, the child needs to be able to utilize syllable indications, accent marks, and sometimes diacritical marks that indicate sound. This can quickly get very complicated, so formal teaching is usually postponed until a third-grade reading level has been achieved. To use dictionary respellings, students must first discover some useful information about syllables, accents, and diacritical markings.

One of the oldest and favorite teaching techniques is to explain that words have parts—the number of which can be heard by clapping as the child says the word: *city* (2 claps, 2 syllables); *happiness* (3 claps, 3 syllables); *turtle* (2 claps, 2 syllables). Once students discover that they can hear syllables, they can be led to understand that every syllable has a sounded vowel. And further, that dictionaries divide words into syllables, marking the sounds of the vowels. At this point, the teacher should look up some words with children to find the syllables and to discover that vowels are marked, substituted (schwa), or missing (silent vowels).

In order to understand accent marks, the students need to hear the emphasis that is placed on certain syllables. The teacher can begin

---

crane (krān), *n.* 1. any of several large birds with long legs and a long neck that live in swamps and marshes. 2. a large machine with a long boom for lifting heavy weights. —*v.,* **craned, cran·ing.** 3. to stretch (the neck) in order to see better.

Whooping crane (height about 5 ft.; wingspread 7½ ft.)

cra·ni·um (krā′nē əm), *n.* 1. another term for **skull.** 2. the part of the skull that encloses the brain. —**cra′ni·al,** *adj.*

crank (krangk), *n.* 1. a bent handle for turning something, such as the drum of a winch or the cutters of a pencil sharpener. 2. *Informal.* a nasty, bad-tempered person. —*v.* 3. to turn or work by means of a crank. 4. to start (an engine) with a crank.

Crankshaft

crank·shaft (krangk′shaft′), *n.* a shaft having one or more cranks, such as that in an automobile engine, which converts the up-and-down motion of the pistons to rotary motion.

crank·y (krang′kē), *adj.,* **crank·i·er, crank·i·est.** *Informal.* grouchy; cross: *a cranky old man.* —**crank′i·ness,** *n.*

cran·ny (kran′ē), *n., pl.* **cran·nies.** a small, narrow opening in a wall, rock, etc.; chink or crack.

crape (krāp), *n.* another spelling of **crepe.**

crash (krash), *v.* 1. to break, strike, or fall with a loud noise: *The tower crashed to the ground. He crashed the vase on the floor.* 2. to collide: *The cars crashed into each other.* 3. to fail, as a business. 4. to gain admittance to (a game, party, etc.) without a ticket or invitation. —*n.* 5. a breaking or falling to pieces with a loud noise. 6. a collision or crashing, as of automobiles, an airplane, etc. 7. a failure of a business. 8. a sudden, loud noise: *the crash of thunder.*

crass (kras), *adj.* coarse, stupid, vulgar, or gross: *crass rudeness and lack of concern for others.* —**crass′ly,** *adv.* —**crass′ness,** *n.*

-crat, a suffix used to form nouns meaning 1. a person who rules or governs: *autocrat; bureaucrat.* 2. a member of a social class: *aristocrat; plutocrat.* 3. a person who belongs to or favors a certain form of government: *democrat.*

crate (krāt), *n.* 1. a box, usually made of wooden slats, used for packing and shipping fruit, dishes, furniture, etc. —*v.,* **crat·ed, crat·ing.** 2. to put in a crate: *to crate oranges.*

cra·ter (krā′tər), *n.* 1. the mouth of a volcano. 2. a bowl-shaped hollow in the surface of the earth made by a meteor, cannonball, etc. 3. a circular, hollowed area on the surface of the moon, usually surrounded by a high ridge.

cra·vat (krə vat′), *n.* a necktie.

crave (krāv), *v.,* **craved, crav·ing.** 1. to long for or desire eagerly. 2. to ask for earnestly; beg: *to crave forgiveness.*

cra·ven (krā′vən), *adj.* 1. cowardly. —*n.* 2. a coward.

crav·ing (krā′ving), *n.* deep longing; great or eager desire: *a craving for food and rest.*

craw (krô), *n.* 1. the crop of a bird or insect. 2. the stomach of an animal.

craw·fish (krô′fish′), *n., pl.* **craw·fish·es** or **craw·fish.** another name for **crayfish.**

crawl (krôl), *v.* 1. to move slowly with the body resting on the ground, as a worm, or on the hands and knees, as a young child. 2. to put out tendrils, as plants or vines; creep. 3. to move slowly: *Cars were crawling along the crowded road.* 4. to be overrun or covered with crawling things: *The cellar is crawling with spiders.* —*n.* 5. the act of crawling; a slow, crawling motion. 6. a stroke in swimming in which the face is kept down and the arms are lifted one after the other from the water.

Crayfish (length 3½ in.)

cray·fish (krā′fish′), *n., pl.* **cray·fish·es** or **cray·fish.** 1. a small freshwater shellfish that looks like a tiny lobster. 2. a larger saltwater shellfish resembling a lobster but having a spiny shell and lacking the lobster's large claws. Also, **crawfish.**

cray·on (krā′on, krā′ən), *n.* 1. a pointed stick or pencil of colored chalk, wax, etc., used for drawing. —*v.,* **cray·oned, cray·on·ing.** 2. to draw or color with crayons.

craze (krāz), *v.,* **crazed, craz·ing.** 1. to drive mad: *to be crazed by hunger and thirst.* —*n.* 2. a widespread, highly popular fad.

cra·zy (krā′zē), *adj.,* **cra·zi·er, cra·zi·est.** 1. mad; insane. 2. very silly or foolish: *a crazy notion.* 3. very enthusiastic: *She's crazy about movies.* 4. very fond. *She's crazy about him.* 5. odd or unusual: *a crazy necktie.* —**cra′zi·ly,** *adv.* —**cra′zi·ness,** *n.*

creak (krēk), *v.* 1. to make a harsh grating or squeaking sound: *The door creaked on its hinges.* —*n.* 2. a creaking sound.

creak·y (krē′kē), *adj.,* **creak·i·er, creak·i·est.** creaking or likely to creak: *creaky steps; a creaky old chair.* —**creak′i·ness,** *n.*

cream (krēm), *n.* 1. the part of whole milk that is rich in butterfat. 2. a soft solid or thick liquid used as a cosmetic. 3. Usually, **creams.** a soft-centered candy coated with chocolate. 4. a soup containing cream or milk. 5. a yellowish white. 6. the best part of anything: *the cream of society.* —*v.* 7. to work (butter and sugar, or the like) to a smooth, creamy mass. 8. to prepare with cream, milk, or a cream sauce. 9. to take the cream from: *to cream whole milk.*

cream·er·y (krē′mə rē), *n., pl.* **cream·er·ies.** 1. a place where milk and cream are processed and

act, āble, dâre, ärt; ebb, ēqual; if, īce; hot, ōver, ôrder; oil; bŏŏk; ōōze; out; up, ûrge; ə = a as in *alone;* ª as in *button* (but′ªn), *fire* (fīªr); chief; shoe; thin; ᵺhat; zh as in *measure* (mezh′ər). See full key inside cover.

---

with the students' names, saying, for example, the names of pupils that have multiple syllables and asking that they listen in order to identify which syllable is stressed: Tommy, Andrea, Robert, Penelope, and so on. Other words can be used that are part of the students' oral vocabulary: names of favorite cartoon characters, television personalities, foods. At this time, the accent mark (´) can be placed after a syllable. Initially, words that have only one accented syllable should be used.

Before formally introducing a dictionary's diacritical marking system, the teacher should find out how much of the system children can figure out on their own, perhaps by writing a mystery message on the board in which all the words are spelled as they appear in the dictionary respelling. The message can be about something that is going to happen in the class that day or it might be a riddle or joke:

thə sko͞ol bəs had a flat tīr än thə wā to͞o sko͞ol this môr′ning.

The school bus had a flat tire on the way to school this morning.

Children who think they have decoded the message can check their dictionaries to verify it. Children can also attempt to write coded messages using dictionary respellings. Recipients must answer in code.

It is often very useful to establish a learning center that contains familiar words and their dictionary respellings, each printed on cards. Children try to match the word with its respelling. There should always be a dictionary available to check the work.

The child's mastery of a dictionary's pronunciation key is demonstrated by his or her ability to meet and pronounce an unknown word using the dictionary. To reiterate, however, use of the pronunciation key is but one small part of word recognition in reading, because reading is not dependent upon pronouncing.

Instruction in the use of the dictionary as a word-recognition technique will be without value if students never turn to the dictionary. For this reason, children need to see the applicability of the dictionary for their own language—both oral and written—and for the language of others. And children should begin to develop dictionary skills and habits as they are learning to read rather than postponing use of a dictionary until intermediate grades.

Dictionary usage can and should be taught through experiences close to children's interests and needs. Ideally, the reader will find language and reading so appealing that a dictionary habit will develop to both sate and whet curiosity.

REFERENCES Austin, Mary C., and Morrison, Coleman. *The First R, the Harvard Report on Reading in Elementary Schools.* New York: Macmillan, 1963.

Bailey, Mildred Hart. "The Utility of Phonic Generalizations in Grades One Through Six." *The Reading Teacher* 20 (February 1967): 413–18.

Clymer, Theodore. "The Utility of Phonic Generalizations in the Primary Grades." *The Reading Teacher* 16 (January 1963): 252–58.

Emans, Robert. "History of Phonics." *Elementary English* 54 (May 1968): 602–08.

———. "The Usefulness of Phonic Generalizations Above the Primary Grades." *The Reading Teacher* 20 (February 1967): 419–25.

Goodman, Kenneth S. "Orthography in a Theory of Reading Instruction." *Elementary English* (December 1972): 1254–61.

Heilman, Arthur W. *Phonics in Proper Perspective*. Columbus, Ohio: Charles E. Merrill, 1964.

Jongsma, Eugene. *The Cloze Procedure as a Teaching Technique*. Newark, Del.: International Reading Association, 1971.

Karlin, Robert. *Teaching Elementary Reading*. 2d ed. New York: Harcourt Brace Jovanovich, 1975.

Marchand, Hans. *The Categories and Types of Present-Day English Word-Formation*. 2d ed. Munich: C. H. Beck, 1969.

Marshbanks, Gabrielle, and Levin, Harry. "Cues by Which Children Recognize Words." *Journal of Educational Psychology* 56 (April 1965): 57–61.

Russell, David H. "Teacher's Views on Phonics." *Elementary English* 32 (1955): 371–76.

Smith, James A. *Adventures in Communication*. Boston: Allyn and Bacon, 1972.

Spache, George D. *Toward Better Reading*. Champaign, Ill.: Garrard Publishing Co., 1963.

Thomson, David S. *Language*. New York: Time-Life, 1975.

Tripp, Susan M., and Miller, Wick R. "Language Development." In *Child Psychology*, edited by Harold Stevenson, Sixty-second Yearbook of the National Society for the Study of Education. Chicago: University of Chicago Press, 1963.

Wardhaugh, Ronald. "Linguistics and Phonics." In *Language, Reading and the Communication Process*, edited by Carl Braun, pp. 105–22. Newark, Del.: International Reading Association, 1971.

Webster, Noah. *The American Spelling Book*. Boston: Isaiah Thomas and Ebenezer Andrews, 1798.

FOR FURTHER READING

Anderson, Paul S. *Language Skills in Elementary Education*. New York: Macmillan, 1972.

Chall, Jeanne. *Learning to Read: The Great Debate*. New York: McGraw-Hill, 1967.

Crutchfield, Marjorie. *Individualized Reading: A Guide for Teaching Word Analysis Skills*. Los Angeles: Gramercy Press, 1975.

Dawson, Mildred A., comp. *Teaching Word Recognition Skills*. Newark Del.: International Reading Association, 1971.

Durkin, Dolores. *Strategies for Identifying Words*. Boston: Allyn and Bacon, 1976.

Gray, William S. *On Their Own in Reading*. Chicago: Scott, Foresman, 1960.

Heilman, Arthur W. *Phonics in Proper Perspective*. 3d ed. Columbus, Ohio: Charles E. Merrill, 1976.

Lamb, Pose. *Linguistics in Proper Perspective*. 2d ed. Columbus, Ohio: Charles E. Merrill, 1976.

3

Understanding the Context

Meaning Is Reading:
Comprehension

"He reads fine. It's just that he doesn't comprehend what he reads!"
We've heard this lament repeatedly from teachers during our own teaching careers. If you accept (as we do) a definition of reading that is based on meaning, you will agree that the notion that someone can read and not comprehend is absurd. Reading is comprehending, and to assume otherwise is to assume that to pronounce words correctly is to read. A six-year-old can be taught to correctly *pronounce* the words of a story written in Russian, but unless the child can *comprehend* written or spoken Russian, he or she cannot *read* the story.

A child who rereads a poem or a joke to enjoy once again the melodic language of the poem or the humor of the joke has comprehended. A child who reviews the grocery list to make sure he or she has found everything on the list has comprehended. A child who feels tearful when the animal hero of a story is mistreated has comprehended. The list could go on, but the examples above are adequate to illustrate that comprehension means reading and reacting. In each of the three examples, the child was doing something when he or she was comprehending. In the first example, the child was enjoying the flow of language in a poem or the nuances of meaning that are usually encountered in a joke. In the second example, the child was comparing the items on a list with those in the grocery cart. And in the third example, the child was responding affectively to the plight of a story character.

Comprehension is an active mental process. It is not something that a reader *has*; rather, it is something that a reader *does*. The teacher's goal, therefore, in helping readers to improve reading comprehension is to set the stage for active reading and responding. Reading comprehension is viewed in this chapter neither as an innate ability nor as a set of skills to be mastered.* This same point of view has been predominant throughout this book—the focus is on instruction to promote reading as an active process rather than mastery of a set of separate skills.

Understanding Comprehension

Reading Comprehension Is Thinking

Many authorities in reading have consistently emphasized a broad definition of reading. As far back as 1949, Arthur Gates stated that reading was neither simply a mechanical skill nor merely a "thought getting" process. Gates said that reading "can and should embrace all types of thinking, evaluating, judging, imagining, reasoning, and problem solving." He further emphasized that the reading act is completed or nears completion when the child uses the reading in some practical way.

Russell G. Stauffer (1969) is another reading authority who has emphasized a broad definition of reading. Like Gates, he sees the teaching of reading as being not merely a process of teaching a set of rote skills but rather as a means of promoting the cognitive and emotional development of each child. Stauffer defines reading as a mental process that builds on the reader's background and on the reader's ability to shift and reassociate meanings "until the constructs or concepts presented are clearly grasped, critically evaluated, accepted and applied or rejected."

Reading comprehension should be broadly defined. To do otherwise would be to ignore a logical process that happens when one reads: building upon the solid background of concepts, experiences, and language that the reader brings to the printed page. In a sense, the author's ideas are seeded in the reader's background. As the reader attempts to explore his or her own ideas, to modify them, to fit new ideas into the organization of his or her thinking, and to construct still new ideas, the reader is involved in a constant process of concept development.

John Dewey's five-part analysis (1933) of thinking as problem solving correlates interestingly with the broad definitions of comprehension

---

* Among the specific skills that many authorities feel are involved in reading comprehension are: finding main ideas, selecting significant details, predicting, organizing, evaluating, and following directions. However, Dale (1969) has suggested that if we accept such lists as a definition of reading comprehension, we will "suffer from hardening of the categories." And Robinson (1970) has said that by considering the separate points of comprehension we may fail to see the whole.

proposed by Gates and Stauffer. According to Dewey, thinking takes place in this way:

(1) One intellectualizes the difficulty or perplexity that he has felt (directly experienced) before into a problem to be solved—a question for which the answer must be sought.

(2) One receives suggestions, in which the mind leaps forward to a possible solution.

(3) The thinker uses one suggestion after another as a leading idea, or hypothesis, to initiate and guide observation and other operations in collection of factual material.

(4) One engages in elaboration of the idea or supposition as an *idea or supposition*. He uses reasoning, in the sense of which reasoning is a part, not the whole, of inference.

(5) One tests the hypothesis with overt imagination and/or action.

Listening Comprehension Is Similar to Reading Comprehension

There is no clear-cut evidence to pinpoint the exact age at which listening comprehension begins, but we do know that a child must comprehend before speaking. We know that by about one year of age, a child can utter one- and two-word sentences that convey meaning (Lenneberg, 1970). It follows, then, that by the time the average child is one year old, he or she has been comprehending literally hundreds of spoken messages.

Study of the development of the child's ability to comprehend spoken messages is far from complete, but there are several aspects of listening generally agreed upon by researchers in this area. The first is that the child listens for a specific purpose. Personal needs and some knowledge of and experience with the speaker motivate the child to listen.

The second aspect of listening is that the listener interacts with the speaker and focuses on both the content of the message and the way it is spoken. The differences between a harsh, "Don't do that!" and a softly spoken, "We don't want to do that, do we?" are easily understood by children at a very young age. Listening is a process by which the child constructs meanings in his or her mind while listening. There is a constant interplay between the child's background (what he or she knows about the subject and the speaker), what the child expects is going to be said, and the content of the message.

Finally, as the child listens, a response is evolving. Thus, the third aspect of listening comprehension: the synthesis of, and response to, what has been heard. The child comprehends, and based on this understanding, synthesizes and reacts. The child may choose to test this comprehension to see if he or she has understood the intent of the speaker. For example, the child might attempt to do something he or she has been told not to do because of a desire to test the meaning of the softly spoken "We don't want to do that, do we?" The child may have learned from experience that such messages usually don't carry the same emphasis as a sharp reprimand. In any event, listening comprehension does include reaction (sometimes internal), which is often evidence that the listener has assimilated what has been heard.

There are some distinctions between reading and listening comprehension,* but despite these differences, the relationship of listening comprehension to reading comprehension is well accepted. Gertrude Hildreth's summary (1964) indicates that the richness of the child's oral language is related to reading success. Nicholas Anastasiow (1971) points out, "The child who at five months learns that speech sounds contain meaning, does exactly that: he *learns* that from all the sounds present in his environment, speech sounds contain meaning." Anastasiow further emphasizes the relationship of this language learning to cognitive development and concomitantly to reading comprehension. It is, of course, the thinking, or comprehension, that is the common purpose for listening and reading.

Three Dimensions of Reading Comprehension

Thus reading *is* comprehension, and, as we shall see, comprehension is a process of thinking and learning that can be analyzed in three dimensions as an organizational aid to instruction:

(1) You can capitalize on and develop the child's background, interests, and purpose(s) for reading.
(2) You can encourage the child to reason actively while reading.
(3) You can encourage the child to assimilate and use what is read.

In teaching reading as comprehension in this way, you will be encouraging children to learn to discover new ideas through printed materials, to cope with a complex technological society, and to entertain

---

* The reaction of the reader is less immediate to the written message because there is time and distance between the reader and the author. The written word, however, seems to have at least one advantage over the spoken in that it can be skimmed so the reader can focus in on the part of the message that is of most immediate importance or interest to him or her. The reader, however, has to supply most of the author's intonations. While punctuation and other graphic cues supply some of these emphases, print cannot carry the same degree of nuance as speech—although the finely tuned lines of the poet can convey the richness of speech.

Another major difference between listening and reading is the difference in function. Spoken language has basically an "interpersonal" function. It is primarily concerned with the communication process as a form and as a channel of social action. On the other hand, written language is, for the most part, ideational. It is primarily a means of imparting knowledge and therefore needs to maintain a coherence and logic that is rarely necessary in conversation. This difference is significant to reading comprehension in that it suggests that there are skills related to logical thinking that are more important to reading comprehension than to listening comprehension.

themselves. These three dimensions should not be thought of as separate and distinct but rather as overlapping and often indistinguishable. The value of considering these three dimensions separately is to provide an organization to discuss teaching procedures that will help you to help students comprehend.

First dimension. Reading comprehension begins with a reader who has a purpose for reading. That purpose and the reader's background and interest in a particular topic is the first dimension of reading comprehension. However, this first dimension is *not* something that merely comes *before* a child reads. Rather, interest and background are being developed before, after, and during the time a child is reading. Further, a reader's unique purpose for reading is often modified as he or she reads.

Second dimension. The second dimension of reading comprehension is that of active reasoning—the reader constantly tests the printed information against his or her own background, experience, expectations, and against the material itself; the reader can also check the validity of statements with established resources.

Third dimension. A comprehender assimilates what is read; something happens as the result of reading. The reaction to print may be as straightforward (and as easily discernible) as a reader who builds a model after reading directions or bakes a cake after reading a recipe. The thing that happens may be an increased knowledge of sailing ships or a better understanding of how people in different parts of the world live. The thing that happens may be an analysis of different story characters and their unique personalities. Or the thing that happens may be the conclusion of an exciting adventure or a happy moment. Whatever involvement is called for, it is important for you to realize that comprehending extends beyond the print—and more important, it is a dimension of reader involvement that you can help readers to develop.

In Figure 7–1, the three dimensions of reading are summarized and compared with both listening comprehension and Dewey's analysis of thinking. In the sections that follow we will provide you with suggestions for developing these three dimensions with each child in your class.

First Dimension: Purpose, Interest, and Background

A second-grade boy once came home from school and was asked by his parents the same questions he had been asked many times before— questions that are asked by most parents. "How was school today? What did you learn today?" Every time before, the little boy had answered, "Fine, everything's great." This was the quickest and easiest way to escape the parental inquisition. But on this particular day, the little boy

Figure 7–1 Summary of the Three Dimensions of Reading Comprehension, Listening Comprehension, and Thinking as Defined by Dewey

Reading Comprehension	Listening Comprehension	Dewey's Analysis of Thinking (Problem Solving)
1. Reader's purpose for reading; interest in the topic; general information and background for a specific story.	1. Child listens for a purpose; his or her own needs and some knowledge of and experience with the speaker motivate the child to listen.	1. A problem or difficulty is felt and an answer is sought.
2. Active reasoning in which the reader uses his background and knowledge to analyze the printed message.	2. The child constructs meaning as he or she listens; constant interplay occurs among the listener's background, what he expects to hear, and the content of the spoken message.	2. The mind leaps to a possible solution; one thought after another is tested; these thoughts guide observation and the collection of factual information.
3. The reader assimilates and reacts to what has been read.	3. The child synthesizes what has been heard and reacts to test his or her understanding.	3. The idea or supposition is elaborated upon; and the idea is tested with overt imagination and/or action.

felt out of sorts and was angry with his parents for one reason or another. So instead of the usual "Fine," the little boy responded, "School was terrible. I hate it. And I hate reading most of all." He knew that reading was the thing his parents were most concerned about.

"But I thought you liked to read," said his mother. "Why just last evening you studied the directions for making a model airplane. And yesterday when you came home from school, you hunted through an encyclopedia for some information and pictures of different kinds of rockets so you could make a drawing of one. And today you wanted to learn to make chocolate chip cookies. You're going to have to read the recipe to make those."

"Oh, those things aren't reading, Mom," answered the boy. "That's making a model airplane, and finding out about rockets, and making cookies."

"Then what's reading?" asked his mother.

"That's what we do in school every morning right after math. We have these dumb stories and the teacher has us sit in a circle and take turns reading. I hate it!"

The point of this story is that when a child reads for some immediate need (that is, when there is a purpose for reading), and when a child is interested in the topic, and when the child has the background to read about a topic, the child will read and will not necessarily view the activity as reading or learning to read. But if there is little immediate purpose for reading—and if interest and background are missing—a child will view reading as a task to be done to satisfy the teacher.

If you want to develop comprehenders, you have to be sure that reading serves the immediate needs of your students and that the students have the interest and background for the reading they will be doing. Purpose for reading grows out of the relevance of the reading for the student as well as from the student's interests and desire for new experiences.

Purpose for Reading Comes from a Child

Teachers build on the immediate needs of a child if they want that child to become a comprehender. Observe carefully the behaviors and attitudes being exhibited by students and teachers alike in the following classroom situations. Try to identify those situations in which the students are reading to learn as opposed to reading because "teacher says to." What are the differences in the interactions between student and material? Teacher and student?

Classroom 1. This teacher is having an individual conference with Jeff about a self-selected book he has just finished reading, *The Biggest Bear* by Lynn Ward (Scholastic Book Services, 1963).

"Why did you choose this book, Jeff?" asked Ms. Larson.

"Oh, Ms. Larson, you know how I like stories about animals—besides, I looked through this before I checked it out and it has some real neat pictures."

"Will you tell me about the story?"

"It's about a boy, Johnny, who wanted a huge bearskin to hang on his barn just like all the other farmers in the valley. And he went out one day to shoot one, only he didn't because he found a little bear cub instead. Here, I'll show you a picture. And he took the cub home to be his pet."

"But the name of this book is the *biggest* bear; this is just a little one in the picture," said Ms. Larson.

"Oh, yeah, but he grew up—and that's when all the trouble started. You see, he ate everything. . . ."

Classroom 2. The teacher is meeting with a group of students who are reading the book, *Little House on the Prairie* by Laura Ingalls Wilder (Harper and Row, 1935). This book has been purchased in paperback form for the classroom because the teacher had overheard some of her students discussing the television series of the same name. Having completed the discussion of what they have read so far, the students and the teacher are discussing the plan for the next day.

"Well, what do you want to read for tomorrow?" asked the teacher.

Two girls pipe up almost in unison, "We're almost to the end—there are only two chapters left—let's read the rest of the book."

Another boy agrees, "Sure, then maybe we can choose one of the chapters and act it out."

The rest of the group is enthusiastic about the suggestion, and they begin choosing their own parts.

"I'd like to be Laura."

"I'd like to be. . . ."

Classroom 3. Two boys are reading a newspaper article on the *Today's News* bulletin board about a tornado.

One says, "I saw a tornado once when I was visiting my cousin in Kansas. It was pretty scary."

"That's nothing," responds the other; "I saw one down in Florida, only there they call them hurricanes."

"Are you sure they are the same? I thought they were different kinds of storms. Let's ask Mrs. Phelps."

They locate Mrs. Phelps who is occupied with other students.

"She looks pretty busy," says one of the boys. "I know, let's check the encyclopedia; that'll tell us if they're the same or not."

Classroom 4. Because of rain, the children in this first-grade classroom are remaining inside for the day. The teacher has passed out special "rainy day" games, that she keeps on hand for these occasions. However, three children have chosen to play "Think of Another Word," which is a reading-center* activity the teacher made using sentences from their instructional-level readers. In this activity, each child pulls a sentence strip from a box; one word is underlined in each sentence, and the child receives a point when he or she can substitute a synonym for the underlined word.

Classroom 5. Five children, with open books on their laps, are seated around the teacher.

"Alan, read the next page," says the teacher. "The rest of you follow along in your books because one of you will read when I tell Alan to stop."

Alan begins reading aloud, only to be interrupted by his teacher.

"Joan and Robert, please stop flicking each other with those rubber bands. Give them to me. Now sit down. Follow along with Alan. Continue reading, Alan."

Alan begins again.

"Joan," interrupts the teacher, "you come over and sit next to me. I told you two to quit fooling around!

"Continue reading, Alan; the last word was not lonely; it was lovely."

Alan begins again.

Classroom 6. In a corner of the room a girl has a worksheet. The exercise asks her to select the main idea from multiple choices for each paragraph. The girl, however, is concentrating her attention outside the window.

---

* Reading centers are described on pages 400–07.

Classroom 7. Four students who have been directed to read the next five pages in their basal reader approach the teacher for discussion. The teacher quickly skims through the story, looking for details to ask questions about.

The teacher says, "Now—since you all read the story—tell me, what was the hint Commander Pott had that the car had a mind of her own?"

Ed mumbles, "Uh-hh . . . I . . . I can't remember."

"Did the car do anything that surprised Commander Potts?"

Ed stares at the floor. "Yes. . . ."

"Well, what?"

"Uh-h-m-m. . . ."

Another girl holds up her hand and answers.

The teacher focuses her attention on Ed again. "How did Chitty-Chitty Bang-Bang get its name, Ed?"

"I can't remember."

"Did you read the story?" asks the teacher.

"Oh, yeah, I *did,* I just can't remember."

Classroom 8. "Okay, I want you to open your books to pages 38 and 39," directs the teacher.

There's a rustle of pages as the students open their books. There are a few groans when the designated pages are found.

"There are two poems on these two pages. Read them silently and be ready to answer questions about them."

"Gee, Mr. Getz, Why do we have to read stupid poems? They're dumb!"

"Yeah, they're for sissies. Can't we do something else?"

"Don't argue with me," says Mr. Getz, "Read the poems. They have a lot of meaning."

"Geesh!" mutters the first boy under his breath.

Which incidents were based on the children's purposes? It is easy to separate those classrooms containing children who were interested and excited about what they were reading from those in which children were marking time or were uninterested in what they were doing—especially the reading part. The children in the last four classrooms (examples five through eight) were disinterested, bored, even argumentative. They wanted to do something other than the tasks they were assigned. They couldn't answer questions about the story; they fooled around; they daydreamed. And, above all, they weren't reading. They were in reading situations, but the only thing they got out of those situations was a negative attitude toward reading.

Contrast this bored behavior with that exemplified by the children in classrooms one through four. "I like stories about animals." "Can't we read the rest of the book?" "Let's check the encyclopedia." Such statements are obvious indications that reading is regarded as a relevant, enjoyable activity. The interactions of the students with the printed materials also resulted in understanding. It should be apparent as well that these children were easier to teach than were the others.

What was it that caused the students in the first four classrooms to be motivated? A number of factors, some of which have already been discussed in the section on informal assessment (pages 23–26) in Chapter 2, were at work. The teachers had no doubt determined the children's interests and reading levels and had provided stories and books based on those assessments. It is obvious that this was done in the first four classrooms because those children were obviously experiencing success with reading. We all tend to continue doing those things that we do well and to avoid those that cause us difficulty. This is true of children who seek reading activities. They do these activities because they find them pleasurable and because they *can* do them. Success motivates.

When children read books and stories that appeal to their immediate needs and interests, these children can find personal value in reading. Interest is a powerful factor that influences not only the motivation to read but also the understanding of what is read. Thus interest promotes comprehension. And it is of vital importance that you identify and further develop the interests of the students in your classroom.

Determine and Develop General Interests

When the students first enter your classroom in the fall, you know very little about them. However, if you have been following the guidelines presented in Chapter 2 (pages 21–37), you already have been familiarizing yourself with the community and with the general background of your students. You should have some idea of the availability of books and other resources in the community that promote ideas, the home environments, and so on. But while this provides you with a good foundation, it is not enough. So how else can you determine interests?

There are numerous ways to elicit information that reveals students' interests. All you need to do is listen to your students. Class discussions provide a good opportunity for students' current interests to be explored. Or, frequently, you overhear snatches of personal exchange between students that also serve to further your knowledge. "What did you do over the weekend?" "Our dog had puppies." "We have a new pony!" "I got to help Dad cook brownies."

Sharing time is a period when the students can talk and listen to their peers. During this period the personal interests of the children become apparent to you while the children develop language skills by talking. The things to be shared need not be anything more than everyday experiences. It may be that one student brings his coin collection, another her stamp collection, while another brings a picture of the plane she traveled in. They show, explain, listen, and ask. Sometimes the things shared are prized treasures, such as the Monarch butterfly discovered on the ground on the way to school, or an empty bird's nest removed from the backyard tree.

Another source of information concerning the children's interests is parents. After all, parents live and interact with their children constantly. Who could be better aware of a child's desires, dreams, ambitions, and activities? You should frequently interact with parents—by telephone, at meetings, and during parent-teacher conferences. Visits to the home can provide additional insights.

By now you should recognize that obtaining knowledge of your students' interests isn't really all that difficult. It merely requires providing time to talk and to listen. As one of the teachers in our example did (Classroom 2, pages 256–57), you should build upon such stated interests as favorite television or radio shows, heroes or heroines, or television or movie stars. Never criticize such interests; exploit them, instead,for all media are powerful interest developers. Movies, television, radio, videotapes, and records are constantly being produced that appeal to children and extend their experiences. Schools generally have access to such materials. These materials can be rented from companies or agencies; they can also be obtained from the local library or from any nearby educational institution or educational service center.

Expand Interests and Background

Don't stop with just finding out the general interests of the students in your class. In fact, discovering general interests is just the beginning; from knowing these you can launch into all kinds of classroom activities—and plan beyond the classroom, too—to find out the specific interests of each child, to develop each child's background, and to expand the interests of the child.

The best beginning is to encourage talk—encourage each child to tell about those things that interest him or her, to ask about things that are unknown, and to engage in discussions and sharing. Perhaps your most vital role is to be a good listener and then to surround your students with an exciting classroom environment. Contrast the sterile classroom with its five rows of desks, faded pictures, and dull bulletin boards with the classroom containing eye-catching bulletin boards about current topics, a science corner, plants and animals, objects related to art activities, cozy areas with rugs and pillows, and a "things" table piled high with old magazines and other salvaged treasures—such as pieces of wood, cloth, rocks, and so on. It is much easier to expand children's interests in the latter classroom where all their senses are aroused.

Plan your classroom carefully to arouse the senses and to awaken curiosity and the desire for more information. Keep the atmosphere dynamic by changing the environment frequently. Learning centers that are static too long fade into insignificance. Perhaps one center can be devoted entirely to the newsworthy events that are constantly occurring in the school and community. In addition, plan time so that children have daily opportunities to browse around on their own and explore the various centers in the room. For example, you can let the students know

that when designated work on their learning plan or contract is completed, each can freely move to other areas of the room, such as the art corner, and use the materials there. Above all, be certain that this "interesting" classroom is not planned and organized by you alone. Each child must be an active partner in developing the classroom displays and the various centers.

Field trips are an effective means of sparking children's attention and increasing experiences. Perhaps you can still remember how the field trip you made to the fire station when you were in the first grade culminated with a ride on the fire truck, or how on the third-grade visit to the botanical gardens you and your classmates were each given a small plant to take home. Field trips are much more than a day away from the regular school routine. The learning that results from these real experiences is lasting. All too often, such field trips are restricted to the lower grades. This is unfortunate since they have the same motivational and educational effect on all ages. So visit museums, zoos, planetariums, factories, farms and so on, but also let your imagination run free concerning other places to visit. Then don't forget the more "ordinary" places right in your school's neighborhood that aren't so ordinary when you help children to experience them fully—perhaps for the first time. For example, most children will have shopped with their parents in a supermarket. But how many have been in the storerooms to watch a truckload of canned goods or vegetables being unloaded, or have visited the meat-cutting section "behind the scenes," or have been taken into a "walk-in" food cooler?

To supplement field experiences and excursions, invite resource people into the classroom to talk about their work or hobbies. Recently we observed a man of ninety-two talking to fifty children about his life in their community over seventy years before. He had brought with him wooden figures that he had been whittling to occupy his time. The children were enthralled with his tale and wanted to read more about what their neighborhood was like many years ago.

The most important method of expanding children's interests is through reading to them. Whether it's a carefully chosen book, a high-interest magazine article, or a current newspaper article that is being read, new interests can result. Just like the field trips, this activity is frequently observed occurring in the primary grades, even though every school-age child should be read to. Reading aloud requires that the teacher practice effective oral reading and keep abreast of children's literature.

One way to keep informed about new books and stories is to develop a good liaison with your school or community librarian. Don't fall into the rut of always reading the same stories to each class each year—although there will be favorites that the children will demand as well as your own all-time favorites that you really do want to share. But when reading a story or book becomes "old hat" and boring to you, you can be sure it will also be to your students. Read stories that you enjoy—and if you enjoy the stories, your enthusiasm will be contagious.

Reading Can Serve a Child's Needs and Interests

Now that you have made provision for expanding your students' interests, you can channel these interests toward print. Connecting the pleasures of reading with the interests of children helps develop a reading habit. Your attempts to help children achieve a purpose for reading should happen naturally and unobtrusively. Let's examine how some of the activities used in the previous sections can be used to further develop an interest in reading.

The first-grade boy who wants very badly to tell his classmates about a trip to a farm only needs to be shown where the books are that might have some pictures of farms or farm animals. He will eagerly hunt through the books to find the ones that will help him show the class what the farm was like.

The second-grade girl who wants to be an astronaut will eagerly devour articles about astronauts. And the boy or girl—and there are usually several at all grade levels—who is out to become the world's greatest expert on dinosaurs will read all that he or she can on the subject.

We once observed a second-grade boy who had decided that the best thing in the world to be was a comedian. So he read—and memorized—

as many joke books as he could get his hands on. Perhaps the boy did bore a few people with his repertoire of jokes, but he was eagerly reading, and the reading was serving his personal needs.

Jon, one of your quieter students, may be excited about art. How do you know? Whenever he has any free time, he heads straight for the art center where he works contentedly. You take a few moments during the day to accompany Jon to the school library where you locate and check out a number of books that will lead him to other art techniques.

When Sarah shows the bird's nest that she found near her house to the rest of her classmates, the question is raised, "What kind of bird made the nest?" Sarah offers to go to the library to find a book about birds and their nests in order to answer this question.

Your task is to find the reading materials at the appropriate reading levels so each child has what he or she needs to meet immediate needs. When you couple the right reading material with an immediate need, you have a dynamic force for developing a comprehender. In all of these examples, the children's interests are being discovered and used to cultivate their interest in reading. These children are seeing reading as relevant—as a means to an end. They have a purpose for engaging in reading. For each, there is a logical reason for finding a book or for reading a newspaper or magazine.

---

try this ▶ Go to a local elementary school and talk to some of the children. (And be a good listener as well.) Without asking directly, see if you can ascertain what their immediate interests are. Make a list of these interests. Can you think of a reading activity that relates to each interest? Does each reading activity serve an immediate need for the child? If you really want to test yourself, see if you can locate a story, book, or magazine that relates to the reading activity. Now is the time in your teaching career to begin making lists of the places where you can locate such materials.

Develop Specific Purposes for Reading

Up to this point, we have outlined the teacher's role in (1) determining and expanding the children's backgrounds and interests, and (2) providing the stories and books to meet their immediate needs. If you accomplish these two tasks, the children's reading activities will focus on specific purposes. There are several things you can do to ensure that children do read for specific purposes.

When you read to the children in your class, discuss the incidents in the story with them; talk to them about the kind of story they're going to be listening to; let them discuss experiences similar to those in the story. In other words, give them a reason for listening. When you read articles or newspaper clippings to individual students or your total class tell them why you are reading each one to them. Perhaps you want to share one that was especially funny, or another that is about a child's or your own special interests. What you are doing is giving the children a model that shows that we read for specific purposes.

When a child is eagerly reading on his or her own because of a personal need, you usually won't need to be concerned about that child's purpose for reading: the child already has one. But sometimes a child needs to share the purpose—he or she needs to tell someone else about the reading. Thus you should be alert to every opportunity to let each child share his or her purpose for reading with you.

Building Background and Purpose with a Group Story

Throughout this book we have been describing an individual child-centered reading program. However, it is not uncommon (nor alien to the philosophy of this text) for elementary-classroom teachers to work with a group of children who have read the same story. In this kind of teaching situation, it is just as important as in the individual situation that the purpose for reading come from the readers and not be forced upon them. And here, too, the purpose must, of course, be relevant to the children's interests and needs.

It is much easier for a child to read when he or she has a reason for doing so. As was pointed out earlier, having a genuine reason develops from an interest or a desire to learn about something. Children have fantastic curiosity about the world surrounding them, as their own questions demonstrate. For example, "Where do butterflies sleep?" "How does a rocket work?" "Why doesn't the grass just stay short after we mow it?" "Why don't people on the bottom of the earth fall off?"

The teacher needs to stimulate this natural curiosity and interest of children as a means of motivating them to read. A variety of techniques are successful in guiding children to find a purpose for reading. The following examples show teachers interacting with students in reading situations. The goal of each of these teachers is the same—arousing the children's interest in reading a particular selection.

The first teacher wants to read a story entitled "Robber in the Night" with the children. It is about a family on vacation who is staying in a cabin in the middle of the forest. During the night, noise awakens them and they find that some of their food has disappeared. However, the robber is gone. This continues for three more nights until they set up a trap. They discover that the robber is really a hungry raccoon.

The teacher is holding up a "Wanted" poster for the children to study. "Do any of you know what this poster is?"

"I know. I've seen them in the post office. It's a paper showing pictures of somebody who has robbed a bank or broken the law or something."

"This particular poster has a picture of a man who robbed a bank.

Now I would like for you to think about this: on this poster we can see the robber's face. But what do robbers usually do so people don't know who they are?"

Janet volunteers. "They wear masks. Like we do at Halloween!"

"Our story for today is about a robber—and the robber has a mask over his eyes. But there's something different about him." And so, using the picture as a way of getting into the story, the teacher launches the reading of the story.

The second teacher regularly brings library or trade books into her classroom in order to bring them to her students' attention. Sometimes she will read the first chapter only; at other times she will read a number of chapters until she arrives at one that introduces a crisis for the leading character. For the past six school days she has been reading *Charlotte's Web* by E. B. White (Dell, 1952).* Today she will conclude her oral reading with Chapter 7, "Bad News." See if you can determine why she has chosen to stop with this chapter. (By the way, Wilbur is a pig.) She reads:

> As the days went by, Wilbur grew and grew. He ate three big meals a day. He spent long hours lying on his side, half asleep, dreaming pleasant dreams. He enjoyed good health and he gained a lot of weight. One afternoon, when Fern was sitting on her stool, the oldest sheep walked into the barn, and stopped to pay a call on Wilbur.
>
> "Hello!" she said. "Seems to me you're putting on weight."
>
> "Yes, I guess I am," replied Wilbur. "At my age it's a good idea to keep gaining."
>
> "Just the same, I don't envy you," said the old sheep. "You know why they're fattening you up, don't you?"
>
> "No," said Wilbur.
>
> "Well, I don't like to spread bad news," said the sheep, "but they're fattening you up because they're going to kill you, that's why."
>
> "They're going to *what*!" screamed Wilbur. Fern grew rigid on her stool.
>
> "Kill you. Turn you into smoked bacon and ham," continued the old sheep. "Almost all young pigs get murdered by the farmer as soon as the real cold weather sets in. There's a regular conspiracy here to kill you at Christmastime. . . ."

When the teacher stops at the end of this chapter, and it has been established that Wilbur is going to be butchered, don't you think that the students will be motivated to pursue the book to the end to see if, or how, Wilbur is saved from this fate? Unfinished introductions leave students hanging; they want to know the conclusion.

* *Charlotte's Web* is perhaps one of the most popular books among elementary school children. One survey estimated that more teachers read *Charlotte's Web* to their students than any other book. It is because the book is so well known that we use it as an example. You will need to make certain that children gain exposure to other books as well.

The third teacher is resorting to the "make it personal" tactic as a means of focusing the children's attention on the story. Because a number of children in this classroom are at the stage of development where they are losing their baby teeth, it is not uncommon to see smiles with gaps on various faces in the room. The teacher wants to help the students in this particular reading group find a purpose to read a selection about a little girl who has lost her two front teeth. Embarrassed by the resulting gap—and knowing that she will be told to smile for the class pictures that are to be taken the next day—she solves her problem in a unique way: she purchases a set of wax teeth at the local dime store.

"I've been noticing something that has been happening to a number of you recently. You've all been losing something. Can you think of what it is?" asks the teacher.

The children look at each other, but no one can think of what it is the teacher means.

"Maybe another clue will help you. The only time I can tell that you have lost something is when you smile or laugh, or sometimes when you talk."

Beth giggles as she holds up her hand, "I know; it's our teeth."

"Right. How many of you have lost a tooth?" Every child's hand in the group goes up.

"I'm even missing three. See?" volunteers Carrie.

"How did you feel when you first lost your teeth?"

"Well, it was okay for me, because I got to put the tooth under my pillow."

The other children respond. "So did I." "Me, too."

"What did you think when you looked into the mirror?" the teacher asks.

"Oh, I looked funny. At first I didn't want to smile or talk to anyone."

The discussion continues as the teacher elicits the feelings from the other children. Gradually she leads the conversation to the story for the day. This teacher is building upon the personal, shared experiences of the children in the group to motivate them to read the story.

These three classroom examples point up the fact that interest and motivation give rise to specific purposes for reading. Without interest, children read because the teacher tells them to, but they will be reading to accomplish the teacher's purpose rather than their own. The teacher must, therefore, help children to develop personal purposes for reading. The teacher can accomplish this by creating strong interest in a good story, by relating children's personal characteristics to those of story characters, and by helping children find reading materials that help them pursue their own activities.

A teacher *should never* assign children a reading assignment without discussing with them the purpose for reading. And once children have a purpose for reading, they will engage in active reasoning while reading. Thus it is important that synthesis activities are planned that relate to the specific purpose for reading.

Second Dimension: Active Reasoning

A second-grade class was preparing for an "Indian week." The idea for Indian week was suggested by several students in the class and was probably the outgrowth of the fact that the teacher had read several Indian stories aloud to the class.

After hearing Indian stories read by the teacher, two children began discussing what it must have been like to live as an Indian many years ago. This discussion led the children to the encyclopedia where they found pictures depicting Indian life. The children were interested to learn that different Indian tribes dressed differently and lived in different kinds of homes.

"Wouldn't it be great to live like the Indians did?" remarked one child.

The other child agreed. The teacher seized on the opportunity and suggested that the children might like to find out more about Indian life and report what they found out to the rest of the class.

"But can't we show them how the Indians lived rather than just telling them?"

"We could dress like the Indians did."

"And show them how the Indians wrote."

"And what they ate."

"And the kinds of homes they lived in."

"Well, I suppose you could do all that," said the teacher. "But you've got a lot to find out about."

The project grew and quickly involved the entire class. The plan was for the children to learn everything they could about a particular Indian tribe and to make all the things they would need to have an Indian week. During Indian week the children were to try to live as the Indians did. They were to participate in Indian ceremonies and learn about the things Indian children learned about. They even decided to have lunch each day made from foods the Indians ate. The children planned the menus, made the foods, and even made Indian eating utensils. The week was to culminate with a presentation for their parents and the other second-grade class in the school.

The search for information began. The encyclopedia and the library were vital resources. The teacher and the librarian searched for as many books and stories as they could find about Indians. Several of the children had books and pictures they brought from home. The children had to sort out the materials related to the Indian tribes they were trying to learn about. They had to skim materials, categorize information, and relate facts and ideas in one book to those in another. Each child, or sometimes groups of two or three children, became interested in a specific aspect of Indian life—cooking, hunting, homes, sign language, and so on. Two children set out to learn the sign language of one tribe. When there weren't any signs for words they wanted to use, they had to make up signs based on the ones they learned from the encyclopedia. These children wondered why the Indians needed a sign language when they had their own spoken language. While their books never gave them the answer, the children decided that because this particular tribe traded with other tribes who spoke a different language the Indians needed a sign language to communicate.

Three children wanted to find out exactly what Indians ate. They studied books from the library and made lists of foods. Sometimes the foods had strange names, and the children had to go to other books to find out what these names meant. They tried to find as many of these foods as they could; and with the help of the cafeteria staff, their parents, and a trip to a market with the teacher, they were able to find samples of many of the foods. They discovered that Indians grew much of their own food. Then the children wondered what Indians ate when their crops failed. Again, the books didn't provide an answer; so the children made up a list of foods that probably were naturally available in the various sections of the country where Indians lived.

One boy was very interested in how Indians made cornbread. He found a book that described each step of the process, and, with the help of the teacher, he was able to demonstrate to the class the steps in making cornbread. His effort was so successful that he made enough cornbread for everyone to taste when the parents came to see the Indian project.

Most of the children got involved in finding out what Indians wore and in making Indian costumes. There was debate among the children about whether Indians wore feathers in their headbands all the time, about the kind of moccasins Indians wore, and about whether Indian men wore beads—and why.

All of these discussions led the children back to their resources for information. There was a great desire on the part of the children to be authentic, so, when faced with contradictory data, they tried to find the information that seemed to make the most sense in relation to other information they had. Some information was directly stated in the books, some had to be inferred, and all of it had to be evaluated in terms of consistency from one reference source to another.

Interest, Motivation, and Background Develop Active Reasoning

The children in the incident above were interested and motivated to read and learn about Indians. The topic had been introduced by the teacher because the teacher knew something about the general interest of second-grade children as well as the specific interest of each child in the class. The Indian week project, which was the culmination of all the preparation, was an idea proposed by the children. And as the students read and prepared, they were constantly expanding their backgrounds.

But there is more to comprehension than just interest, motivation, and background. In the episode above, the students were actively thinking about the information they were reading. They looked for facts and details, such as a list of foods or the Indian sign language. They often had to infer what was not specifically stated. They had to evaluate the ideas they read. They had to discover cause-and-effect relationships (why the Indians needed a sign language), sequence (the steps in making cornbread), and comparison (how did one tribe dress or travel compared to other tribes). Each child was engaged in reasoning while trying to achieve a specific purpose.

An unobservable phenomenon.   Active reasoning is obviously a mental process, and it cannot be observed as a child reads. Despite the fact that the process cannot be directly observed, though, reasoning is the key to reading comprehension. The results of active reasoning can, however, be examined. For example, a child who has been mentally processing the steps in making cornbread as he or she has been reading will be able to describe those steps when the reading is completed (or as each step in the process is ascertained).

If a child is to be an active reasoner, there must be a purpose for reading, there must be interest in the subject matter to be read, and there must be an adequate background of experiences to read about a particular topic. But, in addition, you need to guide each child to follow the author's organization and ideas. You need to foster the development of readers who not only have a purpose for reading but who actively hypothesize, verify, and react to ideas as they are reading.

Reading
as
Reasoning

" 'A good reader is a good cheater.' " This statement begins a chapter on reading by two well-known researchers (Levin and Kaplan, 1970). The point Levin and Kaplan were hoping to make with that statement, and which they go on to explain further, is that good readers sample the elements in a book. Good readers, they state, do not read every letter, syllable, word, or phrase; instead, they select "clues to meaning." But how do "good readers" know what to sample? What guides their reading? The answer, of course, is reasoning.

A reader engaged in active reasoning while reading "continually assigns tentative interpretations to a text or message and checks those interpretations. As the material is grammatically or semantically constrained he is able to formulate correct hypotheses about what will come next. When the prediction is confirmed, the material covered by that prediction can be more easily processed and understood. (p. 132)

Reasoning depends on purpose. As we discussed earlier in this chapter, there is no listing of comprehension skills that should be taught to every child. The guide to developing reasoning is not, therefore, the teaching of specific skills but rather to lead a child to think about the ideas being read based on the child's purpose for reading. Suppose, for example, a child is reading about how Indians made bows and arrows, and discussion has established that the child is eager to learn all about making a bow and arrow. That very valid purpose for reading should lead the child to think about the details and the sequence of steps in making a bow and arrows, so that when he or she has finished reading, his or her comprehension will reflect an understanding of what is entailed. Or, on another topic, if several children are reading a selection about Mexico because they are interested in taking a trip to Mexico or because they are excited that a new child from Mexico is joining the class, they will be eager to learn all they can about that country; and the opportunity to teach attention to detail within a specific setting should be very real.

There are three important points to consider in teaching reasoning while reading. First, as we have just discussed, there is no absolute list of comprehension skills, so nobody can tell you what and when to teach. Second, there are types of reasoning that you can be familiar with. And third, by previewing stories and books, you can decide what types can be highlighted according to a child's purpose for reading them.

Types of Reasoning in Reading Comprehension

Even though there is no discrete listing of comprehension skills, it is important to help young readers follow the organization and ideas in stories and books. For example, in the Indian project some students were reading to determine facts and details while others were reading to determine sequence. The usual listing of comprehension skills is a mixture of thinking and writing techniques. For want of a better term, we shall call them types of reasoning that the reader engages in based on his or her particular purpose for reading.

While the breakdown of reasoning into types is arbitrary (in a very real sense, the reader focuses on his or her individual purpose and not on a type of reasoning), there are three major types of reasoning that you can promote with your students. The first of these is reading to identify and remember facts and details. The second is reading to understand main ideas and generalizations. And the third is reading to understand

the relationships between ideas by using such techniques as sequence and enumeration, cause and effect, and comparison and contrast.

In addition to these three types of reasoning, the information to be obtained may be specifically stated by the author; it may need to be inferred or deduced by the reader from what the author states; or it may need to be critically evaluated by the reader. The Indian project provides numerous examples of the three ways information was related to the reader's purpose (types of food that were specifically stated, reasons for sign language that had to be inferred, and the authenticity of facts to be evaluated).

You may logically ask: But which of these types should I teach? And when? The answer depends primarily on the reader's purpose and secondarily on the organization of the reading materials. In general, recognizing facts or details and building these into main ideas is constant in most reading. Beyond this, the particular reading materials you use and the reader's purpose determine which of the other types you can teach. If a selection uses some form of sequence, it provides the opportunity to emphasize sequence. You will, of course, have some control over the selection of reading materials and may be able to pick stories that are organized in specific ways so that you can emphasize the reasoning related to a child's specific purpose. You will also have the chance to focus on certain types of reasoning within a selection and to ignore others, if necessary, in order to focus on the ones you want to stress and the ones that relate to a child's needs, interests, and purpose for reading.

Identifying and Remembering Facts and Details

Identifying facts and details is done because a reader needs the information for some specific purpose. In addition, facts and details are also needed to develop major ideas and generalizations.

Following directions.   Following directions is an obvious instance when a child needs to identify and remember facts and details. You can help a child with this task by giving him or her categories for remembering information. For example, "materials I need to do this," "things to watch for," "how to use the results," and so on. Categories such as these will both focus the child's reasoning and provide a means for the child to make mental or written notes to remember the information.

Reporting facts and details.   Many times children want to share what they have read. You can encourage a child to consider several means for sharing before he or she begins reading. For example, the child could draw a picture of a story event or characters, or a map depicting a story setting. The child could make models of story characters out of clay or other materials. If a child considers how to share what he or she is reading before beginning, the child will be more apt to identify and remember important details that are worth sharing.

Children often become intrigued with the idea of writing a class newspaper. This is an excellent project to focus children's attention on facts and details, not only in reading stories that children have written for the newspaper, but also in writing and reporting the news.

Validating and supporting ideas.   A very common need that any reader has is to validate his or her ideas. Sometimes this involves going to a reference source such as an encyclopedia or dictionary to identify relevant information. Other times it may mean reading to verify a hypothesis or rereading to find supporting information.

In addition, you can use questioning as one strategy. In a later section in this chapter (pages 293–303), there are a number of suggestions related to questioning as a technique to promote comprehension. The questioning technique is best if it is used sparingly by the teacher, and usually only as a stimulus to discusson. Questions like "How do you know that?" "Are you sure of that?" "What makes you think that?" all may promote discussion and emphasize identifying the facts and details to support ideas.

Categorizing facts and details.   There are times when a child might be reading to find out what it might be like to live in the jungle, a big city, or some future century. When reading for such a purpose, you can help a child to identify facts and details by providing one or two categories for noting the information. The child can provide other categories. For example, you might suggest housing or food as categories. The child might add others—categories will certainly need to be added during the time the child is reading. The child then reads to identify the facts and details in each of the categories—as well as reading to determine if the categories are useful.

Defining descriptive words.   One boy told his teacher that he really liked a particular character in a story. The teacher asked why and the boy replied that the character was "neat." "What do you mean by 'neat,'" asked the teacher? The boy responded that "neat" meant "cool." The teacher said she wasn't really sure what that meant and the boy said, "Here, let me show you in the story." And the boy pointed out numerous adjectives, descriptive phrases, and incidents that described the character. This teacher often used this technique to get her children to identify the facts and details that described not only story characters but story settings and incidents as well.

Together with the children you can develop numerous games that they can play to help them identify facts and details. For example, riddle-type games focus on facts and details. Pantomime or charades focuses on details when a child has to act out the details on a printed card. Also useful are quiz games; in these the children divide into teams and challenge each other with fact and detail questions about stories they have read.

Summary.   Identifying and remembering facts and details serves a number of important purposes for reading. The facts or details may be specifically stated or they may be inferred, and often their relevance or validity needs to be evaluated. In getting a child to focus on facts and details remember that there must be a reader purpose for which the facts and details are needed. In addition, the reader needs some organizational schema to which to relate the facts and details; this schema should develop from the reader's purpose for reading.

Main Ideas and Generalizations

It is difficult to define the difference between a main idea or generalization and a fact or detail. Certainly a fact can be a main idea, and what may be a generalization in one story may be an isolated detail in another story. The definition of each seems, therefore, to be dependent on the relationship of particular information to other information in a story or article. For example, if one article is about elephants, the fact that an elephant has a trunk is only one fact related to the development of the generalization about what an elephant looks like. On the other hand, another article may have as the main idea that an elephant's trunk is very useful; the facts and details in this second article are the ways an elephant uses his trunk.

Thus, the definitions of facts and details as contrasted with main ideas and generalizations are as follows: in a particular story or article facts or details are isolated bits of information; main ideas and generalizations are collections of facts and details.

It is, however, the reader's purpose and not our definitions that dictate instructional strategies. When a child is reading to "find out what this is all about," he or she is reading for a main idea or generalization.

Main ideas and generalizations evolve.   A child needs to learn that main ideas and generalizations develop from facts and details. You can encourage this learning when you read to your students and talk with them about the story characters, the story setting, and the events in a story. Structure your discussions so that a child identifies the facts and details that give rise to main ideas and generalizations or vice versa.

When a child is reading on his or her own, provide many opportunities for the child to tell you—and others—what the story is about, what the story means to the child, what the child would have done in a similar situation, and so on. This can easily happen if you allow a child to talk about the stories he or she is reading. It is the best way to promote thinking about main ideas and generalizations.

Character development.   Children often become very interested in the characters they are reading about. After they are finished reading, they might want to act out roles for these characters. Puppets and role playing are useful ways to let children portray the characters they have been reading about. One way you can encourage a child to generalize about a story character is to ask the child how he or she thinks a particular character would have reacted in a particular situation. Better yet, let the child act it out.

Moods and settings.   Sometimes a child is reading to find out what it would be like to live in a particular place. Asking the child to suggest one word that would describe a place is a useful technique to see if the child has captured the generalization. Or ask the child to decide which of several adjectives best described the story setting. If more than one child reads the same story, and they each arrive at different adjective choices when they are finished reading, you might ask each child what facts in the story led to his or her particular choice.

Describing events.   Perhaps the most common reasons for reading a story are, or should be, for enjoyment and to "find out what happened." There are numerous ways to help a child to think about the events in a story. The most direct method is to merely let an enthusiastic child tell what happened when he or she is bubbling over with excitement. At such times you can suggest several means through which the child can share this excitement. Art work, drama, and even music activities are useful ways to let a child describe an event in a story to others.

Summary.   Main ideas and generalizations are defined by the relationship of various pieces of information to the rest of the information in a story or article. Main ideas and generalizations often need to be inferred by the reader from what the writer has written. You should help a child to think about main ideas and generalizations as he or she is reading. Allow the child to freely discuss what is being read. Provide the child with opportunities to report, show, and demonstrate the things he or she has been reading about. And you should *never ask* what the "main idea" of a story or paragraph is—rather, you might discuss with a child what he or she would have done in the same situation as the story characters, or how the child felt when a certain event occurred; such questions should deal with the child's interests and should focus on the main idea. When you ask a child for the main idea, the child will attempt to figure out what you mean by the "main idea." Rather than reading for his or her purpose, your question will have focused the child's attention on your purpose.

Understanding Relationships

When a reader reads to understand the relationships among facts, main ideas, and generalizations, he or she is searching for an overall organization of the material. The ability to identify the relationships between ideas is not necessarily dependent upon initially recognizing the facts. Sometimes the relationships between generalizations help the reader to understand the facts or details more fully. The reader's purpose will determine the way in which reasoning will occur.

Sequence and enumeration.   It is often important to a reader to know the sequence of events in a story or an article. Certainly this is true in a mystery story or an article on how to make or do something. It is certainly true when a reader is following a sequence of events to determine how a story character got into a particular predicament. In fact, most stories have a chronology of events that is important to an understanding of the story.

Authors alert readers to a sequence in a variety of ways. In writing directions, an author may number the steps. Or the author may indent each new step and indicate it with some special typographical marking, such as a large dot before each step. In stories, the reader is alerted to sequence through words and phrases such as *next, first, a few days later, it wasn't long before, before that happened,* and so on. And while the number of such words and phrases is extensive, they are usually part of a child's spoken vocabulary. If they aren't, you can use some of the suggestions in Chapter 3 (pages 138–40) for teaching the vocabulary of sequence.

There are numerous ways you can help a child to focus on the sequence of events in a story or article. For example, activity or learning centers usually include directions for making or doing things. If you print the directions on a sheet of tagboard, you can ask the child to review the steps when he or she has difficulty.

Another activity stems from the fact that children always enjoy illustrating favorite events in a story. When a child has drawn pictures that depict several events in a story, you can suggest a game in which the pictures have to be placed in the order that they occurred. Children often enjoy developing a similar game by cutting apart favorite comic strips and then challenging the other students to put them in a logical order—which can be indicated on the reverse side.

One activity that many children enjoy is acting out story events. When several children have read the same story, they may be eager to dramatize favorite scenes. Several children present these scenes in a sequence that does not follow the story, and then the other children in the class can be asked which event came first.

Keeping a diary for a favorite story character also focuses attention on sequence. The diary could be for a single day, for a week, or more. The diary of events in a mystery story is certainly important to solving the mystery. When a child is reading a mystery, you might suggest that he or she jot down the events that occur during specified time periods so the mystery can be solved.

When a child is telling you about a recently read story, you can help the child to focus on the sequence by asking questions. For example, "What happened next?" "What might have happened if Bill forgot to do that?" "Was it important that things happened in exactly that order?" "What would have happened if something else didn't happen first?" Through such discussion and questions you are not only able to focus the reader's attention on the sequence but also able to review the sequence of events critically. And based on this questioning technique, one teacher developed a game with her students to help them focus on sequence. The game was called "If It Didn't Happen Like That." For this game, one of the children picks a topic, such as building things. The children then tell what would happen if the usual steps in building something weren't followed. For example, what would happen if the top floor of a building were built first? Of course the game can get quite silly. The children in this class often play the game using stories they have read as the topic. The children have a great time twisting around the events and coming up with unusual conclusions.

Cause and effect. Causal relationships are, in themselves, a kind of sequence with a cause, its effect, and that effect in turn becoming the cause of still another effect. In teaching this aspect of comprehension, the teacher's aim with elementary children is merely to make them aware that frequently one event does not just follow another, but rather that it may stem from a previous event(s) or condition(s).

As young readers become aware of this kind of relationship, their reasoning leads them to look back from an action for its cause. As they mature as readers, this will become an important discriminating skill—particularly when reading nonfiction in which an argument may be based on a false causal relationship. Readers can trace the causal relationship—often only suggested by the author—and check the validity of the cause and effect suggested against their own experience and knowledge. A suspicion that the causal chain suggested may not be valid can lead mature readers to additional reading for verification or confirmation.

At the elementary level, the teacher can prime this alertness to causal logic with various kinds of questioning, for besides often being related to the action line of a story, cause-and-effect relationships are an important tool for analyzing character—the structural aspect most relevant to many young readers. Probably the most important question a teacher can ask to focus on cause and effect is, "Why?" "Why do you think the story character did that?" "Why did that happen?" "Why do you think that didn't happen?"

Many of the same activities for developing attention to sequence are also useful for developing attention to cause and effect. For example, a child might want to draw a series of two-panel drawings in which the first panel is the cause and the second is the effect. Another interesting activity is to ask a child to tell what he or she would have to change in a story to make it come out differently. This should focus the child's attention on causal events in the story that would need to be altered.

Also a kind of charades game can be played with cause-and-effect relationships in a story. One group of children can act out an effect in a story and challenge other students to act out the causes of the event.

One often-used technique when a group of children are reading the same story is to ask them to read silently up to a particular point and then to guess what happens next before reading on. To give reasonable answers the children obviously infer the effect of the events that have occurred thus far in the story. This technique can also be used even before a child starts reading a story. He or she can be asked to read the story title and examine the picture on the title page; from these the child can infer what happens in the story. The child's reading of the story then becomes an active process of reasoning as he or she checks this hypothesis against the real cause-and-effect relationship in the story.

Being alert to a child's critical evaluation of a cause-and-effect relationship is important. Suppose a child responds to a story event by saying "That was a dumb thing to do." You now have an excellent opportunity to ask the child to tell why. Often the child will respond by citing a too weak cause for a behavior—or an alternative behavior for the cause.

Sometimes the omission of a cause from a story creates a mystery that can provoke very interesting discussion—discussion that is based both on reading the story and on the experience of the children. For example, the teacher might ask, "Why do you suppose such and such happened?" "Have you known anyone who did that?" "What do you think made the person you knew do that?" "Have you ever done anything like that?" "What made you do it?" In this instance, once again, literal questions have helped in dealing with causal experience. After the young reader has followed this type of cause-and-effect reasoning with the teacher's encouragement, the child should eventually develop the habit of asking himself or herself such questions.

Comparison and contrast.   In comparison, the similarities between two or more things or ideas are pointed out. And in contrast, differences are pointed out.

A child uses comparison and contrast naturally when he or she tries to grasp and understand ideas. "You mean a fish just like my goldfish?" "Is a school of fish like our school?" "I've been on a boat before—but it had a motor." Questions and comments like these are typical of a child's reaction to ideas. The child compares and contrasts those "new" things he or she hears or reads about with those things that are well known to the child. This natural tendency for children to use comparison and contrast can be used in helping children to understand an author's use of comparison-and-contrast relationships.

When making a list of ways in which two story characters are alike or different, or when making a list of the ways in which a story setting is the same or different from a child's own, focus attention on comparison and contrast. In addition, drawings, which often allow a child to indicate even subtle differences, can be used instead of lists.

Similes and metaphors are, of course, comparisons that authors use even in beginning reading. While there need be no attempt to teach a child what the words *simile* and *metaphor* mean, you can create games that focus on the use of them. For example, "The author says that Bill was angry as a bear. Can you think of some other things that might describe how Bill felt? Bill was as angry as a _____ . Suppose losing the game because of Larry's error had made Bill sad. What could you compare his feeling to in order to describe it? Sadness surrounded Bill like a _____ ." Questions like these can lead to interesting discussions about real-life characters. Children also enjoy drawing pictures of, for example, Bill, who was "angry as a bear." In fact, a game can be played with these drawings; the children illustrate phrases such as, "How is a certain character like an airplane?" or "How is another character like a flower?" Most children enjoy these games and like to try to trick each other—and especially the teacher—with very obscure similarities. Even though the similarities are obscure—and the contrast great—the children are exercising their reasoning powers with comparison and contrast.

Some children enjoy reading stories about similar types of characters such as cowboys, sports heroes, or detectives. Comparing and contrasting the characters in such stories through drama, drawing, and discussion heightens a child's understanding of the characters being read about.

Third Dimension: Assimilating Reading

The third dimension of reading comprehension occurs when a child assimilates, uses, or shares what has been read. Any time a child reads for a purpose, and is actively reasoning while reading, the third dimension of reading comprehension is a natural outcome. Indeed, a continuation of active reasoning is the essence of this phase. The reader assimilates what is read by incorporating it as a part of his or her experience and background. A reader learns from what is read: perspectives are broadened, concepts are expanded or modified, reactions are experienced.

But what a reader learns is not always observable. He or she may mull over the plight of a character, think about personal experiences to try to develop a solution to the problem without ever commenting or demonstrating to the teacher that this kind of reaction to reading has taken place. At other times, it is easy to tell when a reader has interacted purposefully with print. For example, a child who finishes reading a biography of a baseball hero may write to the player asking some unanswered questions; or, readers may prepare a recipe, build a birdhouse, or set up an experiment. These observable responses to print will be discussed throughout this section. These responses range from problem-solving discussions that help readers to assimilate themes, ideas, and events, to the more active demonstrations of reaction—drama, puppets, art, music, movement, and creative writing. Simply stated, the third dimension could be described as:

I have read with understanding. The reading has prompted me to think further. I am acting on my thinking.

Classrooms are full of examples of children busily developing and extending their reading comprehension. Students who have had their interests aroused by a classroom topic of investigation read widely in that area and plan to share their reading with others. That preparation for sharing involves students even further in their reading and helps to strengthen their understanding. For example, in one classroom we found several students planning an African safari. These children used the library to make lists of necessary gear, to draw and find pictures of the animals they might see on their trip, and to determine and trace their intended route. Meantime, they listened to the teacher read African folklore, and they wrote imaginary postcards and letters to their relatives back home. These activities stemmed from reading and generated further reading. In another classroom, a child searched the school library for a record to provide appropriate background music for an adventure story she had read and which she planned to share with her class. She had drawn a series of pictures that, along with the music, would help the listeners to understand and enjoy the story. In yet another classroom we visited, there was an activity center where children could pursue hobbies such as macramé, origami, and pipe cleaner sculpture. "How-to" books on each of these hobbies as well as the materials for making things were included in the center.

Activities such as the ones described above will exist in classrooms where the children's interests and purposes lead to reading; because the reading is for a purpose, children have a clearer notion about how to put that purpose into action. In addition, instruction that encourages children to act upon their reading provides both a purpose for reading and an incentive for the development of ideas.

As you have already discovered, the first dimension is facilitated by ensuring that the child has adequate introduction to the reading, that the reader and author have some common background and concepts, and that the reader has asked a purpose-setting question(s)—that is, has a purpose for reading. In the second dimension, the teacher helps the reader to think about what he or she is reading both by asking pertinent questions and by encouraging the student to make observations that connect the known with the uncertain.

And in the third dimension, by knowing each reader and some of his or her reading and listening experiences, the teacher can help readers pull together common threads, help them to see the relationships among characters and events, and provide each child with an arena in which he or she can react to the material. In this reaction the child's experience becomes an important part of the synthesis. Teachers can act as catalysts by asking insightful questions, by noting inconsistencies in text or illustration when children fail to notice them, by calling up similarities between characters and events in what is being read now and what has been read before, and by encouraging and reinforcing children's observations.

Extending and Expanding Comprehension

In order to get children involved in extending their comprehension, it is necessary to build on their active reasoning. Children of all ages are inquisitive, critical, and perceptive. The following examples are brief teacher-child interactions that are apt to occur in any classroom. These are the kinds of classroom incidents that encourage thinking and discussion of what is read. These examples illustrate reactions to print and teachers' encouragement of thinking.

A *four-year-old* listening to and following the pictures of *The Night Before Christmas*:*

> Child: But how will those children get to their presents in the morning? There aren't any stairs in that house.

Kindergarteners responding to a teacher's questions about *Sylvester and the Magic Pebble*:†

> First child: I don't think this story could really happen, because Sylvester couldn't really turn into a rock. Other things, too. Like his mother wore a dress and they sat in chairs, but they were donkeys.
> Teacher: But some of this story felt real to me. I could almost think that Sylvester was a boy.
> First child: Yeah, because he was lonely and missed his mama and. . .
> Teacher: And. . . ?
> First child: And they loved him and wished hard he'd come back.
> Second child: And because wishes *do* come true sometimes.
> Third child: I have a book about *Three Wishes* at home.
> Second child: You mean about that magic stone and that sausage? Whoo-ee, that's funny!
> Teacher: I know the story, too. If you will bring the book, I'll read it and we'll find out about more wishes that came true.

Second grader reading *Where the Wild Things Are*:‡

> Child: You know why I think Max turned into a wild thing?
> Teacher: Why?
> Child: Because he had to play in his mind.

* Clement C. Moore, *The Night Before Christmas*, illustrated by Gyo Fujikawa (New York: Grosset & Dunlap, 1961).

† William Steig, *Sylvester and the Magic Pebble* (New York: Young Readers Press, 1969).

‡ Maurice Sendak, *Where the Wild Things Are* (New York: Harper & Row, 1963).

Teacher: Why do you say that?

Child: Because he was bad and got sent to his room, and there isn't anything in that room *to do*. You'd *have* to imagine.

Teacher: Maybe that's not his room. Maybe it's a grown-up's room.

Child: Nope. Look right here. (points and reads) "in Max's room."

Third graders discussing *Abraham Lincoln:**

Teacher: And who wrote this book?

First child: The d'Aulaires. They wrote that book about *Trolls* you read us, too.

Teacher: Right. But how do you suppose they learned so much about Lincoln?

Second child: They looked him up in the encyclopedia!

Teacher: Any other way?

Third child: They read other books.

Teacher: Yes?

Fourth child: They asked people who knew him.

Second child: Hey, man, that was over a hundred years ago. All the people who knew Lincoln are dead by now.

Fourth child: But the people could tell their children.

Fifth graders after watching and discussing a story of Wilma Rudolph on television:

Teacher: It seems to me that other young athletes have overcome real setbacks before they earned fame.

First child: Who else?

Second child: Like who?

Teacher: Well, it just happens that I have several of their stories in front of me. Let me tell you a little about each; then you decide if you'd like to know more about some other real-life heroes and heroines.

There are specific guidelines you can follow to make use of these naturally occurring incidents. By following these you will be encouraging children to extend their reading:

Know the children you are teaching as well as possible; know their interests and needs, their backgrounds, strengths, and limitations so that you can guide them to books that will have real meaning in their lives.

Be as familiar with as many children's books as possible so you know how to match children with books. Keep abreast of the many good trade books available.

Read frequently to your children from books that are or may be of interest to them.

* Ingri and Edgar d'Aulaire, *Abraham Lincoln* (Garden City, N.Y.: Doubleday, 1957).

Develop a file of poetry to fit many moods and situations that might develop in your classroom or for your children. Introduce the poems when they are appropriate and encourage the children to express their reactions to the poems—particularly their emotional or personal feelings and reactions.

Make as many books as possible available to your children: tap school and city libraries, build a class library, and use a lot of paperbacks. Take the children on tours of local book stores and, of course, libraries.

Use book clubs or groups that come together to discuss their common reading to broaden your children's interests.

Exploit the vast exposure to mass media that most children have. Rather than your looking on television as a competitor for children's time, encourage them to discuss what they see there in order to uncover their interests. Follow through on the interests developed by mass media and uncovered in discussion by directing the children to books that expand on those interests.

React to reading through various outlets: paint the mood of a story; dance or move to a character's gait; write a spinoff story with different events.

Becoming Familiar with Children's Literature

Arbuthnot, May Hill. *Children's Reading in the Home*. Glenview, Ill.: Scott, Foresman, 1969.

Arbuthnot, May Hill, and Root, Shelton L., Jr. *Time for Poetry*. 3d ed. Glenview, Ill.: Scott, Foresman, 1968.

Belloc, Hillaire. *The Bad Child's Book of Beasts*. New York: Alfred A. Knopf, 1965.

Carlson, Ruth K., ed. *Folklore and Folktale Around the World*. Newark, Del.: International Reading Association, 1972.

Eakin, Mary K., ed. *Good Books for Children*. Chicago: University of Chicago Press, 1966.

Huck, Charlotte S., and Kuhn, Doris Young. *Children's Literature in the Elementary School*. New York: Holt, Rinehart and Winston, 1968.

Johnson, Edna; Sickels, Evelyn R.; and Sayers, Frances Clarke, eds. *Anthology of Children's Literature*. 4th ed. Boston: Houghton Mifflin, 1970.

Purdy, Susan. *Books for You to Make*. Philadelphia: Lippincott, 1973.

Sebesta, Sam Leaton, and Iverson, William J. *Literature for Thursday's Child*. Chicago: Science Research Associates, 1975.

Sutherland, Zena, ed. *The Best in Chldren's Books*. Chicago: University of Chicago Press, 1973.

Activities for Extending Comprehension

When children share stories, books, and information with others, they increase their understanding. In addition, they are motivated to interest others in experiencing what they have read. The categories of extending behaviors that we will discuss are creative dramatics, story time, writing, arts and crafts, and music and poetry.

Creative dramatics. Differing from formal dramatics in its spontaneity, its independence from props or costumes, and its flexibility, creative dramatics requires less class time per production. When children first play in make-believe land, their spontaneity is reminiscent of creative dramatics. And if you use activities throughout the school day to provide children with opportunities to pretend and to dramatize events informally, you will make an author's words come alive with a new perspective. Nursery rhymes are often the first reading to be enacted. This need not be done formally or even in front of an audience; these tales can be acted at will.

Next, the children add speech to their enactment of rhymes or old tales—not the speech of texts but the language of the rhyme or story as they remember its spirit. For example, Debbie, an extremely shy child, was the smallest, quietest girl in the whole school. For a long time, her teacher wasn't sure what Debbie could do because she *wouldn't* do anything. Then the day came to dramatize a story a group had read, retold, and illustrated. The teacher knew that there were parts for four children. "Who wants to be Papa Bear?" "Who wants to be Mama Bear?" "Who wants to be Baby Bear?" Three parts offered and accepted. "Debbie," the teacher asked softly, "what part would you like?" Only the role of Goldilocks was left.

It only took the child a minute to decide. "The bowl," came the answer. Thus, the teacher learned that it was still too soon to ask Debbie to use words in her dramatization! Some time later, when Debbie was finally ready to try spontaneous language with her drama, a group had decided to play "Billy Goats Gruff." The part of the troll was grabbed up by the most extroverted boy. Two girls chose the brothers number one and two. All that was left this time was the part of the youngest Billy Goat Gruff—which the teacher offered to Debbie, who accepted. They rigged up a chair bridge; the troll crept underneath, and Debbie started her "trip-trip" process. "WHO'S THAT GOING ACROSS MY BRIDGE?" came the booming voice of the old troll. Nothing from Debbie. "WHO'S THAT GOING ACROSS MY BRIDGE?" he called louder. Nothing from Debbie. "Debbie," the teacher stage-whispered, "Who ARE you?" "Oh," said Debbie; and leaning far over her chair-bridge, she called: "Who ARE you?" It takes some children—especially those who are extremely shy or self-conscious—months to respond totally. Patience and knowledge of your children will certainly help.

Once children have generated interest and decided on the story, fable, or rhyme to be dramatized, they may need to discuss which part of the room they will use, the sequence of events they will play out, the number of scenes, the number of characters, and the movements. Many of the stories children already love lend themselves to dramatization: For example, scenes from the lives of Tom Sawyer, Robin Hood, Caddie Woodlawn, Homer Price, Rapunzel, or Ferdinand the Bull.

Dramatizing stories involves children completely in their ideas and actions. Children who know that they will dramatize a story seem to read or listen much more intently to the flow of events, the range of feelings, and the development of characters. When they know they will have the opportunity to act out the story, children read with purpose: "I'll read to find out who (or what) I want to be." "I'll read to find out how much space or what characters we'll need."

Dramatizing works well with all age groups and reading levels as well as with many different story types—from high action to make-believe to the improvised conversations of characters.

You should stay alert for stories that lend themselves to dramatization, and soon children will recognize them and suggest dramatics. The kind of dramatization most suitable for sharing reading won't require formally learned lines, elaborate sets, or home-sewn costumes. It will mean the spontaneous acting-out of stories through play.

If you are using dramatization for the first time, you may feel ill at ease with the spontaneity of movement and language that is a part of creative dramatics. Sometimes it helps to start small. For example, have two children make up an interview between the major character and an on-the-street reporter; encourage several children to organize a puppet play of just one scene (paper bag puppets are easy to make and are as effective as more elaborate puppets); help a child who has read an exciting story to make up a radio commercial plugging the upcoming show (story), giving carefully chosen hints as to its excitement and appeal; suggest that, after reading a story, the children make up and tape-record divergent story endings.

A good introductory text on creative dramatics in the classroom may also provide the confidence you need to let children create.* If you feel comfortable with the situation, you can take part with the children in any of these dramatizations. Children are rarely inhibited for long from taking part in dramatics; the younger they are and the earlier they start to dramatize, the more involved they get. Little ones wriggle through the garden like the caterpillar in Eric Carlson's *The Very Hungry Caterpillar*, eating everything in sight, until at last with much reaching, pushing, stretching, fanning, and waving, they too, become butterflies.

Primary children love to dramatize favorite folk and fairytales. Each child, of course, responds in varied ways to drama, but the most frequent response is: "Can we do this again?" Young children don't have to be

* One such text is: Ruth Beall Heinig and Lyda Stillwell, *Dramatics for the Classroom Teacher* (Englewood Cliffs, N.J.: Prentice-Hall, 1974).

taught how to be the straws that the princess must spin to gold; they just jump through the spinning wheel. The younger children can be leaves, as easily as they can be one of the cats in *Millions of Cats,* by Wanda Gag.

Upper-level students also find expressive outlets in drama. They need only be convinced of the receptive environment, the fact that everyone is involved sooner or later, and the active nature of dramatics. The more they come to appreciate dramatics as a means for sharing reading, the more deeply and widely they read.

There are other ways as well to get children involved with the ideas and events they have read about. Tell the children that a make-believe time machine will take them into the past and the future; they must improvise the conversation and the actions of the story characters they have just read about—for example, Pocahontas and Captain John Smith, the interactions of the first human on Pluto and the creature that is found there, and so on. Allow several children to develop and act out a new ending to a story. Take characters from different stories and have the children play, "What if _____ met _____?"

Puppetry, too, provides an outlet for sharing reading, interpreting stories, and for encouraging involvement with books. Simple puppets are a joy to all children. They especially help the shy child to project feelings and to extend verbal experiences. Activities with puppets spark language expression, broaden understanding, deepen feelings and emotions, and develop empathy with the story's characters.

Puppets can be formed in a variety of ways.* The easiest to make is probably the stick puppet, which is made from an ice cream stick or a tongue depressor with the figure drawn on or pasted to the end. Paperbag puppets are easy, too. Sometimes the fold of the bag's end serves as the mouth, so simply flopping the fold produces animation as needed. Other simple puppets are made from paper-towel rolls, spoons, clothespins, or boxes. Some puppets are made from *papier-maché* carefully wrapped around balloons or lightbulbs to make heads. When the *papier-maché* dries, the balloons or lightbulbs are broken and clothing is designed to suit the face that is painted on.

You can make puppets from carrots, potatoes, beets, radishes, apples, and oranges. Faces are cut with a vegetable peeler or you can use cut paper and thumbtacks to make interesting and unusual features. As puppet-making skills increase, try to make sock-puppet characters, stuffed paper-bag puppets on sticks, individual finger puppets, or puppet faces on the fingers of white cotton work gloves.

You don't really need a formal stage; a large packing box with a big hole cut in the top works very well. When a child can have a puppet do the talking while he or she is hidden behind a refrigerator box, the child feels less inhibited in oral expression. Primary-aged children make and use puppets to act out favorite stories and then to make up new stories; older children make and use puppets to share stories with younger children, as stimuli for creative writing, and for helping each other to more fully understand historical events or specific problem-solving episodes.

"How-to" books on puppet-making and puppetry are plentiful. Making puppets, acting out stories with puppets, and writing down stories that are spontaneously enacted can extend and enliven reading for children.

Another drama-related technique for encouraging the creativity of children is pantomime. Pantomime can be one of the earliest forms of creative dramatics. One variation on the pantomiming technique is having a child act out the story while others describe the action. Another is to allow free interpretation of favorite story parts.

Children who are reticent about talking when they first come to school can begin to communicate orally by first moving expressively. Pantomime is expression; it is imitation. Your children are naturally immersed in imitative behavior in living—so it's easy for them to play at driving a car, shopping for groceries, repairing something, or finding the proper television channel. Have them get their whole bodies involved in pantomime by suggesting that they imitate defined movements, such as a rag doll, a tin soldier, a runaway horse, an angry dog, a dish of jello, or a monster (Petty et al., 1973). They will also mime the action in a story or a portion of a story. Others guess the scene or the interaction that is being shared.

---

* Puppets differ from marionettes in that the marionette is usually operated by hand from above.

Story time. We have repeatedly emphasized the importance of reading to children daily. No other event in the day so richly underscores the teacher's own attitude toward books. When the teacher shares the adventures and excitement that books provide, when the characters help students to see that their own feelings aren't so unusual after all, when the exchange of reactions is a part of reading, the payoff is an interest in reading.

In a study designed to rate the quality of teachers' efforts to read aloud to children, the following factors substantially contributed to good oral reading (Lamme, 1976):

(1) Children were characters in the story being read.
(2) There was a good deal of eye contact between reader and listener.
(3) The reader's voice expressed the moods and nuances of the story.
(4) The reader's voice had a pleasing tone and pitch.
(5) The reader was familiar with the story.
(6) The story being read was appropriate to the level and interest of the listeners.
(7) The reader could be seen and heard by all the listeners.
(8) The reader highlighted or emphasized unusual vocabulary or such features as rhythm or rhyme.

Sometimes the book may get in the way of sharing a story. In that case, put the book aside so that the story may be told. Some teachers of young children tell stories with finger plays, or flannel boards, and by using a story rolled through a cardboard-carton television set. Or stories can be accompanied by silhouette cut-out figures moving on a screen while the storyteller moves the figures on the lighted surface of an overhead projector.

Some Books about Storytelling

Jacobs, Leland B., ed. *Using Literature with Young Children*. New York: Teachers College Press, Columbia University, 1965.
Sawyer, Ruth. *The Way of the Storyteller*. New York: Viking, 1975.
Tooze, Ruth. *Storytelling*. Englewood Cliffs, N.J.: Prentice-Hall, 1959.
Wagner, Joseph. *Children's Literature Through Storytelling*. Dubuque, Iowa: Wm. C. Brown, 1970.

The teacher who knows the story very well and enjoys it thoroughly is more likely to tell it well. When the author's language is so masterful, however, that using different words in telling the story might detract from it, the teacher should read it well. Both the teacher's reading and telling of stories show children how favorite books can be shared.

These suggestions for story sharing can be used to tell children stories and to pique their interest in reading. Children can also use these techniques to share books and stories with you and with the other children.

Ask a child to try to sell a book or story to others in the class. Sales success is determined by how many other children decide to read the book. The salesperson can emphasize the exciting parts, describe certain events, lead up to a climax but not reveal the result, or describe an unusual character in the story.

If you or a child can sketch scenes or characters on the chalkboard as you describe them to others, you can increase interest in the story and enhance comprehension. You don't need to be an exceptional artist to sketch as you tell a story. Your listeners' imaginations will complete the pictures for you.

Have the children develop maps that trace a route in a story. Adding landmarks and notes to the maps regarding certain events is useful when these maps are used to help a child share a story with others.

When a story centers on a certain location, such as a haunted mansion, children will be able to describe the story to others more easily if they build a model of the location or setting.

Have children who want to describe a story through pictures select from magazines pictures that help to depict the story. These can be mounted and used to share the story.

Writing.   The writing tasks that are too often attached to children's reading are preparing answers to questions, writing a story summary, or
preparing a written book report. The oft-reported outcome is that interest in both reading and writing wanes. It seems more logical to encourage writing by letting potential writers know that they have something
to say and that writing is another way to be heard.

Readers will write (or dictate so that someone else can write for
them) if their reading and language experiences are meaningful and if
their writing efforts find acceptance. Conversely, *writers will read* their
own thoughts and then the thoughts of others. When writing is viewed
as sharing ideas and reactions rather than as a time-filling exercise that
will be collected, marked, and graded, children will choose to write.

To encourage writing as an extension of that which is read, you may
want to provide children with:

personal journals in which they can record their reading, their reactions, and their ideas

a special writing area or center, stocked with paper of various sizes,
shapes, and colors; writing instruments (felt pens, chalk and black
paper, colored pencils, crayons); and materials for making and
binding books (cardboard, fabric, adhesive-backed paper). Tape
recorders for dictation and a typewriter for transcribing tapes are
bonus features.

opportunities to participate in the action of stories through talking, acting, and doing in order to use the language that is a part of the action; these opportunities should precede writing.

reasons to write that make sense to children. It is more meaningful, for example, to write a newspaper report of a story event and to put out the newspaper than to always write answers to comprehension questions. Have the children write a letter to the author, turn a story into a play, write a new ending, keep a diary as a story character would, or write under art work.

personal dictionaries or "recipe-size" file boxes that will house the words children ask for as they are writing.

Sometimes a teacher will spell out words that children ask for when they are writing and sometimes the teacher will say, "Look it up." Both ways appear to get in the way of the flow of thoughts and to interrupt the writing process. Some children respond well to the teacher's assurance that getting the word down in any spelling is fine for the first draft, because there will be plenty of time to produce a more perfect copy later if need be. Other children seem to skirt words they can say but can't spell, thus affecting their writing. A teacher equipped with a card pad and pen can keep the less secure children equipped with the words they ask for. In addition, the stockpile of word cards the children file will help the children in other reading and writing situations.

Sources for Language Arts Activities	These articles and texts are among many that may spark your own ideas for providing students with opportunities to read and write for better understanding:

Allen, Roach Van, and Allen, Claryce. *Language Experience Activities.* Boston: Houghton Mifflin, 1976.

Carlson, Ruth K. *Writing Aids through the Grades.* New York: Teachers College Press, Columbia University, 1970.

Hennings, Dorothy G., and Grant, Barbara M. *Content and Craft: Written Expression in the Elementary School.* Englewood Cliffs, N.J.: Prentice-Hall, 1973.

Moffett, James, and Wagner, Betty J. *Student-Centered Language Arts and Reading, K-13.* Boston: Houghton Mifflin, 1976.

Perron, Jack. "Beginning Writing: It's All in the Mind." *Language Arts* 53 (September 1976): 652–57.

Petty, Walter T., and Bowen, Mary. *Slithery Snakes and Other Aids to Children's Writing.* New York: Meredith, 1967.

Petty, Walter T.; Petty, Dorothy C.; Becking, Marjorie F., *Experiences in Language: Tools and Techniques for Language Arts Methods.* Boston: Allyn and Bacon, 1973.

Tiedt, Sidney W., and Tiedt, Iris M., *Language Arts Activities for the Classroom.* Boston: Allyn and Bacon, 1978.

Arts and crafts.   Sometimes the logical extension of reading is to react to the author's ideas by drawing, sculpting, and painting. Children can interpret stories visually while their thoughts about a story are still being sifted, as the act of creating may help the child deal with the detail, the characters, and the impact of the story much more fully. Often, too, extending reading with artistic expressions is an outlet through which children can be led to explain their creations clearly and then to write and to read other interpretations. An excellent way to encourage creative responses to reading is to permit the children to experience art.

Of course, not all literature lends itself equally well to every form of artistic expression, but the range of art mediums to choose for expressing story ideas is great. For example, children enjoy designing and making jackets for books they are reading. They also like painting murals and making illustrated timelines of story events. In addition, children can make paper-collage scenes from stories, clay figures of story characters, maps, dioramas, costumes, and mobiles.

It should be noted that the purpose of extending reading through art is the same as extending reading through any creative endeavor. It is to help the reader experience more fully and think more carefully (comprehend) about literature through sharing.

Music and poetry. The rhythm of language finds an outlet in both music and poetry. Often teachers want to show children that literature, music, poetry, art, dance, and dramatics are all related. Children under the guidance of such a teacher will dance stories; sing poems; write poetry based on prose; create, write, and read lyrics; and find infinite ways to express one form through another.

When possible, children should be permitted to listen to music in order to set the mood for a story. They can use the same musical selection to move to and interpret a story that has been read or listened to. Some children like to select or create music that will help others feel what they felt when reading. It is possible and delightful to create the "sounds" of a story, and music opens the door to further imagining and expression.

In addition, there are stories that have become more famous as songs and songs that have been written into stories—for example, Tom Glaser's *On Top of Spaghetti,* Robert Quackenbush's *She'll Be Comin' Round the Mountain,* and Peter Spier's *The Fox Went Out on a Chilly Night.* With these books, beginning readers can literally sing their way into reading.

Part of understanding poetry is feeling it, and creating music for the words of a poem will help the child feel the pulse the poet meant the words to have. Music can also call attention to rhyme in the poem. If children become aware of and sensitive to poetry, they may listen to and love poetry that is read to them, experiment with language to produce poetry, write or dictate poetic expressions, and share poetry with others. Poetry (set to music or not) is easy to introduce when a child is caught up in a story or event. And when it is not assigned, but arises from spontaneous appreciation of a shared reading experience, the enjoyment is heightened.

Summary. Initially, you might examine your students' reading materials and suggest ways in which the reader can show others what the book or story has provided. When several choices of expression are possible, you can demonstrate one method; the children will soon create their own outlets for expressing what they have read. Of course, not every book need be shared, nor must every story or book be followed by questions. Sometimes reading for its own sake is goal enough.

Questioning and Comprehension

Asking questions is an important part of helping students to comprehend. The teacher's goal in asking questions is *not* to test a child's understanding of what has been read. Rather, the goal is to help each child become a self-questioner.

The *right* questions, therefore, are those that a reader asks himself or herself—those based on background, interests, needs, and purposes. Like other important reading behaviors, self-questioning while reading needs to be developed in the child. Effective teacher questioning can help the child both develop this behavior and focus on the relevance of a selection to his or her purposes and needs.

Self-Questioning Is Essential to Basic Comprehension

To better understand the importance of self-questioning, let's consider how it works at a simple level of comprehension. Two children are reading the same passage; both are making miscues, but one of them is engaged in self-questioning.

Betty and Sam each read the following passage aloud:

One morning little Ben Beaver left home all by himself. He went across the pond as fast as he could swim. He wanted to pick something for his mother. He wanted to pick something that would please her.*

Betty reads it this way:

One morning little Ben Beaver *light* home all by himself. He went *after* the pond as fast as he could swim. He wanted to *play* something for his mother. He wanted to *play* something that would please her.

Sam reads it this way:

One morning ladder Ben—no, *little* Ben Beaver left home all by himself. He went across the pond as *fat* as he could—as *fast* as he could swim. He wanted to pick something for his mom. He wanted to pick something that would please her.

Sam and Betty each made about the same number of miscues. However, Sam corrected his. His first attempts didn't make sense to him, so he paused to ask himself questions that led to his picking up the thread of the meaning. When he heard himself say "ladder Ben," Sam knew he had never heard of a person like that. In effect, he was asking himself, "What would Ben be if he were ladder? Does that sound right? No, I must try that word again." "How would Ben swim if he swam *fat*? That can't be; let's have another look." It is important to note that Sam's reasoning in correcting his miscues involves context and structural analysis that relies on his background—his understanding of the other word concepts and how they relate grammatically.

On the other hand, Betty, who made only three miscues, did not question the resulting message. Certainly, her reading could not have been the result of questioning the meaning of what she was reading.

Questions and Discussions Can Promote Self-Questioning

Several children in a second-grade class are interested in detective stories. The teacher has found a story that she thinks might interest the

* William Eller et al., "Little Ben" in *Toothless Dragon*, Laidlaw Reading Program: Level 6 (River Forest, Ill.: Laidlaw Brothers, 1976).

group. The story, "Picture of a Winner," involves a young boy who is a camera bug; and, because he needs money to pursue his hobby, he does all kinds of errands after school. On one of his errands, Jim and his camera happen to be in the right place at the right time. Jim's hobby and quick thinking help to solve a holdup.

Before introducing the story to the children, the teacher shows the students two cameras that she has brought to class. One is a traditional camera and the other a camera that rapidly develops the print. She explains the differences between the two types of cameras, encouraging the children who are knowledgeable about cameras to share information. The teacher allows several children to take and develop pictures with the latter. She also has negatives and prints from pictures she has taken with the traditional camera. By allowing them to examine these cameras, to discuss techniques for developing pictures, and to actively take pictures, the teacher is ensuring that the children have the necessary background and experience to make the reading of the story more successful.

The teacher then asks the children to turn to the first page of the story, which shows the picture of a young boy holding a camera up to his eye.

The teacher asks, "What do you think this story is about?"

One boy answers, "I'll bet it's about taking pictures."

"What makes you think that?" asks the teacher.

"The title of the story is 'Picture of a Winner' and the picture shows a boy about to take a picture," the boy responds.

"I wonder what kind of pictures Jim takes in this story," comments the teacher.

One child volunteers, "I'll bet he takes pictures of sports events. Thats why it says *winner* in the title."

"Maybe he wins a prize for his pictures," offers another child. "Maybe *he* is the winner?"

"Your ideas are good ones," says the teacher; "Let's check your ideas by reading. When you're finished, let's discuss in what ways you were right." The children are directed to read only until their predictions are confirmed. In many basal readers, stories are presented in sections to allow the teacher opportunities to involve children with the story they are reading.

When the children are ready to discuss what they have read, the teacher says, "Let's talk about your guesses."

"It sure is about taking pictures. Jim is a camera bug," one child says.

"What's happened to the camera bug so far?"

A girl answers, "There's a photo contest that Jim wants to enter. But it doesn't look like he's going to be able to take the picture he wants to take to enter."

"Maybe he'll win a prize or something for getting Mrs. Bell her medicine on time," suggests another child.

"I think Jim's plan to take a picture of the fountain with the sunlight shining on it was great. That would make a great picture," suggests the child who had already said earlier that he owned his own camera.

"Maybe Jim will take a picture of his brother Paul. He's on the track team and he plays football; that would be a 'Picture of a Winner.'" offers another child.

"That could be," responds the teacher. "I surely think Jim had a tough decision to make when he decided to get Mrs. Bell's medicine rather than go take the picture. "Do you think the decision Jim made will keep him from getting the picture he wants?" the teacher asks. The children disagree with each other when they answer. The teacher asks the children to explain their answers.

One boy thinks Jim seems to know a lot about taking pictures. A girl says he won't get it done. "What did you read that makes you think that?" the teacher asks.

"Well, you can't be running errands all the time and get your real work done," the girl says, relating a part of the story to her own experience. "I didn't have my homework done yesterday because I had to run some notes around the neighborhood for my mother."

The teacher's questions have sparked a discussion that has forced the children back to the text and to their experiences to support their answers. After reading further, the children reject or accept their own guesses, suggest incidents from the story that support their assumptions, react to Jim's actions and attitudes (as well as to those of other characters), and supply personal experiences that enlarge on the meaning of the story.

The children have been stimulated. The teacher can build on this interest and motivation in numerous ways. Maybe she can find a simple book on cameras or another story with facts about cameras. The children will want to get started planning pictures. In any event, the teacher has an excellent opportunity to provide subsequent situations in which the children can use what they learned in the story as a springboard for continuing to develop a reading program that is based on the children's interests.

Notice that the questions were interspersed throughout the reading of the story and that they emphasized reading for meaning. Thus the reader is constantly concerned with a search for meaning and not just with pronouncing words.

Different Kinds of Questions Encourage Different Kinds of Thinking

Many experts believe that children would develop into better readers if teachers would determine the kinds of thinking they want to develop and ask questions that would promote those kinds of thinking skills (Guszak, 1967). But what kinds of thinking should teachers encourage? Stauffer (1969) has suggested that the kinds of thinking we want children to engage in are not discrete (such as those found on a list) but are continuous, ranging all the way from *reproduction* to *production*. Reproductive thinking, according to Stauffer, occurs when readers reproduce information asked for by the teacher. Productive thinking occurs when the reader provides information based on his or her own purpose. Stauffer strongly urges that we ask production questions—questions that are derived from the child's purpose for reading. We should challenge readers to prove their point, to analyze their answers, and to judge what they have stated. Stauffer suggests that the teacher's role in increasing reading comprehension is that of "an intellectual agitator," who "asks and asks again: 'What do you think?' 'Why do you think so?' 'Read the line(s) that proves it.' " As Stauffer points out, such questions increase the search for meaning.

According to the kind of response they promote in children, questions can be considered to be either *literal, inferential,* or *evaluative.* In other words, one kind of question can be answered by drawing a literal reference from the text. A second encourages the child to draw inferences by relating parts of the text to each other and by relating the text to his or her experience in order to arrive at expectations. The third type encourages the child to evaluate the material against itself, against similar material, and against his or her experience in order to arrive at expectations.

Literal questions. In general, a question is a literal question if it can be answered by just quoting the text as a source. For example, after reading the sentence *The worl glibbed a redkin gratingly,* you could answer such literal questions as:

Who (or what) glibbed a redkin?
How did the worl glib the redkin?
Who (or what) got glibbed?

The use of the nonsense words in the example above emphasizes how a direct quote can be used to answer literal questions. And since the reader determines the answer to literal questions through both the syntax and semantics of the passage, the reader must engage in some linguistic analysis for active reasoning. Even though literal questions ask the reader to reproduce what has been read, they are sometimes essential to analysis. In fact, more often than not, a question that calls for the reader to make an inference or an evaluation develops from a series of literal questions structured to force the analysis.

The answer to an inferential or evaluative question can also be aided or achieved through the asking and answering of several literal questions. Suppose, for example, that a story tells about a child who is under the protective wing of several older brothers and sisters. A series of incidents describe how sisters and brothers direct the child's chores, homework, and so on. He does nothing without first asking whether he may and how to do it. Then one day on the way home from school, the child finds a starving kitten and must decide what to do about it on his own. He brings it home and firmly persuades an objecting family that they should help save the kitten's life. That night an older sister comes to the boy and asks his opinion about how she can help a friend of hers who has a problem.

After building some background with discussion about how the young reader feels about his or her own brothers and sisters, and after the child has read the story, the teacher can help structure the child's understanding of the story's theme by first asking literal questions about the early incidents in the story.

How many older brothers and sisters does Willard have?
How does Nell help Willard with his mathematics? Does he object to her doing the problems for him?
What happens when Willard washes the dishes? Why does Bill wash them over?
What does Betty say when Willard asks if he can spend his money on the book?

Having primed the child with literal questions that focus on details that are important to the theme of the story, the teacher can move to questions that encourage analysis and reaction:

Does Willard ever decide anything for himself?
How do you think Willard feels as he walks home with the kitten?
Was it a good idea for Nell, Bill, and Betty to do everything for Willard?
Do you know anyone like Willard?
What are some things you have decided for yourself? How did you feel?

In subject-area reading there tends to be more emphasis on the literal question in order to get the child to retain important details: dates, names, types, and so on. But such an emphasis on detail should serve to develop the broader concepts of science, history, math, and other areas. Thus, the teacher should use literal questions to help children gather the facts and details necessary for developing broader understanding and concepts.

When the major classroom emphasis is placed on elemental detail by asking mostly literal questions, attention to comprehension of the whole idea suffers. Literal questions should help readers understand a selection beyond the immediate literal question being asked. Such questions should focus on following the events in a story, identifying details that have an important bearing on main ideas, or on facts that may have a bearing on story interpretations.

In using literal questions, then, keep the following guidelines in mind. Be sure that the questions are going to lead to or relate to a main idea or general concept in the reading selection. Use literal questions occasionally to get the child back to the text to verify, support, and exemplify a concept, reaction, or interpretation.

Inferential questions. The reader who has a purpose for reading and is reading to understand a selection in the light of that purpose is inferring throughout the process. He or she is, in effect, asking inferential questions. The teacher can use inferential questions to model for young readers so that they can learn to ask inference questions of themselves. There are two general kinds of inference in reading: one is analytic, the other predictive.

In Chapters 4, 5, and 6 we have seen how the reader uses analytic inference to guess what a word means. This is done by using other words in the text and the structure of the sentence. Consider again the nonsense statement: *The worl glibbed a redkin gratingly.* The reader infers from *the* and *glibbed* that a worl is a thing that can *glib*. The reader infers also from structural analysis that *gratingly* tells how the worl glibbed. In effect, this inference is the answer to: "The *what* did *what* to *what*? Did it *how*?"

Now suppose the sentence reads: *Miriam was delighted to see the worl glib the redkin gratingly.* Through inference within the text, we can assume from *delighted* that *glibbing gratingly* is pleasant in some way. Thus, we ask: "Why was Miriam delighted?" Suppose the next sentences read: *She didn't like the redkin and was happy to see it get its just desserts, but she didn't care to see it have its feelings hurt. She wouldn't have wanted the worl to glib destructively.* By asking, "What can I tell about this redkin and what happened to it?" we can infer from the new information that *to glib* may not be such a pleasant action after all; it may even involve vindication. And, "How does glibbing gratingly make glibbing less objectionable?" We can also infer that *gratingly* takes the edge off the glibbing. Apparently there is something softening, or even pleasant, about doing something gratingly. At least we know that it is constructive for it is contrasted to *destructively*.

This example illustrates the kind of thinking that inferential questions can trigger. The teacher's objective should be to teach a child to ask inferential questions. And this can be accomplished by asking questions to assist the child that will serve as models for the practice.

Inferring, of course, can be more a part of reading comprehension than merely helping in word recognition. In teaching the story about Willard, the teacher has asked for inference with the following questions: How do you think Willard feels as he walks home with the kitten? What are some things you have decided for yourself? How did you feel? (The child can infer how Willard must have felt from any details in the text, which might say, "It seemed to Willard that he was taller" or "Willard's chin was up and he held the kitten tightly." The child can also infer how Willard must feel by recalling how he or she felt making an important decision.) The questions about Betty also lead the child to infer between incidents in the story and between the story and his or her own experience.

A second kind of inference is predictive. From the moment a child reads the title of a selection, the child begins drawing inferences be-

tween his or her background and the selection; and the process operates continually as the reading progresses. Each new idea that the reader comprehends provokes new inferences about what is to follow. What is subsequently read is tested or measured against the inferences to see if they hold up.

Using "Jack and the Beanstalk" as an example (because it is a story with which you are familiar rather than because it is a likely teaching situation), children could be led to predict from illustrations, from the title, from their own experiences, and from initial portions of the story. The story is structured so that it lends itself to a child being able to predict events. As children read, their predictions are confirmed or modified (Jack got away safely twice; can he manage it again?) and new predictions can be formed with teacher guidance or questioning. The teacher can probe for predictions: "I wonder how a small boy will get away from a giant." The teacher can also directly ask for prediction: "Do you suppose Jack's mother will let him go back up the beanstalk?" and probe the response "What makes you think that?" In using questioning to promote analytic and predictive inference, keep these guidelines in mind:

> The inferential question should refer to some specific information in the text, but the reader should not be able to answer merely by repeating this information.
> The inferential question can encourage the synthesis of two ideas in the story in order to get a third idea not actually stated.
> The inferential question should move the child's thinking from specifics in the text to more general concepts, such as the theme or main idea of a story.
> The inferential question should encourage the child to relate his or her own experience to information in the text in order to enlarge on it or predict from it.

Evaluative questions. With evaluative questions, the reader passes judgment on the validity or quality of the reading material.

In forming and answering such questions, the reader invariably lays his or her background (knowledge, experience, beliefs, prejudices) against the material to see if it rings true or is complete. Sometimes such evaluation can lead a child to a resource to clarify, enlarge on, or contradict the text. If the text has provoked an emotional response, the child's evaluation may be affected by that.

It is also vital for the teacher to ask questions that get the child to pass judgment on the action of characters. In doing so, the child is encouraged to relate the reading to what he or she knows and believes. Thus the synthesis that is vital to comprehension takes place, and the role of reading as a vital life activity is evident. If the child finds from continued reading that a judgment is incorrect, he or she is taught to broaden perspectives. In this way, prejudices break down, and the child learns that reactions to situations should be tentative in the sense that they are always open to new information:

Questions that lead the child to evaluate characters

Do you think Jack should have taken the giant's hen, food, harp?

Did Willard have a right to decide to keep the kitten without asking first?

What would you have done about selling Jack's cow?

Questions that lead to other judgments of a story

Where else might this story have taken place?
Could this story have happened today?
What would have happened if Jack had been caught?
How could Willard have helped the cat without taking it home?

Questions that lead to the evaluation of the theme or main idea

Do you think small children should make decisions?
How do you treat your little brother or sister?
How do you know when you are right?

Questions that lead to evaluation of the author

The author says Willard "kept as quiet as an old shoe"; how else could we tell how Willard acted when his brother scolded him?

What kind of a person do you think made up "Jack and the Beanstalk"?

Does the person who wrote about Jack know what it is like to be poor?

In using evaluative questions, keep these considerations in mind:

The question should ask the child only to make judgments that personal experience or the ability to exploit resource material will allow.

The question should be structured to show that writers make judgments when they write and that those judgments can be accepted or rejected.

The question should not force the child into passing a judgment that will be made to look foolish in subsequent reading or discussion; the question should allow the child to make a judgment that is open to refinement, adjustment, or withdrawal when more facts are revealed.

Be Flexible When Asking Questions

To use questioning so that the child recognizes and adopts it as a useful behavior, you must remain flexible in questioning. You must be alert to the synthesis that is taking place in the child as the ideas in the text combine with his or her background. This means that you should often let the discussion take its own course, following the enthusiasm and developing interests of the reader.

try this ▶

Locate a teacher's edition for a basal reader series and examine at least two of the lesson plans for stories. See if you can determine which of the suggested questions for teachers ask that the child *remember* something, which ask for *prediction*, and which ask the reader to make a *judgment*. Which questions (if any) may help the child learn to be a self-questioner? Compare your findings with those of a teacher who examined a different series. Does the relative emphasis on question types vary between stories and levels within one series and among different series?

There will be times when the discussion seems to veer far afield from what you thought the children had developed as their purpose for reading the selection; and you may—after giving them some time to develop what you think is a tangent—want to nudge them back toward that purpose with a question. But that question should not come from some prepared list; you would create it on the spot if you were listening carefully with respect and enthusiasm to what the children were saying. And you might, with this kind of flexible sensitivity, shift the discussion back to the original purpose or incorporate it into a more productive purpose.

The need to be flexible is important in asking questions. Discussions need to relate to each child. Our purpose has been to show you ways that you *might* encourage interest, purpose, active reasoning, action, and reaction through questioning and probes if you are aware of what is developing in the thoughts and feelings of the children who respond to the questions.

REFERENCES

Anastasiow, Nicholas. *Oral Language: Expression of Thought.* Newark, Del.: International Reading Association, 1971.

Barrett, Thomas C. "Taxonomy of Cognitive and Affective Dimensions of Reading Instruction." In "What is 'Reading?' Some Current Concepts," by Theodore Clymer. In *Innovation and Change in Reading Instruction*, edited by Helen M. Robinson, pp. 19–23. Sixty-seventh Yearbook of the National Society for the Study of Education. Chicago: University of Chicago Press, 1968.

Berlyne, D. E. "Conditions of Prequestioning and Retention of Meaningful Material." *Journal of Educational Psychology* 57 (June 1966): 128–32.

Dale, Edgar. "Things to Come." *Newsletter* 13 (1969).

Dallman, Martha; Rouch, Robert; Chang, Lynnette; and DeBoer, John J. *The Teaching of Reading.* 4th ed. New York: Holt, Rinehart and Winston, 1974.

Dewey, John. *How We Think.* Boston: Heath, 1933.

Frase, Lawrence T. "Effect of Question Location, Pacing, and Mode upon Retention of Prose Material." *Journal of Educational Psychology* 59 (August 1968): 244–49.

Gates, Arthur. "General Considerations and Principles." *Reading in the Elementary School*, edited by Nelson B. Henry. Forty-eighth Yearbook of the National Society for the Study of Education. Chicago: University of Chicago Press, 1949.

Goodman, Kenneth S. *The Psycholinguistic Nature of the Reading Process*. Detroit: Wayne State University Press, 1968.

Guszak, Frank J. *Diagnostic Reading Instruction in the Elementary School*. 2d ed. New York: Harper and Row, 1978.

————. "Teacher Questioning and Reading." *The Reading Teacher* 21 (December 1967): 227–34.

Harris, Larry, and Smith, Carl. *Reading Instruction Through Diagnostic Teaching*. New York: Holt, Rinehart and Winston, 1976.

Hildreth, Gertrude. "Linguistic Factors in Early Reading Instruction." *The Reading Teacher* 18 (1964): 172–78.

Lamme, Linda L. "Reading Aloud to Young Children." *Language Arts* 53 (November-December 1976): 886–88.

Lenneberg, Eric H. *The Biological Foundation of Language*. New York: John Wiley and Sons, 1967.

Levin, Harry, and Kaplan, Eleanor L. "Grammatical Structure and Reading." In *Basic Studies on Reading*, edited by Harry Levin and Joanne B. Williams, pp. 119–33. New York: Basic Books, 1970.

Petty, Walter T.; Petty, Dorothy C.; and Becking, Marjorie F. *Experiences in Language: Tools and Techniques for Language Arts Methods*. Boston: Allyn and Bacon, 1973.

Robinson, Helen M. "Significant Unsolved Problems in Reading." *Journal of Reading* 14 (November 1970): 77–82, 134–41.

Rothkopf, Ernest Z., and Bisbicos, Ethel E. "Selective Facilitative Effects of Interspersed Questions on Learning from Written Materials." *Journal of Educational Psychology* 58 (February 1967): 58–61.

Smith, Nila Banton. "The Good Reader Thinks Critically." *The Reading Teacher* 15 (December 1961): 162–71.

Stauffer, Russell G. *Directing Reading Maturity as a Cognitive Process*. New York: Harper and Row, 1969.

FOR FURTHER READING

Griese, Arnold A. *Do You Read Me? Practical Approaches to Teaching Reading Comprehension*. Santa Monica, Cal.: Goodyear Publishing, 1977.

Harris, Larry A., and Smith, Carl. *Reading Instruction: Diagnostic Teaching in the Classroom*. 2d ed. New York: Holt, Rinehart and Winston, 1976.

Johnson, Wendell. *Your Most Enchanted Listener*. New York: Harper and Row, 1956.

Karlin, Robert. *Teaching Elementary Reading: Principles and Strategies*. 2d ed. New York: Harcourt Brace Jovanovich, 1975.

Quandt, Ivan. *Teaching Reading: A Human Process*. Chicago: Rand McNally, 1977. Chaps. 7 and 13.

Russell, David. *Children's Thinking*. Waltham, Mass.: Blaisdell, 1956.

Schubert, Delwyn, and Torgerson, Theodore. *Improving the Reading Process*. 4th ed. Dubuque, Iowa: Wm. C. Brown, 1976.

Sebesta, Sam Leaton, and Iverson, William J. *Literature for Thursday's Child*. Chicago: Science Research Associates, 1975.

Smith, Frank. *Understanding Reading—A Psycholinguistic Analysis of Reading and Learning to Read.* New York: Holt, Rinehart and Winston, 1971.

Spache, George B., and Spache, Evelyn. *Reading in the Elementary School.* 4th ed. Boston: Allyn and Bacon, 1977.

Stauffer, Russell G. *Directing the Reading-Thinking Process.* New York: Harper and Row, 1975.

Teaching Reading for Special Purposes

One of the goals of any reading program is to help students to become successful users of printed materials. We know that the mature reader uses print for many purposes—from pleasurable time filling to seeking critically needed information. Readers read for entertainment, enrichment, to stay abreast, and to fulfill professional goals. As children develop toward becoming mature readers, it is the teacher's responsibility to help young readers set and fulfill their own purposes for reading. The reading skills that are discussed in this chapter stem from the young reader's needs to gain, assimilate, and use information.

Five Useful Study Skills

In order to achieve these special purposes, the child is taught *study skills*—the skills that enable the reader to find, understand, and use information. There are five general study-skill behaviors that will be examined in this chapter:

(1) the ability to comprehend the vocabulary of specialized subjects (science, math, and social studies)
(2) the ability to identify appropriate information resources when questions arise and to find information within those sources
(3) the ability to interpret graphic aids

(4) the ability to adjust reading rate to the varying purposes for reading

(5) the ability to recognize and follow the organizational structure of ideas and information within resources

Principles of Teaching Study Skills

Before discussing these five study-skill behaviors, however, it will be useful to mention some general principles and related considerations that should underlie your instruction.

Teach when the need arises.   This principle restates, in effect, the whole philosophy of child-initiated learning. It means that children will learn study skills best when the focus is not on skill development, but rather on accomplishing some meaningful task. For example, when a fourth-grade child wants to build a model plane and asks if you know of a good "how-to" book, that child can be shown the card catalog in the school library. Teacher and child can locate a book together while they discuss the organization of the card catalog, as well as its usefulness. First graders planning a trip to the fire station really need to make a map of the neighborhood for their bus driver. And a third grader who reads regularly to a younger brother or sister can learn to use a table of contents because it is a faster way to find a story the younger child will like. If you asked these children what they were doing, they wouldn't respond that they were using study skills. Rather, they would say that they were "building a plane," "taking a trip," or "finding a good story." But each is being taught how to locate and use information at the critical moment—when each needs what a particular skill can provide.

Teach what the child needs.   The second principle (which appears simplistic) is to teach a study skill only if the child does not already know it. Obviously, it would be a waste of time to teach a whole class to locate a list of words in a glossary when some of the children will know both the words and how to use a glossary. This principle recommends that the teacher preassess the child's ability to use a particular study skill before undue amounts of time are directed toward teaching that skill. *Preassessment* conveys a technical tone, but in practice refers to time allotted to just watching a particular child look up a word, locate a book, and so on. Teachers learn a great deal about the child's efficiency and familiarity with resources by observing.

Teach skills in a logical sequence.   Some study skills require prerequisite knowledge. It is not logical, for example, to try to teach someone to find a word in a glossary, an entry in an index, or a card in a library catalog when that learner has not yet mastered the sequence of the alphabet. A child must know number sequence before he or she can make successful use of a table of contents. In addition, resources vary in difficulty and thus mandate varying prerequisite word-recognition and comprehension abilities. These examples suggest the value of using a logical sequence for the development of study skills.

Teaching the Necessary Vocabulary

To comprehend the ideas represented by sentences, a reader has to understand the concepts represented by the individual words in the sentences. This is especially true in the content areas of the curriculum. The term *content areas* refers to the subject matter areas of science, mathematics, and social studies. The vocabulary of those content subjects can be especially technical. In addition, words can have meanings peculiar to a given discipline. Building the necessary vocabulary for a special area of study requires that the reader have sufficient background—an important consideration that has been stressed throughout this textbook. An adequate background (and, thus, vocabulary) helps create interest, too; for any reader is more likely to want to read materials that contain familiar concepts.

Vocabulary, in general, is so basic to reading successfully that it has been discussed in several other chapters. Chapter 3 describes a variety of ways to develop the vocabulary of the beginning reader. Chapter 4 stresses the need to be sure that a new word in print is already part of a child's listening vocabulary. Chapter 5 talks of the use of context clues as the essential word-recognition skill. Chapter 6 points up the key role that vocabulary development plays in building comprehension. In this chapter, we will build on these emphases to stress the importance of vocabulary development for reading in the content areas.

Developing Background

One of the first things you will learn in working with children is that the range of vocabularies in any classroom, at any level—regardless of how "homogeneous" the group is supposed to be—is very wide. Some children have extensive experiences and can discuss and richly describe those experiences; others have unique experiences that, for them, give some words very special meanings; many children have poorly developed concepts and may understand only superficial meanings for many words. Since, in a sense, every word is a concept, building a child's vocabulary means providing the experiences that will enable a child to build concepts and the vocabulary to express them. In turn, understanding the concepts represented by words enables the reader to perceive the relationship among words in phrases, clauses, and sentences. Frequently, authors select words that a young reader is likely to know, placing them in relationship to each other around a concept (a word) that may be less familiar in order to explain the difficult word. And this practice represents a key principle for teaching vocabulary—extending the child's concepts by expanding from those that are familiar.

If you have ever attempted to read a technical article in a field in which you had little experience, you may have found that although you were able to pronounce the words, you didn't really comprehend. You were not reading in that situation, and, until you develop an adequate background, you will be unable to read it. This situation is even more likely to occur for a child, whose background is more limited. Thus, if you want your students to gain information from reading, you will have to spend time preparing them. In too many classes students read words but not ideas; they fail to relate to the ideas they read because they do not have the background to grasp the concepts represented by the vocabulary.

Two examples.   An effective teacher can help to build the background to fill such a gap. A fourth-grade teacher was preparing a lesson plan for a section of a social studies unit. She listed the vocabulary words that she believed were crucial for meeting the objectives of the session and that might lie outside student experiences. The session was to deal with the effects of a fur trading monopoly granted by the King of France to Canadian fur trappers. Preliminary query (preassessment) had revealed that no student knew what a monopoly was. The teacher realized that without such understanding, the discussion and follow-up reading wouldn't have meaning. So, she planned to help children to derive a meaningful explanation for monopoly from their own experiences. A discussion was initiated that compared what it was like to buy milk in the supermarket as opposed to the school cafeteria. Someone mentioned that only one brand of milk was sold in the cafeteria. Some of the children checked on this and learned that the milk supplying company had an agreement with the school system. The children were becoming better able to read about the fur trading monopolies once they had the conceptual background needed for the reading to make sense.

Another teacher wanted to make sure that the children in his second-grade class had the necessary vocabulary to profit from a study of *weather*. This teacher began the science unit with an emphasis on daily weather, the experience that was most familiar to each child. The children kept charts of the weather, making their charts reflect what they experienced about the weather on their way to school each day. Pictures of puddles, hats blowing, and smog-covered cities cropped up. At the end of two weeks, the children discussed their charts. They were ready to ask some questions, to learn more about weather, and for more effective reading in content materials. These two examples illustrate building background with concrete experiences. Concrete activities are ideal because they provide for the most compelling learning situations. But when you are unable to have children engage in concrete activities, vicarious experiences are the next best alternative: films, television programs, filmstrips, records, and pictures related to the concepts of the reading material are more effective in building vocabulary than is the practice of defining words for children and assuming that a concept has been implanted.

try this ▶

Pick a selection from a content-area text for an elementary grade. Examine it for the vocabulary that you think may be new for some children at that level or may represent difficult concepts. Plan several activities to build background for that new vocabulary. Try to ensure that children will be actively involved with learning those words. Share your plan with others and collect some more ideas.

Guides for Meaningful Instruction of Vocabulary

In building background and in teaching vocabulary in the content areas, there are several general principles that have bearing on children's learning and motivations. There is overlap in these considerations in that each stresses beginning with the known and working toward the unfamiliar.

Begin with the tangible and move to the vicarious. As has already been mentioned, whenever possible, background development should begin with real experiences. The rural child who has never seen an escalator will never fully develop a concept of "moving stairs" until that child rides an escalator. Children need to have experiences in which they touch, taste, hear, see, and manipulate their world. The richer, broader, and more varied the experiences children have before reading, the more they have in common with the author, and the better they understand that author's terminology.

Begin with the particular and move to the generalization. Some vocabulary terms in science, social studies, and mathematics are quite abstract. Examples include *climate*, *government*, *community*, *area*, and *democracy*. You can help children discover these abstract generalizations by capitalizing on that which is already familiar to children, the knowledge of which contributes to an understanding of the difficult generalization. Climate, for example, includes the more familiar *weather*, and the still more familiar *wind*, *rain*, *sunshine*, and *clouds*. Pulling specifics together is what making generalizations is all about. Get started with understanding democracy by voting on the refreshments for an upcoming party. Work through experiments in science and then deal with the principle (using the vocabulary) that explains the results. Discover the mean-

ing of *multiply* by calling on what you already know about *addition.* Use the vocabulary that is already known in order to build toward the less familiar.

Begin with the egocentric and move to the social. This principle, too, is closely related to the previous ones, because in introducing vocabulary you will naturally be searching for ways to deal with ideas that are closest to the child's interests. A very young child learns that a fire is hot from the consequences to that child rather than to another member of the family. When children develop vocabulary, it is because they need it to express their feelings and desires. Teachers must capitalize on this natural egocentricity to ensure that children feel the need to learn and use new vocabulary: "After we have collected the leaves, we'll find their names in these books so we can make books of our own"; "When we've discovered ways in which the Indians used maize, perhaps we can try some of the recipes"; "Let's think of some of the things we may see when we get to the fire station."

Concepts of Vocabulary Development

In thinking of concept development primarily in terms of vocabulary development, we need to understand that each child has a listening vocabulary, a speaking vocabulary, a reading vocabulary, and a writing vocabulary. When a child enters school, the listening vocabulary is the largest and the speaking vocabulary is next largest. As a child progresses through school, the reading vocabulary increases rapidly until, by approximately fourth grade, this vocabulary is usually larger than the speaking vocabulary. The importance of the relative size of a child's vocabulary is important as a guide to instruction. The usual development of vocabulary follows this hierarchy:

A very young child who is learning to talk understands more words than he or she is able to verbalize. Parents teach the child to say words for which the child already has referents.

With a beginning reader, the task is to develop the child's reading vocabulary by learning to read words the child knows as part of a listening and speaking vocabulary.

For a successful reader, reading becomes a means of learning new words that can be added to the listening and speaking vocabularies.

After about fourth grade, the order of vocabularies tends to be listening, reading, speaking, writing.

Activities for Developing Vocabulary

In developing vocabulary, the conventional activity has been for teachers to assign lists of words to students, telling them to look up the words in a dictionary and copy the meanings. Such exercises are not usually appropriate, particularly in the content areas, where special terms represent concepts that need to be fully experienced. A dictionary can be a useful aid to verify the meanings of words, but it is not a very lively developer of vocabulary. It would be much better, for example, to divide the children into groups and have them discuss certain words, perhaps finding the words in print or drawing pictures of them. Or the children could be encouraged to devise a skit that represents their understanding of particular words and to present that skit to others. The dictionary could be used as a check on the meanings the small groups developed, but the first definitions would spring from the children's frames of reference.

Dramatization and pantomime are particularly excellent ways for children to express their understanding of vocabulary. In one first-grade class, we observed four children dramatizing the season *spring*. One child ran about and blew "like the wind"; another shivered, bundled into a make-believe rain coat, then opened an umbrella; a third child went through the fluttering-fingers routine that expressed rain; a fourth child shed a coat and dug a garden.

Children like to play games with words. One vocabulary-building game has the teacher suggest a word and then challenge the children to find pictures that represent that word. A stack of old magazines is all that is needed for a supply of pictures. The reverse of this game is fun, too. Let the children find several pictures they feel are related in some way, and then ask others to guess what the collection of pictures has in common, such as *softness*.

A variation is to ask one child to think of and tell a describing word. Other children must name something that the word describes. For example, take the adjective *gooey*. Children offer examples such as "the inside of a toasted marshmallow," "a muddy field between your toes," or "a candy bar in the sun." Such games encourage the development of the child's vocabulary.

Crossword puzzles that review words from a science or social studies unit can be useful beginning with third- and fourth-grade children. You may want to encourage some of the children to try to make their own puzzles for others to complete.

Labelling pictures, creating topical newspapers, writing and answering riddles, completing analogies, and categorizing and classifying words are additional ways to develop vocabulary.

Teaching the Child to Locate Information

"Where can I find the information on the voter-registration requirements for this town?"

"Does anyone know where there's a good discussion of how to recognize fake antiques?"

"I know I could make a hummingbird feeder if I could find a pattern for one."

"I wish I knew more about dragons."

Almost everyone has information needs. If we are unable to locate and use the resources we need, we sometimes become frustrated. Have you ever heard comments like these?

"The library doesn't have the material I need. At least I couldn't find it."

"I've looked through this entire book and I can't find the information."

"I know the question, but don't know where to look for the answer."

Perhaps the necessary information doesn't exist in the places that were searched or perhaps these complaints are a result of not knowing how to locate the information in available sources. Learning *how to find out* is one of the most important skills teachers provide students. To help children become readers who can learn for themselves, you need to develop instruction that achieves the following aims:

(1) *Your instruction should introduce children to the use of location skills as soon as they begin reading.* This can be done by helping children to locate their own library books, to develop simple picture dictionaries, to use the table of contents in basal readers and trade books, and to organize a classroom library.

(2) *Your instruction should introduce location skills when they are based on information needs that arise incidentally.* This is accomplished by helping children to answer their own questions through the use of appropriate reference materials. When a child wants to see a picture of a skyscraper in order to make a drawing of one, that is the time to introduce a junior encyclopedia. When a boy or girl who was just given a new puppy as a birthday present wants to know when puppies are old enough to start training, that is the time to demonstrate the use of the card catalog in the school library.

(3) *Your instruction should promote opportunities for continual experience with location skills.* Obviously, if you rely totally upon incidental teaching of location skills, you cannot ensure either systematic introduction of all skills or adequate practice. Therefore, your instruction must create opportunities for the meaningful use of card catalogs, indexes, glossaries, tables of contents, and reference books in all subject areas.

(4) *Your instruction should focus first on materials that are important to children.* For example, Cub Scouts, Brownies, and 4-H clubs have manuals that include indexes and tables of contents, while *TV Guide*, the evening newspaper, and children's magazines are all organized somewhat differently. Help children to learn the organization of the materials that they are most likely to use.

Guiding Children in a Library

Surprisingly, to many children a library can be just "rooms filled with books"; a place in which you become confused in a forbidding tangle of shelves, files, and rules; or a place in which laborious assignments are carried out. Your assignment (should you care to accept it) is to make library time pleasurable.

The classroom library. Introducing students to a library can start on a very small scale. Classroom libraries should be a part of every classroom, beginnning with preschool. And even if the classroom library is limited in size and variety, it can be arranged so that it generally follows the organization of the school or community library. For example, all of the reference books—the picture dictionaries, the elementary-level dictionaries, and the junior encyclopedias—could be kept in one section. Fiction books may be grouped together in another section, arranged alphabetically by the author's last name. The nonfiction books may be

arranged by subject. Children can help to classify the books and to decide where new acquisitions will be shelved. By helping to organize the classroom library, children learn that libraries are arranged according to a system. And by encouraging a child to use the organization not only to find books but also to return books to their proper space, the system is reinforced.

The school or community library.   Continued experience with the classroom library will help make the school or community library a more comfortable place to visit. You may even hear the children make comments such as, "This library keeps all of their picture books in one place just like we do!"

A child's introduction to the library should provide a general overview. There should be time to talk with the librarian; pehaps to hear a story; and then time to browse, to select books to read, look at, or listen to, and then to check some books out. This freedom to browse helps the child to feel that the library is a valuable place—a place to find stories just by looking around.

A child who has had experience with a classroom library and/or the school library may want to look through a greater variety of books to find one to meet his or her interests. That child can be guided to the appropriate section of the library and shown the shelves of books that might be of interest. There shouldn't be pressure on a child to "Find the book you want and bring it to the desk so it can be signed out. Hurry now, you only have ten minutes." Even worse would be to introduce a child to a library by trying to teach the organization of the total library and how to use the card catalog. Those skills will come, but if that's where you start, you will only emphasize the technicality of a library.

Another way to make the library an appealing resource for children is to know it well yourself. Know the services it provides—puppet shows, story times, and media presentations. Learn about the nonprint resources that the library provides, such as films, records, tapes, art, or a vertical file of useful pictures. Be certain, too, that you visit the library often, keeping abreast of its organization, its acquisitions that serve your purposes, and its policies. Continual contact with the school and community librarians will make them aware of your children's information needs and your proposed units of instruction in the months ahead and prepare them to better serve those needs.

Introducing the card catalog.   When a child is drawn to the library because of interest in some particular subject but doesn't know where to look for books on that subject, or when a child seeks another book by his or her favorite author, each has indicated a readiness to learn to use the card catalog. Some children may need to use the card catalog in second and third grade; others may not be ready until later. However, this useful key to locating materials in a library should not be forced on children who don't have some real need to use it.

One way to introduce children to the use of the card catalog is to help children develop a simple card catalog for the classroom library. You might start your classroom card catalog with just title cards. Later, when a child seeks other books by a favorite author, it may be an appropriate time to learn about author cards and to begin to make a second card for each book in the library. Finally, if your classroom library is large enough, and when needs dictate, you could discuss with the class a third card for each book—the subject card.

Here are the three card-catalog cards for a children's book:

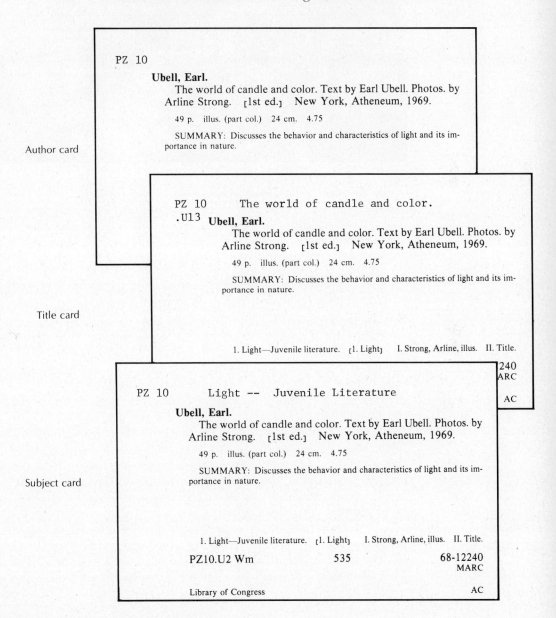

Author card

PZ 10

Ubell, Earl.
    The world of candle and color. Text by Earl Ubell. Photos. by Arline Strong. ₁1st ed.₎ New York, Atheneum, 1969.

    49 p. illus. (part col.) 24 cm. 4.75

    SUMMARY: Discusses the behavior and characteristics of light and its importance in nature.

Title card

PZ 10   The world of candle and color.
.U13 **Ubell, Earl.**
        The world of candle and color. Text by Earl Ubell. Photos. by Arline Strong. ₁1st ed.₎ New York, Atheneum, 1969.

        49 p. illus. (part col.) 24 cm. 4.75

        SUMMARY: Discusses the behavior and characteristics of light and its importance in nature.

    1. Light—Juvenile literature. ₁1. Light₎   I. Strong, Arline, illus. II. Title.

Subject card

PZ 10   Light -- Juvenile Literature
Ubell, Earl.
    The world of candle and color. Text by Earl Ubell. Photos. by Arline Strong. ₁1st ed.₎ New York, Atheneum, 1969.

    49 p. illus. (part col.) 24 cm. 4.75

    SUMMARY: Discusses the behavior and characteristics of light and its importance in nature.

    1. Light—Juvenile literature. ₁1. Light₎   I. Strong, Arline, illus. II. Title.
    PZ10.U2 Wm   535   68-12240
                                                MARC

    Library of Congress   AC

In addition to learning about each of the three types of cards, you can use your classroom card catalog to familiarize the children with the process of locating a book by its call number. Your classroom system ought to use the same call number for the book that your library uses. If your classroom library is on loan from the school or community library, it will already have call numbers.

As we have said many times, when students are taught to use the classroom card catalog or the card catalog in the school or community library, the instruction should be based on the usefulness of the card catalog to fulfill the child's purpose. For example, a child may want (or you may encourage him or her) to read something else by an author named in a textbook and can then be shown the use of author cards. Be sure to take time to show the pupil any description of the book on the card, pointing out how this description can be very useful in determining whether this book will serve the reader's needs.

A more likely opportunity for teaching the card catalog will arise when one or more of the pupils become interested in having more information on a specific topic—thus leading to the use of the subject-card catalog. Once again, descriptive information on the cards can help lead to an appropriate selection, as well as to other topical headings that may be of interest.

Introducing a library's system. After the child can locate a card-catalog entry, the teacher should demonstrate how to jot down the call number. That new code can easily be shown to correspond with the order of the books on the library shelves. The cataloging system used in many elementary and community libraries has traditionally been the Dewey Decimal System, although some libraries are changing to the more standard Library of Congress system. When a child locates an entry in the card catalog, all that he or she initially needs to understand is that the number on the card refers to the location of the book in the library. And since most school libraries arrange books sequentially, memorizing the major classification subjects is unnecessary. It is, however, useful to learn that the fiction books are all kept in one section in most libraries and are arranged alphabetically by the author's last name. The more browsing a child does, the more familiar he or she is with where topics and types of books are kept, and the more rapidly associations are made with the classification system.

Some school and community librarians permit intermediate-level students to assist in the task of reshelving books. Just by arranging unshelved books by catalog numbers or alphabetically by the author's last name, children can learn more about both the library's organization and its collection.

try this ▶

Visit a school or community library and watch children as they use the card catalog. Observe them as they browse through shelves, finding a book and becoming engrossed in it or putting it back on the shelf. Make a list of your observations and determine what skills you think the children need to learn in order to use the library more effectively. Finally, devise several activities for teaching those skills. Compare the skills you identify with those selected by others. Compare the activities you create with those that are suggested below.

Practicing use of the system. Some teacher-made games can provide children with additional practice in locating books in a library. While serving to improve some children's location skills, such games may also provide opportunities for the teacher to find out which children haven't yet mastered the system. Games based on locating books in your own classroom or school libraries will help to familiarize children with available materials:

(1) *Look-It-Up.* The teacher makes a set of laminated game cards similar to the one below. The cards are left in a basket in the library corner or can sit on the card-catalog cabinet in the school library. Children select a card, look up the answers, then either leave it with the teacher or self-check with a posted answer key.

How many books by Mercer Mayer are in our library?___
Who published a book called It's Only Arnold?_____
Under what number could I look for a biography of
  Martin Luther King, Jr.?
                                                           ___

(2) *I've Got a Problem.* Children will write these problems themselves, given a few teacher-made examples. The idea is to come
up with a terrible problem that can only be solved by finding a
particular book.

My Aunt Myrtle says that the Bill Collector is going to take
away her house unless somebody can tell her who wrote
"Elephant in a Well." Can YOU help? Author _____
P.S. She says five extra jellybeans for the kid who can
tell her who saved Elephant.

Sally Fedderson says that she has incurable giggles. She
can only stop laughing if someone will tell her the
name of Johanna Spyri's most famous story.
Can YOU help?   Title _____

Benny McNichol's goat won't come out of the swimming
pool. Benny says he's trying to contact the Greek god
of the seas. Benny doesn't know his name.
Can YOU help? Name of god (mythology)_____

(3) *Scavenger Hunt.* This is a team approach to finding a book or books from a set of clues.

Find the secret book

The call number of the book is 921.

It was written by an author named Vincent Sheean.

It is a book about the third American president.

(4) *Be an Author.* Pretend that the card below is an author card for budding authors. Let children fill in their names and complete the author card with the name of a book that they want to write.

_____, _____.

_____

_____

◯

How to Introduce Reference Books

Children can learn about reference books as soon as schooling begins. Each time a prepared unit of study or a child's own interests raise questions that can lead you to reference materials, take the opportunity to let children see you use reference books to find answers to the questions. All children, even the very young, can learn that special books have special information.

As children develop reading skills, they will learn that each reference tool will have specific contents as well as a specific organization. The most natural way to learn the contents and organization of reference books is to have them available in your classroom and to use them (or demonstrate their use) regularly. If you consult an atlas while children observe, and mention its name, even beginners will learn that the atlas is where to look when you want to find a place. The children don't have to use the atlas themselves at this stage. They need to watch and to listen as the teacher clearly restates the problem: "Bill wants to know if Nagasaki is in Japan or China," and then offers a solution: "Let's look in the atlas to find out."

One frequently made mistake in using reference books is to expect children to read and understand a reference book that is too difficult for them. You can avoid this by reading to children from reference books when there is information that they need and can understand. While some reference books are written at first- or second-grade reading levels, most are not, and their information must be interpreted. Search for reference materials that vary in difficulty for your class. The school and community libraries may be of help to you in this search.

But rather than just relying on a recommended list of reference tools in print, you should stay alert to new reference publications, assessing them for their reading levels, attractiveness, and usefulness for the children in your class. We shall briefly discuss the general types of reference books, indicating how you might teach a child to use them regularly.

Dictionaries. The dictionary is the easiest reference in which to find written materials at varying levels of difficulty. In addition, it is the tool you will probably use most frequently with children. You should also let children see you turn to the dictionary for help.

As Chapter 6 points out, the child must know (or be learning) the alphabet as he or she learns how to use the picture dictionary; as reading skills develop, more advanced dictionaries can be introduced—for example, those that offer words that have the first two or three letters the same and that offer multiple meanings of words.

The location skills that enable beginners to use picture dictionaries efficiently include: knowledge of alphabet sequence, ability to turn to sections of the dictionary in order to locate a word (as opposed to turning every page), and use of the pictures to help gain meaning for a word.

As children achieve a reading level of about second grade, they are ready to learn to use dictionaries that include words that begin with the same two- and three-letter sequences, open to the appropriate section of the dictionary, and find and read simple definitions of words.

By the time children reach third-grade reading level, they need to continue to review the preceding skills, as well as to learn to locate words by using guide words; select from two different meanings the one that fits the context of a given sentence; and use the pronunciation key that the dictionary provides in order to recognize the purpose of a dictionary respelling, identify silent letters in words, identify the syllabic divisions, and identify the primary accent in words.

Intermediate-level students continue to practice the above dictionary skills of locating, pronouncing, and acquiring meaning. By the time a fourth-grade reading level has been achieved, students are usually able to use the dictionary independently to find the pronunciation and meaning for unfamiliar words they encounter in their reading. Additional skills to be mastered during the intermediate grades include the ability to use special sections of the dictionary, such as lists of geographic names, tables of weights and measures, or lists of common signs, such as those used in music or mathematics; determine the pronunciation of a word by using the phonetic respelling, accent marks, and pronunciation key; identify the root or base word; attach meaning to common prefixes and suffixes; offer more than one definition for some words; and select an appropriate definition for an unknown word in order to unlock the meaning of a phrase, sentence, or paragraph.

Procedures and ideas for teaching use of the dictionary are suggested in Chapter 6.

Encyclopedias. Offering a comprehensive source of facts, encyclopedias provide students with concise information about people, places, things, and events. Some teachers are fortunate enough to have a set of encyclopedias within their own classroom. Whether you find yourself in that situation or not, the school library usually has one or more sets of major encyclopedias to serve your students' information needs.

Some librarians favor one set of encyclopedias over others, but their opinions vary; in fact, there appear to be several sets that have enjoyed good reputations.*

Some encyclopedias that have widespread popularity are *The World Book Encyclopedia, Britannica Junior, The New Book of Knowledge, Compton's Encyclopedia,* and *Childcraft* (although not exactly an encyclopedia, *Childcraft* serves as reference material for the preschool and early elementary ages).

Children enjoy paging through encyclopedias at any age, finding photographs that intrigue them, illustrations that tell stories, or something of interest to comment on or to ask about. These informal experiences are an ideal way to be introduced to encyclopedias and should be encouraged. Encyclopedia browsing is one way in which children discover the organization of the encyclopedia for themselves; in fact, some elementary children immediately draw the parallel between dictionary and encyclopedia use and begin to locate in an encyclopedia as soon as their developing reading skill permits.

But for other children, those who have not yet discovered how to use encyclopedias but who want to satisfy specific information needs, the following skills are prerequisite for encyclopedia use:

All encyclopedias are arranged in alphabetical order by the main subject entry, so each independent user must have mastered the sequence of the alphabet.

* For an excellent annotated bibliography (as well as critical reviews) of reference books for children, see Carolyn S. Peterson, *Reference Books for Elementary and Junior High School Libraries,* 2d ed. (Metuchen, N.J.: Scarecrow Press, 1975). Critical reviews of reference books can also be found regularly in issues of *The Booklist* and *Wilson Library Bulletin.*

Because of the number of entries beginning with identical letter sequences, each independent user should be able to alphabetize to the third and fourth letter.

Because of the need for efficiency in locating information within comparatively thick volumes, each user should be able to locate entries using guidewords.

Because the purpose of the encyclopedia search is to find specific information or add to general knowledge, the independent user should be able to successfully read the entry when it has been located.

There are probably several reasons that use of the encyclopedia changes in some children's perceptions from "interesting encounters with interesting books" to drudgery. The attitudes are shaped in part by how the encyclopedia is introduced. Is it viewed as a rich opportunity or a potential source of endless look-it-up assignments? Are important questions that stem from the children's experiences used to introduce the encyclopedia? Or are the stimulus activities prepared dutifully by the teacher with no child's "burning question" in mind?

There are other potential hazards that can cause children to experience failure with the encyclopedia. A child will have difficulty in locating if any of the prerequisite skills listed above are lacking. Difficulty can also stem from inability to focus the search, to understand the organization of the contents, or even the inability to spell the entry word. But perhaps the most frustrating experience of all is to have mastery of all the skills necessary for locating and then be unable to read the entry.

It is the teacher's responsibility not only to ensure the adequacy of the prerequisite skills and (as stated many times) to ensure that the child feels a need to answer a question or find information, but also to be certain that he or she is not required to read independently from sources that are far beyond that child's instructional reading level.*

You can check the adequacy of the match between the child's instructional level and the difficulty of the available encyclopedias by using the process of the informal reading inventory described in Chapter 2. Ask that a child either read aloud to you or read silently for a specific purpose from a short entry on a familiar topic. If you choose oral reading, monitor and tally the miscues, listen for a breakdown in fluency, and watch for signs of strain or physical fatigue. If you offer silent reading, ask the child to read for a specific purpose; note whether an undue amount of time is required for that reading and whether or not the child has achieved the purpose when the reading is finished—that is, can the child answer the question?

For the children who appear to find the use of the encyclopedia a frustrating experience when they use it independently, choose simpler

---

* Many children's encyclopedias claim to have reading levels of high third or fourth grade, but to have interest levels that will take a child through elementary, junior high, and high school years.

reference materials for them to read on their own. And make certain that you guide their future encyclopedia work, reading to them, discussing, and interpreting as necessary. You should not withhold encyclopedias from any child, regardless of reading level.

For students who demonstrate success with the informal assessment process, the teaching task becomes one of facilitating the independent use of the encyclopedia. You can do this by helping learners to focus their search, as well as to use subtopics, cross-references, and the encyclopedia's index.

Help the child to state the focus of the search concisely, identifying key words:

> Child: Do you know how long ago it was that Babe Ruth hit his last home run?
> Teacher: No, but I think I know where to find out.
> Child: In the library?
> Teacher: Right. We could probably find a book on George Herman Ruth in the library, but there's also a reference in this room you could try first.
> Child: The encyclopedia?
> Teacher: Let's do start there. You want to know the year that Babe Ruth hit his last home run. What volume will you pick to look it up?
> Child: I guess *B* for *Babe*.
> Teacher: You might find something about Babe Ruth in the *B* volume, but it would probably be under *baseball*. When you look for a famous person in an encyclopedia, you look under the person's last name.
> Child: *R* for *Ruth*.
> Teacher: I'd like to look it up with you. I'm interested in finding out, too.

(The teacher will use the opportunity to observe the child's use of guide words as well as to do some further teaching.)

Help the child to use the subtopics, if necessary:

> Teacher: There is quite a bit of information here. There are sections about his early life, the teams he played on, and his records. What section should we read first?
> Child: Let's read the records. That might have it.
> Teacher: Let's each read it silently. We'll stop if we find it.

(They read.)

> Child: It's not here. It says how many home runs in a season, but not the year of the last home run.

Help the child to use cross-references if necessary:

Teacher: I don't see an answer to your question either. Do you think we could find it somewhere else?

Child: It says down here we could see *Baseball, Historic Era*.

Teacher: In what volume would that be?

Child: *B*. But under *baseball*, not *Babe*.

Help the child to use the index of the encyclopedia:

Teacher: If we don't find the answer under *baseball*, we can check the encyclopedia's index. It may tell another place to look for the information.

Child: Maybe in another volume.

Teacher: Yes, or we may need another reference book.

The following activities that can help children practice using encyclopedias are offered with a caution: too much emphasis on isolated exercises tends to make encyclopedia usage a chore rather than a quest, and an end in itself rather than a means to an end. The best source for becoming familiar with encyclopedias remains the child's curiosity:

(1) *Class Pass.* Children are handed a cut-out of different familiar shapes with a label on each. Each child selects the appropriate volume of the encyclopedia, looks up the word the shape represents, and then quickly passes the book and the shape to the next child.

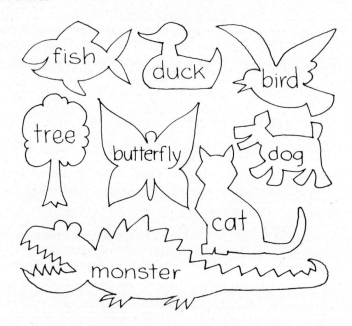

(2) *Look in What Book?* Make silly rhymes that require children to put in the letter(s) of the correct volumes, and then check their guesses by looking up the answers.

If you needed a lollipop
    (and had not one <u>penny</u>)
You could look under _____
    to see if there's any.
(1) P for penny (2) C for cent (3) M for money

You want a pet <u>hippo</u>
    Your mother said, "No".
Just look under _____
    That one won't grow.
(1) H for hippopotamus (2) A for animals (3) Z for zoo

There's a saying they have
    near Waverly Sea:
"To know <u>tortoise</u> from <u>turtle</u>,
    Just look under_____."
(1) R for Reptiles (2) T for turtles/tortoises (3) S for sea

"If I looked under_____,"
    asked Sweet Milly McGoo,
"Could I find the <u>flag</u>
    of South Timbuktu?"
(1) F for flag (2) C for countries (3) S for states

(3) *I've Always Wanted to Be.* Children think of an animal, fish, insect, or bird that they might like to be. They discover facts about that living thing in the encyclopedia. The facts are collected, organized, and listed. Then children take turns telling about themselves as that creature, offering one fact at a time until their identity is guessed.

(4) *What Volume Please?* Make a large poster like this one. Then play a variation of a Quiz Show with children writing the questions. For example, In what volume will you find *Snakes?* Put the questions in a box. Then, divide the group into teams and let each team take turns drawing a question. The team can huddle and decide the answer.

A 1	B 2	C– Ch 3	Cl– Cz 4	D 5	E 6	F 7	G 8	H 9	I 10
J–K 11	L 12	M 13	N 14	O–P 15	Q–R 16	S– Sn 17	So Sz 18	T 19	U–V 20	W–X Y–Z 21

The game gets more difficult if you add another step. In this example, if the first team says Volume 17, they earn one point, but then the second team gets a chance to propose *another* volume where they could learn about snakes. If that team can come up with a second volume and prove it by looking in the encyclopedia, they earn two points (for example, Volume 16, because a snake is a reptile). The first team then has a chance to earn three points by suggesting still another volume and verifying it.*

Other reference sources. Besides learning to use dictionaries and encyclopedias, children in the intermediate grades will find that the reference shelf in the school and community library offers them other sources of information. But even when children have the necessary skills to use these references, they often don't unless some other conditions are satisfied: the references must be easily accessible, the children must have a need for them, and their use must be demonstrated in a meaningful way. Because reference materials vary in their content, organization, and format, those of potential value to your students should be introduced with emphasis on the type of information the reference contains

* Other group and individual activities designed for locating information in encyclopedias are collected in *The Encyclopedia: A Resource for Creative Teaching and Independent Learning,* available from Educational Services, Station 8, Field Enterprises Educational Corporation, Merchandise Mart, Chicago, Illinois 60654.

and its importance. A teacher demonstration of various references is effective when questions arise that signal a need for a particular reference, and timely when an upcoming unit of study can be supplemented with an available reference book. For these reasons, try to spend some time becoming aware of and comfortable with those references yourself. When you know what is available, you will be able to cue children more successfully.

When locations, climates, or crops are in question, help children to learn about atlases.

When children want to identify the members of the President's cabinet, the names of endangered species, the Baseball Rookie of the Year, or the population of New York City, show them almanacs.

When they want to know more about a favorite author, or to see that author's picture, there's the *Junior Book of Authors, More Junior Authors,* and the *Third Book of Junior Authors.**

Atlases, almanacs, yearbooks, special indexes, biographical and geographical dictionaries, foreign-language source books, as well as information specific to the community (its wildlife, plantlife, history, industries, and attractions) are likely to be among a library's references and should not be overlooked.†

Periodicals.   The presence of magazines in your classroom will introduce children to their types and distinctions. Some children's magazines serve as literary forums, others as outlets for children's writing, and still others provide information that will spark interest and send the child to other sources. Reading about porpoises in *National Geographic World* may pique curiosity so that the young reader will search for further reading materials. Some school libraries and most public libraries file back issues of such useful children's and adults' information magazines as *Ranger Rick, Natural History,* the *Smithsonian,* and *National Geographic.*

Learning to use the *National Geographic*'s large print and easy-to-use index (published separately at regular intervals and then compiled) serves as an excellent introduction for preparing upper-elementary level children for the *Readers' Guide to Periodical Literature.*

If your school or community library has a *Readers' Guide,* you may want to introduce its use as early as fifth grade. Again, the use should be demonstrated when the need for information is real, sparked by units of study or by needs for current information. An important distinction

---

* Stanley J. Kunitz and Howard Haycraft, eds., *The Junior Book of Authors* (New York: H. W. Wilson, 1956). Muriel Fuller, ed., *More Junior Authors* (New York: H. W. Wilson, 1964). Doris De Montreville, and Donna Hill, eds., *The Third Book of Junior Authors* (New York: H. W. Wilson, 1972).

† A "comprehensive annual reviewing service for reference books published in the United States" for both children and adults is provided by the *American Reference Books Annual,* edited by Bohdan S. Wynar (Littleton, Col.: Libraries Unlimited).

Some Magazines for Children	Title	Address
	Scienceland	501 Fifth Avenue Suite 2101 New York, NY 10017
	Boy's Life	Boy Scouts of America North Brunswick, NJ 08902
	Children's Playmate Jack and Jill Young World	1100 Waterway Blvd. P.O. Box 567 B Indianapolis, IN 46206
	Ranger Rick	National Wildlife Federation 1412 16th Street, N.W. Washington, DC 20036
	Highlights for Children	2300 W. Fifth Avenue P.O. Box 269 Columbus, OH 43216
	Humpty Dumpty Children's Digest	Subscription Office Bergenfield, NJ 07621
	Ebony Jr!	820 S. Michigan Avenue Chicago, IL 60605
	National Geographic World	Department 00577 17th and M Streets N.W. Washington, DC 20036
	Cricket	P.O. Box 100 LaSalle, IL 61301
	Stone Soup	Box 83 Santa Cruz, CA 95063

that should be drawn by students between the card catalog and the *Readers' Guide* is that the former is a listing of books, while the latter is for periodicals.

Locating Information Within Sources

Three parts of books can provide ways of locating information efficiently. These tools are the table of contents,* the glossary, and the index. In the following sections, we will discuss how each of these aids can be introduced and reinforced.

* The table of contents also provides the reader with an overview of a book's organization. This skill will be discussed later in this chapter (page 332).

Figure 8-1 A Checklist of Location Skills Using Book Parts

Table of Contents

1. knows that the table of contents includes titles and page numbers.
2. can use the table of contents to locate a given section
3. can describe how selections are grouped, or classified, in units
4. can skim a table of contents to gain an overview of the book
5. can skim a table of contents of a book that is a collection for names of authors

Glossary

1. can alphabetize
2. can describe the function of the glossary
3. can locate words in a glossary
4. can use guide words effectively
5. can use the pronunciation guide in a glossary
6. can select the most appropriate meaning from several choices

Index

1. can alphabetize
2. can describe the purpose of the index
3. can identify key words for locating specific information
4. can locate information using an index
5. can use cross references

Sequence of instruction. The time to begin teaching the use of the table of contents is at the very beginning of the reading program. The glossary and the index are introduced later, at the time when the books children are using contain these tools.

One logical sequence in which skills could be developed in using the table of contents, glossary, and index is presented in Figure 8–1. As you work with children, you can observe the degree to which each seems to possess the locational skills necessary for efficient use of books as resources, and plan accordingly. You can also ask information-yielding questions at key spots that will cue you to instructional needs:

(Table of Contents)	"The story that I'm going to read to you today is 'The Cap That Mother Made.' Can you think of a way that I could find it quickly in this story book?"
(Glossary)	"The word that you have asked me about is *Arctic*. There's a place in your book to look up the meaning. Do you know where?"
(Index)	"We can find out more about Alaska in this book, but in another place. Do you know where to look to find those page numbers quickly?"

Your observations and informal questions should help you to determine and record each child's ability to use parts of books to locate information efficiently.

Table of contents. The table of contents in a book can be introduced as soon as children begin to read books that include them. In addition to helping the reader locate specific sections, a table of contents can also provide information about the types of stories or information included in a book, the organization of a book, and the relative emphasis of topics within the book. And this information can answer questions such as: What are the titles of selections in this book? What kind of writing is in this book? stories? articles? poems? What can I learn from this book? Is there a main idea for this book? If so, how does the author look at it? How is it divided? How do the units relate to the main focus of the book?

Below and to the right are examples of tables of contents from two low-level elementary texts. The first, *Sun Up*, is a basal reader preprimer by one author. And while the second example, *Going Places, Seeing People*, is simple too, it could better serve to answer more of the questions above.

Stories

From *Sun Up* by Margaret Early et al. (New York: Harcourt Brace Jovanovich, 1974). Reprinted by permission of the publisher.

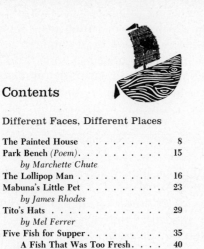

Contents

Different Faces, Different Places

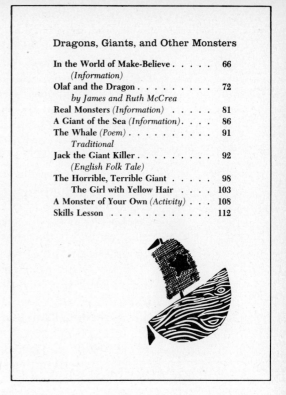

Dragons, Giants, and Other Monsters

From *Going Places, Seeing People* by Margaret Early et al. (New York: Harcourt Brace Jovanovich, 1974). Reprinted by permission of the publisher.

When the teacher guides the beginning reader, the instruction can start with the contents page. "Here's a book that may have some stories you like. Right here at the front is a list of them. Let me tell you some of the stories that are listed in this table of contents. (Reads from the list.) Today's story is 'Sun Up.' Can you guess the page number where we'll find the first page of the story?"

The child either guesses successfully or is told; regular reference to the table before reading will reinforce the understanding that the tool helps to locate. After the basic understanding of the table of contents as a list of what is inside and where it is located, children can learn to use it to "shop" a book, locating stories of interest or information needed for unit studies in the content areas.

Among the practice activities that can reinforce using the table of contents are those that involve children in locating a story and opening the book to where they think the story might begin, finding given titles and calling out the page number, and using the subtitles to guess unit titles that have been blocked out by small strips of paper. The best experience with contents pages, however, occurs when a book is read for a purpose, and the contents page facilitates that reading.

Glossary. Like the use of dictionaries, use of the glossary is one means of recognizing and learning the meaning of a word. The child usually comes to think of the glossary as a particularly handy little dictionary because it is right at the back of the book. The most common level for the introduction of glossaries into children's texts has been third grade. There are some published content materials, however, that include glossaries at lower levels. The time to teach glossaries, then, is when they are there, when children need them, and when the prerequisite dictionary skills are in order.

Ideally, the new vocabulary of content-area reading has been introduced prior to reading through concrete or vicarious experiences. If the child has some problem identifying the word when it reoccurs in print, and seems to have only a vague understanding of its meaning, that child can be led to the glossary. To guide children to the glossary with vocabulary words that they already recognize may teach the existence of the glossary but do little to transfer any awareness of its usefulness.

Because the use of a glossary involves the same skills as the use of a dictionary, it is likely that the majority of children will have acquired some dictionary knowledge before they meet their first glossary. Thus, they need only learn that some authors save the reader time by providing an alphabetical list of words and their meanings at the back of the book. These words are the ones the authors judge to be important to their readers' understanding of the book's ideas.

A Glossary

From "The Green Kingdom" volume of *Childcraft—The How and Why Library.* © 1976 Field Enterprises Educational Corporation.

290

New Words

Here are some of the words you've met in this book. They may be new to you. Many of them are words you'll meet again in other books—so they're good words to know. Some of them are flower names that may be hard for you to pronounce. Next to each word you are shown how to say it correctly: acid (AS ihd) Put the emphasis on the part of the word shown in capital letters. Under each word, the meaning is given in a complete sentence.

acid (AS ihd)
An acid is a chemical substance strong enough to dissolve things.

agronomist (uh GRAHN uh mihst)
An agronomist is a person who studies how to improve the soil so that crops can grow better.

algae (AL jee)
Algae are green plants without stems, roots, or leaves. They live in water or moist soil and make their own food.

alyssum (uh LIHS uhm)
Alyssum is a plant of the mustard family. It has small yellow, pink, rose, or white flowers.

annual (AN you uhl)
An annual is a plant that lives only one year.

anther (AN thuhr)
The anther is a tiny sack on a stem inside a flower. The anthers hold the pollen.

biochemist (BY oh KEHM ihst)
A biochemist is a person who studies the actions and changes of substances in living things.

biologist (by AHL uh jihst)
A biologist is a person who studies living things.

biome (BY ohm)
In nature, a place where certain kinds of plants and animals live together is called a biome. The weather limits the kinds of plants and animals that can live there.

botanist (BAHT uh nihst)
A botanist is a person who studies plants.

broccoli (BRAHK uh lee)
Broccoli is an annual plant that is eaten as a vegetable.

bulrush (BULL ruhsh)
Bulrush is a tall, slender plant that grows in or near water.

cacao (kuh KAY oh)
The cacao is a kind of evergreen tree. Cocoa and chocolate are made from its seeds.

calamus (KAL uh muhs)
Calamus is a plant with long, sword-shaped leaves.

carbon dioxide
(KAHR buhn dy AHK syde)
Carbon dioxide is a heavy, colorless gas that does not have an odor.

carotene (KAR uh teen) or
carotin (KAR uh tihn)
Carotene is a red or yellow color found in plants and animals. Carrots have carotene.

cauliflower (KAW luh flou uhr)
Cauliflower is an annual plant that is eaten as a vegetable.

Like the dictionary, a glossary may give multiple meanings for a word and provide pronunciation aid. Some glossaries give examples of how a word has been or can be used. Other glossaries include page numbers that refer to examples of the word's use in the text, creating an index of terms. Teaching the child to become aware of and to use the glossary involves the introduction of its placement in the book, the practical nature of its entries, and the value of "looking up" terms for added understanding.

Index. Like the other parts of print resources that are used to locate information, indexes vary in complexity. The simplest index and the one that is probably the most familiar to chidren is a newspaper's index. A child's introduction to an index could consist of being asked to locate the comics, the movies, the weather map, and the sports.

index

Amusements	*time out*
Ann Landers	C2
Church	C6-7
Classified Ads	E7-24
Comics	E4-5
Deaths	B6
Editorials	A8
Ellie Rucker	C1
Garden	C3-5
Horoscope	C4
Life/Style	C1-8
Personalities	C2
Sports	D1-8
TV Log	*time out*

A Newspaper Index

The Austin American-Statesman, March 4, 1978. Reprinted by permission.

As already noted, some elementary textbook glossaries carry page numbers at the end of the entry, and this combination of glossary-index is probably the next type of index that a child will encounter. During the middle elementary years, however, children begin to use a variety of content texts and library references that vary significantly in the organization and difficulty of their indexes, making systematic instruction with the index more difficult.

Simple Entry	*More Difficult Entry*
animals, 111–115 astronauts, 85–90 automobiles, 97–102	*animals,* domestic 44–45, 49, 50; endangered species, 58–59; food (see animals by name); homes of, 51–54; hunting by 63, 67–69; mammals, 71; map of (wild), 60; protection, 61–63, 67; wild, 58–69; young, 43, 58; *see also* mammals, reptiles.

It is important that the child's first experiences with a content index system stem from a genuine information search. So you must listen carefully to the child's oral reactions to what is being read in order to determine if there is an interest in more information. For example, "Where does a badger live?" "How does a beaver cut down a tree?" "What animals are enemies to lion cubs?" You can suggest that the book in hand may contain an answer on some other page and then demonstrate where to find the index.

With such a beginning, you are ready to help the child focus on a basic behavior leading to full exploitation of the index: the ability to select the entries or key words most likely to supply page numbers for reference. Suppose, for example, that the child is reading about wild animals and indicates an interest in lions and how lionesses protect their cubs for as long as two years (a fact gained from reading). Rather than supplying an answer, you can suggest that the book might answer the question on another page. The alternatives are to actually look on every page or to turn to the index. The index usually appears to be the most efficient solution.

You may add, "If you can decide on the most important word in your question, we could look under that word first." The child may suspect that *lions* is the key word. You may then suggest that the reader generate some alternative key words and help the child to list other possibilities for finding the information within the book.

"Besides looking under lions, what other words might lead us to information about the cubs' enemies?"

"Let's find out if your first choice gives us results." The thinking, talking, and listing should be interpreted by both you and the child as detective work, in other words, as fun rather than as an exercise that has importance in and of itself.

During early experiences with the index, you should watch the reaction to the new experience of consulting an index, noting any inefficiency or frustration that may signal need for more fully developed prerequisite skills (knowledge of alphabetic sequence, use of guide words, and ability to enter the index with an appropriate term). The children who experience difficulty will require more teacher direction, more guidance, and some reteaching of basic dictionary usage.

The efficient index user can be introduced to more aspects of the index, such as these:

Typographic techniques, such as boldface print, signal major and longer sections.
Persons are entered under their last names.
The more subcategories an entry has, the more emphasis there is on that topic within the book.
There are often-used abbreviations within indexes that should be understood (*illus., diag., pict.*).
Semicolons usually mark the division between entries in an index; commas mark divisions within an entry.
There are cross-references in indexes that are signaled by *see also.*

A delightful index that provides simplicity along with high interest information is that from the *Guinness Book of World Records*.

Wouldn't you like to know the longest snake, the longest sled ride, and the highest paid singer? (Kids would.)

Signatures, see Autographs
Signs, advertising 279–280
Silence, Musical, longest 223
Silver, largest nugget 178, biggest mine 283, most expensive dinner service 360, single piece, highest-priced English 366
Singer, highest-paid 224, opera 224, 240, youngest 224, 225, oldest 225, most successful recording artist 239, 240, group 240; see also Records (Phonograph)
Singing, highest and lowest notes 47, longest marathon 482
Siphon, longest 187
Sitting, unsupported in circle 490
Sit-Ups, most 581
Skateboarding, fastest 482, jumps 482, 483
Skid Marks, longest 305
Skiing, origins, duration 616, highest speed 616, 617, most world titles 616–618, longest jump 618, most Olympic victories 618, 619, cross-country, greatest descent, highest altitude, longest run 619, steepest descent, "hot dog," longest lift, skijoring, ski parachuting 620, ski-bob,

snowmobiling 621; see also **Water Skiing**
Ski Lift, worst accident 436
Skipping Rope 481
Sky-Diving, fastest sport 503; see also **Parachuting**
Sky-Writing, largest letters, earliest 200
Sled Journey, longest 445, 447; see also **Bobsledding**
Sleeplessness, longest period of 52
Slide Rule, longest 184, 185
Slimming 23
Slinging 482
Sloganeer, most successful 212
Sloth, slowest land mammal 61
Smell, most acute sense of 102, chemical compound, most pungent 172, smelliest substance 173
"Smelling Out" 400
Smoker, most voracious 358, G
Smoke-Ring Blowing 482
Snail, most ancient 104, largest, fastest 105, eating 494
Snake, longest 89, longest venomous, shortest, heaviest 90, oldest, fastest-moving, most venomous, longest fangs 91, longest extinct 112

From the *Guinness Book of World Records*. © 1977 by Sterling Publishing Co., Inc., New York.

Summary. Locating information can be fun for children as they get caught up in the mystery of the search and then solve it. The natural reinforcement of "finding just what I looked for" is the best push of all toward more frequent use of the table of contents, glossary, and index. And if the use of all references grows from real needs of children, you will find a natural motivation that can be built upon. There is no limit to the interest or curiosity of children. Listen to them when they speak to you as well as when they talk with one another. You will never stop being amazed at the breadth of their interest and their willingness to seek more information.

Teaching the Child to Understand and Use Graphic Aids

The early humans who painted aspects of their lives on the walls of their caves used pictures to record and communicate information. Discovered thousands of years later, these cave drawings have provided contemporary humans with a richer understanding and appreciation of that period. These paintings alone underscore the significance of the statement that a picture is worth a thousand words. Further significance can be seen from the extensive use of pictures and other graphic aids today as a means for communicating ideas.

Just take a look around you. Graphics are everywhere. Illustrations, symbols, maps, logos, and signs speed messages. Graphics signal where to park, to walk, to drive, to smoke, and to eat. Graphics abound in children's lives also. The earliest reading is usually of the "golden arches," the front of the cereal box, the shape of the ice cream store's sign, and picture maps at a zoo.

The widespread appearance of graphs, pictures, maps, and typographic displays means that readers must be equipped with the knowledge necessary to interpret them. Woe to the driver cruising along at 55 mph in rain who fails to understand the bent arrow on a diamond shape. Precious time is wasted by the shopper who must wander all around the shopping mall because of a lack of understanding of a floor plan. To function efficiently today, one needs to be able to interpret graphics.

When graphic presentations accompany printed text, the ability to read graphics helps the reader comprehend the printed message. Conversely, many graphic aids include text within the graphic display that helps the reader understand the graphic. In most content areas, reading and understanding graphics and relating them to text is an essential part of comprehension. In science, figures, tables, and illustrations are among the many graphic aids that gather detail, support points, and amplify concepts. In the social sciences, maps, charts, figures, tables, and graphs are frequent adjuncts to the printed material; occasionally they summarize what is in the printed matter, but most often they carry significant additional material and the text refers the reader to the graphic aid for more content.

Because so much communication is offered in our lives through graphics and because school materials make continuous use of them, relevant learning situations must be provided by teachers that guide readers to develop the appropriate skills for interpreting and utilizing graphic aids.

The graphic aids that will be discussed in this section are maps, tables, graphs, and illustrations.

Maps of Familiar Places

Maps are graphic descriptions of where things are located in relation to one another. Children need to learn first that maps represent reality, that they can provide a variety of information, and that they are like a bird's-eye view.

To ensure the understanding of these concepts, the initial experience with maps should be as representations of the child's most familiar spaces, such as his or her own bedroom or the classroom.

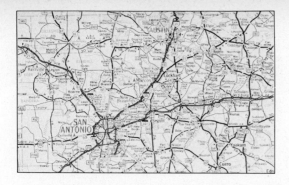

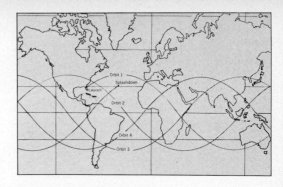

Maps are used by many people and can show many things.

Maps can help you find the easiest route when travelling by car.

Maps are used by airline pilots and ship captains.

They are used for tracking astronauts . . .

Maps are even used to show the weather . . .

There is a lot to know about maps. So let's look at some maps and find out what they tell us.

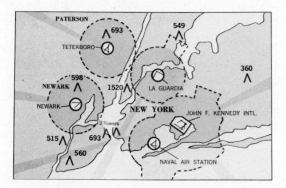

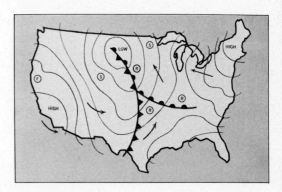

From *What We Find When We Look At Maps* by John Oliver, illustrated by Robert Galster. Copyright © 1970 by John Oliver and Robert Galster. Used with permission of McGraw-Hill Book Company. Detail of map of Texas © AAA. Reproduced by permission.

A map of the classroom. Kindergarten and first-grade children are sometimes led to make a map of their classroom to help visitors, substitute teachers, and new students to locate materials and to feel comfortable. The children may work on one map together. A large piece of paper representing the general dimensions of the classroom can be spread on the floor. At this point, you need not try to teach scale directly; the initial emphasis will be on spatial representations. Find the door and the windows and mark them on the paper. Then provide the children with blocks and help them to arrange the blocks on the paper to represent the furniture and equipment in the room: "This block will be the clay-work table. Where does it go?" "This block is the rocking chair. In what corner does it go?"

After the blocks are placed on the paper in a manner that satisfies the children's sense of space, you can ask whether anyone would like to substitute a smaller or larger block for any that are on the map. As children discuss the relative sizes of tables, shelves, cupboards, the sink, and the chairs, they are introducing themselves to scale. When all is in place, ask several children to draw around the blocks. When the block is lifted away, you can label the shape with the name the child provides. Individual children can make maps of the classroom in two dimensions when provided with an outline shape and colored-paper shapes to arrange. If the shapes are attached with tape, they can be adjusted as the room is rearranged.

In the classroom map below, different shapes for the various types of furniture are used to introduce a simple key for the map.

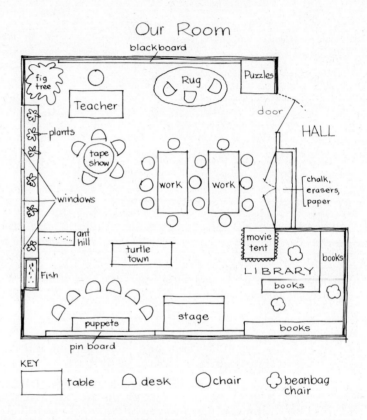

More abstract maps. After children are familiar with the idea of a classroom map, you can introduce maps of more abstraction, such as the school or the community. Such maps are more abstract than a classroom map because the child can look at the classroom map and then immediately look about the room to see how the map represents the room. With a school map, the child can't see the entire plan at once and so must attempt to conceptualize it.

In producing maps of larger and more abstract places, you can teach the notion of scale. If you ask children to sketch a free-hand map of the school, they will discover that some of their maps show classrooms larger than the gymnasium, others have sidewalks wider than classrooms, while others show playground equipment to be smaller than sidewalks. That is the logical time to introduce a unit of measure in order that children can resketch maps to scale. The unit of measure need not be

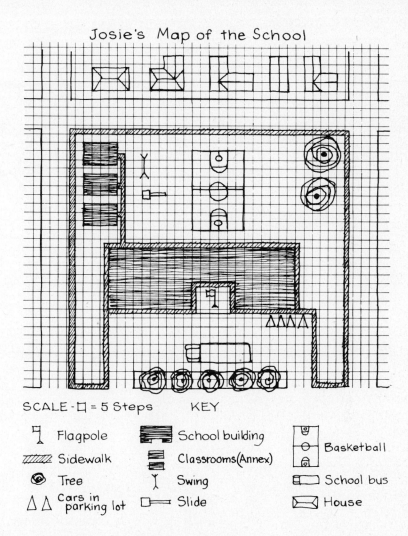

Josie's Map of the School

SCALE - ☐ = 5 Steps   KEY

Flagpole   School building   Basketball

Sidewalk   Classrooms(Annex)   School bus

Tree   Swing

Cars in parking lot   Slide   House

a foot or a meter. It can be steps, a piece of rope, or the length of a table: "This room is six tables long and five tables wide." "The school is 125 steps long and 220 steps wide."

If children decide that they will use steps to measure the school building, you can help them decide how many steps will be equal to one block on some graph paper and then to measure (with steps) other parts of the school's grounds. All of the information they gain that is transferred to graph paper provides them with an introduction to scale and an understanding of how maps communicate.

Children can usually read a map of their own community easier than a map of a more distant or less familiar place. Reading the map of the community for a purpose—to plan a trip, to locate homes or familiar sites—has the same validity as reading print for a purpose: it increases interest and improves comprehension.

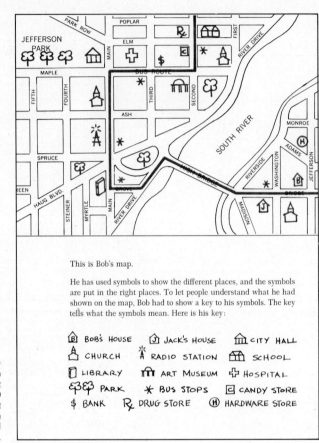

This is Bob's map.

He has used symbols to show the different places, and the symbols are put in the right places. To let people understand what he had shown on the map, Bob had to show a key to his symbols. The key tells what the symbols mean. Here is his key:

From *What We Find When We Look At Maps* by John Oliver, illustrated by Robert Galster. Copyright © 1970 by John Oliver and Robert Galster. Used with permission of McGraw-Hill Book Company.

With the maps of the school and then the community, children can mark the compass directions on a map. By planning the route for a proposed trip, they can talk about (and demonstrate) use of those directions.

Other useful maps. The road map is the most commonly used map by mature readers. But children find many different kinds of maps in their content-area texts. As early as second grade, but especially through the intermediate grades, children can engage in activities that will introduce them to different kinds of maps to interpret.

Some of the maps you will be helping your children to use include road maps that show roads and distances between cities and towns;

physical maps that show the roughness of the earth's surface; distances above sea levels, rainfall, or temperature; political maps, which show different states or countries by their political boundaries; and special maps for showing special features or events such as weather, travel routes, geological features, and population distribution.

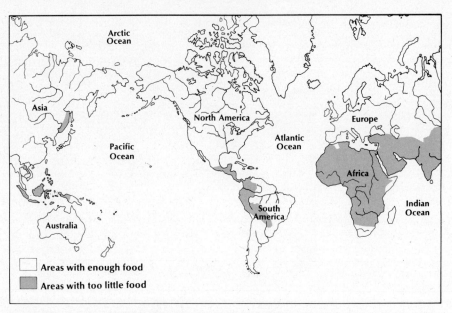

Excerpted from *Biology: Patterns in Living Things* by Evelyn L. Morholt and Paul F. Brandwein. Copyright © 1976 by Harcourt Brace Jovanovich, Inc. and reprinted and reproduced with their permission.

The understanding of these maps is based on the same three concepts for understanding a classroom map. That is, a map is a scaled representation, a map shows relative direction, and a map uses symbols to indicate places. If children develop these concepts with simple classroom, school building, and community maps, learning to use all kinds of maps will be easier for them.

Help Children to Develop Tables

Readers need to understand tables as a concise yet comprehensive method of displaying related facts and information. The occurrence of tables in content-area material gives the reader with the ability to interpret them additional or clarified information. Tables also appear in references such as encyclopedias, almanacs, and research reports. Tables report many things: calories and carbohydrates, the bus schedules, the rise and fall of stocks, and the roomiest car with the best gas mileage.

The basic concepts to be taught about tables are that tables serve several levels of communication and the formulation of ideas and information. Specifically, a reader should understand that from tables:

Specific information can be found.
Information can be used comparatively.
Additional information can be calculated from the information given.
The overall implications or point of the table can be surmised.

Making useful tables. In order to teach children the importance of tables, the tables themselves must be important to children. One way to begin is to help primary children make a chart that will remind each child of the daily maintenance tasks in the classroom and provide each with a chance to serve as caretaker.

Room Helpers

JOB	Monday	Tuesday	Wednesday	Thursday	Friday
Water plants	Tassy			Jay	
Erase boards	Dan	Julie	Tim	Leonard	Ann
Feed fish	Randy	Kathy	Jim	Elaine	Laurie
Run Errands	David	Erin	Mike	Diane	Barbie
Turn off lights	Ken	Jeff	Linda	Paula	Stacy

"Today is Thursday. Who's supposed to feed the fish? What will you do to help today, Leonard?" Note that without any lecture about how tables are made up of rows and columns, the children learn both that tables have them and that one uses the intersection of rows and columns to find needed information.

As the above example suggests, the development of tables for the purpose of teaching how to read and understand them should be a joint activity for teacher and children. When a group of first graders studied pets, they decided to make a list of the pets that each owned and another list that tallied the pets their classmates would like to own. When the lists got longer, one or two of the youngsters began to see duplication. They made comments like these:

"I think more people own dogs than anything else."

"I think cats are second."

"Uh-uh. Fish. Bobby has twenty-seven fish. That's more pets than we've all got together."

Our Pets

	Dogs	Cats	Fish	Gerbils	Guinea Pigs	Turtles	Mice
Jan		2			1		
Tommy			3				4
Sarah	2	1					
Rene			7				
Lisa				1			
Jeffrey			15				
Chris		3			1		2
Michelle	2						
Bobby		1	27				
Marilyn	2						
Kent				3			
Sean	1					1	
Mandy	3			1			
Total	10	7	52	5	2	1	6

The teacher could tell that these children were interested in comparisons and helped them to develop some tables. The children used the columns for the different kind of pets that were represented in the room and the rows for each child's name who had a pet. Another table listed the children who wished for pets and the columns represented their wishes (elephants, lions, and even skunks).

As children become more familiar with the structure of tables, they will need less teacher guidance in the preparation or completion of them. Second graders, for example, practice addition facts by completing mathematics tables:

Addition Table

	0	1	2	3	4	5	6	7	8	9
1	2	3								
2										
3										
4										
5										
6										
7										
8										
9										

Middle graders readily make and use tables that contain information that they need, such as sports statistics, bus timetables, and television schedules. As a part of a study on the effects of television on children, third graders monitored their television viewing by compiling tables that each child filled in, reporting his or her own daily viewing.

Television Tonight

Time	Channel 6	Channel 12	Channel 34	Channel 24
5:00		Mickey Mouse		
5:30				
6:00				
6:30				News
7:00		Happy Days		
7:30				
8:00				
8:30				
9:00				
9:30				
10:00				

These are shows I watched ——————————.
                                    date

My name ——————————.

Upper-elementary youngsters learn to translate print into tables for the purposes of clarification, consolidation, and rapid presentation of data. Children reading a prose paragraph in a science text that presented the class and weight of eggs in the supermarket were encouraged by the teacher to come up with a way to make the information easier to compare and interpret for consumers.

Weigh Your Eggs Before They're Hatched!

Weight class	Minimum weight per dozen eggs in	
	Ounces	Grams
Jumbo	30	850
Extra Large	27	765
Large	24	680
Medium	21	595
Small	18	510
Pee-wee	15	425

In the following example, children listed characters from several stories they read and recorded words that described them.

We Had Words to Describe

	Words that describe appearance	Words that describe feelings	Words that describe actions
Susie	winsome lively	indignant regretful	speedily
Mrs. Willins	meddlesome	cranky nervous	mockingly
Tom	handsome	solemn	politely gently

Teaching tables in texts. Although beginning readers encounter few tables in their reading, they can discover quite early the basic concepts underlying the interpretation of tables. So by the time children reach the middle- and upper-elementary grades, they can interpret more easily the tables encountered in their content texts. To obtain maximum information from tables, the child should learn through repeated contacts with many kinds of tables that the table allows one to: obtain data directly from a concise source; make comparisons between different sets of data; and draw conclusions from existing data.

In the following example, children are required to interpret the table from a science text at the fourth-grade level and to draw a conclusion.

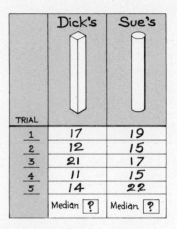

Dick stated a hypothesis. He said his magnet was stronger than Sue's because it was square and hers was round. They made many trials to see how many washers each could pick up. Here are the results. Is Dick's hypothesis correct? What would Dick's conclusion be?

TRIAL	Dick's	Sue's
1	17	19
2	12	15
3	21	17
4	11	15
5	14	22
	Median [?]	Median [?]

From *Elementary Science: Learning by Investigation, Level 4* by A. C. Brewer, Nell Garland, and Jerome J. Notkin (Chicago: Rand McNally, 1972). Reprinted with permission of Rand McNally & Company.

Another example from an elementary science book allows ready comparisons of temperatures for the reader who can use tables.

CITY	WINTER		SUMMER	
Bismarck, North Dakota	9°F	−13°C	71°F	22°C
Detroit, Michigan	26°F	−3°C	74°F	23°C
Albuquerque, New Mexico	35°F	2°C	78°F	26°C
Boise, Idaho	29°F	−2°C	75°F	24°C
Miami, Florida	66°F	19°C	82°F	28°C
New York, New York	32°F	0°C	76°F	25°C
Madrid, Spain	40°F	5°C	74°F	23°C
Nairobi, Kenya	60°F	16°C	67°F	19°C
Tokyo, Japan	34°F	1°C	79°F	26°C
London, England	39°F	4°C	64°F	18°C
San Juan, Puerto Rico	75°F	24°C	80°F	27°C
Nassau, Bahama Islands	70°F	21°C	82°F	28°C

Excerpted from *Biology: Patterns in Living Things* by Evelyn L. Morholt and Paul F. Brandwein. Copyright © 1976 by Harcourt Brace Jovanovich, Inc. and reprinted and reproduced with their permission.

In the social studies, tables are used to report such information as mileage between cities, rainfall rates, height above sea level, and average temperature.

mileage chart

Abilene	Amarillo	Anthony	Austin	Beaumont	Brownsville	Corpus Christi	Dallas	Del Rio	Denison	Eagle Pass	El Paso	Fort Worth	Gainesville	Galveston	Houston	Laredo	Lubbock	McAllen	Odessa	Orange	San Antonio	Temple	Texarkana	Waco	Waskom	Wichita Falls
269																										
473	452																									
216	485	605																								
432	651	854	249																							
524	792	832	332	444																						
392	661	726	197	306	160																					
183	369	656	203	279	535	396																				
248	455	446	233	437	384	281	406																			
242	355	705	278	323	610	471	75	481																		
304	511	502	222	426	328	225	425	56	500																	
453	432	20	585	834	812	707	636	426	695	482																
151	345	624	191	306	523	384	32	373	101	408	604															
200	313	673	259	349	591	452	70	441	42	476	653	68														
402	659	810	211	74	408	248	291	402	366	440	790	314	360													
351	608	765	160	87	357	218	240	350	315	339	745	263	309	51												
381	630	627	233	399	203	144	436	181	511	125	607	419	487	365	312											
167	122	359	390	598	679	548	325	333	332	389	339	293	290	561	510	508										
485	754	773	303	436	59	152	508	325	583	269	753	494	562	397	349	144	641									
168	260	295	339	588	633	495	351	249	410	305	275	319	368	550	499	426	138	570								
458	664	880	276	26	469	332	295	463	339	452	860	327	364	96	113	425	620	462	614							
247	520	595	80	284	276	145	283	153	358	142	575	266	334	249	197	153	403	238	350	310						
182	451	637	69	249	404	265	134	302	209	291	617	122	190	220	169	302	349	372	342	275	149					
367	503	840	341	272	648	509	184	574	157	563	820	216	190	342	291	574	480	640	535	264	421	280				
186	431	641	105	253	437	298	98	338	173	327	621	86	154	234	183	339	355	408	346	279	185	36	244			
349	536	829	298	209	586	447	166	531	192	520	802	198	225	283	229	531	491	578	517	198	378	241	86	205		
143	229	565	286	422	614	483	142	391	126	447	545	116	84	430	379	491	206	576	296	437	338	238	274	202	307	

From *Texas: Land of Contrasts* (Austin: State Department of Highways and Information), p. 158.

In math, tables show relationships such as units of measure. Science tables report experimental results and environmental relationships.

The teacher's responsibility is to be certain the children will encounter the tables of their texts with a purpose for reading the table and the background skills necessary for reading it successfully. With a definite purpose in mind, the interpretation of tables is undertaken more eagerly; with a background in making and reading simple tables, the reader knows how to attack the task. The teacher can guide discussion to promote rereading of such tables to demonstrate their power to reveal their comparative information and to provoke questions that only additional reading can answer.

Teach That Graphs Show Relative Amounts

Graphs, like some tables, show quantitative relationships. As children learn to interpret graphs, the understanding that they must gain is that graphs show how much of something exists compared with something else: How much money has been collected compared with the fund-raising goal? How many children are involved in accidents within the home as compared with accidents at school? There are three other concepts that need to be understood in using the information from any graph:

(1) the kind of information that is being presented—for example, amount of money, number of children, or amounts of time
(2) the unit of measurement used for reporting—for example, thousands of dollars, number of children, or percentage of a total
(3) the significance of the information—what can be learned from the graph?

Types of graphs. Graphs are primarily of four types: picture, bar, line, and circle or pie. Children need to have experience with all of these types; and, as with maps and tables, it is best to start by developing graphs with children that relate to topics that are concrete and familiar to them.

Children enjoy keeping track of information. Discovering ways to share that information helps to teach the utility of graphs. For example, the number of sunny, cloudy, partly cloudy, or rainy days in a month can be recorded in a *picture graph*.

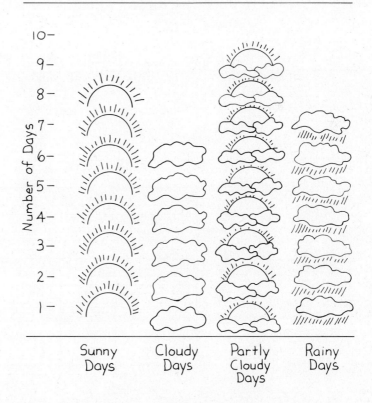

Number of Sunny, Cloudy, Partly Cloudy, and Rainy School Days in April

Another example of a picture graph (pictograph) is this one made by fourth graders to illustrate relative milk consumption by grade.

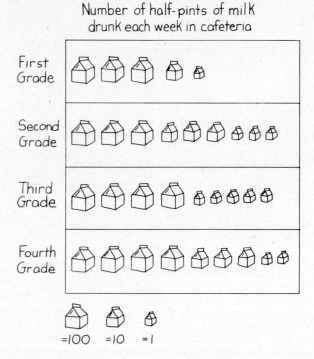

Number of half-pints of milk
drunk each week in cafeteria

Every beginner (who can count) can help to make a graph that shows how many boys and girls are in the class. A simple *bar graph* is the result.

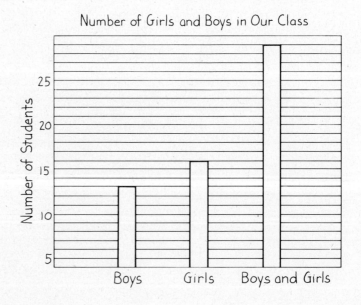

Number of Girls and Boys in Our Class

Line graphs can be developed to keep track of information such as the number of children who attend school each day.

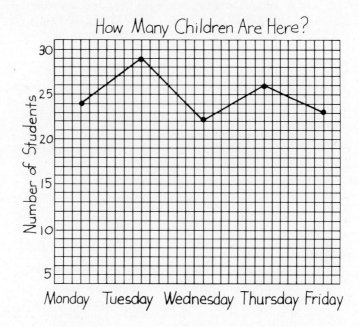

Monday   Tuesday   Wednesday   Thursday   Friday

Circle or pie graphs are more difficult to learn to read because they often deal with percentages or fractions. The picture, bar, and line graphs can be introduced as early as first or second grade, especially if they deal with very concrete information. Interpretation of the circle graph, however, depends upon children's understanding of parts of a whole. In many schools, fractions are taught in second and third grade, and this is the time that circle graphs can be introduced.

When children have experienced percentages, the picture graph on page 352 should become a circle graph.

Percentage of Sunny, Cloudy, Partly Cloudy, and Rainy School Days in April

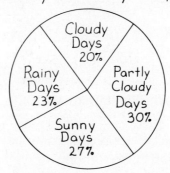

The significance of graphs. Authors tend to include graphs when they feel the text needs to be clarified or expanded. Sometimes graphs provide more impact than the text alone. In other instances, graphs provide the reader with specific information and the data to make comparisons, projections, and to draw conclusions. Careful reading of a graph can help the reader to survey or to preview the accompanying print. Graphs provide the teacher with an opportunity to encourage students to predict the content and then read to verify those predictions. After reading a passage, rereading a graph serves as a check on the reader's grasp of the author's explanation.

Children who can make their own graphs will learn to read the graphs included in content material more quickly. The following graph (and the language-experience story that explains it) was done by kindergarten children.

Tiburcio said, "We color the cup."
Sarah said, "We plant the bean."
Felicia said, "We put water in the cup."
Cheryl said, "The bean grew up."
Yvonne said, "The bean made a leaf."

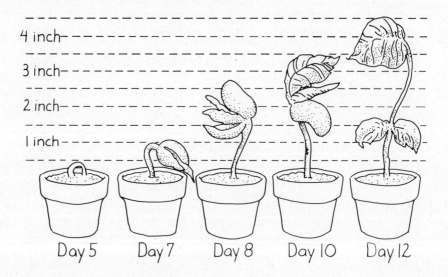

Teach Illustrations with the Text

There are several kinds of graphics that expand and clarify texts—among them are diagrams and pictures. (Maps and charts are, of course, illustrations and they have been discussed earlier.) For the most part, authors provide illustrations in order to supplement and explain the text. The fact that an author felt the need to use a diagram, for example, may mean that the information can be clarified with a picture. Skillful reading of illustrations, then, should improve comprehension of print.

Attention to illustration can be taught in several ways. The teacher may choose to call attention to the picture, diagram, or chart as a kind of preorganizer for the reading. The discussion would serve to relate the illustration with the text, so that the picture helps the reader to focus upon the likely main idea of the selection. Another technique is to use follow-up questioning to direct attention to the illustration, again tying the graphic presentation to the written referent. By providing for the student to reread the material after discussion of the illustration, the teacher can ensure that main points can be located.

Teaching a diagram.   Diagrams are most common in children's science and social studies books where they serve to clarify new vocabulary or illustrate difficult concepts. Children learn to attend to diagrams and receive their messages by being asked to label them. Given the diagram below, the most direct teacher question is: "What does this diagram show?" The child who can answer "parts of a grasshopper" reveals a grasp of the message and is ready to discuss the details of the diagram.

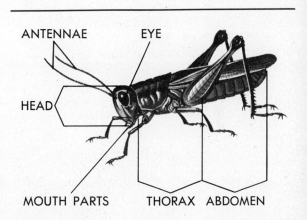

From *Exploring and Understanding Insects* by Barbara J. Collins (Westchester, Ill.: Benefic Press, 1970), p. 8. Used by permission.

Growth in ability to read a diagram may, however, depend upon guided observations and focused questions that the teacher provides. Thus, while some children are ready to label the diagram, identify its details, and predict its relationship to the text, other children must be led: "What are some of the labels that you see here?" "Why has a drawing been included here?" "What is the illustrator showing us?"

In addition to labeling the diagrams of others, middle- and upper-elementary children can create diagrams of their own to clarify or interpret text.

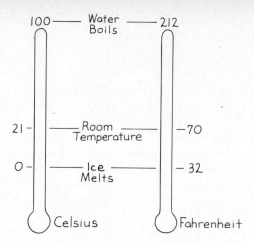

Teaching the reading of pictures. Reading a picture is much like interpreting a diagram or a map. Readers can preview the picture to provide them with clues to the text. By noting the detail in the picture, children are more alert for those same details in the reading. When the teacher helps the child to ask questions about the picture, yet leaves those questions unanswered, there is purpose for reading. When pictures enhance details, there is basis for discussion. Good picture-reading skill is similar to good text-reading skill: it is the habit of predicting content so that the reading can serve to verify or modify hunches.

The steps in effective picture reading that are offered below represent only one example of teacher-directed picture interpretation.

Level 1 is an overview of the picture: "What is going on here?"

Level 2 is encouraging children's questions about the picture that may be answered in the text: "What is the boy doing?" "Why does the child look frightened?" "What may have just happened?"

Level 3 is reading the text to answer some of the questions and to verify the main hypothesis: "What was going on?"

Level 4 is incorporating details from both the text and the picture to promote thinking that ranges beyond both: "I'm not sure that child really would have felt frightened at this point, because . . ."

Promoting Flexible Rates of Reading Comprehension

> Some books are to be tasted, others to be swallowed, and some few to be chewed and digested. (Francis Bacon, *On Studies*)

A reader's purpose for reading a particular book or article should determine the rate at which he or she reads. That purpose can range from the need for deliberate analysis in order to comprehend thoroughly to the need for speed in order to glean only a main idea. Fitting the rate to the kind of comprehension that purpose dictates is an important reading and study skill for all children to learn. In order to achieve the goal of helping readers achieve different rates for different purposes, the teacher's goal should be to teach the child to reflect on the purpose for reading each time that he or she reads, and then consciously select the reading rate necessary to achieve that purpose. Teaching children how and when to vary their reading rates will help them to achieve their purposes for reading more efficiently.

Purpose Determines Reading Rate

If curling up with good literature is the goal, the reader reads slowly, stopping to savor the language of the author and to let mental images seep in. If trying to get an overview of the daily news before an 8:00 A.M. appointment is the goal, the reading speed is rapid, the eyes make jumping motions across columns, and detail is forsaken in favor of main ideas. If gaining familiarity with a difficult subject is the goal, the reader may preview a selection by reading the table of contents, then the title and paragraph heads of one chapter, followed by a rapid skimming for main ideas, and finally, a careful speed to put together details that illustrate and support major headings. Not all readers have different rates of reading for different purposes. Some just have one gear and do all their reading at one rate regardless of purpose.

In addition to purpose, other factors influence reading rate:

Difficulty of the material.   The difficulty of the reading selection* as compared with the reader's instructional level affects the rate of reading comprehension. A reader with a fourth-grade instructional level who attempts to read a seventh-grade text will certainly be slowed considerably. As any reader's prowess develops, however, the range of material that can slow the reading rate narrows.

Familiarity with the topic.   Even if a selection is written at a difficult level, a reader who has considerable background experience with that topic will be able to increase the rate of reading comprehension. Similarly, lack of familiarity will slow a reader's rate. As we have stressed earlier, this factor can be influenced by the teacher who attempts to build the reader's interest, purpose, and background.

Reading habits.   Many children learn to read in a word-by-word fashion, carefully identifying each word, even subvocalizing when the reading is silent. While word-by-word reading can be useful when reading a difficult content text, it is not appropriate for all purposes. If children develop the habit of reading everything at the same pace (whether too rapidly or too slowly), they will not be able to easily adjust their reading

* The level of difficulty of material is often judged by readability formulas. The formulas, which judge difficulty of a passage by such factors as average length of sentences and number of difficult words, vary in complexity and ease of application. This is briefly discussed in Chapter 9.

rates for different purposes. Providing children with opportunities to practice flexibility will help solve this problem. In the following section, we will discuss several guidelines for helping readers to gain flexibility.

Controlling the Purpose

When a child learns that there are different reasons for reading and that the reader can determine the appropriate rate, that child is ready for opportunities to skim, scan, and read closely. The young reader will need practice with all three rates, and you can help develop the reasons and provide the appropriate materials.

Skimming. Skimming is a type of reading in which the material is covered rapidly in order to grasp main ideas. A good skimmer learns to pick out the main ideas by rapidly collecting key words, phrases, and sentences. Internal heads (subheads) are useful to the skimmer because they summarize the following subsection so that the skimmer's speed increases to verify the content that has been signaled. Recognizing and following the organization of the writing—which is discussed on pages 363–66—is a particularly useful skill to the skimmer.

There are various reasons for skimming. Often the reader is under time constraints. And even without time constraints, the reader may want to examine the material quickly to see if he or she wants to read it at a slower rate for more thorough comprehension.

To encourage the child to practice skimming, you must offer as valid and real a purpose as possible:

Skim a selection to see if this writer includes information that will answer your question.

Skim through the story and tell me about it. Then read at a regular rate; did you find out more information?

Skim a selection to determine if it has any material related to a topic you're studying.

Skim the table of contents and describe the book.

Skim a newspaper or a magazine to find more information about something you're studying in class.

Skim a chapter or article and tell me the sequence of events.

Browse through a collection of books in the classroom library, pick one or more to read, and tell me why you picked it.

Find the shelf area in the library that is likely to contain books that are of interest to you.

Scanning. Scanning is the perusal of material for the purpose of finding specific information. The scanning technique depends on some preset purpose or question. The scanner moves his or her eyes quickly over the page, alert for specific terms or key phrases that fulfill the purpose or answer the question. Often scanning is combined with a skimming technique—for example, the reader may scan a selection to locate paragraph heads which signal needed content, then skim those paragraphs to determine if their contents are applicable to the problem.

No body of research information exists to substantiate when a child is ready to scan. Many children are never taught this skill that provides them with an alternative rate: they pick it up for themselves later in life as the demands of adult reading increase. Other readers are likely to maintain one reading rate for all material unless given specific demonstrations and instructions with scanning; in this case, even some second-grade-level readers are successful with scanning. Usually, initial instruction in scanning provides that the reader have suitable material (an information article, for example, from a child's text, tradebook, periodical, or newspaper) and a stated purpose for scanning.

The simplest scanning task is to locate numerals in print. So young readers are often asked to: "Read fast to see if you can find how old the giant sequoias are." or "Read to find out the length of a newborn whale."

The next logical step in developing scanning skills is to locate proper nouns in print. Capital letters seem to announce themselves: "Read to find the name of the capital city of Italy."

When children seem to be able to adjust their reading rates to scan for numerals and proper nouns, you can ask the child to rapidly locate the answer to a question that you frame in the exact language of the text. For example, suppose the text reads in some part, "The City Council wants to add a chemical called fluoride to the city's water supply." Your question (or purpose statement) may be: "Scan the paragraph to find out what chemical the City Council wants to add to the city's water supply."

Finally, children can scan for information that is based on a less literal translation of the text: "Is there any information here about what a gerbil will eat?" As children begin to set their own purposes for reading, they can choose to scan when scanning will serve their purpose. If you stay in touch with the children's reading material, however, you will be able to spot opportunities to encourage children to scan.

Close reading.   Much of the content reading in school-type situations is done in an attempt to remember the author's ideas.* Other reasons for reading closely include reading to analyze characters, to understand special-content concepts, to draw relationships, to seek patterns, and to analyze style. Close reading of content material usually means that the reader is attempting to be aware of the organization, the relationship of subordinate ideas to main ideas, and is making an effort to weave newly encountered information into an existing framework.

This is the rate that children learn first and they often get stuck in this gear. In certain cases when children do *not* seem to be reading closely enough to get the message, you should check for other potential

* Much of the emphasis in Chapter 7 was on helping readers to grasp an author's ideas and to interpret them.

"Two funny things happen on this page. Put one clothespin on the page next to each funny thing."

"Here are four steps that you will take to make the cookies. When you have read the recipe, put the steps in order."

| Wash your hands |
| Turn on the oven |
| Measure the ingredients |
| Put the dough on the cookie sheets |

"There are questions on these cards about this article. As you read, if you find an answer, paperclip the question to that page."

| How will you know if the plant gets too much water? |

| What should happen to the seeds in the closet? |

"A letter addressed to you is in your book. It has questions about the story. As you read, write the page number that tells the answer. If you add up the page numbers you write, the secret total is 272."

Dear Andy,
Here are some questions about your reading today. When you find an answer, write the page number next to the questions.
                                        Page
What does a newborn
    whale look like?   ___
Does a baby whale know
    how to swim as
    soon as it is born?   ___
What kinds of danger
    threaten whales?   ___
About how large does
    the blue whale get?   ___
                    Total <u>272</u>

causes of the difficulty rather than encourage the child to slow the reading rate. Some of the potential causes may be an inappropriately difficult text, the child's need for a specific purpose for reading, for a shorter reading selection before responding, for guided silent reading, or for more background and vocabulary development before reading.

Flexibility Means More Than Speed

There are some general concerns about reading rate which you should be aware of.

Breaking old habits and building new ones.   Many children are convinced that they must read every word on a page, that they must start at the first word and end with the last, and that they should never skip ahead. Sometimes the reliance upon one rate is the result of instruction and sometimes it is the result of habit. Whatever the cause, children need to develop flexibility by matching their rates to their changing purposes for reading. Many of the procedures suggested above will encourage the child to adjust rate according to the reason for which he or she reads.

Using timed exercises. Timed reading exercises can be used to teach rate flexibility, but they should be used only with those children who have mastered basic word-recognition skills and who show an interest in rate improvement. No child should ever be pressured into timed reading exercises; and when timed exercises are used, some type of comprehension check should follow the reading—for example, questions, retelling, or discussion of the reading. It is also important that timed reading exercises should be at the reader's independent reading level. Some students enjoy charting their increasing reading rates.

Using mechanical aids. Machines or hardware, such as reading pacers, are useful in helping students improve and maintain rate as long as the machine is used. However, the gains in rate using mechanical devices don't always transfer to print. An alternative to the machines is to encourage intermediate-level readers to try to read faster (when a faster rate is called for) by moving their eyes more rapidly over the page of print, or by using their finger in a sweeping back-and-forth motion across the page with the eye keeping pace. Emphasis on changing eye movements by machines is not recommended by most reading authorities. The major advantage of the pacing machines designed to improve reading rate is that children often like to manipulate them, so machines can serve as expensive motivators.

Emphasizing reading speed. Most of us are intrigued by the concept of "speed reading." The appeal of being able to read an entire novel in less than an hour or to read lengthy assignments in just a few minutes is attractive. But there is evidence that the physiological and psychological limits of reading speed are about 800–1,000 words per minute. This does not mean that we cannot improve our reading speed: the average reading speed for adults is about 250–300 words per minute.

There are several important points to consider before attempting to increase the reading speed of the children you teach. First, you should set as your goal the improvement of the rate of reading comprehension. Reading speed should never be considered separately from comprehension. Merely speeding the eyes over print without comprehending is not reading at all.

Flexible reading rate means shifting rate gears when the purposes for reading change and sometimes even changing purposes within the same materials. For example, when readers find specific information by scanning, they may slow to read that section closely. And what the reader learns in that close reading may create new interest and modify the original purpose for reading. This type of shift is more likely to occur between skimming and close reading. As readers grasp the main ideas

Speed Reading?

There has been a continuing debate about "speed reading programs." The debate has focused primarily on how fast people can read. Reading researchers have concluded that the most rapid reading cannot exceed 800–1,000 words per minute. Ronald P. Carver, a noted reading researcher, summarizes the evidence this way:

> When we read normally, our eye movements are under immediate control of the material being read. Our eyes do not move faster than our information-processing ability functions. We usually read at a rate that makes complete sense of written material. Several researchers have shown that an intelligent individual reading very easy material cannot comprehend most of the material at rates above 500 to 600 words per minute. There is evidence that suggests that persons who read normally at 200 to 300 words per minute cannot function at faster rates because of the distracting influence of conscious eye movement. If we become conscious of the individual parts that make up the act of reading, we are no longer reading. Most reading researchers agree that reading rates above 800 to 1,000 words per minute are physiologically impossible. (1972, p. 25)

The claims of the advertisers of speed reading courses and materials often run counter to Carver's conclusions. The claims are made that John F. Kennedy learned to read 12,000 words per minute and that you can do the same. Such claims notwithstanding, controversy will continue.

by skimming, they may be enticed to begin reading (or to reread) closely, looking for the elaboration of ideas.

In encouraging flexibility, remember to help children to begin to define their own purposes for reading ("I'm reading this to find out who won the game.") and to select an appropriate rate ("I can read fast and look for the score.").

Practice in shifting rates can be promoted, too. When a child discusses what has been scanned or skimmed, watch for opportunities to intensify interest in the material that will promote close reading. In teaching close reading, watch for chances to promote predictions that will send the child ahead at a rapid pace—skimming or scanning for verification.

Briefly, the discussion on reading rate can be summarized by the following points:

Reading rate is determined by one's purpose for reading.

Rate flexibility means not only using different rates for different predetermined purposes, but also shifting rates when purposes change.

To get a quick grasp of main ideas, one skims.

To find specific information quickly, one scans.

Comprehension is the ultimate goal—not the rate.

Reading closely is the way to get full comprehension. Reading fast at the expense of comprehension is no asset to the reader.

Organizing Thinking in Writing

The mature reader enhances comprehension by identifying, following, and using the author's organization. As children become independent learners, they must acquire the ability to follow the author's organization of a content text in order to better understand and recall the information.

When we discussed the table of contents earlier in this chapter (pages 332–33), we noted that not only does it serve as a tool for locating parts of the book but it can also provide information as to how the book's contents are organized.

In the following example of a contents page from *This Is Man*, the unit titles, chapter titles, and subheads help to give an overview of the organization and help the reader to be alert to the patterns in which ideas are developed and related.

In a guided overview of a book's contents, you should encourage the child to draw inferences from the table and to make some assumptions about the scope of the book and its organization.

From *This Is Man* by Vincent R. Rogers (Morristown: N.J.: Silver Burdett, 1972), pp. 2–3. Used by permission.

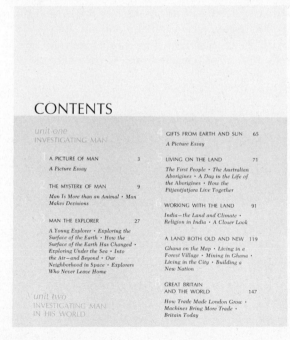

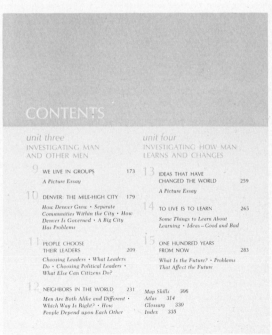

CONTENTS

The first chapter's title sets up the distinction between mankind and other living things as a mystery that is explained by the subtitles. Those intellectual qualities lead to the second chapter's consideration of man as a searcher, and the subtitles indicate a treatment that is organized both by aspects of environment and by history. The last of these, however, brings the reader back to earth to consider in the second unit how mankind has coped with and developed the world. The chapter titles in this unit are intriguing because, with their subtitles, they force a reader to consider survival, as exemplified by the Aborigines; the basic uses of land, as exemplified by India; the development of civilization, as exemplified in Ghana; and modern exploitation of the world, as exemplified by Great Britain.

The table of contents of this book begs questions like, "Why Denver?" And its subtitles indicate answers, such as "This is an example of how mankind's way of living together developed." By reading and studying this table of contents, a child could both predict the overall theme and subthemes of the book and expect that the development of ideas would follow picture essays with examples of places portrayed in some historical order. Not all tables of contents provoke thinking about themes as much as this one does, but any can be used to lead young readers to an assessment of how a book is organized.

In addition to the overview of organization, content authors tend to draw from a set of organizational techniques to present information within books. The most common types of organization include sequence, enumeration, cause and effect, and comparison and contrast (see Chapter 7).

By examining the materials children will be using, you can watch for segments that use an identifiable organization pattern and can guide the reader to some familiarity with it. In addition, you can encourage discussions and provide materials that offer introductions to the other ways of organizing information.

How to Teach Organization

There are six general considerations that should guide you in teaching the use of organization.

The first is to teach recognition of the way an author organizes the material only when that understanding will enhance the child's enjoyment and/or understanding. For example, a mystery story that begins with an event and moves ahead to unravel the cause of that event is a common cause-and-effect organization that does not necessarily have to be pointed out to the reader in order to allow the reader to follow and get sense from the reading. But a social studies text that uses cause and effect might offer a valid opportunity to call attention to its organization. For example, if a unit begins by describing how uncomfortable and hungry the Pilgrims were by the beginning of their first spring in America, the logical organizing behavior is to look for the cause of the effects. The teacher's task is to note the organizational pattern before children read in order to stir the interests of the reader to make guesses about the causes of these hardships before going on to find what the author said caused the difficulties. In that social studies text, the reader's comprehension of the unit will be at least partially dependent on understanding the organization.

The second consideration is to avoid using technical terminology to teach organization. The point is to get the child to understand and use various patterns of organization—not to be able to label the patterns as *enumeration* or *cause and effect*.

The third thing to keep in mind is to encourage the child to test an author's thinking. Too often, perhaps, teachers miss opportunities to receive the child's reactions because of adherence to a predetermined plan or set of questions. If the child's experience or previous reading has provided information that is in conflict with an author's statements, there ought to be time provided for investigation, rechecking, and appraisal of sources.

The fourth consideration when teaching organization is to tie it into activities that teach the child skills of outlining. As soon as a reader can list the author's main points, he or she has mastered the first step in outlining a text.

The fifth consideration in helping readers to use the author's organization is to focus attention on boldface subheads or paragraph heads. Again, if the reader can turn the subhead into a question, he or she may predict what information that section will provide, then read to answer the question and confirm the prediction.

The sixth point is to take note when student texts provide study guides that describe the organization and sometimes guide the reader by providing marginal notations, questions, and cautions ("This is important; review."). These guides can be used just as subheads are—as indicators of the main ideas and as ways to predict content.

Most Children Can Follow Sequence

Sequence and chronology are closely related organizational schemes, dealing with the order of events over time. Sequence is a common method of organizing elementary texts even within the primary grades. Math and science texts that offer activities that stress following steps or directions are prescribing a sequence for activity.

At other times, texts aren't nearly so explicit in the prescription of the sequence. Words like *first, now, next, then,* and *after* signal that the discussion is following some sequential presentation. Locating those key words when they occur in children's reading and discussing their significance is one way to help children learn to attend to sequential organization.

Another opportunity for calling attention to sequential organization is to provide the child with an out-of-order sequence of a selection that is to be read and then ask that the correct sequence be established by reading—for example:

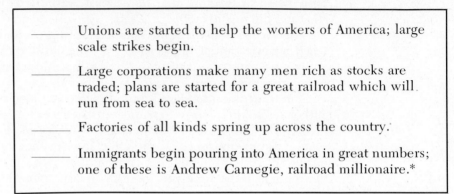

_____ Unions are started to help the workers of America; large scale strikes begin.

_____ Large corporations make many men rich as stocks are traded; plans are started for a great railroad which will run from sea to sea.

_____ Factories of all kinds spring up across the country.

_____ Immigrants begin pouring into America in great numbers; one of these is Andrew Carnegie, railroad millionaire.*

Finally, it should be established that when a child's attention is directed to any sequence, that sequence should be important in the presentation of ideas or else it should be ignored.

When to Teach Enumeration

To recognize enumeration, the child needs to be alerted to cue words or phrases that introduce the enumeration. Sometimes the cue to an upcoming enumeration is as simple as a cardinal number: The sun helps plants grow in three ways.

The teacher's prompting can alert the reader to watch for such number cues. Often the subsequent points are set off with ordinal numbers: *first, second,* and so on.

Other cues that signal enumeration are more general, such as words like *several, many, some,* and *a few.* When less specific words are first encountered, the teacher may guide the reading by a question: "The author says that there were many reasons that people left England and came to America. How many are discussed and what are they?" As the reader becomes more self-directed, he or she may learn to turn the cue automatically into a question to guide reading.

All of the uses of organization presented here are only valuable to readers who are meeting various types of organizational patterns within their reading. The needs of these readers will be served if they are cued to the way in which the selection or content text is presenting ideas and leading the thinking. Better comprehension should be a result of the ability to follow and predict the presentation of ideas.

*Naunerle Farr and Dennis Dostert, *The Industrial Era: 1865–1915* (West Haven, Conn.: Pendulum Press, 1976).

REFERENCES   Anastasiow, Nicholas J., and Hanes, Michael T. *Language Patterns of Poverty Children*. Springfield, Ill.: Charles C. Thomas, 1976.

Carver, Ronald P. "Speed Readers Don't Read; They Skim." *Psychology Today* (August 1972): 22–30.

Cheyney, Arnold B. *Teaching Reading Skills Through the Newspaper*. Newark, Del.: International Reading Association, 1971.

Fay, Leo. "How Can We Develop Reading Study Skills for the Different Curriculum Areas?" In *Individualizing Reading Instruction: A Reader*, edited by Larry A. Harris and Carl B. Smith. New York: Holt, Rinehart and Winston, 1972.

————, and Jared, Lee Ann, comps. *Reading in the Content Fields: An Annotated Bibliography*. Newark, Del.: International Reading Association, 1975.

Henry, George. *Teaching Reading as Concept Development: With Emphasis on Affective Thinking*. Newark, Del.: International Reading Association, 1974.

Herber, Harold L. *Teaching Reading in Content Areas*. Englewood Cliffs, N.J.: Prentice-Hall, 1970.

Maxwell, Martha J. *Skimming and Scanning Improvement*. New York: McGraw-Hill, 1969.

Russell, David H. "Concepts." In *Encyclopedia of Educational Research*, 3d ed., edited by C. W. Harris. New York: Macmillan, 1960.

Thelen, Judith. *Improving Reading in Science*. Newark, Del.: International Reading Association, 1976.

Vernon, Magdalen D. "The Value of Pictorial Illustration." *British Journal of Educational Psychology* 23 (1953): 180–87.

FOR FURTHER READING   Berger, Allen, and Peebles, James D., comps. *Rate of Comprehension*. Newark, Del.: International Reading Association, 1976.

Burmeister, Lou E. *Reading Strategies for Secondary School Teachers*. Reading, Mass.: Addison-Wesley, 1974.

Hafner, Lawrence E. *Improving Reading in Middle and Secondary Schools*. New York: Macmillan, 1974.

Herber, Harold L. *Teaching Reading in Content Areas*. Englewood Cliffs, N.J.: Prentice-Hall, 1978.

Karlin, Robert. *Teaching Elementary Reading: Principles and Strategies*. New York: Harcourt Brace Jovanovich, 1975.

Laffey, James L., ed. *Reading in the Content Areas*. Newark, Del.: International Reading Association, 1974.

Richards, I. A. "Powers and Limits of Signs." In *Media and Symbols: The Forms of Expression, Communication, and Education,* edited by D. R. Olson. The Seventy-third Yearbook of the National Society for the Study of Education. Chicago: University of Chicago Press, 1974.

Robinson, H. Alan. *Teaching Reading and Study Strategies: The Content Areas*. Boston: Allyn and Bacon, 1975.

Thelen, Judith. *Improving Reading in Science*. Newark, Del.: International Reading Association, 1976.

Thomas, Ellen Lamar, and Robinson, H. Alan. *Improving Reading in Every Class*. Boston: Allyn and Bacon, 1977.

4

Planning the Program

9) Organizing for Instruction: Students, Time, Space, and Materials

Perhaps the most difficult task facing the new teacher, and one that necessitates great expenditures of time and energy, is the preparation for the organization and management of the classroom reading program. The payoff for the effort expended in organizing, however, will be increased efficiency and more effective reading instruction. This chapter considers the task of organizing and managing the reading program in terms of *who* and *what* can be organized and discusses the steps toward effecting an efficient, pupil-centered reading program. Aspects of organization that will be considered are: organization of students (both group and individual patterns); organization of time; organization of space; and organization of materials.

Some Guidelines for Organization

It would be easier to lapse into a more "traditional" mode by relying upon published and packaged materials to define your reading program than it will be to consider the unique strengths and needs among children under your direction and to select materials accordingly. It would be easier to apply instruction in a blanket fashion than it will be to consider individual differences among learners. And it would be easier not to accept the challenge to plan and carry through programs of instruction geared to the individual interests of children. The problems that result from the easier way out are evidenced by the child who falters, the child who needs special help, the child with different interests, or the child who learns best in a unique way. Ultimately, each child falls into one or more of those categories.

No one knows for certain how to determine the ways in which children learn best. Learning styles may be as diverse as the children themselves. Nor does reading research seem to support any *one* prescribed sequence of skill-development activities, any one combination of materials, or any one method. Remembering that "experts" aren't certain, perhaps you will be less in awe of the prescribed sequence of instructional objectives and activities in published materials and will begin to draw upon guides, teachers' editions, and kits as tools to supplement your own experiences—and intuition.

Paradoxically, freedom to learn will result from organization and careful planning. Provision for individuals is the strongest impetus for extending your efforts. These guidelines for effective organization should also increase the efficiency of learning:

(1) Organization should provide for the specific instructional needs of each child.
(2) Organization should build on the interests of children.

Providing for Each Child's Specific Instructional Needs

There is no one best organizational system for any classroom. You have been reminded repeatedly that children vary markedly. This is true even when schools place children into similar achievement groups. Any organizational system you devise will be valid to the extent that it allows you to provide for differences. Ultimately, the teacher relies upon initial diagnostic information and the results of informal assessments, observations, and interviews to make judgments about reading interests, attitudes, and needs as well as to determine an instructional reading level for each child. But the initial organization may be the assignment of children to groups based *just* on instructional reading level. Unfortunately, what should be merely a starting point has been consistently adhered to as *the* organizational schema by many teachers. When (and if) the organization changes, it is often to reduce the total number of instructional groups–not to expand or to refine the system. The underlying premise for those teachers may be that, given good instruction, individual differences will be eradicated and children will be brought "up to grade level" in reading. A better premise is: given appropriate instruction, the range of differences within each classroom should broaden as time goes by. No one-criterion grouping system (by achievement, for example) can provide for the divergence. As your own skills increase, you will find that you can meet children's needs flexibly on the bases of many grouping criteria (interest, instructional need, problem-solving, friendship) and that you have increased time to deal with each child as his or her individuality dictates.

Specific instructional needs are partially uncovered during initial informal assessments. As large groups (or groups based on instructional reading levels) meet, as children are given opportunities to read to you, to talk about their reading, and to perform related tasks, you will have further information for augmenting and revising the organizational plan. It is important that you collect and use this information as you work to develop an organizational system based on individuals rather than upon static groups. The record keeping, however, can bog down if you don't resolve to keep records *handy, simple,* and *short.* Examples of record keeping based on observations of students' reading behaviors are included on pages 380–88 of this chapter and on pages 50–75 of Chapter 2.

Finally, don't be misled by glossy kits or packaged materials that offer you an organizational system within a box. The individualization that results from one of these packaged programs goes only so far as to offer students different entry points and a different pacing through identical materials. Your organizational system should provide for differentiated assignments as well as pacing. When students move through the same sets of books, skills pages, tapes, and filmstrips, the same learning centers, projects, and learning contracts, but vary only in the rate at which the tasks are accomplished, individual differences have not been recognized. By taking the whole child into consideration, you accept the fact that children will learn in different ways, at different times, and in different orders (even though the ways, times, and order don't always appear logical to the adult mind). This means that some children can learn easily with any adopted basal reader and skills book; others flourish when they realize the connection between speech and print via language experience; others can blend speech sounds to decode print; while still others appear to learn easily in other ways. Combinations of approaches, of styles, and of materials must be tried out and adjusted. Organization that provides for individuals does not refer to the differentiated rate (fast, medium, or slow) through which pupils progress in *identical* materials.

Providing for Each Child's Reading Interests

We have repeatedly said that instruction should be geared to the individual interests of each child—but certainly this is easier to say than to put into practice. However, children whose interests are being tapped, sparked, and provided for are easier to teach. Instruction based on a child's interests means planning for book sharing, problem-solving, and outlets for curiosity. It means considering all sources of print for the reading program as well as breaking away from dependence upon one series, one manual, and one source of supplementary aids. It also means freedom to deviate from a prescribed plan, to recognize that children learn to read by reading, and that they will most likely read what they have interest in.

A student teacher once said to a second grader, who was hiding a book about modeling clay in his lap, "Put your book away; it's time for reading." Reading to this teacher wasn't figuring out how to make a clay figure from a book; reading meant something prescriptive, controlled, and not necessarily child-initiated. Teachers must capture the interest of children and must help them to develop new interests, planning the reading program to ensure that this occurs. But the time set aside for reading instruction should not be just the culmination of the teacher's planning. ("These are the activities and materials I have gathered for today.") Rather, instruction that considers the child follows the child's curiosity and permits exploration with print, continuous investigation to answer his or her own questions, and the recognition and encouragement of children's interests.

Before any organizational schema can be initiated or implemented, the organizer must decide on his or her priorities, asking the most important question: What is it that I want to accomplish with children? There can be no effective organization without specifying the goals for the learners under your direction.

What Are Goals?

Goals are broad statements of what the teacher hopes to accomplish through instruction. Referred to also as general objectives or just objectives, these statements guide the entire learning-teaching process. Goals deal with the outcomes of instruction; they encompass the application of what is to be learned. Rather than describing specific behaviors, goals are general statements of the expected results of education.

The development and understanding of goals for a reading program may seem to be an impossible and confusing task to you. There is some evidence that practicing teachers regard them as pointless and futile. In an article in which she reports on her observations of several classrooms Durkin (1975) concluded that much reading instruction appears not to have a goal other than "filling up a day."

It seems rather simple to state that goals are needed so that instructional time can be planned to meet them. But that is exactly the case. Durkin, in fact, asserts that if teachers had time to ask themselves one question, it should be: Why am I doing what I'm doing? She further suggests that this question be asked once every hour that school is in session. While we are not saying that you should set an alarm clock in your classroom to ring as a reminder to ask, Why am I doing what I'm doing? we do feel that this question should certainly be asked continually. And one of the best times to ask the question is when you are planning the use of instructional time—for stating your goals provides you with the framework for selecting materials, developing teaching procedures, selecting appropriate activities, and formulating more specific instructional objectives.

Goals for reading instruction will grow from both your knowledge of the reading process and your beliefs about the purpose of education.* These two concepts will be constantly developing and changing throughout your professional career. Your emerging definition of reading is not only a place for you to begin but also an initial pivot to reexamine continually.

In addition, your belief about the purpose of education will also exert an influence on the development of what you believe should be the major goals of reading instruction. For example, if you believe that schools should not concern themselves with the development of values but rather should leave those to the home and other agencies, such as the church, then your statement of goals would reflect this position.

Figure 9–1 indicates the process that moves your definition of reading and your beliefs about education to the identification of the broad goals for reading instruction. As you can see, the goals for reading instruction are applied to a particular situation. However, they should not merely be imposed upon the situation—they should be adapted to it. It is essential that you recognize the fact that your goals will need to be modified for each unique teaching situation in which you find yourself. This modification is determined by the goals of the school you teach in, by the goals of the other teachers, and by the attitudes and beliefs of

Figure 9–1   Goals as Guides to Instructional Organization

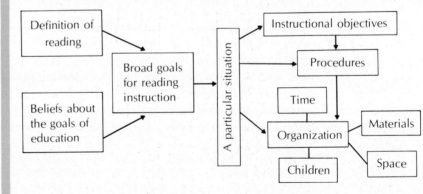

* While stating goals is your individual responsibility, it is important for teachers and administrators in a single school to meet and discuss their goals so that a program that has a common thrust can be developed. In many schools and school districts, parents and students are also involved in the development of the goals for reading instruction. This is commendable, because when all groups are included in the process of developing goals, it is more likely that greater personal commitment to the accomplishment of the goals will result.

the community you find yourself in. Any modification should, however, be guided by a recognition of what you yourself believe about education and reading.

What Are Instructional Objectives?

With goals clearly established, both in mind and in print, you are equipped to prepare more specific instructional objectives that will guide your planning the wise use of time. Probably the term *instructional objective* is familiar to you. And although this term is often used synonymously with *performance objective* or *behavioral objective*,* we prefer *instructional objective* because it emphasizes the use of objectives in planning instruction; and that is their main purpose. An instructional objective specifies that under certain conditions a learner will perform a task with a degree of competency that allows an observer to decide whether or not the objective has been mastered. As we discussed the teaching of specific areas of reading in other chapters, we have kept our instructional objectives clearly in mind. At this point, however, we will show how instructional objectives grow from broad goals and influence your decisions as you determine how much emphasis to give to certain areas as you prepare your schedule.

One goal that most people generally agree upon in the area of reading is that each child should develop readiness for reading at all levels. Among the specific instructional objectives that need to be defined to help one achieve this goal are:

(1) The child should be able to state a reason for reading anything he or she reads.
(2) The child should be able to provide orally or in writing information that is essential to understanding the selection he or she is about to read.
(3) The child should be able to read at a level that is appropriate for the selection he or she is about to read.

The list could go on, but it is not important to do so at this point. What is important is for you to be able to recognize how this list of objectives is based on a single broad goal and how the objectives could then be used to do the daily and weekly planning that is so necessary to effective reading instruction.

Similarly, *each* of your own broad goals could generate sets of *instructional objectives*. Each of these objectives will imply sets of learning activities that will help learners to meet the objectives. And you will determine—based on your knowledge of the children assigned to you— the priorities for individuals.

* If you are unfamiliar with the concept of behavioral objectives, you should read *Preparing Instructional Objectives* by Robert F. Mager (Palo Alto, Cal.: Fearon Publishers, 1962).

try this ▶

Obtain the teacher's edition for one or more basal readers and find the instructional goals that are listed in the front of the book. You may also be able to find both the author's definition of reading and point of view about the teaching of reading. Examine the manual as well as the student materials to see if the broad goals are reflected in the teaching suggestions and student activities. You might notice particular instructional activities that do not seem consistent with the broad goals. Why do you think this happens? Are there reasons for including certain instructional activities even if they don't match a particular point of view about reading? Could you suggest instructional activities that might be appropriate to develop the broad goals?

Establishing Instructional Priorities

It has seemed like a long road from asking a deceptively simple question: What is it that I want to accomplish with children? to establishing instructional priorities. But it is a necessary trip. If you are forced to decide that, for example, children's enjoyment and pleasure from reading and sharing books has greater priority in your program than children's ability to assign meanings to given prefixes, you are on your way to determining how and when to schedule learning experiences, to plan space, and to use materials. Conversely, if your definition of reading, your broad goals, and your instructional objectives result in the decision to place priority on children becoming efficient decoders, that decision will also affect your classroom organization—your use of time, space, and materials. And the teacher who makes these decisions is less dependent on the predetermined goals and objectives of basal series and other packaged programs. The drawback in full-scale adoption of one existing series or program is that no basal-reader or curriculum-guide author knows your children (and you) as well as you know your children (and you). These sources might better serve you as tools or resources from which you may select, expand, ignore, or deviate as you plan your own instructional priorities.

Organizing Children

The organizational plan developed for any classroom should have effective instruction as its major goal. Increased efficiency, increased amounts of time spent with individual needs, and capitalizing on the interests of children are all aspects of this goal. Determining both where your learners are on the irregular learning-to-read continuum as well as their long- and short-term interests are the first steps in organizing for effective instruction. Chapters 2 and 3 have already provided you with some of the data-collection techniques that you are now ready to use.

Schoolwide Grouping for Flexibility

Before you accept your first teaching assignment, it is likely that some interclass, or *between-class*, grouping has determined how the children are grouped in the school where you will teach. These methods by which children are shuffled and dealt to classrooms may depend upon administrative policy or school organization. During your first year of teaching this a priori constituency of your class is something over which you have least control. Whether homogeneously or heterogeneously,* whether alphabetically, by achievement-test scores, or birthdates—by whatever means children are assigned to you, there will still be critical differences among them, for individual differences are never (and shouldn't be) eradicated.

Common examples of interclass (between-class) grouping are contained in Figure 9–2.

Figure 9–2   Methods of Between-Class Grouping

Joplin Plan	Children throughout a school (or unit) experience reading instruction at the same time. Provides for shifting children in order to read with others (regardless of age differences) who read at the same level.
Modified Joplin Plan	Children regroup by achievement within primary grades and, similarly, within intermediate grades.
	or
	Children are regrouped for reading only within one designated grade level. (One first-grade teacher takes "high group," another the "middle," a third the "lows.")
Nongraded, Ungraded or Continuous-Progress Curriculum	Attempts to shake traditional grade-level designations and to provide a continuous flow of curricular experiences as dictated by each child's achievement and needs. Child moves ahead at his or her own pace and begins each succeeding school year at the point he or she left off the year before.
Open Classroom, Open Space, or Open Concept	Schoolwide organization that goes by any of these names is usually closely related to the category above, but such organization is more likely to be dictated by the physical nature of the school, which is designed to facilitate still other features, such as team teaching. Sometimes applied incorrectly to schools with a minimum of interior walls, the term is more correctly used to describe continuous progress controlled by the learner, a movement toward independent learning, departure from group instruction; often characterized by team teaching (4 teachers to 120 students), flexible organization, and alternative means to reach goals.

* Homogeneous grouping is an attempt to put children of similar learning potential together for instruction. Heterogeneous grouping allows the achievement of the children in each class to cover a broader range.

Results of research (Bryan, 1971) and our own experiences pinpoint at least two potential pitfalls that may accompany some between-class grouping systems. The first is that schoolwide ability grouping, whether based on the results of standardized reading tests or on a specific criterion (such as instructional reading level) will tend to mask individual differences in the children if instruction proceeds without attention to additional information. The second potential difficulty may be a tendency on the teacher's part to treat all members of the group the same because they have been assigned on the basis of a single criterion.

In addition, there may be some other instructional disadvantages to a homogeneous between-class grouping, and being alert for these potential difficulties may help you to avoid them: for one, if children change classrooms or shift to different spaces or teachers for reading, the time period designated for reading instruction must be fairly rigidly adhered to. Smooth flow is dependent upon strict scheduling. Some teachers complain that reading must be terminated by the dictates of a clock rather than by a more meaningful or logical conclusion. Reading tends to become a separate subject rather than a part of the total school day. Others have suggested that it is difficult to assess the application of a child's reading skills within the content demands of other subject areas. At times, communication between teachers falls victim to crowded schedules so that the careful monitoring of individual pupil progress suffers (Bamman et al., 1973).

Regardless of the schoolwide or between-class organization imposed, however, the within-class organization will be the means through which children are taught to read.

Organization for Individualization Within the Class

Even experienced teachers recognize the magnitude of the task facing them at the start of each school year as they begin the organizational planning for twenty-five to thirty (or more) children. The effectiveness of your own plan is dependent upon the systematic compilation of diagnostic information for each child. Among other information, you will need some indication of the instructional and independent reading levels for each child. Until you can muster the time to hear each child read, you may want to begin reading instruction in a less systematic way that works for you. It sometimes takes the beginning teacher as long as six weeks to arrive at decisions about each child's reading levels, specific needs, interests, and attitudes. Even then the picture is not completed. A continuous flow of information is imperative for maintaining an effective organization. Two examples of classroom organization offer models for beginning to meet individual needs and interests.

Classroom model 1. One successful teacher we know organizes the initial reading program by forming two large instructional groups on the first day of class. He does this during an art activity by moving quickly around the room with a class roster and a basal reader for the grade level he teaches. Stopping by each chair, he asks each child to read a brief paragraph aloud. Using only his ear (and of course, it is an experienced ear), he decides one of two things: either the child reads *at* or *above*, grade level, or the child reads *below* the grade-level placement. A mark on the roster (+ or −) indicates the child's first organization group. This teacher uses that one basal reader (along with some supplementary materials) to teach the "at or above" group and picks a lower-level book to begin instruction with the "belows." Using this highly traditional organizational plan (where some children will struggle and others breeze), he begins instruction as the teacher's edition suggests: he teaches the new vocabulary words, provides for silent and oral reading, asks questions to tap comprehension, and assigns the related practice materials. From the performance of the children, he can quickly locate the extremes. Extremes in this case are the immediately identifiable children for whom the lower-level book is too difficult, and those for whom the grade-level text is much too easy. The majority of the children will succeed with grade-level materials and can continue to be taught in a large instructional group until more information is collected and their specific instructional needs and interests planned for.

The teacher chooses first to determine the instructional level, specific skill needs, attitudes, and interests of the strugglers and the breezers. These children, he believes, deviate enough from the norm to either reach frustration with or not be sufficiently challenged by the large-group organizational beginning. These extremes are identified through performance in the large groups and still more subjective decision making. Once these children are identified, this teacher employs some of the same systematic data-collection techniques that you read about in Chapter 2. He wants to know these children in terms of their interests, attitudes, reading level, and specific needs. Eventually, when the other children are reading silently, looking at books, visiting the library, completing practice work, writing, or illustrating, he meets individually with each child in order to collect the information that will permit a more individualized program to emerge.

Classroom model 2.   The teacher in the second model also takes some time to discover where her pupils are in terms of reading achievement, interests, and needs. But rather than begin with a basal reader, she brings trade books into the classroom. For her class, reading time means browsing through the books that were selected to represent a range of reading levels and potential interests—folklore, fantasy, sports, picture books, biographies, cookbooks, old favorites, science books, and so on. In addition, reading *to* children to spark interest in these books is a part of her initial organization. She also observes what children read, their attention span for browsing and reading, and their probable tastes. She listens to children read to her and makes judgments about their potential needs in reading.

Figure 9–3 | Susan's Reading Record

NAME	BOOK	DATE	LEVEL	COMMENTS
Susan M.	Madeline in London	9/6	3'	Read silently. Retold with excellent comprehension.
	Madeline's Rescue	9/7	3'	Read silently. 50 word sample orally.
	In the Forest	9/8	2'	Preparing to read this book to Kindergarten—100% word recognition

Word Recognition

vocabulary	suffix
vengeance	-er (sooner)
disgrace	

Record keeping for this teacher is a loose-leaf notebook with anecdotal records listing the books read, responses to the books, estimates of the difficulty level, and types of reading errors (Figure 9–3). On Susan's record, the teacher enters the books read, the date she began them, and the approximate level of their reading difficulty. The notes under "Comments" are for diagnostic information. Note that when Susan read orally, she had trouble with -er suffixes, exemplified by *sooner*. Also she did not know the words *vengeance* or *disgrace*. (Such a record might also note how Susan attacked the unknown word—whether she used context clues, for example.) Note, too, that with *In the Forest*, a lower-level book, Susan recognized every word. This reading record is a variation of the informal records detailed in Chapter 2 (pages 69–70).

She will continue to rely on trade books, pupil conferences, and individual teaching in her organizational plan. Observation and monitoring of children's reading will help her to decide what to teach and how to teach it.

Criteria for Organizing Children

Beginning to organize children for reading instruction, then, is dependent upon:

(1) knowing each child's reading level, specific strengths and needs, and reading interests
(2) meeting each child's needs through the organizational plan, that is, through group instruction, individual instruction, and a combination of both types of instruction.

Because the perfect organizational plan for the classroom reading program has yet to be discovered, and because successful teachers have implemented a variety of plans, in the following section we will describe some approaches to establishing a classroom organization that have worked for others and may be helpful to you. The approaches to organization will be discussed as they approximate these categories: management based on groups, management that depends upon individual instruction, and a combination of group and individual instruction.

Management Based on Group Instruction

The teacher described in the first classroom model was collecting data in order to "peel away" students with similar reading levels from his two initial groups. He wanted the instruction for these children to be based on more appropriate books and materials. If he continues with this type of organization, his reading program will rely on (at least somewhat) group instruction.

The effective use of groups for reading instruction is usually based on a clear-cut purpose for grouping, a structure that allows for flexible or changing groups, constant attention to individual differences within groups, and participation and feedback for each member of the group.

To achieve an effective organization for the group, there are four criteria that should be met. First, the groups should be flexible (once a Bluejay, not always a Bluejay). Second, groups should be formed for specific purposes (for example, mutual interest, to work with friends, to discuss a story, or to plan a project). Third, the groups should be disbanded after the purpose has been achieved. And fourth, the size of the group should be dependent on the type of learning activity; for example, listening to a story can be an effective large group activity while hearing a child read may mandate a "group" of one.

The type of group that will be formed is dependent, then, on the instructional priorities and the type of learning activity that is to occur. And the more the teacher knows about the children's needs, levels, interests, and attitudes, the better the teacher can bring children together in ways that will enhance learning. Similarly, groups that have specific purposes and then disband after achieving those purposes tend to meet their objectives more efficiently than do static groups. We will be considering several types of groups in more detail.

Groups Based on Mutual Interests

When teachers encourage children with common interests to meet together in order to discuss those interests and to share their reading, those teachers are supporting both children and learning. Regardless of reading achievement level, children who share a lively interest in or curiosity about reptiles, ecology, or even television, for example, can meet together to pursue those interests, to prepare a project, or to make presentations based on what they have read.

Diamondback Rattlesnake

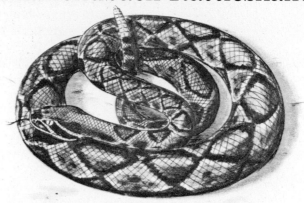

The diamondback, largest of all rattlers, can grow 6 feet long or more. The Eastern diamondback rattlesnake has a pattern of dark brown or black diamonds with a light edge. A Western diamondback is less dark. The poisonous bite of a diamondback is very dangerous, and can kill a man. When disturbed, a diamondback coils up and makes a loud, buzzing sound with the rattles on its tail.

Diamondbacks are born alive.

Eastern diamondback rattlesnakes are poisonous. When disturbed, they coil up and buzz their rattles.

Children who are interested in the same topics can read books of varying difficulty levels, yet receive similar information.

These groups are sometimes called sharing groups, book clubs, or literary guilds. They meet primarily to share their pleasure in reading about a particular topic. Although groups that share reading interests may be just one part of an organizational plan, it is an important part. The teacher may form these interest groups in a variety of ways—for example, by using results of informal interest inventories, interviews, or surveys as a basis for inviting children to join an interest group; by listening to and observing children's conversations and behavior in informal situations to get clues to either established or passing interests; by encouraging children to sign up for and attend interest-group meetings (space travel, sports heroes, folk tales, news events, and so on); or by initiating and joining an interest group based on the teacher's own interests. When interest groups are a part of the classroom organization, the teacher has additional responsibilities. For example, the teacher

The Rattlesnake—PIT VIPER

THE SNAKE did not look at all well. Its colors were dull, its scales had an oddly swollen look, and its eyes were clouded and bluish. It lay motionless, coiled in a secluded hiding place between a low bush and a large boulder.

Days passed during which the snake hardly moved. Then, slowly, its appearance changed. The cloudiness disappeared from its eyes, and they again became golden and catlike. The puffiness of its scales went down. Its color seemed to brighten.

It began to move, pushing its head against the rough side of the boulder, rubbing nose and chin against the rock much as a cat rubs its head against a chair leg. The skin on the snake's nose slowly split from the friction of rubbing. The break widened, and, as the snake continued to rub against the rock, the skin was pushed back over its head.

The snake started to crawl, and as it crawled, the loose skin folded backward, turning inside out, sliding back along the snake's body. As the old skin was pushed off, new skin was revealed, shiny and bright with the tan, yellow, and dark brown of an eastern diamondback rattlesnake.

In minutes, the snake's old skin dragged from the reptile's tail in a single, long piece. As the tail slid over a rough bit of bark, the skin was torn loose and left behind, a pale snake-ghost, to be slowly tattered to shreds by wind and rain.

Resplendent in the bright new skin that had formed beneath the old one, the snake slithered on. It was vigorous, now, and ravenous. The process of molting, shedding its skin, had taken more than 10 days, and during most of that time the snake had not moved from its place of seclusion and had not eaten. Now it sought food.

A red, forked tongue flickered in and out, in and out, of the slit between the lips of its closed mouth. The tongue was a hunting tool. It gathered in scents from the air and carried them to a special place in the snake's mouth. The snake was seeking the scent of warm life—a rat, rabbit, or other living creature that could end its hunger.

It continued to crawl, moving through the night's darkness with a steady, sinuous curving of its body. It was a creature of the night; this was its natural hunting time. Constantly, its tongue flickered, seeking.

Abruptly, the snake found what it sought: the strong scent of an animal close by.

At most other times the rattler would

20   EASTERN DIAMONDBACK RATTLESNAKE

From Album of Reptiles by Tom McGowen, illustrated by Rod Ruth. Copyright 1978 Rand McNally & Company.

must plan a time for the groups to meet. Meetings should be regular but not necessarily rigid. The teacher should also ensure that the group establishes a purpose for meeting. One valid culmination of the group's reading activity is to share the interest in some way (through a graphic presentation, a display, a newsletter, a panel discussion, a television or radio show, or a drama). In addition, the teacher must alert the school librarian to an upcoming siege on books on a particular topic to ensure that books will be available. The teacher must preview the difficulty levels of these books so that children will not be frustrated in their search for appropriate material. Use of the public library can supplement in either popular or obscure interest areas. Finally, the teacher must monitor group activity to ensure that the group fulfills its purposes, continues if the interests developed are still keen, and is rechanneled as new interests develop.

Groups Based on Friendship

Just recently a teacher we know was attempting to group some university students randomly for an activity in a reading-methods class. Some one piped up and asked, "Hey, could we work with our friends?" Indeed, why not? If classroom groups are sometimes formed based on strong friendships (or potential new friendships), the teacher is encour-

aging children's decisions and avoiding a total adherence to a stereotypic ability-grouping pattern. Like mutual-interest groups, however, the friendship group works best when each child has reading materials of the appropriate level and the group is project or activity oriented.

Friendship groups are sometimes no more complex than permitting children to choose partners to read with. Some teachers refer to this practice as "buddy reading." At other times, friends work together on practice (skill-building) activities, or create together—original stories, poems, songs or plays. It's a popular form of grouping among children and one that you may want to employ, making sure that no one is isolated or excluded from a group.

Groups Based on Common Reading Levels

The most prevalent grouping format employed by teachers is one that provides that all children with the same instructional reading level shall be brought together for instruction. And that makes some sense. For if several children—say, three—who need the same vocabulary words in order to read a story successfully were taught those vocabulary words individually, the teacher would have used three times the amount of time and energy than if the children experienced the introduction together.

The organizational pattern that relies on grouping by instructional reading level usually presupposes use of some basal reader system, but this is not always so. The groupings are formed by reviewing the initial assessment data, identifying children whose levels are fairly comparable, and then selecting an appropriate instructional level text. A criticism that has frequently been leveled against this method of grouping is that it often leads teachers to deal with several children as though they were one. Some teachers, however, seem to be able to treat a group of readers with similar abilities as individuals. In the following comparison, notice how two alternative approaches to grouping on the basis of instructional level vary in their attention to individuals.

Approach A	Approach B
(1) Children are introduced to the story and the vocabulary that the basal reader author thinks may be "new" for the children.	(1) Children are introduced to a story and helped to learn vocabulary words that are new to them.
(2) They are told to read the story and each is given the *same* purpose for reading.	(2) They are helped to set their own purposes for reading.
(3) They initially read silently while the teacher waits.	(3) They move to other parts of the room to read, freeing the teacher to check on and guide other children, or to meet with another small group.
(4) The children are asked questions as a group to determine their degree of comprehension.	(4) As children read silently (or even to a friend), the teacher moves to each of them and listens to a portion of the story read aloud, asking: Does the reading sound reasonably fluent? Are the children using new vocabulary? Are the children comprehending what they read? Children may then come together to share their reactions.
(5) The group works on skill-building activities, or the children are prepared to read the next story.	(5) Instructional needs that are uncovered may be unique to one child or fit a pattern with several others. In any case, the needs may constitute the makings of a new group.

Grouping by instructional reading level is one way in which children can be prepared to read the same story. Generally speaking, however, it is more efficient to listen to children's oral reading and to determine literal comprehension on a one-to-one basis.

Groups Based on Similar Skill Needs

Groups formed to work on a particular skill may be the most challenging to the teacher. This is because of the difficulty in deciding what specific skill should be taught and in keeping constant track of who is where in demonstrating competence in those skills. Some teachers use some kind of specific skill assessment. Other teachers attempt to categorize oral-reading miscues according to their likely cause and to record those categorizations so that a scan of children's records will suggest instructional groups based on common miscue patterns. For such purposes the use of a notebook page for each child as described on pages 379–80 is quite useful. Alternatively, or in addition, there may be a master list of children and skill needs. Through the monitoring of specific needs (in the case of Figure 9–4, by using the vertical axis to identify children with similar needs), groups could be formed, taught, disbanded and reformed as necessary. *Never lose sight of the possibility that a "group" may be just one child who demonstrates a specific need.*

Figure 9–4	Recording Format for Individual Skill Needs

Attacks words containing
INITIAL CONSONANTS

	B	C	D	F	G	H	J	K	L	M	N	P	R	S	T	V	W	Y
Alex	+	+		+		+	+	+	+	+		+		+	+	−	+	−
Andy	+	−	+	+	+	+	−	+	+	+	−	+	+		−			
Barbara	+		+	+	−	−	+		+	−	+	+		−	+	−		−
Betty	+		+	+		+		−		+	+		+	+	−		+	+
Christine		+		+	−					−			+			+		+
David	+	+	+		+	+	+	+	−	+	+	+	−	+	+	−	+	+
Dominic		−	+					+				−	+	−				+
Elsie	−		−	−	+	+			+	−	+	+		−		+	−	−
Gayle		−		+	+	−				−			−	+	+		−	
JoAnn	−	−	+	+		−	+		+		+	−		−		+		−
Kelly	+		−		+		+	+					+		−	−	−	−
Lisa			+	+		+			+		+	+	+	+			−	+
Martha			+				−		−	+	+	+	+			+	+	
Michael	+		+	+		−			−	+			−	+	+	−		+
Robert	+		+	−		+			+	−	−	+	+		+	−	+	+
Sandra	+		+	−	+	+	+	+	−	−	+	+		+	−	+		−
Shannon		+		+	+	−	−	+	−	+	−	−	+	+	−	−	−	
Theresa	+			+		+				+		−			+		−	+
Thomas		+		+	+	−		+		−			+		+	+	−	−

+ = mastered
− = incomplete mastery
☐ = not taught

try this ▶

React critically to the following grouping practices used in Mr. Kay's beginning fourth-grade classroom. In addition, list any questions you feel you would like to have answered about the grouping procedure. Then suggest a different organization that might result if you assume some of the answers to your questions.

The thirty children in Mr. Kay's classroom have been grouped for reading on the basis of scores on a reading achievement test given in the spring of grade three. Three reading groups have been formed. Children in groups 1 and 2 are using the beginning fourth-grade reader of the same basal series. Group 2 is proceeding through the reader at a somewhat slower pace than is group 1. Group 3 is using the reader written for the second half of grade 3. There are eight children in group 1, fifteen in group 2, and seven in group 3. The range of scores on the achievement tests is given below. The scores are equivalent to grade levels and the tenths are months of the school year (3.9 means third grade, ninth month).

Groups	Vocabulary	Comprehension	Total
1	3.9 - 6.9	4.8 - 8.0	4.7 - 7.5
2	3.0 - 5.2	3.7 - 5.0	3.5 - 4.5
3	1.8 - 4.1	2.0 - 3.9	1.8 - 3.5

The reading groups in this class meet approximately thirty minutes each day. While one group is meeting, the others work on activities related to their basal reader selection. Typical activities include the use of the workbook and writing answers to questions over reading selections.

Individual Instruction and Pupil-Managed Activities

As mentioned earlier, the size of any group should depend upon individual needs and the task itself. Individualized instruction does not mean the same thing as each-one-teach-one. Rather *individualizing* your instruction will mean that you are dedicated to the idea that children are different and that, to the extent that you are able, you will provide for those differences. Some listening and book-sharing experiences could involve the whole class; at other times, just one teacher and one child might work together. Still other learning can go on with any size group, even the whole class, without abdicating a dedication to individualizing instruction. (Both Classroom Models 1 and 2 had teachers dedicated to achieving eventual individualization of instruction, whether through small groups or on a one-to-one basis.) So whether you organize for reading instruction primarily through use of flexible groups or primarily through instruction of individuals, the extent to which you have individualized instruction will depend upon how well you can accommodate the strengths and needs of each child.

Before going further, we need to establish clearly the difference between independent activities and individualized instruction. Independent activities usually mean that the student can complete a task without the direct aid of the teacher. To its fullest extension, it means that the child can *locate* material (from shelves, files, or workfolders), can *read* the directions (or knows them in advance), can *perform* the task, and can then *check* the results.

There are degrees of independence, of course. The teacher is still needed to give initial instruction, but children who manage some of their own activities independently do not need constant supervision. In a classroom where independent activities are going on, materials are accessible to students and there is some means of communicating how the student is to manage time other than through the teacher's oral directions. For example, the students may rotate through learning centers or select and complete packets of materials. In any case, the teacher is freed to do small-group or individual teaching.

But students who are busily at work on independent activities may not necessarily be recipients of individualized instruction. It is just as faulty to assume that working alone means "individualized" as it is to assume that working in groups implies the absence of individualization. An individualized classroom, as noted earlier, operates on the premise that each child has distinct learning needs and that these needs are met at a time when the child is ready to learn. It is conceivable that every child could need something different from every other child. Each child could have different practice activities and different projects. As far as our experience has led us, we have concluded that "ideal individualized instruction" has never been achieved anywhere.

The most efficient condition appears to be some mixture of independent activities and individualized instruction. With this combination, learning tasks will aim at the individual developmental need of each child, will follow direct teacher instruction, and will then be pupil-directed. As some children learn alone, the teacher is freed to work with other children who need immediate help, without forcing anyone into an unproductive wait. Children who know what their daily goals are can select another task if they become puzzled or need clarification and yet see that the teacher is busy with another child. They know that the teacher will be available for consultation soon.

Developing the independence that is required to move from one task to another without teacher reinforcement or guidance is a big step. For very young children, the movement toward independence is slow because almost *all* children love to have attention and reinforcement from the teacher. Some independence must be achieved, however, if the teacher is to do small-group or individual teaching. At the beginning, before this new teacher has an organizational pattern established, it is conceivable that the independent work could be geared simply toward teaching the child to be independent. That is, the self-directed tasks should be easy enough and reinforcing enough so as to discourage interruption of the teacher. The students may all be doing nearly the same things at first, but they are learning to do these tasks independently. Independent work habits in children are prerequisite to individualizing the reading program; otherwise, it doesn't seem possible for a teacher to meet and dismiss groups, or to hear individuals read and discuss their reading without ensuring that the other children—not working directly with the teacher at that moment—can manage themselves and their materials.

Setting up a classroom in this way is not an easy task. Teaching children to be responsible for themselves, finding and building enough constructive and interesting materials, keeping records, and evaluating continuously are all time-consuming and challenging tasks. Once established, however, an efficient organizational plan pays off in student attitude and achievement—and in the teacher's sense of accomplishment.

Learning Contracts

Once the decision is made to help children develop into more independent learners, a system must be developed to communicate with the child in order to free both teacher and learner from the time-consuming task of relating, "Now, here is what you will do today. . . ."

A learning contract is educationally defined as a work agreement between a student and the teacher to do certain things—to complete projects and to engage in activities. As it was originally conceived, the learning contract was a negotiated work agreement, involving both "management" and "labor." Today, many contracts look more like individualized assignment sheets or work orders.

Having already made an initial assessment of a child's reading level, interests, and needs, the teacher may rely upon a learning contract to direct the child's activities when he or she is not working with the teacher. The contract itself can be just a piece of paper that is marked off in some way (by days, time, or events) with the suggested activities entered in various slots.

Contracts vary in format and messages depending upon the age, interests, reading ability, and needs of the learner. Generally speaking, children of all ages can follow the sequence of events on a learning contract if the design is appropriate. Even kindergarteners can use a learning contract as soon as they are ready to work independently and can follow a suggested sequence by matching colors or shapes on a contract with the activity that those cues signal.

On the following four pages are a few examples of learning contracts, showing both variety in form and the adjustment of the contract to different levels.

Kindergarten-early primary contract. Children who are not yet reading can be directed to stations, corners, or activities when the teacher is occupied elsewhere. Barry will start at the "Circle Center" designated by that shape in the room. At some point while he is working there (with puppets, blocks, books, paint, or whatever the center contains), his teacher will call him to come and work together (perhaps to dictate, read back, or listen to a story). Finishing with that, he can find an area in the room marked with a rectangle and move there to continue his work.

This contract format also sends beginners to specific centers in the room that are coded to the contract. The center activities may change, but the child consults his slip to help him to change spaces. Each center in this kindergarten has been introduced systematically so that children have become familiar with their use and the care of materials in each.

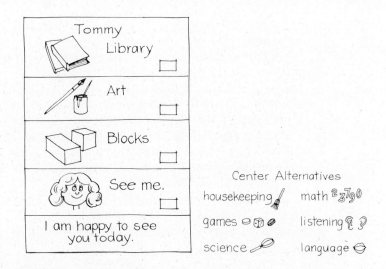

Primary-grade contracts for beginning readers. These contracts have been made with sturdy poster board, then laminated both for durability and because each day a new sequence of activities can be drawn and written after wiping off the previous day's activities.

Intermediate contract. As John progressed on the daily work, the teacher has monitored that progress and given written praise for specific accomplishments. This kind of checking up comes at times between the teacher's direct instruction to groups or individuals. This teacher moves about the classroom guiding, redirecting, and reinforcing both orally and in the spaces left over on the learning contract. The teacher can't specifically gauge the exact minute when John will get individual help that day to write his story, but John knows that he is free to select the activities on his contract in any order and free to select any or none of the activities at the bottom.

The following example of a learning contract is for a child who can read well enough to follow printed directions. The box in the upper right-hand corner is meant to allow the child to check off (√) his or her accomplishments.

FRIDAY

Hi, John. I think you will like your work today!

Come and see me. Let's write a story about "Star Wars"! ✓
You remembered a lot.

Will you draw a picture to go with your story?

Find a paper with blanks on it in your folder. Fill in the blanks. Then check your work. ✓
Perfect! Was it hard?

Now read "Martin and the Spaceship." What's funny about the story? Write something here. ✓
Nobody believed that he saw a real spaceship.
You did some careful reading!

Some things to choose:
☒ go to the library
☒ put your new words on the spaceship
○ play the game in your folder
Let's read your new book tomorrow.

Advanced contract. This is an example of a negotiated contract.

I, the undersigned, having declared my interest in the study of ___fossils___, do hereby declare my intentions for the week of ___March 2-6___. Provided that good health is my fortune, I will:

(1) _find and read all or part of three books on fossils in the school library,_

(2) _use the information to label some of the fossils in my own collection, and_

(3) _think of a way to illustrate life in my community 100 million years ago._
To achieve this I may:

(4) _visit the museum, ask the science teacher for help, and visit the public library._

With all good faith that I can accomplish my goals, I sign myself this ___second___ day of ___March___ in the year ___1978___.

Witnessed and agreed to by

___Larry Alan Bates___   ___Rodney Walters___
student   teacher

Children who read better than others at their level or who are able to work independently might learn to use contracts first. For the less independent children, watching more independent learners work provides an example: "I see! When I finish this, I may do _____ or _____ or _____. I can check my own work! I can work alone, with my teacher, or with other children."

The teacher who is initiating a contract system generally continues to meet with the other children in whatever grouping pattern has been developed. If the teacher proceeds slowly, making certain that children understand what is required, can follow directions, and have sufficient materials with which to operate, there is little reason to doubt success. Contracts should continue to be made by the teacher until the children become aware of the choices available to them—and then they can be negotiated, as effective contracts should be. As with any language-arts lesson plan, the contracts should be balanced to ensure that children have listening, speaking, reading, and writing assignments that are pertinent to their interests and skill needs. Most contracts are planned by the week and revised as the week progresses. Some teachers prefer to write a few contracts each afternoon rather than face a large pile of them on the weekend.

Activities can be reviewed as they are completed, at the end of the day, or when the student meets with the teacher. The information gleaned in this manner is used to plan further instruction and is transferred to the current classroom notebook. The daily work is used as one means for the teacher to determine progress and to provide feedback to the child.

As more and more children begin to work with individual learning contracts, they should also be spending more time on appropriate reading and reading-related activities. Teachers should find increased opportunity for instruction that is less interrupted by pupils seeking directions. Ultimately, learners gain satisfaction in knowing the game plan, in assuming responsibility for their independent work, and in having some input into the choice of activities.

Peer-Tutoring

Peer-tutoring or pair-learning are terms that refer to a one-to-one, teaching-learning situation involving students. The tutor could be the

same age as the tutee or older—from a different grade level; the amount of guidance that the tutor is given can vary; the kind of instruction that the tutor gives may depend on the abilities of the tutor and the needs of the tutee; and the number of children tutored may range from one to a small group.

Setting up a simple program for buddy-reading, times for children to listen to a partner read, is one interpretation of peer-tutoring. Whether it is with another student of the same or a different age, it is fun for children and expedient for the teacher. In addition, the learning appears to go both ways—both reader and listener benefit. Although research that substantiates the value of tutoring as it relates to a child's reading improvement is limited, there are positive benefits that center around the tutor. Daniel Fader argues for the use of students as teachers:

> Failure to use students as teachers of students is made more remarkable by the nature of an experience shared by all teachers. No one who has taught has been able to avoid the humbling, edifying experience of learning through teaching. . . . What are plans for smaller classes about if not about attention to children who need it most and receive it least? No teacher can pay sufficient attention to the learning needs of twenty-five children, much less the customary thirty-five and more. But classes may be halved when budgets are doubled; doubled budgets and the millennium will arrive together. Until they do, teachers will have classes that are impossibly large so long as they do not enlist the aid of their students as teachers. When they solicit that aid, they may discover that neither the millennium nor a doubled budget is necessary. (1971, pp. 160–61)

Organizing Time

Successfully organizing a reading program that takes the similarities and differences among children into account, that brings together those who share a need or an interest, that helps them individually, and that manages their activities, depends upon the efficient organization of *time* by the teacher.

Questions that new teachers sometimes ask when faced with the task of planning instructional time are:

When do I meet with groups?
How often do I need to hear each child read orally?
When and for how long do specific skill groups meet?
When do children meet to discuss their reading?
How often do interest groups meet?
When do I schedule individual conferences?
When do I monitor (or check up on) independent work?
How much time should be devoted to reading books and stories as opposed to practice activities, creative projects, writing, and so on?

Unfortunately, there are no answers to these questions that will be as specific as the new teacher would like and still be generalizable to any teaching situation. What we can offer, however, will be sample organizational plans (pages 397–400) that can be adapted to many teaching situations.

Planning Instructional Time—Short Term

In reassessing your goals and in establishing priorities, you might have phrased and answered several important questions for yourself about planning instructional time. Let's suppose that priority time has been assigned to providing children time to *read* every day, providing children with vocabulary instruction at their instructional level as needs dictate; providing children with skill instruction as it relates to their reading; and providing children time to think, extrapolate, and create based on their reading.

There will undoubtedly be other priorities, but identification of these four can serve to illustrate, in the following examples, how teachers begin to apportion time and to spread themselves among so many learner needs.

Time study 1.   Ms. McGuire faced a classroom of thirty third graders with nine different instructional reading levels, ranging from preprimer three through approximately fifth grade. She recognized that the children's needs were diverse; she had recorded evidence related to their special interests and specific needs. Her problem was neither identification of need (she had done that) nor how to teach to need (she felt comfortable with her teaching skill). What she felt she needed was an organizational system that would allow her to work with children who represented that range of difference in some reasonable time frame. So Ms. McGuire attacked her organizational problem by setting priorities. She knew that she wanted her children to be comfortable with books, to seek them out, and to use print for pleasure and information. So she went in search of books, and she stocked her room with books—using public and school libraries, her own books, the children's books, garage sales, and used book stores as sources. That seems like such a logical first step as to be almost embarrassingly simple. But there are still an inordinately large number of "fully equipped" classrooms—full of games, hardware, skills-sheets of every description—that are bookless except for the series that has been adopted.

Ms. McGuire found books—books to read to children, books to look things up in, books to just look at, and books for children to read. She developed her organizational system by allowing children to read or browse through books on their own while she "encountered" individuals and small groups. The time she spent with pupils was devoted to discussing stories, to listening to a child read, or to teaching to discovered needs. Sometimes she took dictation from children and encouraged them to read stories. As they moved away to illustrate their stories, she was up and about the room, helping one child make a book selection, guiding another to plan for sharing a book with the class, helping a third to tape record his story for later listening. She found her program strenuous, yet exciting. She was hesitant to form her program completely independent of a basal series, so each child had a reader of appropriate difficulty; but, at the same time, she was also hesitant to rely on an adopted series totally, so she used the books and the teaching suggestions contained in the teacher's edition selectively, as children demonstrated specific needs. Ms. McGuire found that she did not remain for long periods with a group—and also discovered that she was working with each child daily as she moved about. She found that her children had time to read and that she had time to facilitate and encourage that reading because of her flexibility.

Time study 2. Josh Carter teaches twenty-five lively first graders. When asked for his priorities for reading instruction, he said that he hoped each child would develop a "solid start" in reading. He defined a solid start as each child's development of a sight vocabulary that would permit inductive teaching of sound-symbol relationships—which, in turn, would enable children to become independent users of print. After assessing the reading levels of his class, he found one child already reading at about beginning second-grade level, two others at about primer level, and seven more who were "print-aware"—that is, they could read "McDonald's," "Coke," their own names, names of brothers and sisters, and so on. Seven more could recognize just their own names. The others seemed not yet to have found any need for print.

In developing his initial program, Josh used language experience, relied on learning centers for organization, and gathered a selection of preprimers (and other appropriate level texts) for the children. Aware that all activities are real opportunities to develop reading interests and to have children actually read, Josh established five learning centers in early September: for listening (to stories, poems, and songs); for science (magnets, plants, books, simple experiments); for art (colored paper, scissors, paint, clay, glue, felt pens, and crayons); for reading (books, pillows, rugs, and a rocker); and for writing (sand, paper, chalkboards, laminated strips, and writing instruments.) He also put five same-color clothespins in each learning center. As children arrived, they found a colored card in their individual mailboxes. That card indicated which matching-color learning center was to be their first activity of the day. As they entered the center, each child clipped a clothespin onto his or her clothing—five children in and the center was full. In order to change centers, a child had to wait for a vacancy, which would occur when Josh called some children to come and work with him. In teacher-directed time, Josh provided stimulus situations for children's language-experience stories, taught new vocabulary words, or let children work with sentence strips, with dictating, writing, or copying their own books, or reading to him.

The times Josh spent with individual children were extremely short at first while he moved about to ensure that children knew the acceptable procedures for operating in and moving between centers. (Suggestions for making centers in your own classroom are discussed on pages 404–07 of this chapter.) Josh used individual and small-group instruction. As children began to indicate more spread in abilities, he provided appropriate reinforcement activities in their mailboxes at the beginning of each day. Like Ms. McGuire, he used time flexibly and knew that he was "teaching" as he moved about the classroom checking and reinforcing students' work, guiding activities, and answering questions.

Time study 3. Alicia Salazar's fifth graders also demonstrated various reading levels and individual needs. Alicia had spent one entire summer building and laminating materials that students could work with independently to practice specific skills (for example, identifying meanings for prefixes, using the pronunciation key in a dictionary, and so on). She filed these materials by categories so that they could be retrieved and refiled by children.

For the first five to fifteen minutes, she handed out individual work folders that included instructional tasks that were appropriate to the children's current needs. For the next thirty minutes on most days, Alicia met with two or three small groups, teaching needed skills. After Alicia finished with a group, the children moved back to independent work. On other days, Alicia met with individual children during this time to preassess, to teach new vocabulary words, to help children to define purposes for reading, to listen to children read orally, or to discuss some reading with them.

There was also opportunity in her room for children to listen to stories being read on tape and to record themselves. Alicia and her aide transcribed these tapes after school and presented the "storytellers" with their tapescripts to read. After the thirty-minute instructional period, Alicia circulated around the room to check on written work, to check reading, to clarify, or to redirect. She used about ten to fifteen minutes to make herself available to all the children before she again began short direct-teaching sessions based on demonstrated needs. If, for example, a child needed help with vocabulary, structural-analysis clues in word recognition, or locational skills, he or she got that help. Children finishing written work were then spot-checked, praised for their accomplishments, directed to related reading or self-selected activities. The library corner and the listening center were more heavily trafficked toward the end of the second thirty-minute direct-teaching period. Work folders were returned to a designated spot as children completed assigned tasks and moved into such free-choice activities.

Alternative 1	*Alternative 2*
(1) See me. We'll get ready to read.	Hi—find a book in this stack that would make a good radio play.
(2) Read your story. Look for the new words you've learned.	Read it over.
(3) Find the question cards. Slip them into the page where you find the answer.	Who else could be in it? _____ , _____ , _____
(4) Do the practice page. Remember to look at the example I worked for you.	What part would you like? _____ Come and read part of it to me. Now, let's see if you can make a list of some of the sound effects you may need _____ _____
(5) File new words in your card file.	_____ _____
	Get started!

In these situations, Alternative 1 prescribes each step in a skills-oriented program. Alternative 2 provides for the use of a similar amount of time, but allows for pupil input and creative participation.

Organizing time takes time. One of the ironies of planning use of time to save time is the amount of time you will spend trying to save it. It does take a break-in period before your schedule will work properly. We can't specify exactly how long before you will be running smoothly, but our experience indicates that the range is from three to six weeks. While you are struggling, try to remember that it gets easier with practice.

To boost your morale, you can also tell yourself that in your classroom, fewer children are "marking time" while someone else is learning, fewer children sit around taking it easy while the one who gets called on does all the thinking; fewer children lose their places while they are waiting for their turn to read; fewer children are "lumped" into groups and their real needs ignored even though their group meets regularly.

Efficient planning of time is based upon all the other aspects of classroom organization: children, space, and materials. Therefore, there is no *one* best way to use time. Establishing *your* priorities and learning about your children are first steps. Then, organizing your space and your materials will contribute to the effective use of time.

Organizing Classroom Space

The basic design for many of our current educational facilities harks back to legitimate spatial needs as they existed in the early 1900s. The rectangular room that may greet you someday was intended to provide "ventilation, light, quick departure, ease of surveillance and a host of other legitimate needs" (Sommer, 1969, p. 98).

Before the advent of electricity, rooms were narrow to get light across and were designed to bring light over the left shoulder. In addition, the school's physical plant supposedly mirrored its educational philosophy, so attention centered on the teacher who dispensed information, gave directions, and monitored behavior. The teacher had the most space, the greatest freedom of movement, and the most commanding perspective.

Educational philosophy has changed considerably since then, and new school buildings attempt to reflect these changes—although their success is being debated. New classrooms provide areas for the child to move around, to learn in many places, and to be instructed by a teacher within touching distance.

Regardless as to whether the shape of your classroom is rectilinear or amorphous, with fixed or with movable walls, or whether you gaze out your window on grazing sheep or on a factory, the inside is up to you—how you use color and form, how you route traffic and arrange furniture, how you block off areas. In short, how you use space influences the creative production in your language-arts program. Centers for reading and writing need to be relatively quiet. Activity centers can be placed nearest heavy traffic flow. Familiar activities of the room are not the things that distract students; generally, it is the flow of visitors or messengers that create distractions. In essence, you must plan for places and spaces to read.

> Your activity centers can be as imaginative and as plentiful as your facilities and your ingenuity allow. Try to make reading areas comfortable and cozy places which call out for someone to stretch out and read a book on an old piece of carpet or an attractive floor pillow. Large, sturdy cardboard boxes can be cut to simulate houses, stores, etc., to create private places for children. Smaller ones can also be painted and varnished and used as large building blocks which children can arrange as walls, barricades, writing tables, etc. You can hammer nails or have a friend who can do so, you can build all kinds of intriguing structures from plywood. Do not miss any opportunity to build upward. We waste so much space above the first six feet from the floor. Children love to get off the ground. Perhaps because they are always lower than adults, it is a wonderful feeling for them to suddenly be up higher than those giants they must deal with all the time. It is up to you and your students to experiment in any way you can to make your room assist you in achieving your educational aims. (Blitz, 1973, pp. 107–08)

It is sometimes difficult for adults to realize that what may be attractive and inviting to them may be perceived differently by children. As you plan the organization of your own classroom, you should be aware that children's eye levels are lower than yours; children's storage facilities should be within their reach, promoting independent access to materials; the amount and kinds of activities children will be involved

A bird's-eye view of an experience-centered classroom in a traditional setting.

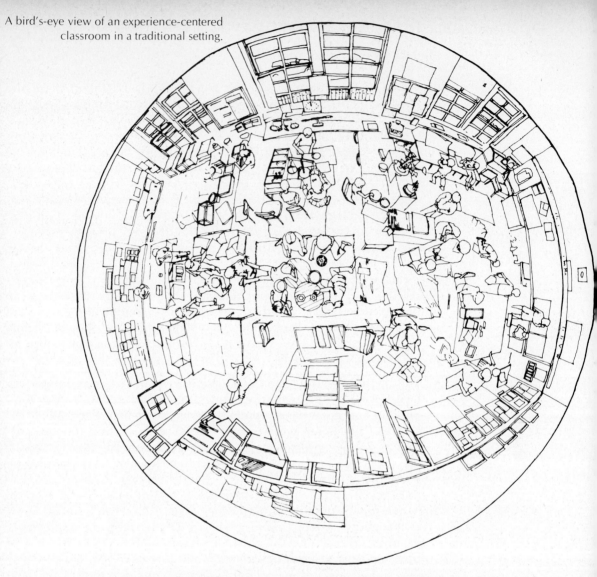

in should help you design "zones"* for those activities; the way you plan use of space (whatever your space may be) reflects your instructional priorities; and children can be a part of the planning process.

All over America, children are reading in bathtubs, in pirate ships, and in racing cars without ever leaving their classrooms. Teachers and children are creating spaces for books and children to get together.

* Zones are defined areas that receive minimum interference from other zones and from paths of circulation.

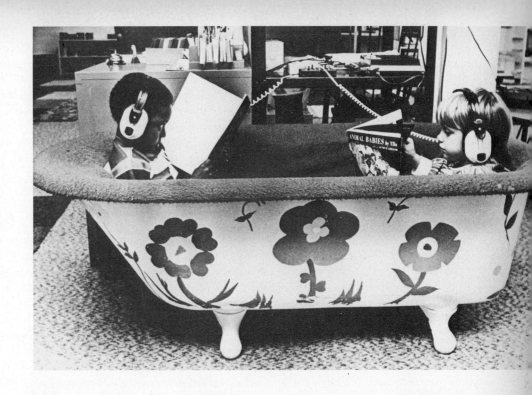

Helping children to make special spaces for independent reading communicates that reading is a special thing to do. Together you can build an airplane cockpit, a rocket ship, a corral, a submarine, a sportscaster's booth, a stable, a barn, a jungle, a castle, or a hollow tree—to point out just a few examples. And you can use cardboard cartons, plywood, empty closets, unused tables, and left-over paint. Inside each space should be books—books that you supply as well as those brought in by children. Keep in mind, though, that any place or space to read should be inviting, quiet, isolated from traffic, comfortable, and well lighted.

Classroom Space Should Provide Active Learning Centers

Learning centers in classrooms are sometimes referred to as learning stations or activity centers. The activities that are planned for the centers are usually designed for independent work. The closer the activity matches a child's real need, the more individualized it is. The use of the center—or the physical space given over to a learning activity that requires special equipment, material, or stimulus—is different from the use of direct teaching space—and *may* be different from the spaces where children read independently or complete written assignments.

Learning centers are usually created within the room but may utilize hallways and other areas. A learning center provides the space and materials for special activities. For example, a learning center may be as simple as a study carrel formed by framed pegboard dividers, shelves, screens, movable chalkboards, display boards, or the back of a piano. The learning center may be a table with a cassette recorder, a record player, and headphones to serve its users. Or it may consist of a desk

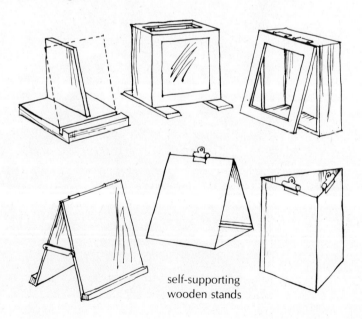

self-supporting
wooden stands

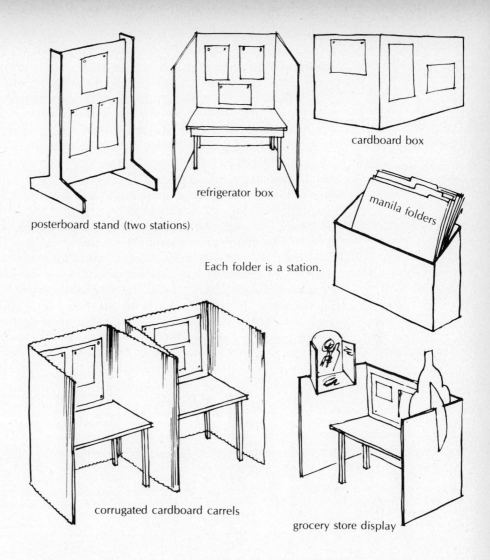

posterboard stand (two stations)

refrigerator box

cardboard box

manila folders

Each folder is a station.

corrugated cardboard carrels

grocery store display

with an activity board, a shelf and beanbag chair, or just some materials placed on the floor. The point is that how the center looks or what form it takes is not nearly so important as the choice of activities that will take place there, and the teacher tries to make the area invite the activity.

Setting up an activity center. The kinds of experiences that you provide for children's independent activities and explorations are dependent upon your broad goals, instructional objectives, and priorities—as well as on children's levels, interests, and needs. This means that you must develop worthwhile and reinforcing activities that grow from your objectives and are appropriate for your learners.

In a center, you might find pictures to write about, directions to make something, puppets and a stage, film and filmstrip projectors, learning machines, gameboards and word games, phonic activities, poetry to listen to, tape recorders, and typewriters. Thus, it is important for you to remember that an activity center is constructed with a purpose or objective, that the purpose is evident to the learner, and that the activity is such that it can be carried through without continuous teacher direction. This implies clear directions, models, or demonstrations, but it also allows for each child's involvement in deciding exactly what to do.

Before children use a center for the first time, teachers often give a general orientation of its purpose, its equipment, and the procedures that a child might follow there. The degree of explicitness in the directions will depend on the expected product. For example, directions for completing a cloze exercise could be clarified by display of a sample sentence. But directions for an activity that invites creative response must be clear enough to communicate the intent and yet open enough to encourage divergent products. Directions for use of a center may also suggest some system for evaluating results. Keys for self-checking a prescriptive practice activity could be provided. Sometimes teachers ask that the child share products or consult with peers. Still other activities lend themselves to teacher-pupil consultation over the product, so papers or products are filed for later perusal and discussion.

There are many recent books that prescribe ideas for learning centers. Some titles are suggested in the box below. Other contemporary books not necessarily including learning centers as their major focus also have valuable suggestions.

References to Help You Plan Learning Centers

Allen, Roach Van, and Allen, Claryce. *Language Experience Activities*. Boston: Houghton Mifflin, 1976.

Burie, Audrey Ann, and Heltshe, Mary Ann. *Reading with a Smile: 90 Reading Games that Work*. Washington, D.C.: Acropolis Books, 1975.

Carson, Patti, and Dellosa, Janet. *Stick Out Your Neck*. Write care of the authors, 8488 Glenridge Avenue, Clinton, Ohio 44216.

Don, Sue et al. *Individualizing Reading Instruction with Learning Stations and Centers*. Evansville, Ind.: Riverside Learning Associates, 1973.

Fisk, Lori, and Lindgren, Henry C. *Learning Centers*. Glen Ridge, N.J.: Exceptional Press, 1974.

Forgan, Harry W. *The Reading Corner: Ideas, Games, and Activities for Individualizing Reading*. Santa Monica, Cal.: Goodyear Publishing, 1977.

Greff, Kasper N., and Askov, Eunice N. *Learning Centers: An Ideabook for Reading and Language Arts*. Dubuque, Iowa: Kendall/ Hunt Publishing, 1974.

Heilman, Arthur W., and Holmes, Elizabeth. *Smuggling Language into the Teaching of Reading*. Columbus, Ohio: Charles E. Merrill, 1972.

Herr, Selma E. *Learning Activities for Reading*. Dubuque, Iowa: Wm. C. Brown, 1977.

Spache, Evelyn. *Reading Activities for Child Involvement*. 2d ed. Boston: Allyn and Bacon, 1976.

As you locate and use helpful references remember:

Start with a learning objective based on the needs of a child you know rather than an appealing idea.

Design some independent-activity centers that extend or reinforce a teacher-pupil learning encounter.

Design some independent-activity centers that allow all children to create—regardless of level.

Design centers that include imaginative, varied, and purposeful materials.

Design centers that can be used by learners in various ways.

Design centers where tasks are evident through example, demonstration, or models.

Design centers that are independent, that is, appropriate to level, self-checking, or "no wrong answer."

Successful use of centers depends upon careful selection and development as well as wise deployment of children to specific activities based upon interest and need.

Organizing Materials

The effective implementation of a program geared toward individualization of instruction relies heavily upon a wide variety of instructional materials. The materials help children to practice what you have taught; they also help the children to review and to reinforce. In addition, materials are the means through which individualization is accomplished when a child is working on his or her own and the teacher is working with some other child.

Such materials are gathered from the school library and the dusty shelves of book storage rooms. They are reclaimed from refuse heaps and attics. They are constructed using old magazines, catalogs, and telephone books. They are pulled from outdated readers and workbooks. From many unexpected places you will find the makings of instructional materials that match children's interest, provide for a range of individual abilities, represent a variety of skill needs, and encourage self-direction and self-correction.

The kinds of materials you have and the way in which you choose to organize those materials will affect the program. The ease with which you and your children can retrieve and use materials will depend on their types, their locations, and the organizational system you employ.

Materials organized by types refer primarily to your possible use of the material. For example, you will probably have some books and magazines, or other materials, that you will want children to use regularly. Still other materials may be for certain children only when they need to practice certain behaviors. Reference materials will be placed in one section of the classroom so children will know where they are located and how they are arranged.

Some of the types of materials include:

Books. Above all else, have a good collection of children's trade books.

Texts. You may need more than one series and many levels of basal readers.

Children's magazines and newspapers.

References. A good supply of dictionaries, including picture dictionaries, encyclopedias, an atlas, an almanac, and information books of all types would provide an ideal set.

Practice materials. These are the skills pages, games, cards, reading laboratories or kits, and the teacher-made materials that help children to practice a skill.

Hardware. This is the common name for the media—learning machines, filmstrip projector, tape recorder and tapes, record player and headset, even the overhead projector—used to reinforce learning or for more exposure to literature.

You will also find it useful to organize reading materials in other ways. For example, some teachers find that they can efficiently retrieve the exact aid if they file or shelve materials according to the reading skill for which that material provides practice. Some teachers cut apart workbooks and file the pages according to the reading skills that can be practiced with the pages. Others make games, manipulative materials, and other practice activities that can be shelved according to their function. For example, one section of such a file may contain pictures, games, and practice sheets that allow children to match initial consonants with pictures of words beginning with that consonant; another section may provide practice with plural endings, and so on.

Some teachers also code the reading materials according to the reading difficulty of the content by using a readability formula, such as the Fry formula (see page 415).

The most important point, however, is that the organization of materials should relate to the organizational pattern of your classroom and the way you and the students use reading materials. Materials should be located so that everyone can draw upon them, so that they can be easily returned, and so that your class schedule moves smoothly—avoiding delays because a child doesn't know how to use the organizational system, or because only you can distribute the reading materials.

Selecting and Evaluating Materials

In deciding how you are going to organize materials, you need first to decide what materials are available and what additional materials will be needed in the classroom. That will be determined by the reading levels and interests of your students. What books will you need to provide material for independent reading? What materials will be needed for specific learning centers you are planning? The answers to both of these questions, of course, depend greatly on the interests of the individual children in your class as well as on the reading skills that individual children need to develop. In organizing materials, you will want to consider how children use them and how frequently they are used.

Consider books as the core of your material and extend your classroom activities to the school library. The library provides the greatest support and the strongest impact on the reading program. The American Association of School Librarians* suggests how:

> The school library, in addition to doing its vital work of individual reading guidance and development of the school curriculum, should serve the school as a center for instructional materials. Instructional materials include books—the literature of children, young people, and adults—other printed materials, films, recordings, and newer media developed to aid learning.

* American Association of School Librarians. *Standards for School Library Programs.* Chicago: American Library Association, 1960, p. 11.

A library such as this one has a vital, active role in the education of children. You should familiarize yourself with the library in your school to see to what extent it can support your reading instruction.

Evaluating materials. There is no other subject area of the curriculum, from the preschool level through graduate school, for which more materials have been published than for teaching reading. There are many thousands of books, kits, practice dittos, games, machines, and audio-visual materials that have been produced for this specific purpose.

But quantity does not promise quality. While it is safe to say that the majority of such materials are good, even excellent, it is also realistic to point out that some are inadequate. Further, some materials will be excellent for one situation and useless in another. Your job of evaluating and selecting materials is thus of primary importance.

In the following pages, we shall discuss some guiding questions that a teacher may ask when selecting and evaluating instructional materials.

(1) *What is the popular name, publisher, and type of material?* This includes the range of materials under one heading, the total number of pieces, and the general purpose of the total set. If a piece of material is part of a larger program, each part should be examined separately. It is neither practical nor reasonable, for example, to attempt to describe and evaluate a total set of basal readers and accompanying instructional aids that comprise one of the major basal programs on the basis of examining one or two pieces of material. It is important to note the general type of

material—basal series, boxed skills kits, learning machines, packaged games, and audio-visual materials. Each type may conceivably be designed to serve different purposes, to be the core or a supplement to the reading program, and should be examined with those purposes in mind.

(2) *For what levels are the materials appropriate?* You may have to dig into the materials somewhat to determine this. Many publishers have abandoned the use of grade-level designations and are instead describing their materials by levels or by skills for which the materials provide; for instance, the Laidlaw Reading Program (1976) has thirteen levels that span grades one to six. This range emphasizes the fact that a particular book or practice material may not be designated for general use at a particular grade level. Similarly, an item labelled "practice with initial consonants" may be designed for children across a range of grades who need additional practice. Labelling their materials by levels and skills, publishers feel, will enable a teacher to use a wider range of materials in the classroom with less stigma attached to not being "on grade level." This is a compelling reason to support this change on the part of the publishers.

However, the dropping of grade-level designations for basal readers has caused one problem. For years, reading teachers and specialists have described their pupils' reading ability as being approximately 2^2, 3^1, or fourth-grade level, for example. Readability formulas—methods for determining the reading difficulty of written material—have also designated materials as being of third-grade difficulty, sixth-grade difficulty, and so fourth. These designations provided practical help for the teacher; by simply matching the reading level of the student with the reading-grade level of the material, the teacher had a method for making a judgment about reading material. The elimination of grade-level designations on basal readers has resulted in some confusion for teachers. They wonder just what a level-eight reader is. In other words, they want to know the approximate reading difficulty in terms of a grade level it would generally be used in. Figure 10–1 (pages 432–35) should help to alleviate this confusion. It indicates the general grade-level designations for many of the basal readers that are widely used in elementary classrooms today.

(3) *What are the general goals and objectives of the materials?* You will need to examine the goals and objectives that are given in the instructional materials or the accompanying teacher's manuals. Sometimes these are difficult to find, and at other times they are not given at all. Of course, a note should be made to indicate whether either of these is missing. Your use of materials should be based on the degree to which the goals and objectives that are presented by the publisher match your priorities for reading instruction. You also need to review the materials to see what goals and objectives can logically be met using these materials. The goals and objectives that you list might be quite different from those listed by the publisher, or they may merely be an expansion of the publisher's list.

You may need to examine sample lessons and exercises to determine what is being taught. Although this may seem like a lengthy task, it is really not too difficult because of the internal similarity of many materials. And, at the end, you may even find that your analysis of the goals and objectives agrees almost totally with that of the publisher.

A page from a phonics workbook is reproduced below. The publisher's stated performance objectives for this page are that the lesson will enable each child: (1) to identify the consonant combination /br/ and /cr/ at the beginning of words, (2) to match the consonant combinations /br/ and /cr/ with the graphemes br and cr, and (3) to write those graphemes. The publisher's general goal for this page and similar pages is that each child should be able to associate the consonant graphemes with the consonant phonemes in initial and final positions.

From *Sounds, Letters, and Words*, Level Two, by Ana Myra Seaver (River Forest, Ill.: Laidlaw Brothers, 1975), p. 53. Reprinted by permission of Laidlaw Brothers, a Division of Doubleday and Company, Inc.

Work with one section at a time. Name the key picture. Have the children listen for the initial sounds in its name and complete the word under the picture by tracing the initial letters. Then name each small picture with the children. If its name has the same beginning sounds as <u>brush</u> or <u>crab</u>, the children are to write the letter combination in the space. If not, they are to cross out the space.

brush	(br) (bracelet)	(br) (broom)	X (clock)
	X (blindfold)	(br) (brick)	(br) (bridge)
crab	(cr) (crown)	X (flag)	(cr) (crayons)
	X (plate)	(cr) (cross)	(cr) (crocodile)

For additional teaching helps, see T16.

Introducing initial consonant combinations **br** and **cr**.

In examining this page you might try to ascertain the instructional objectives for yourself. You might start by asking yourself what the child will be doing when he or she works on this page. What behaviors will be exhibited? What will the child have to know in order to complete the task? By actually doing the exercise mentally you can get a good idea of what the task entails and what the actual objective is.

(4) *Are the materials representative of varying cultures?* We usually associate attention to culture and ethnic-group representation with stories when talking about reading materials. That is easily understood. All stories have settings. And so it is with stories in books used in reading instruction. Most basal readers on the market today have included a great variety of social and cultural settings for stories, ranging from the inner city to the rural area. But cultural representation is not limited to this obvious illustration. All instructional materials have some type of setting. Phonics workbooks and kits use pictures to illustrate letter sounds (phonemes) and include specific words to teach the written (graphic) representation of those sounds. Middle-class suburban America is presented in some of these pictures while others attempt to avoid the use of cultural-value symbols by using animals or imaginary characters.

Careful examination of the materials allows you to determine whether a broad or narrow sampling has been achieved. You should note whether the number of settings is limited in scope or whether the selections cover a range of settings. In general, better reading materials expose children to many different settings and opportunities to identify.

You will also note the possible children's interests that the material may appeal to. Many books and studies have examined children's reading interests at a variety of age levels. They have found, for example, that boys are generally interested in such subjects as sports, transportation, and science, while girls like to read stories about people and make-believe. Both boys and girls like mysteries and stories about animals. These studies are helpful in indicating the general trend of children's interests, but it is our experience that the general topics children frequently state a preference for aren't always the specific topics they want to read about. Suppose that one of your students, a boy in fourth grade, has mentioned his interest in horses. You want to make reading relevant, so you go to the library and obtain *Blind Colt* by Glen Rounds. But when you show this book to your student, you are met with a lack of enthusiasm. Perhaps it is because this boy owns his own horse and is more interested in learning proper ways to groom his horse or methods of training his horse for showing than in reading a touching horse story. This point cannot be stressed enough: reading has to make sense to children if they are to become avid and able readers.

(5) *What is the difficulty of this material?* Estimating the difficulty of materials for the students in your class is another important consideration. This is especially true in learning to read. If a child experiences success when reading a particular selection, there is a strong possibility

that he or she will be encouraged to continue developing this reading ability. If, on the other hand, this same child invariably encounters difficulty and failure with the reading material, it is probable that he or she will come to view reading as a frustrating experience and will avoid subsequent reading situations. Not only is a dislike for reading being cultivated but the child's reading development is being stymied. Therefore, knowledge of the readability of materials is necessary for competent planning.

Readability formulas help you to estimate the difficulty of selections before trying them out with children. While readability formulas only provide estimates, they are helpful to approximate the reading difficulty of material. Readability formulas have been developed, studied, researched, and written about for over fifty years. George Klare discusses readability formulas and their use in this way:

> One of the problems in public education and mass communication is how to tell whether a particular piece of writing is likely to be readable to a particular group of readers. Several possible solutions are available.
>
> A first is to guess. Writers and teachers have long been making estimates of readability with skills probably developed largely from experience and feedback from readers. A second solution—particularly suitable when a precise index of readability is needed—is a test. In this case, a comprehension test covering the material must usually be built and refined before readability can be determined. With the large amount of reading material being published and available today, still another approach is needed. Readability formulas have come to provide a third possible solution to the problem.
>
> A readability formula uses counts of language variables in a piece of writing in order to provide an index of probable difficulty for readers. It is a predictive device in the sense that no actual participation by readers is needed. (1974–75, p. 64)

But exactly what is meant by language variables? This term refers to such things as the length of sentences, the difficulty of the vocabulary, the number of prepositions, the number of meaning units, and the number of syllables. A readability formula uses one, two, or more of these variables to provide an estimation of the reading difficulty of a writing selection.

There are many readability formulas. These vary both in complexity and in the language variables they incorporate. Each of these formulas has its proponents who state the advantages of the respective formula. Most of these formulas are validated by determining how well they compare with the other available formulas.

One of the easiest methods for determining readability has been devised by Edward Fry (1977). His formula, which is presented here, uses two language variables: the average number of syllables per

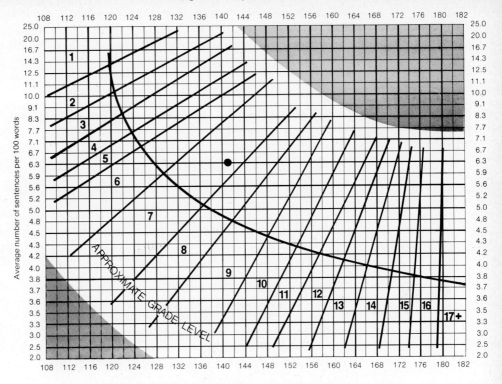

Average number of syllables per 100 words

DIRECTIONS: Randomly select 3 one hundred word passages from a book or an article. Plot average number of syllables and average number of sentences per 100 words on graph to determine the grade level of the material. Choose more passages per book if great variability is observed and conclude that the book has uneven readability. Few books will fall in gray area but when they do grade level scores are invalid.

Count proper nouns, numerals and initializations as words. Count a syllable for each symbol. For example, "1945" is 1 word and 4 syllables and "IRA" is 1 word and 3 syllables.

EXAMPLE:		SYLLABLES	SENTENCES
1st Hundred Words		124	6.6
2nd Hundred Words		141	5.5
3rd Hundred Words		158	6.8
	AVERAGE	141	6.3

READABILITY 7th GRADE (see dot plotted on graph)

Graph for Estimating Readability by Edward Fry.

hundred words and the average number of sentences per hundred words. An obvious result of this formula is that if the words and the sentences are long, the reading material will be designated difficult. In contrast, reading material composed of short words and short sentences will be easier. An advantage of Fry's formula is its simplicity. When correlated with other formulas, some that are more complex and lengthy, Fry's formula has been shown to result in similar estimates of reading difficulty.

The directions for the use of this formula suggest the selection of many samples when a great degree of accuracy is needed. It is not unusual for various samples from a book or story to produce different readability estimates. When this happens, the average should be computed to obtain the estimate of reading difficulty.

Klare strongly supports the use of Fry's formula in determining readability when he states:

> It may seem surprising that counts of the two simple variables of word length and sentence length are sufficient to make relatively good predictions of readability. No argument that they cause ease or difficulty is intended; they are merely good indices of difficulty. Consequently, altering word or sentence length, of themselves, can provide no assurance of improving readability. How to achieve more readable writing is another and much more complex endeavor. But as long as predictions are all that is needed, the evidence that simple word and sentence counts can provide satisfactory predictions for most purposes is now quite conclusive. (1974–75, pp. 97–98)

But the best way to assess whether reading material is appropriate for children is to have them actually sample it in your presence. Matching materials to children in this way is often described as administering an informal reading inventory (see Chapter 2, pages 39–71). It is evident that students must be present when using the informal-reading-inventory approach. Therefore, this method is not feasible when you are in the process of evaluating materials prior to their use with children. For this reason, readability formulas may provide useful information.

(6) *How does the material attempt to provide for individual differences?* Assigning a group of children to the same reading material is, in effect, indicating that such children are similar. Children in your class *will* be similar in some respects. For example, a particular group of children may have developed to the same general instructional reading level, and they may be interested in somewhat similar topics. But, while such factors are shared, it is also evident that major differences between children exist.

There are many factors that cause each child to be different; these variables are found in children's physical, mental, emotional, and intellectual makeup. Since all of these factors are brought by the child to the act of reading, every child is a unique reader. You should evaluate your materials to see if any provision has been made for these individual differences. Does the material have broad appeal? Does the material provide for additional instruction in specific areas that individual children may need? Does the material provide for individual learning rates? Does it lend itself to flexible use? If it does this to a great extent, it is probable that such material will be relevant to the varied children in your classroom.

Because children invariably progress at their own rate, even among children who read at the same general level, some will need to be introduced to a new concept only once, while others will need additional instruction and practice to master the concept. Further, some children will want to learn about a topic or concept in greater detail. Look at the material you are studying. Does it allow the children who have mastered the concept to continue on to something new? Are there suggestions or supplementary activities for those children who need additional instruction and practice? Are descriptions of relevant games, worksheets, or other materials that cover the same concept provided? Are there lists of other resources that will let a child explore a topic in greater depth? Generally, you should know the extent to which reading material provides for meeting individual needs of children; the more the instructional material you select does this, the more useful to you it is.

(7) *Does the material provide for self-instruction?* This item is closely related to item six in that it is also emphasizing the needs of the individual child. However, it focuses on the amount of self-direction or self-instruction the child is allowed to do. When you study materials to see if any provision has been made for self-instruction, you will be looking for two things: the first is the degree to which you, the teacher, must interact with the child; the second is the amount of additional suggestions that enable the interested child to explore a topic on his or her own. Thus, when evaluating reading materials to see what provisions are made for self-instruction, you should observe not only how much instruction the teacher must provide but also whether additional references are given that will allow a child, acting alone, to expand his or her knowledge.

Materials vary in the amount of instruction that the teacher is expected to provide. There are those that require the teacher to be available to all children at all times because their completed exercises must pass the teacher's inspection. This eats up teacher time that could be spent tending to individual needs. It leaves little time for the teacher to be spontaneous and creative or for the children to be self-directing. At the other extreme are the materials that require the child to be completely self-directing to the complete exclusion of the teacher. This leaves the teacher at the mercy of the material, with no influence on the child's learning, and may result in haphazard, hit-and-miss learning. As you can see, both extremes are inadequate.

The teacher has value when he or she interacts with the child and thus facilitates the child's learning. This interaction is important in guiding the child to fulfill needs and aspirations. Materials should allow for self-instruction on the part of the child, but not to the exclusion of the teacher.

One final word about your evaluation. It is important to evaluate materials prior to using them in instruction. Later, after you have had some classroom experience with them, take time to reevaluate them. A comparison of your evaluations before and after you use the materials will increase your ability to understand reading materials and their use with specific children in particular learning situations.

Organizing Yourself

In addition to becoming aware of all the factors that make each of your students unique, it is also important to strive constantly to become more aware of yourself. No other factor is more important than you are in the teaching-learning situation. It is the teacher who makes the ultimate difference in reading instruction. While the overall learning climate fostered by the school system is important—and ample and adequate materials are essential—your pupils' successes will be a function of your ability to blend your knowledge of the child and of his or her specific reading development with your awareness of the reading process. This begins with the acknowledgment that you have much to find out—that your understanding of that process will grow as you teach and learn about individual children. As well as knowing how much you know and need to learn, you must also be aware of other aspects of yourself. In short, you need to know your own strengths and how you can handle the instructional program for each child while remaining sane and cheerful.

try this ▶

One way to assess how ready you are to teach reading is to create a checklist similar to the one that follows. The questions on this checklist are rhetorical, but being able to answer these honestly to yourself should give you an idea of the information you yet want to acquire before beginning to teach.

Teacher Readiness Checklist

		Yes	No
(1)	Do you have a general awareness of the scope and goals of the reading program througout the total range of reading development?	____	____
(2)	Do you know a variety of approaches to reading instruction?	____	____
(3)	Can you devise an organizational plan for diagnostic reading instruction?	____	____
(4)	Are you acquainted with a wide variety of materials?	____	____
(5)	Can you evaluate reading materials?	____	____
(6)	Are you sensitive to and able to assess children's physical needs? Are you cognizant of:		
	a. vision problems frequently experienced by children?	____	____
	b. the effect auditory problems may have on a child's learning?	____	____

c. the effect speech differences may have on a child's academic achievement as well as on adjustment? _____ _____

d. the effect poor health may have on a child's attitude toward and interest in achievement and academic work? _____ _____

(7) Are you sensitive to children's emotional status?

a. Can you usually tell when a child is disturbed and can you usually find ways to reassure the child? _____ _____

b. Do you recognize children's needs to rid themselves of pent-up energy and to let off steam? _____ _____

c. Can you correct children's errors without making them feel inadequate or embarrassed? _____ _____

d. Do you recognize and provide for every child's need to feel acceptance and success? _____ _____

(8) Do you possess the necessary background and have command of the skills necessary for effective teaching of reading?

a. Do you have a solid background in and understanding of:

word-recognition skills and techniques for teaching? _____ _____

reading–study-skills and techniques for teaching? _____ _____

ways to evaluate progress _____ _____

methods of analyzing reading problems?

ways to motivate learning and identify and expand children's interests and tastes? _____ _____

b. Do you have a basic knowledge of sequence in reading-skill development? _____ _____

(9) Do you keep abreast of current developments in reading materials and instructional strategies by reading in professional journals, attending professional conferences and so on? _____ _____

In this chapter we have described the management and grouping procedures to provide structure for a reading program—a structure that will enable creative responses to come forth. Within this structure, children are encouraged to become more self-directing—to initiate and to complete projects. Some work is done alone, some with another child, some with a small group, and some only with the teacher. The teacher serves to monitor progress, to ascertain whether learning has occurred, to gather small and flexible groups for instruction, and to disband the group as objectives are met. The teacher serves as the initiator, director, and redirector. When interest wanes, the teacher has a wealth of resources to spark new interests. When interest skyrockets, the teacher stands discreetly aside to see what direction the propulsion will take. The teacher is helping children grow in reading skill without suffering a loss of interest. The teacher has worked to develop organization and to make organization work for children.

REFERENCES Bamman, Henry A.; Dawson, Mildred A.; and McGovern, J. J., *Fundamentals of Basic Reading Instruction.* New York: David McKay, 1973.

Blitz, Barbara. *The Open Classroom: Making It Work.* Boston: Allyn and Bacon, 1973.

Bryan, Miriam. *Ability Grouping: Status, Impact, and Alternatives.* ERIC Clearinghouse on Tests, Measurement, and Evaluation. Princeton, N.J.: Educational Testing Service, June 1971.

Durkin, Dolores. "The Importance of Goals for Reading Instruction." *The Reading Teacher* 28 (January 1975): 380–83.

Fader, Daniel. *The Naked Children.* New York: Macmillan, 1971.

Fry, Edward B. "Fry's Readability Graph: Clarifications, Validity, and Extension to Level 17." *Journal of Reading* 21 (December 1977): 242–52.

Klare, George R. "Assessing Readability." *Reading Research Quarterly* 10, no. 1 (1974–75): 62–102.

———. *The Measurement of Readability.* Ames, Iowa: Iowa State University Press, 1963.

Mager, Robert F. *Preparing Instructional Objectives.* Belmont, Cal.: Fearon Publishers, 1962.

Russell, David H. *The Dynamics of Reading.* Waltham, Mass.: Ginn, 1970.

Sommer, Robert. *Personal Space: The Behavioral Basis of Design.* Englewood Cliffs, N.J.: Prentice-Hall, 1969.

FOR FURTHER READING Durkin, Dolores. *Teaching Young Children to Read.* Boston: Allyn and Bacon, 1972.

———. "A Six Year Study of Children Who Learned to Read in School at the Age of Four." *Reading Research Quarterly,* 10, no. 1 (1974–75): 9–61.

Goodlad, John, and Anderson, Robert. *The Non-graded Elementary School.* New York: Harcourt Brace Jovanovich, 1959.

Lapp, Diane. *The Use of Behavioral Objectives in Education.* Newark, Del.: International Reading Association, 1972.

Ramsey, Wallace Z., ed. *Organizing for Individual Differences.* Newark, Del.: International Reading Association, 1967.

Russell, David H. *The Dynamics of Reading.* Waltham, Mass.: Ginn, 1970.

Stauffer, Russell G. "The Library." In *The Language-experience Approach to the Teaching of Reading.* New York: Harper and Row, 1970.

Tanyzer, Harold; Tanyzer, Karl; and Tanyzer, Jean, eds. *Reading Children's Books and Our Pluralistic Society.* Newark, Del.: International Reading Association, 1972.

Taylor, Anne P., and Vlastos, George. *School Zone.* New York: Van Nostrand Reinhold, 1975.

Thorenson, Louis B.; Gibbons, John Patrick, Sr.; and Kackley, Mary. "How the Janitor Can Help in the Reading Program." *The Reading Teacher* 27 (February 1974): 458–61.

10) Programs for Teaching Reading

If you were to review the list of topics to be presented at a teacher orientation conference at the beginning of the school year, an in-service education program, a teacher institute, or a professional conference on reading, you would almost certainly find a few sessions devoted to "programs for teaching reading." And many of these sessions would center on a specific method, program, approach, or set of materials— some of which would be labelled "innovative." Each speaker would present arguments and data to support the conclusion that the particular program being discussed guarantees results far superior to those you can expect from another program. The speakers promoting "innovative programs" would compare their programs to less effective "traditional" types. The enthusiasm of the speakers and their seeming concern for the reading development of children might even rub off on you, so that you would find yourself looking forward to trying one or more of these "innovations."

Such conferences and institutes often include publisher's exhibits, which you might find time to visit and where you would find a myriad of published reading programs. Most of the publishers would be passing out attractive brochures proclaiming that their materials represent the most carefully researched and theoretically sound "program for teaching reading." The various brochures would describe such programs as a "modified linguistics program," a "language experience program," a "total language program"—the list could go on and on. If you are like us, you might become just a bit confused—perhaps even overwhelmed—with all of the hard-sell surrounding so many different programs.

Understanding Some Terms

Already, you have encountered *program, approach, method,* and *materials* used vaguely as synonyms. Exactly *what,* you may wonder, constitutes a program for teaching reading and how do programs relate to approaches, methods, and materials? Once you have an answer to this, of course, you may wonder what the various programs represent pedagogically and which programs can best serve each child in your class. This chapter will attempt to explain what programs are so that you can better select them. First, let's try to clarify the relationship of the terms that cluster around the loose concept of *programs for teaching reading.*

In this chapter, we will be using the following definitions:

Approach is a general term that indicates the educational philosophy influencing or underlying a program. Throughout this book, for example, we have been advocating an individualized, child-centered approach to teaching reading.

Program is a set of related materials for instruction. Most programs are put together by educational publishers; however, programs are also developed by educational-research laboratories and individual school districts. Programs often include descriptions of specified skills to be taught to children and specific teaching procedures or methods for teaching those skills. Some programs very carefully control the language or sequence the difficulty of the children's reading materials.

Procedures is a term that we use synonymously with *method* and denotes a specific teaching activity. For example, in Chapter 6 we described the analytic and synthetic procedures, or methods, for teaching phonics. As noted in the definition of *program,* particular procedures (or methods) are often prescribed as a part of a program; but *procedure* or *method* can also refer to a classroom teaching activity devised by the teacher to meet the needs of a child. For example, it is *method* when a teacher introduces a new vocabulary word in context or creates a practice game for a particular word-recognition behavior.

In the following section, we will examine more completely the definition and contents of reading programs.

What Is a Program for Teaching Reading?

As we shall see, the particular materials and prescribed methods that are used to teach reading are sometimes components of a program selected to meet the needs of a particular child or group of children. Therefore, a program is either a set of packaged instructional materials, a collection of recommended methods, or both materials and methods used to teach reading. The particular program that provides materials and recommends methods has some unifying aspect to it. The unifying aspect may be that the program uses only certain types of materials, emphasizes the teaching of certain reading skills, emphasizes certain teaching methods, or perhaps uses reading selections that follow a particular format.

Obviously, then, you can use different methods regardless of the specific program you are using. Therefore, in reading this chapter, you should not get caught up in the concept of selecting a program and having that program dictate all your materials and teaching methods. You will need to modify your methods and materials. Sometimes you will find yourself in a situation where you cannot select the program because the school district has mandated that a particular program be used. In such a situation, it is even more vital that you be aware of the modifications you can and should be making within a given program.

At this point you may be wondering how an approach fits in with the idea of a program. As we mentioned earlier, our general approach to teaching reading is to focus on determining the needs of each child, to provide instruction to meet those needs, and to encourage the use of interesting and appropriate reading materials for children. Our total approach is to individualize instruction regardless of the specific program in use. And we believe that any program can be adapted to the individual needs of the children in your class.

While most programs for teaching reading seem to suggest that each can stand alone without the need for other materials or teaching procedures, such is not the case. You will find that many of them are alike in important ways. For example, you have certainly heard or read about something called a *phonics* program. Phonics is not a program for teaching reading; rather, phonics is a set of generalizations about the relationships between letters and sounds that are taught to children. Phonics are taught with all kinds of materials and through a variety of teaching activities as a part of many programs. What most people mean when they talk or write about the phonics program is any reading program with an emphasis on teaching phonics.

Another example is what educators often describe as the *basal reader program*. This term can be quite misleading because there is no one reader or program. A basal program is any graded set of materials for teaching reading that is accompanied by teacher's manuals for using those materials. Some basals emphasize phonics skills; others emphasize comprehension. And almost all basals include both of these—although with varying emphasis.

Programed materials (or *systems programs*) are also often cited. Programed materials, however, can be developed to emphasize phonics skills or reading comprehension. A systems program means a particular set of teaching procedures will be used—often with a particular set of materials; but the skills that can be taught using such a program can vary considerably.

In a very real sense, then, all programs represent aspects of reading instruction—and the relative attention to these aspects must be considered before adopting a program to teach reading to a child. These aspects, which will be the basis of our review of the more commonly discussed types of programs for teaching reading, include special materials, specified skills, specific teaching procedures, and control of the language of reading materials.

What Is the Best Program for You?

The question, Which reading program should I use? often crops up before a teacher has a chance to learn what all those labels mean. Experience with various materials and with children demonstrates that there is no one best program for teaching reading and that there is no one best program for a single class. The task for most teachers is to obtain as many materials as possible and adapt different programs to meet the needs of each child in the classroom.

As you form your definition of reading and increase your understanding of how reading ability is best developed in a child, however, you will come to have more appreciation for some programs than for others. As an effective teacher, you will study children's reading and language-processes; you will establish the goals and objectives of your reading program; and you will develop a variety of techniques for helping children meet those objectives. In short, you will put together a reading program that reaches past the limitations of any single program. Thus, it is easy to understand why no single program has been shown to be consistently more effective than any other. Indeed, the teacher who knows and understands a variety of programs and how they develop various reading skills supercedes the program.

Knowing many programs and how to modify these for each child is a big order, we agree; and the first step toward building your own is to understand what the methods and materials billed as programs are and how they operate instructionally. In the sections that follow, we are going to review some commonly discussed types of programs for teaching reading. For each of these, we will consider the four aspects mentioned above: specified materials, skills, teaching procedures, and the control of the language of the reading materials. In addition, we will summarize some of the potential strengths and weaknesses of each type of program. Finally, each section will describe some of the ways you could implement features of a program of that type in your classroom. We believe that when a program becomes something with a set of directions to be followed precisely—a set of materials to be introduced in an exact order or a set of skills to be taught in an absolute order—the teacher will no longer be a teacher. The developer of the packaged program will dictate the teaching, and the classroom "teacher" will act as a monitor who could be replaced by a minimally trained aide or even a computerized tape recording.

There has been no paucity of attempts to determine the best program for teaching reading. For example, one of the longest sections of the *Reading Research Quarterly*'s annual "Summary of Investigations Relating to Reading" is the section that collects and reviews the published research on approaches to teaching reading. In the 1975–76 edition of the summary (Weintraub et al., 1976) there are 16 reported studies that deal with the teaching of reading in the primary grades alone. At that rate, by 1986 there would have been about 160 additional studies that have attempted to determine the best program or approach to teaching reading.

Another recent indication of the plethora of comparative studies is an annotated bibliography published by the International Reading Association (Laffey, 1971), which includes an extensive list of references on reading approaches that appeared in the published research literature between 1950 and 1970. The bibliography is divided into three parts: elementary, secondary, and college and adult reading. The elementary part is divided into sections that deal with general programs (53 entries), basal programs (44 entries), individualized programs (38 entries), language-linguistics programs (36 entries), programed approaches (11 entries), phonics programs (35 entries), and artificial orthographies (alphabets) and other programs (40 entries).

Regardless of the quantity of research, however, there are no definitive answers to the question of the best program because the results of various studies support different programs, and nothing conclusive can be shown about which programs are superior.

A major effort to research the effectiveness of various programs for teaching beginning reading was the "Cooperative Research Program in First-Grade Reading Instruction" (Bond and Dykstra, 1967). One of three major objectives of this study was to determine "which of the many approaches to initial reading instruction produces superior reading and spelling achievement at the end of first grade." The examined approaches included basal, basal plus phonics, initial teaching alphabet, linguistics, language experience, and phonic-linguistics. The major conclusions of this study were that all beginning-reading programs should include a systematic approach to word-study skills, that combinations of programs are often superior to single programs, that linguistics programs are especially effective in the area of word recognition, that reading programs are not effective in all situations, and that reading achievement is related to factors other than the particular program being used. Another major conclusion was that future research might well center on teacher and learning situation characteristics rather than on methods and materials. The findings of the study stressed that the tremendous range among classrooms using any one method is just one of several key elements in the learning situation that are more

(continued from
page 426)

significant than the methods employed. To improve reading instruction, it seems more important to educate better teachers of reading than it is to expect a solution in the form of materials.

Because the teacher is (and should be) vastly more important than the program, the enthusiasm of the teacher for the general approach being used is almost always a strong enough factor to produce better results with one program than another. This enthusiasm for the "new" or "untried," commonly referred to as the "Hawthorne effect" by researchers, results from the dedication and interest teachers develop when they begin using a new program—if they are supportive of the new program and believe it will produce better results.

In addition to the strong overriding influence of the teacher, another major reason that research has not been able to provide definitive answers about the best program for teaching reading is that much of the language learning of children (including reading) takes place outside classrooms—as does the greatest amount of practice of language skills. Thus, many factors are influencing the child who is a subject in a study, and it is difficult, if not impossible, to control or account for all these influences in a research study that is examining the effect of some program used in the classroom.

Finally, research in classrooms is quite difficult to conduct because of the inability of the researcher to "control" the program the teacher is using. To determine if a program is actually producing results, the researcher needs to insure that the program is implemented in a very precise manner with almost no variation. If a teacher varies the program, the researcher is often at a loss to know whether the particular program or the program plus the teacher's variation produced the results. Many researchers feel that definitive results can only be produced in a laboratory setting. Classrooms are not laboratories, however; they are dynamic and active places. For this reason, educators generally place little faith in the results of studies conducted in laboratories. They feel that studies conducted in highly controlled laboratories often have little relation to the real world of the classroom.

Even though few definitive answers are available from the research, the continued interest in new programs has created an environment where teachers, materials developers, and researchers are constantly developing, trying out, and studying different programs. Not only does this continuous effort cause an examination of what works and what doesn't work; it also leads to a kind of constant "Hawthorne environment," where many teachers are enthusiastically developing and redeveloping their reading programs. If such change and invention is thoughtful and orderly, it can lead to teacher enthusiasm for specially tailored methods that will help to produce effective readers.

The Basal Reading Program

Basal readers are primarily sets of published materials organized to teach reading. Some basal reading programs emphasize the teaching of word recognition through synthetic phonics, while others suggest teaching procedures emphasizing analytic phonics. Some basals place a great deal of emphasis on reproducing the natural language patterns of children, while others use programed materials. Our point is that if you use a particular publisher's basal reading program, you will not be using the same program another teacher is using if that teacher is using a different publisher's basal reading program. The term "basal" signifies a general type of program and does not specify what each specific program contains. Most important is that the materials in a basal reading program can be used flexibly (and more than one series can be used); each should be adapted to fit your beliefs about teaching reading and the needs of your students.

Basal reading programs have been the most common instructional materials in classrooms for over a hundred and twenty-five years. McGuffey's readers* were first published about 1840 and dominated the American public schools for the next forty years (Smith, 1965). Other basal programs soon appeared on the market and began to compete with the McGuffey readers. However, basal programs continued to provide the structure for classroom reading instruction.

In a landmark study, Mary Austin and Coleman Morrison (1963) reported that

> despite discordant views over its value, the basal reader is unquestionably the predominant tool of instruction in most of the school systems sampled throughout this study. . . . In only one school system visited during the original field study were basal readers not used as the major tools of reading instruction. In fact, for many teachers it would be unthinkable and impossible to teach without them. (p. 54)

There is much evidence to support the conclusion that basal readers continue to dominate reading instruction and that they will do so for some time to come. This is probably true for two major reasons. The first is that basal readers have continuously been modified to meet the changing pedagogical and social influences in the United States. Second, basal programs attempt to provide a total set of materials and instructional suggestions for teaching reading. Examination of each of these points will help you to understand basal reading programs more fully.

The flexibility of basal readers in reflecting nationwide influences was shown by Nila Banton Smith in *American Reading Instruction*

---

* McGuffey's readers were not the first basal readers. That honor, according to Nila Banton Smith (1965), goes to Noah Webster, who in 1790 published "three books which constituted the first set of consecutive readers in the history of American reading instruction." McGuffey's readers, however, pioneered many of the concepts of today's basal reading programs.

(1965). For example, Smith describes the period in American history from 1776 to about 1840 as the period of nationalistic-moralistic emphasis. This was the time in our nation's history when the colonies had broken their ties with Great Britain and established themselves as a new nation. Politics and the development of a strong and independent nation replaced earlier concerns with religion. The titles of some selections from *The North American Reader* (1835) show how the reading materials of that time reflected the national mood of patriotism and moralism.

> The Love of Country and Home
> My Country
> The Danger of Altering the Constitution
> The Debt Due to the Soldiers of the Revolution
> Little Things Destroy Character
> Advice to the Young
> Danger of Bad Habits

By the late 1800s the nation could pursue the benefits of its independence and wealth. Smith describes this period in our history as one of the pursuit of culture. Again the basal reading programs reflected the national mood. One of the popular reading programs of the period was *Stepping Stones to Literature* (Silver, Burdett and Company, 1897). The preface to these readers describes the content:

> In the Fourth Book the child is given his first distinct introduction to mythology. In the earlier books, fables and fairy stories have been used, and there has been a little suggestion of mythology; but in the Fourth, myth and wonder—those subjects which appeal to the child's imagination and carry him out of his limited environment into a larger world—are emphasized. We believe that this is in accord with whatever truth exists in the culture epoch theory of education. . . .
>
> In the Fifth Book the use of the myth which is found in the Fourth is continued, but the myths here used are mainly historical, leading directly to the study of history. . . .
>
> In the Sixth Book the pure myth does not appear, but in its place is much of history, especially of the legendary lore which appeals to the developing imagination of the child,—such as the tales of ancient Rome and Scott's poems.

Not only have social and historical influences affected the content and organization of basal readers but changes in educational theory have also been very influential. Smith describes the period from 1925 to 1935 as the time of the expansion and application of educational research to reading instruction. For example, she cites the research of William S. Gray, who concluded that few adults spent much time reading orally, while much primary grade reading instruction was spent in oral reading. The result was that about 1930, when Gray became coauthor of the Elson-Gray readers, silent reading was emphasized as a primary mode for reading instruction.

In addition to the numerous social and pedagogical influences pointed out by Smith, there are many that have occurred since the publication of her book. When educators became vocally critical of the prescriptive lock-step curriculum that basal readers reflected (around 1960), many publishers dropped the traditional grade-level designations and replaced them with letters, a numerical sequence, or with some coded indication of each book's difficulty level. These changes were intended to remove some of the stigma from using different levels of books within one class. The newer designations are discussed more thoroughly below.

Other societal changes and the findings of educational research resulted in even more changes in basal readers: the illustrations and content began to reflect varying lifestyles and different races; the language began to reflect more natural patterns; and the strict controls on vocabulary were somewhat eased. As a result of the latter change, more children's literature could be included in the texts.

Materials Are the Key to the Four Aspects of Basal Readers

In the following sections we will describe basal readers in regard to the four aspects of any program that were explained earlier in this chapter: the use of special materials, the teaching of specified skills, the use of specific teaching procedures, and the control of language.

As you read, you will discover that basal reading programs include many different instructional materials. In fact, basal reading programs are more nearly collections of materials than they are specific teaching procedures. Basals do emphasize the teaching of specified skills, but there is variation in the number, the sequence, and the suggested procedures for teaching the specific skills introduced in each basal. Because recommended teaching procedures vary from basal to basal, teachers are encouraged to supplement the teaching procedures described in the teacher's manuals. Finally, the language of the instructional materials is heavily controlled. The introduction of vocabulary, the length of sentences, and the content of stories are all sequenced to match the expected reading development of children. Each publisher of a basal reader uses its own controls, but there is a great deal of similarity in the controls used by different publishers.

As you read about basal readers, keep in mind that the individual basal programs offered by the various publishers can vary greatly in emphasis. That is, while all basal programs will offer a collection of readings grouped or organized in some way, one may emphasize a linguistics approach in its teacher's manuals and skills books, another may build skills in some programed way, and still another may focus on the comprehension of the concepts that the organization of its contents hopes to build. Other basal programs may stress any combination of the other general approaches we will be considering in this chapter. As you can see, the term "basal program" is not specific enough for you to base your choice on.

Special materials. The continuous modification of basal reading programs, however, only partially explains their popularity. A second reason, and perhaps the more important, is that basal reading programs provide a fairly complete array of teaching materials, including comprehensive teacher guides.

There are at least sixteen major basal reading programs published. These programs all differ to some extent in their educational philosophy; thus, these materials place somewhat different emphases on the various reading skills and on the content of the stories. In addition, the type of instructional materials included in each program varies. You should examine several basal programs to understand these differences by looking at the children's books, teacher's guides, workbooks or skills books, and supplementary materials.

The major components of a basal reading program are the books read by the children. These basals, or readers as they are sometimes called, are graded in terms of difficulty from preprimers to books of from sixth- to eighth-grade difficulty. As mentioned earlier, readers were commonly labelled according to the grade in which they were to be used, such as fourth reader, fifth reader, and so on. Today, most publishers have abandoned the use of grade designations and are instead describing their materials by levels. For instance, the Houghton-Mifflin Reading Program has thirteen levels that span grades one to six. This type of designation emphasizes that a particular book is not necessarily limited to use in a particular grade level. Children in the second grade are more homogeneous with respect to age than to reading ability. A group of thirty children in this grade, for example, may represent developmental reading abilities that span the beginning reader through the fifth-grade text. To use a single "second-grade" book with these children would be not only inappropriate, it would be professional malpractice. The child who should be in a beginning reader would be frustrated, while the child who could read fifth-grade material may be bored. Publishers feel that by indicating their books by levels rather than grades, they will free the teacher to use a wider range of books in the classroom.

The dropping of grade-level designations for books has caused one problem, however. For years, reading teachers and specialists have described their pupils' reading ability as being approximately second-grade level, fifth-grade level, or some other grade level. Readability formulas, which are methods for determining the reading difficulty of written material, have also designated materials as being of specific grade difficulty. All this was helpful to the teacher, who could match the reading level of the student with the reading grade level of the material. The elimination of grade-level designations of materials, however, has resulted in some confusion for teachers. They now wonder just what a "level eight" reader is. In other words, they want to know its approximate reading difficulty and the grade level in which it would generally be used. Figure 10–1 indicates the general grade level designations for basal readers widely used in elementary classrooms today.

Figure 10–1 Relationship Between Basal Reader Levels* and Instructional Reading Levels

Publisher	Series	Date of Publication	Instructional Reading Level										
			Readiness	Preprimer† 1	Preprimer† 2	Primer	Grade 1	Grade 2	Grade 3	Grade 4	Grade 5	Grade 6	Grade 7–8
Allyn and Bacon	Pathfinder	1978	1–3 (read aloud) 4,5	6 (Preprimer 3) 7–8	7	8–9	9–10	10–12	12–14	14–16	16–18	18–20	
	Sheldon Reading Series	1973	Picture Stories / More Picture Stories	At Home (Preprimer 3) Here and Away	Here and Near	Our School	Our Town	Fields and Fences / Town and Country	Magic Windows / Story Caravan	Believe and Make-Believe	Finding the Way	Arrivals and Departures	
American Book Company	American Book Reading Program	1977	A B	C (Preprimer 3) E	D	F	G	H, I	J, K	L	M	N	(To be published in 1979)
	The Read System	1968 1971	First Step Second Step Third Step	A (Preprimer 3) C	B	D	E	F, G	H, I	J	K	L	
The Economy Company	The Key-text Program	1978	Lev. 1	Lev. 2	Lev. 3	Lev. 4	(Levels 1–4)	Lev. 5 Lev. 6	Lev. 7 Lev. 8	Lev. 9 Lev. 10	Lev. 11 Lev. 12	Lev. 13 Lev. 14	
	Keys to Reading Program	1975 (2d ed.)	Lev. 1	Lev. 2 (Preprimer 3) 4	Lev. 3	Lev. 5	Lev. 6	Levels 7, 8	Levels 9, 10	Lev. 11	Lev. 12	Levels 13a, 13b	Levels 14, 15
Ginn	Reading 720	1976	1	2	3	4	5	6–7	8–9	10–11	12–13	14–15	

Publisher	Series	Date	(Readiness)	1	2 / 3	4	5	6, 7	8, 9	10	11	12	(To be published in 1979)
Harcourt Brace Jovanovich	*Bookmark* (2d ed.)	1977–1978	*Look, Listen, and Learn*	(Preprimer 3)	3 (Preprimer 3)	4	5	6, 7	8, 9	10	11	12	
Harper & Row	*Reading Basics Plus*	1976	*Get Ready! Get Set! Go Read!*	Aa	Ab (Preprimer 3) Ac	Ad	Ae	BAa Ba	CAa Ca	Da	Ea	Fa	Ga Ha
	Design for Reading	1972	Level 1 Level 2 Level 3	Lev. 4	Lev. 5 (Preprimer 3) Level 6	Level 7	Level 8	Levels 9, 10	Levels 11, 12	Levels 13, 14	Levels 15, 16	Levels 17, 18	Levels 19, 20
D. C. Heath	*Reading Perspectives* (Supplementary)	1975				Primer	Book 1	Book 2	Book 3	Book 4	Book 5	Book 6	
	Reading: Beginnings, Patterns/ Explorations (Supplementary)	1974					A	A & B	Explorations				
	Bookshops (Supplementary)	1973					A	B	C				
Holt, Rinehart, and Winston	*Basic Reading Systems*	1977 (rvd.) (1973 ed. same levels)	1, 2	3–6		7	8	9, 10	11, 12	13	14	15	16, 17
Houghton Mifflin	*Houghton Mifflin Reading Series*	1976	*Ready Steps* GRTR- Lev. A	Lev. B	Lev. C (Preprimer 3) Level D	A–F	F–H	H–J	J–K	K–L	L–M	M–N	N–O
	Houghton Mifflin Readers	1971, 1974	*Ready Steps* GRTR Lev. 2	Lev. 3a	Lev. 3b (Preprimer 3) Level 3C	2–5	5–7	7–9	9–10	10–11	11–12	12–13	13–14

* Basal reader levels are indicated by number, letter, color, and/or title whichever is appropriate for the series.

† Some basal series include a third book which is estimated to be at Preprimer level.

Adapted and reproduced from the Metropolitan Achievement Tests. Copyright © 1978 by Harcourt Brace Jovanovich, Inc. Reproduced by special permission by the publisher.

Figure 10–1 (continued)

Publisher	Series	Date of Publication	Readiness	Preprimer		Primer	Grade 1	Grade 2	Grade 3	Grade 4	Grade 5	Grade 6	Grade 7–8
				1	2								
Laidlaw	Reading Program	1976–77 –78	1, 2		4	5	6	7, 8	9, 10	11	12	13	
J. B. Lippincott	Basic Reading Program	(See Grade Levels)	Beginning to Read, Write and Listen (1975)			A	B–D (1975)	E, F	G, H	I	J (1978 rvd.)	K	L, M 1971 (last revision)
Macmillan	Series r	1975	3, 3+	4–6		7, 8	9, 10 (1st Reader)	11–14	15–18	19–24	25–30	31–36	
	The Macmillan Reading Program	1974	1, 2	3–5		6	7–7A	8, 9A	10–11 11A	12	13	14	
McGraw-Hill	New Practice Readers (2d Ed. Supple.)	1978					A	B	C	D	E F	G	
	Reading for Concepts (2d Ed. Supple.)	1977						A B	C	D	E F	G H	
	American Language Today	1976					Scout Hand	Tiger Tree	Emerald Snowflakes	Orange Rain	Purple Sand	Flying Free	
Charles E. Merrill	Linguistic Reading Program	1975	My Alphabet Book	A		B	C–D	E–F	G–H	I	J	K	

Instructional Reading Level

Publisher	Basal Series												
Open Court		1976, 1977			5	1:1:1 1:1:2 1:2	2:1 2:2	3:1 3:2	4	5	6		
Rand McNally	Rand McNally Reading Program (Young America Basic Series)	1978	1	2	3 (Preprimer 3) 4	5	6	7, 8	9, 10	11	12	13	14, 15
Rand McNally (Lyons & Carnahan)	Young America Basic Reading Program	1972, 1974	1	2	3 (Preprimer 3) 4	5	6	7, 8	9, 10	11	12	13	14, 15
Science Research Associates	Basic Reading Series	1976 (Revision)	Readiness Book, Alphabet Book	A (Parts 1 & 2)	B	C	D	E, F					
	Comprehensive Reading Series	1971						G	H, I	J	K	L	
Scott, Foresman	Basics in Reading Program	1978	Kinder-garten Readiness	Prep. 1 Preprimer 1	Prep. 2 Preprimer 2 3	Primer	Book 1	2-1 2-2	3-1 3-2	4	5	6	7, 8 (To be published in 1979)
	Reading Unlimited	1976 (Revision of S-F Reading Systems)	K, 1	2	2	3	4	5-8	9-12	13-15	16-18	19-21	22-24 25-27

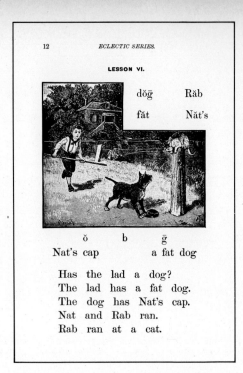

The first readers that were graded in difficulty were the McGuffey readers, which went from grades one to six. These 1840 readers introduced the concept of a controlled vocabulary with the gradual introduction and repetition of increasingly more difficult words. McGuffey's vocabulary control was based on his own common sense and the actual number of letters in each word. For example, in his primer the reading selection above appears.

McGuffey's principles of controlled vocabulary and the use of repetition are continued today to varying degrees in almost all basal readers; they led to the development of the famous Scott, Foresman series, which included stories like the one reproduced on page 437.

While the concept of the control of vocabulary difficulty has been central to the development of basal readers since the days of the McGuffey readers, the sophistication of vocabulary control has changed. Researchers have attempted to determine the most common words in children's speaking vocabularies, the most common words in the stories and books written for children, and which words children learn most easily. In addition, linguists have demonstrated that the syntax of a sentence also has a great deal to do with reading difficulty. All these factors are now considered when basal readers are written. The language of the stories in basals today more closely resembles the everyday speech patterns of children rather than the primers of bygone days. Still, many

Jane said, "Look, Dick.
Look at this.
Puff can ride with me.
Spot can ride with you.
Come and ride."

From *Fun Wherever We Are* by
Helen M. Robinson, Marion
Monroe, A. Sterl Artley, et al.
Copyright© 1965 by Scott,
Foresman and Company. Reprinted
by permission.

children learned to read well with the stilted style of the basal preprimers and primers of a decade or two ago. In fact, even today some children have more success with these old, heavily controlled readers than with the "natural language pattern" books of today.

For many years the content of children's books focused on the white, middle-class family. Most included serial-type stories of a family made up of an intact suburban family: a mother and father, two or three exemplary children (usually a brother and sister and a baby girl), a dog, and a cat. Minority groups were almost totally excluded, and city and rural settings were used only when the family took "A Trip to Grandmother's Farm" or "A Trip to the City."

Today's books have changed considerably. The stories take place in a wide range of settings; minority families are included; and females are depicted in a wide range of roles and occupations. One of the major changes in content has been the inclusion of a wider variety of forms: fiction, fairy tales, how-to-do-it stories, factual stories about real people and events, and poetry.

The teacher's editions that accompany the children's books include lesson plans for teaching each of the selections in the readers. Sometimes the teacher's editions of texts are printed adjacent to a facsimile of the student's book. In this way, the teacher can read and follow the teaching suggestions along with the student's reading selection.

From *Whispering Ghosts: Teacher's Edition*
by William Eller et al. (River Forest, Ill.:
Laidlaw Brothers, 1976), p. T114. Reprinted
by permission of Laidlaw Brothers, a
Division of Doubleday and Company, Inc.

Pages 98–105

TO ENSURE PUPIL INVOLVEMENT

Have the story located in the children's book and
the title read. Encourage speculation about the
man in the picture. Tell the children that the man
is a Parsee. Write *Parsee* on the chalkboard, and
explain that this word refers to a member of a
group of people who live in India.

Reading the Story

Suggest that this "how" story is similar to the
"why" stories that have been read previously. Ask
the children to read the story and then to be ready
to tell how the rhinoceros happened to lose his
smooth skin. Excuse the independent readers, as-
suring them that they will rejoin the group later for
"Talking It Over." Provide guidance for the other
children, as suggested below.

Read to Find Out   Pages 98–99

What did the Parsee do on this particular
day?

What was special about the Parsee's cake?

What else did you find out about the Parsee?

Read to Find Out   Pages 100–101

Let the children speculate about what is happening, using clues from the picture. Then ask,

How did the author describe the rhinoceros?

How did the rhinoceros show his poor manners?

What did the Parsee do when he first saw the
rhinoceros?

What did the Parsee do after the rhinoceros
walked away?

Encourage volunteers to tell what the last sentence on page 101 suggests.

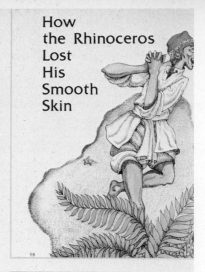

How the Rhinoceros Lost His Smooth Skin

98

Just as the Parsee was about to
eat the cake, there came walking
down to the beach an ugly rhinoceros.
In those days the rhinoceros had
smooth skin which fit him quite
tight. There were no folds to be
seen in it. He had huge jaws, a
great horn on his nose, and very
poor manners. He had no manners
then, he has no manners now, and
he never will have any manners.

The rhinoceros said, "How!"
and frightened the Parsee. When
the Parsee saw the ugly rhinoceros,
he climbed up the trunk of the nearest
tree, leaving the cake behind.

The rhinoceros upset the oven
with his nose, and the cake rolled
in the sand. He lifted the cake with
the tip of his horn, and it disappeared
inside his huge jaws. Then he went
away, waving his tail as he walked
up the beach.

Most basal reader programs include a practice book, or skills book,
to accompany each of the readers, the use of which is usually described
in the teacher's manual. Skills books provide practice for the reading
skills that are introduced with the basal reader stories. The skills books
usually follow the same prescribed order of skills as does the basal series
itself. Examples of these skills lessons can be found in both Chapters
5 and 6. Skills books are often consumable; that is, the students write
in the books and a new set must be purchased for use the next year.

Accompanying most basal reading books are a wide variety of supplementary materials to help students practice word-recognition skills,
including games, word and phrase cards, and pictures to be used to
introduce stories. Commonly, tests are provided that are used to assess
each student's mastery of the reading skills at each level and readiness
to advance to the next level of the program.

Specified skills. Basal readers are developed to introduce and teach all of the skills their authors believe a child needs to become an independent reader. While basal readers do include a wide range of skills, the individual bias of the authors who develop a particular series is demonstrated by the relative emphasis on certain reading skills, by the order of presentation, and by the suggested procedures for teaching and reteaching.

Most important is that basal readers emphasize reading comprehension—at least at the literal level. Most lessons—even those that are designed to teach word-recognition skills—involve the student in reading as a means to gain meaning. In addition, the teaching of word-recognition skills in most present-day basals is usually done in a meaningful context.

Specific teaching procedures. The teaching procedures outlined in the teacher's manuals vary from series to series. Here, the series diverge, reflect their variant philosophies, and lend support to our earlier statement that there is no single identifiable basal reader program. Still, most lesson plans suggested by the various series do have a few elements in common. These lesson plans focus on the reading of a specific selection and are divided into four major steps: (1) developing the child's background, readiness, and motivation to read a particular selection; (2) introducing new vocabulary; (3) guided silent reading; and (4) rereading for specific purpose and/or follow-up activities.

The first step is often accomplished by encouraging the teacher to discuss the subject matter or setting that is the focus of the story. Student involvement is emphasized by asking the child to talk about experiences he or she has had that are similar to those of the story. The lesson plan will also describe ways to arouse the child's interest in reading the story by asking questions that cause the child to make inferences about the story. The child then reads to check the validity of the hunches.

The second step, introducing new vocabulary, often combines the introduction or practice of word-recognition skills with an emphasis on the meanings of words as they are used in the particular story. Sometimes the lesson plan will suggest teaching specific word-recognition skills prior to the reading of the story. Such word-recognition skills will be introduced using words that the child will later read in the story. In addition, the lesson plan often provides suggestions for discussing the new words that are introduced in the story. The meanings of the words— especially as they are used in the story—are emphasized.

The third step in a lesson plan emphasizes guided reading of the selection. The teacher's manual will often suggest appropriate places in the story to have the child stop reading in order to discuss what has been read. The child is encouraged to locate and read aloud passages from the story that support conclusions about action, character, and so on. At these points, the child is also encouraged to think about what comes next in the story and to discuss his or her reasons for predicting this action. Teachers are provided with questions that focus on the child's inferential and evaluative comprehension as well as questions aimed at developing literal comprehension. A common concern about the teacher's questions included with basal readers, as well as a concern with teachers' questioning strategies generally, is that they focus much too often on literal questions to the exclusion of other types of comprehension questions (Guszak, 1974).

The fourth step in a basal lesson plan is often the follow-up of what has been read. The lesson plan encourages the teacher to relate follow-up activities to the purposes that were established for reading the selection by referring back to them. Quite often the follow-up activities involve the child's rereading parts of the story for modified or even new purposes. Other follow-up activities include discussions, creative activities, further reading, and storytelling. Sometimes the follow-up sets the stage for reading the next selection, thus becoming the first step of the next lesson.

In addition to these four steps, a basal reader lesson plan is often designed to teach, or reinforce through practice, specific reading skills. These suggestions to the teacher of skills to be practiced are sometimes placed at the beginning of the story, when the new words are being introduced. Sometimes they come at the end of the story as part of the follow-up activities. The specific reading activities may include either instruction or practice with word-recognition skills or provisions for improving comprehension by extending the reading. Examples of these may be seen in Chapters 6 and 7.

Control of the language of the reading materials. Basal reader authors and publishers have generally carefully controlled the language of the materials to be read by the children through the control of vocabulary and reading difficulty. However, the amount and specific type of control (for example, sentence length, difficulty of vocabulary, sentence patterns, rate of introduction of new vocabulary, and number of repetitions of new words) vary from one basal program to another.

The control of vocabulary and of reading difficulty in basal readers has often been the focus of criticism. Critics of vocabulary control contend that it imposes the use of unnatural language patterns onto the stories. Furthermore, they claim, a child's extensive oral-vocabulary background is broader than the limited vocabulary in the stories and should be capitalized on when he or she begins reading instruction. Consequently, the critics would have a much broader range of vocabulary and language used in the basal stories that reflects the language of real children.

The supporters of the gradual introduction of vocabulary believe that such control is necessary in many cases so that each child can experience maximum success as he or she encounters each new story. They point out that basal stories should always be accompanied by the use of supplementary stories where vocabulary is much less controlled. Spache (1972) points out that great variation continues in basal readers in regard to vocabulary.

> Recent changes in basal readers in the area of vocabulary control have taken the form of an increase in the breadth and depth of the words presented, some changes in the manner of teaching, and less repetition. Some recent reading series, of course, have swung to the opposite view and introduce as many words in the first grade as the child has learned in the preceding six years. (p. 39)

Today's Basals Are More Representative

Over the years basal materials have been changed in an effort to have their content represent society more accurately. This has been particularly true in the way females have been presented and in the inclusion and treatment of minority groups. How successful this effort has been is still an issue, but a recent analysis by Houghton Mifflin, which compares their reading programs from 1966 and 1976, clearly indicates an attempt to avoid stereotyping in the portrayal of men and women and to include ethnic groups in balance as major characters.* In addition, the analysis examined the tendency to use more natural language in more recent series.

* The analysis was conducted for inclusion here by John T. Ridley, Editor-in-Chief of Houghton Mifflin's Reading Department, and by his staff. The series analyzed were *Reading to Meaning* (1966) and the *Houghton Mifflin Reading Series* (1977).

Portrayal of males and females.   The analysis shows that in the 1966 series—from the first preprimer through the Level 6 reader—boys and men were portrayed in active roles, whereas girls and women were more passive: playing with dolls, cooking, and asking for help and information. The female characters were always of smaller stature and in dresses—often in aprons. They were often silly, fearful, and dependent; on the other hand, the male characters were resourceful, and took commanding roles. Interestingly, men were often depicted reading while relaxing, but women were shown relaxing by doing needlework. Just as there were few strong female characters in the 1966 series, these basals contained few biographies of famous women.

In the 1976 series, by comparison, girls and women appear more often than not as leaders and problem solvers. They are ingenious and courageous. Females excel in athletics, drive buses, own shops, work on automobiles, and so on. They sometimes wear slacks or jeans instead of dresses.

Several stories in the 1976 series have female characters who rebel at traditional roles; included in these are biographies of strong women. The following examples from the 1966 and 1976 basals give some idea of how the portrayal of the sexes changed in textbooks over a ten-year period.

In the 1966 first preprimer, boys were pictured in active play while girls in dresses were confined to roles of playing tea party. A 1966 illustration from a story about "Tip" exemplifies this analysis:

No, no! No, Tip!
Go home. Go home.
I will not play with you.
Go home, Tip.

From *Reading for Meaning,* 4th ed., by Paul McKee et al. (Boston: Houghton Mifflin, 1966), p. 46. Reprinted by permission.

Here is the zoo bus!
You will not have to get on the bus.
We can see where the bus will go.

You are a real help, Jill.

Tigers, here we come!

Can you help?
We want to go to the zoo.

Go to the bus stop.
You have to go to the zoo on a bus.

We can't go on a bus.

From *Rockets* by William K. Durr et al. (Boston: Houghton Mifflin, 1976), pp. 36 (left) and 38 (right). Reprinted by permission.

In a 1976 first preprimer story called "Tiger, Here We Come," (above left) a little girl in shorts and T-shirt is a leader of a group that includes three boys. Also in this 1976 first reader are examples of women in a variety of professional roles. Page 38 (above right) shows a policewoman. In the 1966 book, women were almost always housewives.

Ethnic representation. The Houghton Mifflin analysis shows that the major difference in ethnic representation is not so much in the number of different ethnic groups represented as in the number of such characters and their treatment. The story of "Tip," for example, has one black girl as a minor character, but in "Tiger," blacks are key characters in the action. The survey shows that while the 1966 series depicted American Indians, Eskimos, Asians, Costa Ricans, and French Canadians as major characters, the 1976 series includes these plus Afro-American, Puerto Rican, Middle Eastern, Asian-American, African, European, West Indian, Mexican, Mexican-American, and Hawaiian characters.

Stilted versus natural language. Using an American Heritage study of word frequencies, Houghton Mifflin tried to use words of highest frequencies in the 1976 series. This extended the vocabulary of the texts, limiting the amount of repetition. This development, plus the use of contractions, led to what the publishers believe is a more natural language than that in the 1966 series.

You Can Adapt the Basal Reader to Meet Individual Needs

In many schools, a single basal reader series is used in all grades and in all classrooms. Each school—usually through a committee made up of teachers, administrators, and parents—reviews the basal readers and adopts the one the committee decides is most appropriate for the children and teachers. Most schools use the same basal program for at least five years before considering a change. Despite the fact that a single basal in a school has been the predominant practice, there is evidence to suggest that this situation is changing. Some schools now adopt two or three (or more) basal series and allow the teachers to use whichever they choose—or all of them.

As we have stressed throughout this book, you need to adapt all reading materials to meet the needs of each child as well as your own definition of reading. Modifying a basal program should include these general considerations:

finding the appropriate reading materials for each child within the basal program

establishing instructional yet flexible groups—(including a group of one)

monitoring oral reading to determine if children need the prescribed skills, adjusting as necessary

adjusting the supplementary practice books as need dictates

reorganizing the practice books—even by cutting them apart and filing them by skill or by omitting sections and pages altogether

A basal program allows you great flexibility if used selectively. Don't assume that every child needs to be introduced to every skill. Rather, rely on continuous informal diagnosis as we have suggested in Chapter 2. And don't rely on the materials of the basal program exclusively. Children need to try out their reading ability with a wide range of reading materials.

Be sure you study the basal program to ascertain exactly what the developers of the program are attempting to help you accomplish. Do their aims fit your goals for reading instruction? Certainly you should not be tied to the basal program, but you do need to be fully aware of what you are modifying. The teacher's manual for most basal readers contains numerous suggestions for creating additional materials and varying teaching procedures.

The greatest strength of basal readers is that they provide a carefully sequenced set of instructional materials with complete teacher's guides for supporting a continuous program. Basal readers may be especially helpful to beginning teachers who need a clearly laid out plan for teaching reading for the first time. However, as is often the case, this strength can turn into a weakness if overused. When teachers stop thinking about what they are trying to accomplish and quit searching for alternative materials and methods because of total reliance on the step-by-step lesson plan, the basal reader is being misused.

Another important item you need to remember in using a basal reader is that some basals continue to focus only on middle-class, suburban story settings, giving children the misconception that that is all life is made up of. The middle-class child encounters no expanding experience, and children who are growing up in other environments find it hard to relate to the content. On the other hand, many basal readers have been modified extensively in this respect. The stories they include cover a wide range of story settings in which the social, economic, geographic, and even psychological situations vary. Such readers also provide extensive lists of books and stories as suggested reading that can broaden the range of reading interests even further. When basal readers don't provide the stories to meet the needs of your children, you need to find stories that do.

You also need to review constantly the skill exercises and supplementary aids to be sure the materials used are pertinent to the backgrounds and experiences of the children in your classroom. You will need to develop these materials when appropriate ones are not available. Teacher-made materials are sometimes more pertinent to the needs and interests of individual children and can be less expensive than purchased materials.

Strong supporters of basal readers might argue that teachers don't have time to find or build all those materials; and even if they could, all teachers are not equally adept at constructing good instructional materials. A commercial publisher can employ outstanding artists, expert teachers, and experienced instructional-materials developers to design a program to meet the needs and interests of most children. Furthermore, they point out, the teacher's manuals encourage the development of supplementary, teacher-made materials to personalize the program for each class in which the program is used. We believe that your modification of some materials in the basal program, the development of some of your own materials, the selection of materials from other programs, and the use of some existing materials from published sources will provide you with a program to meet the needs of each child.

Controversies about the use of basal readers will no doubt continue for some time to come; yet basal readers have been used since 1840 in most classrooms in the United States as the major set of materials for teaching reading, and it is expected that they will continue to dominate for some time into the future.* Despite the dominance of basals, keep

* Spache (1972) states, "Studies indicate that about 95–98 percent of our primary and 80 percent of our intermediate grades use graded readers. In fact, the basal reader is the only major instructional program in about seven out of ten of all our elementary classes."

in mind that basals are a tool for you to use and not a prescription for all reading needs. It is your task to modify and adapt this tool to meet the needs of your children.

The Individualized Reading Program

The Individualized Reading Program* most commonly refers to the practice of allowing children to select and read books of their own choice at their own pace. This program probably got its greatest push in the period between 1910 and 1920 with the development of standardized tests in reading. These tests emphasized both the wide range of children's reading abilities in any single grade and the differing rates at which children learned to read. The findings from standardized tests led educators to propose various means for allowing each child to progress at his or her own rate. This emphasis on providing for individual rates of development has continued until today, with, for example, the practice of grouping children for reading instruction, of individualizing the pacing of instruction, and of determining each child's interests and then matching those interests with reading materials.

Individualized reading is a fairly universally-agreed-upon program, perhaps most clearly represented by two of its strongest proponents, Jeannette Veatch and Philip Acinapuro (1966). Although the Individualized Reading Program has been diversified in its implementation, basically the program revolves around a classroom or school library. The child is encouraged to seek and select materials related to his or her interests. Thus the child paces himself or herself with a variety of reading materials. This process is accompanied by teacher-child conferences, the most important part of the program.

As with all of the seven general reading programs we are reviewing, there are variations of the Individualized Reading Program. Some proponents contend that reading skills should not be taught; they argue that these skills will be learned as the child reads. But other programs that are described as individualized reading use additional material (besides books) to teach reading skills. Still other programs have taken the label "individualized" when they added a free-reading period to a traditional basal reading program.

A truly individualized program focuses on teaching each child to read by surrounding the child with books and setting aside not only time for reading but also time to talk about that which was read. You would begin by reading interesting and entertaining stories to the child. And as he or she became more interested and motivated to learn, you would help the child read some of the same books. You would spend time

---

* The *Individualized Reading Program* suggests a particular strategy for organizing and meeting with children. It should not be confused with *individualizing* reading instruction, a practice that means teaching children what they need when they need it, and can be a part of any program.

talking with the child about what both of you had read; you would provide help in doing and making things that you had read about; and you would both go to some of the places mentioned in your reading. You would continue to read to the child in order to generate interest in new stories, and you would restock the supply of reading materials periodically, making sure they dealt with many topics, especially those that most interested the child. These reading materials would, of course, need to be written at a difficulty level that the child could read without too much assistance. During the teacher-pupil conference, you would ask the child to read aloud to you something he or she especially enjoyed reading, and you would listen to determine if the child was having difficulty with specific word-recognition skills. This kind of attention also relies on keeping a careful record of how the child is developing in the specific skills. As skills were identified, you would schedule time to help the child learn them.

Using an individualized program in the classroom requires generalizing the procedure described above to a situation where you are responsible for numerous children. It requires that a teacher know well the intended objectives for each child, know children's books, and be a good organizer.

Teaching Procedures Are the Key to Individualization

The Individualized Reading Program obviously does not rely on the use of special materials. On the other hand, a wide variety of reading materials must be available to implement the program. In addition, skills are not prescribed in some guide but rather introduced by the teacher as each child needs them. The Individualized Reading Program relies on several generally accepted teaching and organizational procedures—for example, child-teacher conferences, individual diagnosis, and flexible grouping. The language control of the reading materials is as variable as the materials that are used in the program—and they should be extensive. The only control concerning the materials is that the teacher must help each child to select books that match his or her reading level and interests.

Clearly the Individualized Reading Program offers great flexibility. It can, and must, be modified to meet the needs of each child, and it must be adapted to your definition of reading. The next sections examine more closely each of these four aspects.

Special materials. If you decide to implement the Individualized Reading Program, you will need to collect and become familiar with a great number of children's books and stories. Large amounts of reading materials covering a variety of topics and reading levels are the heart of the Individualized Reading Program. You will need to be familiar with these materials so you can guide each child to the reading materials that are of possible interest to him or her and that match his or her reading ability; in addition, you will use conference times to discuss the stories and books the child is reading. Extensive classroom libraries are a must. Some experts recommend from three to ten books for each child in the program. The reading and maturity levels of the children may account for these different recommendations. There are a number of means of getting these books and making them available to your children (see pages 281–89).

Learning centers for encouraging children's interests and for providing opportunities for follow-up activities are useful variations in an individualized program. Such centers could include places to read and create and allow children to explore new topics, such as farming, astronomy, or sports. These centers expand on selections read and motivate the child for further reading. Learning centers are described more fully in Chapter 9.

Specified skills.   As with the basal reader, the individualized program provides opportunities for teaching all reading skills that a child needs to become an independent reader. However, in contrast to the sequenced hierarchical presentation of reading skills in a traditional basal program, the individualized program provides for the teaching of those skills that a child needs in order to progress in his or her reading development; and those skills are taught when a child is ready to learn them. Proponents of the individualized program argue that if a child continues to make progress in reading development without being taught isolated reading skills, the child need *not* be taught separate reading skills because he or she is obviously demonstrating the needed skills simply by continuing to read.

The overall emphasis in the individualized program is always on comprehension—on having the child apply and extend the ideas in the story or on being able to relate to the ideas and characters in the reading, not just on having the child answer questions about what he or she has read. Reading materials are self-selected and are, therefore, seen by the child as being important.

Individualized reading, then, means more than self-pacing of instruction and self-selection of reading materials. It goes beyond those to the point where reading is a very personal experience for each reader.

Specific teaching procedures.   The teaching procedures in the individualized program center on the individual teacher-student conference. These conferences vary in frequency and length, with most teachers meeting with each child once or twice a week for ten to fifteen minutes. During the conference, the teacher and child discuss what the child is reading, the child may read aloud, and specific word-recognition and comprehension help is given as needed. Sometimes the teacher may group several children for instruction in a particular reading skill. The individual conference is also an opportunity for the teacher to suggest and to discuss follow-up activities for the child's reading. Plans for sharing what the child has been reading with the other children can also be developed. As has already been suggested, the teaching procedures in an individualized program emphasize broadening the experiences of children so they will develop interests in a wide variety of topics.

In brief, the individualized program includes individual conferences, oral reading by the teacher to small groups of children, the possibility of individual and small group reading-skills lessons, individual and group follow-up activities, and sharing periods. Obviously, careful planning by the teacher is needed to see that all of these activities mesh into a worthwhile reading program for each child.

Control of the language of the reading materials.   Because the reading materials used in the individualized program are not prescribed, there is no control over the way the materials are patterned. There are two aspects of the selected materials that proponents of the individualized program consider both strengths and requirements. The first is that the materials should deal with the topics and ideas that are interesting to children. The second is that the teacher should know how to assess the relative ease or difficulty with which children read the materials.

Implementing the Individualized Program

While the individualized program is an interesting and attractive alternative to other programs because it focuses on the individual child and his or her personal reading development, it is a program that calls for careful and extensive planning. Moreover, individualized reading calls for a wealth of reading materials, a teacher who is willing to read extensively and become very familiar with books and stories for children, and a teacher who is knowledgeable about the sequence of reading skill development (Robinson, 1960). If you decide to begin an individualized program, you should certainly start slowly. A completely individualized program is difficult for some teachers to manage. Such a program can be started as an extension of a basal reader program. For example, you could plan one day a week for individualized reading, using materials that the children select themselves; then you could let them pace their own reading. Individual conferences can be begun as the children are reading. When you feel comfortable with the "one day a week" tryout, you can expand the program.

Another way to ease into an individualized program is to start with just one group of students. Usually the better readers in a class are able to profit more readily from such an approach. Again, you can extend the program to other groups. With appropriate materials available and a good match between children's interests and reading materials, one aspect of the program is easy—just let kids read.

The strengths of this program grow out of its focus on the individual child. A child is always more highly motivated by materials that he or she selects because of a current and real interest. When a child can discuss what he or she has read on a one-to-one basis, this interest can be capitalized on. And when the ideas that a child reads about cover a variety of activities, interests lead to other reading.

In implementing the individualized program, it is vital that each child be allowed to progress at his or her own pace without being compared with other children in the class. Teaching each child the reading skills he or she needs when they are needed is generally regarded as being superior in both its efficiency and effect to teaching skills to groups of children just because the skill lesson comes next in a particular instructional program (Sartain, 1960).

Studies of the individualized program report that children read more and read a greater variety of materials. Furthermore, research (McDonald et al., 1966) points out that children read more for their own enjoyment and interest rather than because reading is assigned.

Individualized reading demands a great deal of the teacher. Becoming familiar with a vast number of children's stories and books, being able to diagnose the individual reading development of each child, planning individual skills lessons, understanding the unique reading development of each child, and keeping track of all this information for twenty to thirty children—all of these are obviously quite demanding.

In a study of teachers' reactions to using the individualized program, Harry W. Sartain (1960) found that the teachers:

> were concerned about the lack of a systematic program in word-recognition skills
>
> were unsure of their ability to plan an effective word-recognition program
>
> were bothered by their inability to find time to hold enough individual student conferences

Yet none of these weaknesses is the sole fault of the program. Rather, they result from the teacher's lack of basic knowledge about reading and how it is taught, as well as from the lack of time to plan and implement a total individualized program. Better teacher training and reduced class size, coupled with adequate planning time in a teacher's daily schedule, could overcome most of these weaknesses. In addition, it should be pointed out that the teachers in Sartain's research felt the individual conference was very important in helping them to learn about each child and to plan better reading instruction.

The Language Experience Program

In Chapter 3, we described the language experience program, which stems from the direct *experiences* of children and uses the language those experiences evoke to teach children to read what they have said.

The language experience program is not a recent development. The idea of putting children's language into print was suggested many years ago as an essential step from prereading to actual reading. In a book on teaching reading published over twenty-five years ago, Fay Adams, Lillian Gray, and Dora Reese (1949) described the development of a language experience story that grew out of an experience some children had in baking cookies in the school kitchen.

As these activities went on, the children were led to compose many stories describing what they were doing. With the children dictating what they wanted to say, the teacher printed their stories on the blackboard. Print was used, since it is not wise to burden the inexperienced reader with the need for learning to read script before print when starting preprimers.

These stories, called experience stories because of their source, are first recorded on the blackboard by the teacher as the children dictate them. After the first recording, the stories are printed by the teacher on oak tag, a fairly durable grade of paper. . . . Occasionally the children themselves want to reread their experience stories. But the teacher did not use the little self-made stories for drill. It should be stressed at this point that if experience stories are used for word drills, they are misused. Their purpose is to give the children a *feeling for reading,* not a mastery of the technique of the reading process itself. (p. 166)

Proponents of the language experience program emphasize it as a total program. These proponents argue that if a child reads his or her own story or a story he or she has had a part in dictating, that child will learn what reading is all about. The emphasis will by definition be on reading for meaning and the language of what is read will be the child's own language because the child has authored it.

Supporters of language experience further contend that reading skills will be learned much more quickly if the child is reading ideas made up of words that are part of his or her oral language. Some proponents of the language experience program suggest that a child's reading of an experience story can be used to diagnose word-recognition needs. This diagnosis can then be used to plan instruction to develop the word-recognition skills.

As for the argument that reading experience stories is not reading to find out anything new, the response is that we all like to read about those things that we know best, and we often reread to enjoy an experience a second or third time. Furthermore, proponents argue, if each child develops his or her own set of stories and then exchanges them with another child, there is a sharing of ideas and reading to learn about the experiences of others.

The experience story, however, is only the springboard for the language experience program. From developing a story related to a specific incident, the children are ready to be read to, to read when they are able, to discuss, and to expand their experiences by any means that is provided. Once a child has visited a bakery, baked cookies, made up a story about the experience, and read the story, he or she may be interested in reading other stories about baking.

In recent years the strongest proponents and developers of the language experience program have been Russell Stauffer (1970) and Roach Van Allen (1962). In an often quoted statement, Allen has summed up the theory behind the language experience approach as follows:

(1) What I can think about, I can talk about.
(2) What I can say, I can write—or someone can write for me.
(3) What I can write, I can read.
(4) I can read what I write, and what other people write for me to read.

Stories Dictated by a Child Are Fundamental

The fundamental component of the language experience program is the story a child dictates. These stories are based on the child's everyday experiences as well as on experiences the teacher and child share. The language experience program does not require specified skills that need to be taught to a child. Instead, skills to be taught are determined by the teacher's diagnosis as a child reads his or her own stories, as well as those developed by other children. The teacher procedures for eliciting experience stories from children are fairly well specified. However, the procedures for teaching word-recognition skills are left unspecified. Finally, the reading materials grow out of the children's language, and as a result, there is little control of the language structure of those materials.

Special materials. In order to use language experience as the base for your reading program you need to explore and discuss the experiences of your students. You must organize and share new experiences with them. Because of rich experiences, the children will talk, and because of their language, stories will be developed that they will want to share with you and the other children in the class. You can help to promote interests by using every opportunity to pique the children's curiosity and to encourage language. The initial materials you will need include large sheets of paper or charts and felt pens for writing and illustrating the experience stories dictated by the children.

Once you have helped children to develop their own stories, you will need to provide independent reading materials for the children to expand their interests. This means having a great deal of reading materials available on a wide range of topics. These should include stories you can read to the children and they can read independently.

There are sets of published materials available that you may want to examine if you decide to implement a language experience program or use language experience to supplement another program. A good collection of published suggestions for experiences is in *Language Expe-*

(9)

(10)

words to show their perception of the difference between sounds we make and symbols we choose to represent the sounds. Example: Ssss-ssk--RRRR-UMMG!

Activities with the pupil book

1. Give the children the page "Thunder and Lightning."
   Review ways of describing thunder and lightning and ask each child to write one descriptive statement in the spaces provided.

2. On the back of the page write stories about storms.
   A few children can tell stories about storms to set the mood for writing. Encourage them to use descriptions of thunder and lightning on the front side of the page if these descriptions are appropriate to the stories. Try to have them make the stories exciting!
   Call attention again to the beginning of a paragraph by indenting the first line. See if some children remember to indent for other paragraphs.
   A few children will need additional paper for their stories.
   Continue to take dictation if there are some who cannot do their own writing.

3. Children orally read their stories about storms.
   The oral reading of these stories should lend itself to dramatic expression and deep feeling. Encourage children to read just as if they were telling their stories to friends.

4. Bind the stories into books for the library.

Choosing reading and improving reading skills

1. Children select books and stories for independent reading.

2. Schedule individual and/or small-group conferences with a few children each day.
   Continue to emphasize sequence and main ideas as described in Lesson 4.

Additional activities

1. Lightning pictures
   Color pieces of red, orange, or yellow paper with a heavy coat of black crayon. (A slick surface paper is best.) Scratch off two or more streaks with an instrument or fingernail. The color will show through like lightning. (9)
   Crayon the streaks and/or flashes of lightning with heavy strokes on white paper. Cover the paper with a wash of black water paint. The paint will not adhere to the crayon surface, leaving a dramatic picture.

2. Individual books about storms
   Children can make individual books.

3. News clippings
   Make a folder to hold news clippings about storms. These can be pasted in the book to become a source of information and as a guide for the correct spelling of words. (10)

riences in Reading: (LEIR) Teachers' Source Book (Allen and Allen, 1966). But remember that published materials can take you a step away from the overriding strength of language experience—its focus on unique individuals. An example of a page from the *LEIR* program is shown above.

Specified skills. The emphasis in the language experience program is on reading for meaning. In fact, reading for meaning is ensured because readers develop their own material. In addition, the language experience program helps children to develop all communication skills as children listen to the stories being read by others, read their own stories, discuss their experiences, and write (or dictate) their experiences. But there is no prescribed sequence of reading skills through which each child is led.

The proponents of the language experience program claim also that because children develop their own stories and then see those stories

printed, they develop good self-concepts. In addition, the children have a chance to develop their own creativity as they express themselves through experience stories. Finally, as we mentioned earlier, language experience can be supplemented with an ongoing reading skills program in which the teacher diagnoses word-recognition needs and then plans individual and group instruction.

Specific teaching procedures. The child comes to school with two means of communication already fairly well established—speaking and drawing. The language experience teaching method uses these two as a means of teaching other language arts—listening, reading, and writing. The child's first step in learning to read is giving oral expression to his or her own ideas. This is done through the medium of storytelling, through sharing personal experiences, and through such experiences as telling about a picture he or she has made. The child is also learning listening skills as the other children talk about their own experiences and tell their stories. The teacher helps the children find new ideas to express by reading stories and poems to them; by telling them stories; by developing classroom units in social living, science, and math; by introducing music into the classroom and generating discussion about it; by encouraging classmates to share; and by utilizing picture books from the classroom library.

One effective way to begin helping children to see the relationship between language and print is to enlist their help in the timeworn, but proven, act of labelling objects and areas in the classroom with carefully lettered signs.

A follow-up to beginning their exposure to the printed word might include the production of student books, such as "All About Me" or "The Me Book." For example, after the child draws a picture of himself on a sheet of paper, the teacher writes "My name is David" or "This is me." Pages in the book are added as children's artwork expands to include the family, pets, home, school, and so on. When finished, David has authored his first book. The children can then read what they have said and what other children have "written." These books are bound for later rereading or for a proud "I can read" trip home.

When a child dictates a story, the teacher writes exactly what the child says, but doesn't include misspellings, in order to represent exactly the child's "natural language." For example:

Child dictates: "Harry said he's not gonna go!"
Teacher writes: "Harry said he's not going to go!"

When the child reads back what the teacher has written, the teacher should accept the natural language of "gonna" and avoid correcting usage or dialect because of a mistaken notion that this correction is teaching. To correct would contradict the prime advantage of the language experience material—its validity with the child.

The development of experience stories with a group of children can be a very enjoyable sharing experience for them and can help them to develop their language skills by listening, talking, and discussing an experience they have had. The development of group stories can easily grow out of a group experience. After returning from a field trip, for example, such as a trip to the airport, the children are often bubbling over with excitement—especially if they can tell someone about their trip. A suggestion from the teacher that they write a story, a letter, or a diary about their trip so they can share it with children in other classes, their parents, or with brothers and sisters is usually ample motivation. The children are given the opportunity to recall and to share their own perceptions of the experience. When they are ready, individuals contribute to the story and the teacher writes the story that evolves as different ideas or events are added to the story. The children can then title the story and listen as the teacher reads it aloud from the chart paper or chalkboard. Sometimes this modeling is followed by the children reading aloud or by individuals reading their contributions. Later the teacher can mimeograph the story so that it could be copied by the children, illustrated, and taken home for sharing with the family.

As several children come to the point of independent reading, the teacher offers easy-to-read books and materials. The child can now choose a book to read. And since he or she has already built a fairly extensive vocabulary from reading experience stories, some begin to read books with ease. Interest in reading other authors was first stimulated by the interest the child had in his or her own ideas.

When a child decides to write his or her own stories, the teacher may help with words the child is not sure of. Both word attack skills and vocabulary can be developed through the writing experience. At the same time, the teacher should point out other readily available sources of words—the bound books of the children's picture stories, charts, bulletin boards, labels, word lists, and picture dictionaries.

Control of the language of the reading materials. Materials that are dictated by the children will reflect the language patterns of the children who dictated them. There is, then, no external control on the language. Sometimes difficulty is encountered when a child with a more extensive vocabulary than the others in the class develops a story using terms and concepts that the rest of the children are not familiar with. This event is in fact an advantage—because of the opportunity it provides to expand the vocabularies of other children. The lack of control over vocabulary (except for the constraints that the experience itself provided) is one of the factors that proponents of language experience cite most frequently as a strength.

The independent reading materials that are brought to the classroom by the teacher to be used with the experience stories should attempt to match the reading abilities of the children and should deal with topics that will relate to the children's experience stories.

Implementing the Language Experience Program

Using experience stories with beginning readers appears to be an excellent procedure. You may even want to consider using experience stories as a supplement to a more materials-dependent program. The management of a total language experience program is challenging, and it requires thorough planning and a knowledgeable, committed teacher.

There are numerous ways you can use language experiences in the classroom. Here are a few examples:

Discuss plans for a field trip about to be taken.

Give directions for carrying out some classroom activity—how to fix up the aquarium, what is needed, who will bring the different things; how to make apple butter; how to churn butter.

Keep diaries about special projects—such as raising pets.

Post news events of importance to the class.

Make labels and captions for pictures on the bulletin board.

Send notices of special projects to other rooms—programs to be given, or "Come to our room to see a film. It is 'The Monarch Butterfly.' "

Keep diaries of seasonal activities—The grass is green around the walk, April 10; Tulips are up, April 11; and so on.

Record jokes made up or told by the children.

Keep simple records of science experiments—the object of the experiment, how it was done, what the results were (for example, The Thermometer Study).

Make large calendars that record the weather and other interesting events.

John DeBoer and Martha Dallman have outlined eleven steps that could be implemented over a two-day period to develop and use experience stories.

First Day

(1) The boys and girls participate in an interesting and significant experience.

(2) The children discuss the experience.

(3) The pupils, with the help of the teacher, plan the title, general content, and the exact sentences for the chart as the teacher does the writing on the board.

(4) The chart as a whole is read first by the teacher, then by the pupils and the teacher together, and finally by the boys and girls alone.

Second Day

(5) Before class the teacher has copied onto chart paper the writing for the experience chart that she had put on the board the preceding day. The teacher has also copied on separate strips of tagboard each of the lines of the chart, so that they can be matched later with the writing on the chart. These are placed on the chalk tray or in a word-card holder. On tagboard word cards, the teacher has also written a few of the words on which she plans to give special practice.

(6) The new chart is then read by the teacher and pupils together.

(7) The teacher reads sentences for the pupils to find, and they point to each one as they read it.

(8) After the teacher has read the sentences out of the regular order, the pupils match the sentence strips with the sentences on the chart and read them.

(9) As the teacher shows the boys and girls each of the several word cards containing those words on which she thinks it is important to provide practice, she pronounces the word and has the pupils say it after her. A pupil then matches the word on the card with the same word on the chart. Further practice on the words can be given if before class the teacher writes these words on the board. In that case the pupils can name the words as the teacher points to them.

(10) Review of words used in the chart that the boys and girls have studied earlier can then be made.

(11) Before the period is over one or more pupils can read the chart alone. (1960, p. 87)

The Advantages and Disadvantages of the Language Experience Program

The strengths of the language experience program include the following:

Through the writing of stories, each child's creativity and originality is enhanced.

The program builds on the experiences and understanding of each child.

Listening, writing, speaking, and reading are developed in an integrated fashion.

The program can provide for individual differences because each child can progress at his or her own pace.

The limitations of the language experience program include the following:

Such a program requires more teacher initiative and organization skills.

The teacher must guide children's experiences, encourage language, and teach needed reading skills without benefit of prescriptive guides. Thus, much teacher time is devoted to providing a rich language environment—helping children to experience, to expand, and to express those experiences in order to compose their own reading materials.

The program requires more teacher skill than does rote application of published material.

The lack of repetition of the vocabulary may not allow all children to have enough repetitions with new words to make them part of their recognition vocabulary.

Another complaint lodged against the language experience program is that it inhibits the cultural growth of children. Such critics say that it limits the teacher's opportunity to select materials that present themes and stories that add to a child's vicarious background and understanding of other peoples and cultures.

Phonics Programs

In Chapter 6, we defined phonics as the teaching of generalizations between printed letters (graphemes) and spoken sounds (phonemes). In that chapter we described phonics as one aspect of word recognition. Most authors of published reading series agree with this and include phonics in their reading programs. Therefore, to some extent almost all reading programs are phonics programs. It would be very difficult to find a primary-grade classroom in which some phonics is not being taught.

Advantages of the Language Experience Program

The potential advantages of using the language experience program have been demonstrated by the research of Russell G. Stauffer (1967). As reported in 1972 by George D. Spache:

> Russell G. Stauffer's study indicated that at the end of the first grade the language experience pupils were superior in practically all of the formal test measures used in the *First Grade Reading Studies*. These differences persisted into the second grade. Language experience pupils achieved higher scores in word meaning and paragraph meaning, in writing mechanics, and in the number of running and different words as well as spelling in the children's own compositions. (p. 69)

The results in another study (Harris, 1969), however, favored language experience less conclusively. Spache also reported on the three-year study by Harris, who contrasted the language experience program, both alone and enriched by a variety of audio-visual aids, with a basal reader program.

> The results at the end of the three years were negative in that there were no significant differences in any of the tests. There was a trend toward better paragraph meaning scores and better attitudes among the basal students at the end of the first grade, but even these small differences disappeared in the second and third grades. (p. 68)

On the other hand, Spache points out that Harris did find positive effects on teacher behaviors:

> The author (Harris) also noted that these teachers were more permissive, less rigid, and more creative. Other studies confirm these effects on teachers and the social climate of the classroom, indicating that the language experience method is conducive to a less authoritarian climate than basal or even individualized reading programs. (p. 70)

However, some instructional programs have systematically emphasized phonics. These are generally the ones that have been labelled *phonics programs*. Therefore, if a debate about phonics *versus* whole-word rages in your school community, as it almost certainly has in the past, the point to remember is that the issue is really one of the amount and method of phonics instruction rather than a no-phonics program *versus* a phonics program. During the past hundred years, professional articles, research reports, popular magazine and newspaper articles, and television and radio programs have added fuel to this heated debate.

In a review of the teaching of phonics, Arthur W. Heilman points out that:

(1) Teaching phonics is an important part of teaching reading.

(2) Teachers should be knowledgeable about the purpose of phonic instruction as it relates to reading (what to teach) and about the rationale or justification for the practices they follow.

(3) There are a number of psychologically sound principles which should be followed in phonics instruction.

(4) In recent years, there has been no legitimate basis for a debate on phonetic methods *versus* sight word methods, as these terms actually have no identifiable referents.

(5) The spurious debate on the above polar positions has tended to obscure real educational issues such as:

(a) the proper concentration of analysis that is desirable for the beginning reading period,

(b) the desirability of teaching rules or generalizations which have very limited applications, and

(c) the logical order in which the "steps" in phonics instruction should be introduced. (1964, pp. vii–viii)

While the research and debate concerning when to begin teaching phonics, how to teach phonics, how much phonics to teach, and which phonic elements should be taught will almost certainly continue, there are still those who will advocate "a phonics program" as the only way to teach reading.

Skills Are the Essential Aspect of the Phonics Program

Special materials are sometimes used in a phonics program; the teaching procedures can, however, be quite varied; and because of the need for sequential introduction of words to develop the relationship between sound and symbol, there is more control of the language structure at the early stages in phonics materials than in materials designed for more advanced stages. It is the sequential and systematic introduction of phonic generalizations that is the key to the phonics programs. In Chapter 6, we provided sequential lists of the most commonly taught phonic generalizations. Most publishers of phonics materials follow this general pattern, but there are variations. We do not believe there is any evidence to support one of the variations over another.

Special materials. The published materials for teaching phonics can generally be classified as falling into one of two categories: synthetic phonics or analytic phonics. This is true whether the phonics materials are part of some more general program, such as the basal reader program, or whether they are separate programs. Examples of synthetic and analytic phonics materials are included below in the subsection on procedure, where the two emphases are more fully explained.

All phonics programs include a wide variety of materials. Some of them look much like the basal reader programs that we described earlier. Others include just workbooks and perhaps several wall charts depicting vowels and consonants in various patterns. An example of the use of wall charts is shown in the Open Court program.

Exact reproductions of the art on the Wall Sound Cards are included in the first Foundation Workbook, Learning to Read and Write [We call it the Blue Book]. In this exercise children practice writing the letters that represent the sounds to which they have just been introduced.

From *Open Court Foundation Sampler* (LaSalle, Ill.: Open Court Publishing Company, 1976). Reprinted with permission. Copyright© Open Court Publishing Company 1971.

Other materials that publishers often include in phonics programs are phonograph records or audio tapes that give students practice in hearing letter sounds. These are usually coordinated with filmstrips, workbooks, or some other printed form. Sometimes such programs are developed so that they can be used by individual children at learning stations that are equipped with a small projector and headphones to allow children to listen to records and tapes.

Specified skills. Certainly the focus of phonics programs is on the children's mastery of sound-symbol relationships. Usually phonics programs begin with a strong emphasis on auditory and visual discrimination, and students are encouraged to recognize and name the letters of the alphabet. The teaching of phonic generalizations is to help children understand the relation between sounds and symbols.

Phonics programs vary in their emphasis and in their introduction to phonic skills. The order of the teaching of phonic generalizations also varies from program to program as does the reliance on synthetic or analytic teaching procedures. Most phonics programs are very systemized—some more than others.

Specific teaching procedures. Teaching phonics is accomplished either through synthetic or analytic procedures. Synthetic phonics begins with teaching sounds associated with letters. These letter-sound generalizations are then used to teach the blending of sounds into words—as in the following example:

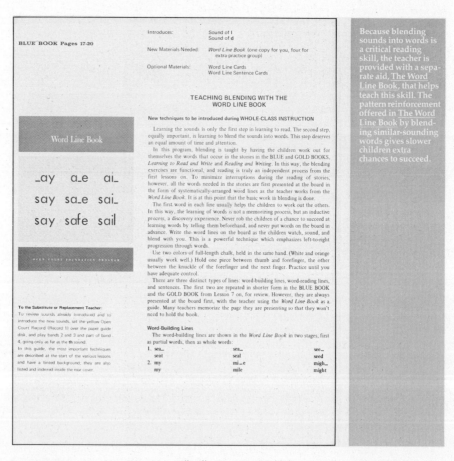

From *Open Court Foundation Sampler* (LaSalle, Ill.: Open Court Publishing Company, 1976). Reprinted with permission. Copyright © Open Court Publishing Company 1971.

From *Studybook for One to Grow On* of the Reading 720 series by Theodore Clymer and others, © Copyright, 1976, by Ginn and Company (Xerox Corporation). Used with permission.

Analytic phonics, on the other hand, begins with the teaching of some words. These words are then analyzed to deduce phonic generalizations. For example, the children can discern the phonic generalization that the sound at the beginning of *dog, day, door,* and *desk* is the same and is represented by the grapheme *d.* Most basal reader programs also emphasize analytic phonics procedures, as can be seen from the example above.

To summarize the main teaching procedures for both synthetic and analytic phonics:

Synthetic Phonics

(1) Prereading emphasis is on developing auditory and visual discrimination.
(2) Children learn the names and sounds of the letters.
(3) These sounds are blended into words.

(4) Children then apply their phonic skills to a wide range of reading materials.

(5) Children are encouraged to "sound out" any word they do not know.

Analytic Phonics

(1) Prereading emphasis is on helping children recognize the relation between print and speech.

(2) Some sight vocabulary words are taught to children.

(3) These sight words are used to deduce phonic generalizations.

(4) Generalizations are then applied to a wide range of reading materials.

(5) Children are encouraged to use phonic generalizations as one word-recognition cue.

Control of the language of the reading materials.   The phonic generalizations (sound-symbol relationships) are introduced one at a time and usually follow a clearly defined hierarchy. Easier sound-symbol associations (for example, initial consonants) are introduced and mastered by the children, and then more difficult elements are taught (for example, "silent e"). The language structure of the material follows this sequential pattern and sometimes results in very stilted wording in the beginning

Dad and Mim

Dad rests.

Dad rests in the tent.

Mim rests.

Mim is not in the tent.

Mim rests on the mat.

Dad and Mim rest.

From *The Red Book* by Glenn McCracken and Charles C. Walcutt (Philadelphia: Lippincott, 1972), p. 8. Reprinted by permission.

material—as shown on page 464. At upper levels, the language is natural because children have supposedly mastered the sound-symbol relationships that enable them to attack any word.

Phonics Should Always Be Tied to Meaning

The most frequently cited strength of programs with a heavy phonics emphasis is that children do learn to "sound out," or decode words and gain early independence in word recognition. This achievement is reflected in studies in which phonics approaches usually result in children's superior performance on word analysis tests at the end of the program. These superior results don't always hold up in tests measuring the reading of continuous words and sentences rather than just sounding out words. Proponents of a strong emphasis on phonics believe that children need to learn sound-symbol relationships as quickly and efficiently as possible so they can become independent readers. Effective phonics instruction, they argue, will achieve that goal.

The major limitation of synthetic phonics programs is their somewhat narrow definition of reading at the beginning stages, particularly as it effects word recognition. Word-recognition instruction that overemphasizes phoneme-grapheme relationships and limits, or even excludes, context can produce some readers who fail to see reading as a search for meaning; in addition, they may laboriously sound out words, slowing the rate and interfering with comprehension of the writer's thoughts. This limitation does not seem to be true for analytic phonics programs.

The lack of vocabulary control has also been cited as a limitation of phonics programs. In discussing the Lippincott Basic Reading Program (a strong phonics-emphasis program), Spache (1972) states:

> The vocabulary includes approximately 2,000 words in the first year, all supposed to be read handily by the child because of the phonic training. The first grader is expected to recognize and understand such words as *cog, punt, din,* and *ram,* since he has been taught the sounds which compose them. (p. 64)

The crux of such criticisms is based on teaching and learning phonics as an instructional goal valid in itself. Most phonics programs, however, posit that phonics is a tool or a means to an end, and that end is effective reading for meaning. Comprehension is not forsaken in most phonics programs; it is placed on a back burner during the initial phases of reading instruction.

Modified Alphabet Programs

For many years there has been much debate about the need for simplifying the English spelling system. Perhaps the best known of the alphabet reformers was George Bernard Shaw, whose famous bequest, offering large prize monies to people who would devise a system of spelling that was consistent with pronunciation, has not had results (Pei, 1965). However, linguists say that there are consistent patterns to the spelling-pronunciation relation in the English language, but these patterns are not always easily recognizable to the beginning reader.

Nonetheless, there are probably several reasons that alphabet reform has not succeeded. First, people in general seem to be quite conservative and traditional about their spelling system. Second, if alphabet reform were adopted, most of the books in our libraries would eventually need to be reprinted for generations that are trained to read by a new or modified alphabet.

Despite the lack of any total alphabet reform, some educators have proposed modifying the alphabet for use in teaching beginning reading. These educators have argued that if a child can learn to read with an alphabet that is consistent between spelling and pronunciation, the child will learn to read more easily because he or she will be able to rely on the consistent pronunciation of graphemes.

There have been a number of modified alphabets proposed for use in materials for beginning reading. Their objective has been to develop a consistent alphabet in which each symbol or letter represents only one phoneme.* Using such a symbol system, the proponents of modified alphabet approaches argue, the learning of sound-symbol generalizations—and therefore learning to read—will be much easier.

Modifying alphabets is certainly not a new idea.† Nila B. Smith (1965) described some of these as they developed in the United States:

> In the United States the "Fonotype" devised by Sir Isaac Pitman and A. J. Ellis was used to teach beginning reading in ten schools in Waltham, Massachusetts between 1852 and 1860. . . . Schools in St. Louis used a modified alphabet from 1866 to 1886. . . . Between 1870 and 1920 several Americans developed expanded alphabets, prepared reading books and experimented in having reading taught with the use of books printed in their respective alphabets. (p. 394)

The Modified Alphabets' Special Materials

The printing of materials in a modified alphabet is the key aspect of these programs that aim primarily at beginning readers. Obviously, special materials are needed. However, specified skills and teaching procedures vary among the programs. The special materials are developed using the modified alphabet for coding the language; the teaching pro-

---

* In Chapter 6, phonemes were defined as those sounds in words which make a difference in a particular language. Linguists agree that there are about forty-five different phonemes in English.

† The noted linguist Charles C. Fries, in *Linguistics and Reading* (New York: Holt, Rinehart and Winston, 1963), described various alphabet reforms in England dating as early as the 1500s.

cedures generally center upon helping children to decode. This is not always the case, however. We will examine several modified alphabets and their varied teaching procedures in the following section.

Special materials.   Rather than describing the various materials that have been developed using modified alphabets, we will describe several of the modified alphabets that have been developed for use in teaching beginning reading, since these are really the most important aspect of the programs.

Probably the initial teaching alphabet (i.t.a.) is the best known of these alphabets. The i.t.a. (also known as the Augmented Roman Alphabet), developed by Sir James Pitman, includes forty-three different

THE AUGMENTED ROMAN ALPHABET

Number	Character	Name	Example	Traditional spelling
1	æ	ae	ræt	rate
2	b	bee	big	big
3	c	kee	cat	cat
4	d	dee	dog	dog
5	ee	ee	meet	meet
6	f	ef	fill	fill
7	g	gae	gun	gun
8	h	hae	hat	hat
9	ie	ie	tie	tie
10	j	jae	jelly	jelly
11	k	kae	kit	kit
12	l	el	lamp	lamp
13	m	em	man	man
14	n	en	net	net
15	œ	oe	tœ	toe
16	p	pee	pig	pig
17	r	rae	run	run
18	s	ess	sad	sad
19	t	tee	tap	tap
20	ue	ue	due	due
21	v	vee	van	van
22	w	wae	will	will

THE AUGMENTED ROMAN ALPHABET (Continued)

Number	Character	Name	Example	Traditional spelling
23	y	i-ae	yell	yell
24	z	zed or zee	fizz	fizz
25	ʂ	zess	houʂes	houses
26	wh	whae	when	when
27	ch	chae	chick	chick
28	th	ith	thaut	thought
29	th	thee	the	the
30	ʃh	ish	ʃhip	ship
31	ʒ	zhee	meʒuer	measure
32	ŋ	ing	siŋ	sing
33	a	ah	far	far
34	au	au	autum	autumn
35	a	at	appl	apple
36	e	et	egg	egg
37	i	it	dip	dip
38	o	ot	hot	hot
39	u	ut	ugly	ugly
40	ω	oot	bωk	book
41	ⲱ	oo	mⲱn	moon
42	ou	ow	bou	bough
43	oi	oi	toi	toy

From *New Perspectives in Reading Instruction* by Albert J. Mazurkiewicz (New York: Fearon-Pitman Publishers), pp. 543–44. Reprinted by permission.

symbols. In addition, words are spelled according to a set of rules that, for example, eliminate the writing of silent letters and that use large-type, lower-case letters in place of capital letters. The following example from *Œlaf Reedz* demonstrates what i.t.a. looks like in a children's book.

craʃh! aull ᵻhe bœks fell ḍoun.
"œ, ᵻhær yœ ɑr," ʃhɛɛ seḍ. "ie ʃhɷḍ
hav nœn. whot ɑr yœ gœiŋ tɷ dœ
wiᵻh aull ʃhœʃ bœks, œlaf?"
"rɛɛḍ ᵻhem?" askt œlaf.

From *Olaf Reads* by Joan Lexau, illustrated by Harvey Weiss. ⓒ copyright 1961 by Joan Lexau. Reprinted by permission of Dial Press.

In the early 1960s Albert Mazurkiewicz and Harold Tanyzer—after visiting English schools that were experimenting with i.t.a.—started the development of several i.t.a. tryouts in the United States. Mazurkiewicz and Tanyzer developed a reading program known as the I/T/A Early-to-Read Series. As a result of the considerable research conducted in England (Downing, 1966), extensive tryouts in the United States (Mazurkiewicz, 1964), the development of a complete i.t.a. reading series, and much publicity, i.t.a. became the most widely adopted of all of the modified alphabets. Today, it continues to be used in some schools throughout the country.

There are, however, other modified alphabets. A forty-symbol alphabet called Unifon was developed by John R. Malone of Park Forest, Illinois. Unifon, in contrast with i.t.a., uses only capital letters and adds some new symbols for vowel phonemes. Malone developed his alphabet to help his son with sound-letter relationships. Unifon is an acronym for *uniformly phonetic;* and the alphabet is, as its name indicates, a uniformly phonetic representation of the sounds of the English language.

Instead of changing the alphabet by adding new letters, Words in Color—devised by Caleb Gattegno—modified the alphabet through the use of color. Gattegno's alphabet uses a different color for each of the forty-seven different phonemes that he feels comprise spoken English.

Gattegno's alphabet, which was copyrighted in 1962, was first used in an instructional program published by the Encyclopedia Britannica Press. The advantage of Words in Color is that the transition to the regular alphabet is made easier because the regular alphabet is not changed; all the different spellings of the same phoneme are merely printed in the same color on large wall charts. However, the colored letters do not appear in the WIC books; they are printed only on the charts with all accompanying phonetic spellings of the letter printed in the same color; for example, the sound of *a* in c*a*ne, r*ai*n, and l*ay* are the same so *a*, *ai*, and *ay* in those words would be the same color. The child identifies and then begins to blend sounds to make words. For example, t-a-p, tuh-aaah-puh. The phonics instruction emphasized by Words in Color is a synthetic method. Words in Color has been tried out in schools in different sections of the country, although it has not been researched extensively.

Edward Fry devised the Diacritical Marking System (DMS). In describing his system, Fry states:

> The Diacritical Marking System (DMS) that I have developed has over 99 percent phoneme-grapheme regularity and aims at achieving essentially the same goals as the Initial Teaching Alphabet without distortion in word form or change in spelling.
>
> The DMS is somewhat simpler than the diacritical marking systems found in most dictionaries, since the intention is to aid beginning readers rather than to give extreme accuracy. Regular consonants and short vowels have a bar over them. Regular two-letter combinations which make unique sounds such as the consonant digraphs and diphthongs have a bar under both letters. Silent letters have a slash mark through them. These marks plus a few others, such as those used for the broad *a* and other sounds of *u*, constitute the bulk of the marks used. Nearly every word used in first-grade reading books is marked; likewise, all work that a teacher duplicates or puts on the board contains the DMS marks. In writing, children have the option of using or not using the marks. (1972, p. 394)

Specified skills. Modified alphabet programs tend to emphasize the teaching of phonic skills. This is because most of these alphabets have been developed to help children more easily master sound-symbol relationships. However, because i.t.a. was not initially developed as a method, its proponents say that the i.t.a. alphabet lends itself well to various methods. All materials can be rewritten in i.t.a., whether they emphasize decoding or meaning. A point to remember in regard to all of these modified alphabets is that they are still alphabets and, as such, can be used to teach any reading skills that can be taught with a traditional alphabet.

Specific teaching procedures. Each published program using a modified alphabet describes certain teaching procedures. There are, however, no general teaching procedures that are applicable to all of these programs. Each program seems to emphasize some teaching procedures over others. For example, the Words in Color alphabet relies on a synthetic phonics approach, while instruction in i.t.a. may emphasize either analytic or synthetic phonics as well as earlier reading and writing.

Control of the language of the reading materials. Certainly the key element of any of the various modified alphabets is the attempt to use an alphabet that has consistent spelling patterns and a one-to-one sound-symbol relationship. In most of these programs, it appears that neither the vocabulary nor the syntax of the reading selections is systematically controlled. In some cases, such as for i.t.a., a traditional basal reader has been reprinted entirely in the modified alphabet.

Implementing Modified Alphabet Programs

The research regarding the use of modified alphabet programs is equivocal. The obvious strength of modified alphabets is the one-to-one correspondence they attempt to achieve between graphemes and phonemes. For this reason, modified alphabet programs are sometimes useful with children who have failed to see consistency in traditional spelling-pronunciation relationships. A modified alphabet can also be a motivating factor for a child who has been experiencing limited success in learning to read or in literacy programs. Given a special code to learn to read—one that is unknown to others—learning to read sometimes becomes a new experience for the child who has failed (and a manageable task for the adult illiterate). Once a learner masters the special code, he or she often transfers this knowledge to the regular alphabet code with little difficulty or setback. As with all programs, the value of modified alphabet programs lies with the type of child who may do well with such a program. As we have consistently pointed out throughout this chapter, no single program is best for all children and each program can be adapted to fit the needs of each child.

The major problem in implementing modified alphabet programs is fairly obvious. The use of a modified alphabet seems to limit the beginning reader to reading only those materials that have been printed using the modified alphabet. With the possible exception of i.t.a., there have been very few materials—other than those published specifically to teach that system—that have been published using modified alphabets. Because of the need to have children—especially beginning readers—read outside of their instructional materials as much as possible, this is a serious limitation.

Another implementation problem is the transition that students must make from reading materials printed in the modified alphabet to materials using the traditional alphabet. This occurs at different times in each

"Today we started on the
all-digit alphabet."

© 1979 Sidney Harris

of the programs, but for many of the programs it is about the middle of the second grade. However, program reports by teachers and administrators using these approaches, as well as some research reports, indicate that this is not a major problem for most children.

Linguistic Programs

Most linguists have been concerned when educators refer to something called linguistic programs for teaching reading (Shuy, 1977). Linguists contend that they study language behavior as psychologists study all types of behavior and sociologists study social behavior, and that as a science of behavior, linguistics is not meant to be a prescription. Perhaps one of the reasons for this is that in 1961 two linguists, Leonard Bloomfield and Clarence Barnhart, wrote *Let's Read, A Linguistic Approach* in an attempt to apply their knowledge of language to new ways of teaching reading. From this book, and other similar ones, grew the linguistic programs.

There are also great variations in the teaching procedures offered by those programs labelled linguistic. Among the linguists who first proposed their science as the basis for reading programs were those who emphasized the sound-symbol relationships of language. Their methods focused on small language units—letters, syllables, and words. More recently, linguists have emphasized the importance of larger language units—the sentence, the paragraph, and total story units. These linguists have emphasized teaching methods that help a child to use the meaning (semantics) and the organization, or word order (syntax), of what is being read.

Therefore, it should not be surprising to discover that linguistic programs are the least well defined of all the programs we have discussed up to this point. There does not seem to be a single definition that adequately describes all existing linguistic programs, but there appears to be an evolving set of linguistic beliefs about the reading processes that are being applied to the teaching of reading. Most of these beliefs have been set forth by linguists who have developed an interest in the reading process as a language process. Linguists, it seems, have been interested in the teaching of reading for some time. In her history of reading instruction, Smith (1965) identified M. V. O'Shea (1927) as the first person to write about the application of linguistics to reading.

However, it was not until 1961, when Bloomfield and Barnhart published *Let's Read, A Linguistic Approach,* that linguistics began to have a strong impact on the teaching of reading. The Bloomfield-Barnhart procedures emphasized the teaching of reading through methods that are similar to analytic phonics procedures in that they emphasize the teaching of sound-symbol relationships and begin with the teaching of the alphabet. The relationships are taught through practice exercises on lists of words that have similar spelling patterns. In their methodology, letter sounds are always in sentence contexts; comprehension is of secondary importance in the early stages of reading, with the primary emphasis on decoding (associating the phonemes of our language with their most regular grapheme representations).

Fries (1963), who endorsed the same general teaching methods set forth by Bloomfield and Barnhart, became a coauthor of a basal reader series, the *Merrill Linguistic Readers* (1966), that was one of the first developed following a linguistic theory. This program (examples of which appear below) was based on the following principles that appear in the teacher's manual:

- (1) Learning to read must begin with and build upon the language control already achieved by the pupils.
- (2) The periods of school time devoted to learning to read should use only the language already controlled by the pupils.
- (3) Many non-readers are not aware that the "talk" they have learned is made up of separate units called "words."
- (4) The most important first step in preparing to learn to read is the "learning" of the alphabet.
- (5) From the very beginning, reading is developed as a means of acquiring meanings—not only the meanings of the separate "words," but these meaningful "words" always in "sentences" and therefore with the grammatical meanings that attach to whole sentences; and, in addition, these sentences in sequences of small units of from three to eight sentences with the cumulative meanings of connected discourse.
- (6) Reading with "expression" depends upon the grasp of the cumulative meaning of sentences in sequence.

(7) All the significant matters of language are matters of contrast. Contrast, therefore, and especially minimum contrast, constitutes the fundamental principle of this teaching method from the very beginning.

(8) The spelling-pattern approach differs fundamentally from the commonly used practices of "word-method," of "word-families," and of "phonics."

(9) Wherever pictures are used, as they are in the Practice Books, the pupil does not proceed from the pictures as clues to the "words" of the text to be read, but rather from the words and sentences that must be read to the pictures he must mark to demonstrate the correctness of his reading.

Points seven and eight in Fries' list dictate the emphases on the two text pages below, which train the reader to note minimal differences.

Left: from *Dig In*, Level B, p. 63. Right: from *Skills Book* for *Dig In*, Level B, p. 38. Both in Merrill Linguistic Reading Program (Columbus, Ohio: Merrill Publishing Company, 1976). Reprinted by permission.

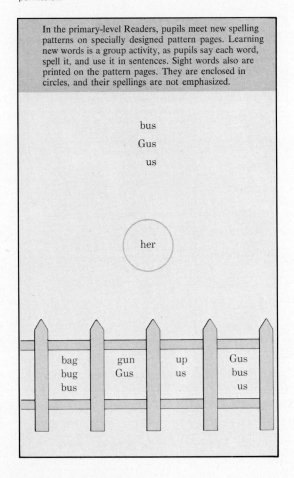

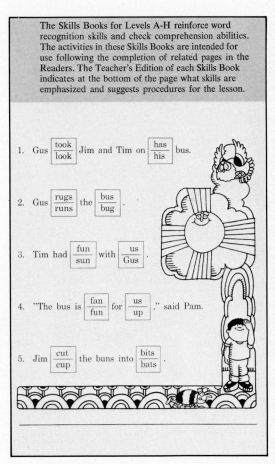

Other linguistic programs published at about the same time as the *Merrill Linguistic Readers* include the *SRA Basic Reading Series* (1964) published by Science Research Associates; the *Linguistic Readers* (1965) published by Harper & Row; *Programmed Reading* (1963), which is a programed linguistics series published by McGraw-Hill; and the *Miami Linguistic Readers* (1966) published by D. C. Heath.

Most of these programs include stories that emphasize the gradual introduction and numerous repetition of sound-symbol relationships. For example, the page below from the *Merrill Linguistic Readers* gives students practice with the consonant-vowel-consonant (c-v-c) pattern. In this program, as well as in most early linguistic programs, the regular patterns are introduced before the irregular, and the simple before the complex.

After meeting new words on the pattern pages, pupils read stories employing the words. The Teacher's Editions of the Readers include suggestions for discussion of the stories and comprehension-checking.

Six on a Bus

Jim and Tim are on a bus.
Jim said, "Look at us
on a big bus.
Gus is with us
and he runs the bus.
Dan and his dad are with us.
Six of us are on the bus."

Tim said, "It's not six,
is it?"

Dan said, "It is six.
Rags got on with us."

From *Dig In*, Level B, Merrill Linguistic Reading Program (Columbus, Ohio: Merrill Publishing Company, 1976), p. 66. Reprinted by permission.

While sound-symbol consistency is the emphasis of these programs, meaning is not; and many of these linguistic programs are found in classrooms as supplementary materials to give students practice in applying phonic skills.

Following the first flourish of linguistic programs, some reading specialists decided that linguists were just a new brand of phonics proponents. In recent years, however, linguistics is gaining a different perspective. The linguist's knowledge of language is being coupled with that of learning specialists by a new group of reading theorists. This group of specialists with the combined expertise has given rise to a new field—psycholinguistics. In his introduction to *Psycholinguistics and the Teaching of Reading* (1969), James T. Fleming lists a number of issues that should be studied by this new cadre of psychologists, linguists, and educators. The attention of these psycholinguists has moved from spelling-symbol relationships to the relation between total language and reading. According to Fleming, the psycholinguists are concerned with:

the question of whether (or to what degree) dialectal variations pose a barrier for some children learning to read

the necessity of constructing a convincing, comprehensive model of just what reading is all about

a close look at the oral reading errors made by mature as well as by immature readers in a variety of circumstances—their hesitation, false starts and omissions (of parts of a text); their insertions (of parts which do not appear in the text); and their self-corrections

a searching reconsideration of the worth of phonic generalization including a more basic examination of the English spelling system as it relates to oral language

the need to know what language "knowledge" a child brings to his reading tasks; that is, what he is best capable of using

The result of this broader perspective has been greater attention to the purpose for reading—the communication of meaning. Kenneth S. Goodman's (1970) definition of reading includes this emphasis on meaning: "Reading is a complex process by which a reader reconstructs, to some degree, a message encoded by a writer in graphic language." Goodman's model of reading—which we discussed in previous chapters, especially Chapter 4—describes how a reader uses syntax, semantics, and phonological cues to decode printed messages. It appears that most of the psycholinguists are moving to this emphasis on defining reading as a purposeful reconstruction of meaning rather than decoding symbols to sounds. Thus linguistics or psycholinguistics no longer can be seen as a single set of procedures for the teaching of reading. Rather they represent a set of understandings about language that can be used to develop reading programs.

There are six major generalizations about reading instruction that can be made about the work of linguists from 1961 (when Bloomfield and Barnhart published their book) to the present. Obviously, such a list is a simplification of the contributions of many individuals and may even obscure many of the differences in the work of various individuals. Such a list, however, can guide you in examining the different "schools of thought" that are the linguists' contributions to reading instruction.

(1) Reading is based on oral language development and follows some of the same principles. Reading instruction should be based on the oral language development of children.
(2) Reading instruction should be based on an inductive approach.
(3) There is a sound-symbol consistency in the English language if one understands all of the generalizations. The development of instructional materials in reading should emphasize this consistency.
(4) Reading should be taught as one aspect of a total language program and should not be separated from speaking, listening, and writing.
(5) Readers combine syntactic, semantic, and phonological cues to decode printed messages.
(6) The focus of reading and reading instruction should be on reading for specific purposes and on receiving an author's message.

Control of the Language of the Reading Materials

The linguists' influence on reading programs has been to focus attention on the language structure of the reading materials. While earlier linguists emphasized spelling or sound-symbol relationships, later linguists emphasized the reader's use of the meaning and structure of language in decoding meaning rather than just decoding individual sounds and words. Some linguists, as we discussed here and in Chapter 6, have attempted to control the language of reading materials so that they match the normal oral language patterns of the children who will be taught to read using the materials.

Because of the control of the language of the reading materials, linguistic programs do use special materials and tend to emphasize the teaching of specified skills growing out of the language-control emphasis. However, the linguistic programs do not conform to the same teaching procedures.

Special materials. Because there are a number of quite different linguistic programs available and each of them includes different materials, it is difficult to make any generalizations about the types of materials. However, many linguistic programs do include practice materials such as the example on the next page.

The purpose of these practice materials is to help the child learn the patterns (sound-symbol as well as syntactic and semantic) of the printed language.

Linguistic programs offer approximately the same variety or types of material that basal programs provide, including texts, placement tests, duplicating masters, vocabulary charts and cards.

From *Skills Book* for *Lift Off*, Level F, Merrill Linguistic Reading Program (Columbus, Ohio: Merrill Publishing Company, 1976), p. 68. Reprinted by permission.

hoped — hopped

1. The little frog _____ hopped _____ quickly into the pond.

2. The girls _____ hoped _____ for a good day for the picnic.

3. Pete _____ hoped _____ to take a train to camp.

taped — tapped

4. Gail _____ taped _____ the snapshots into her book.

5. The baker _____ tapped _____ the nuts to crack the shells.

6. A tag was _____ taped _____ to each bunch of bananas.

biter — bitter

7. The lemon drink tasted _____ bitter _____

8. That dog could be a _____ biter _____.

9. A gumdrop is sweet, not _____ bitter _____.

68   *Use after LIFT OFF page 112.* **Completing Sentences:** Have pupils read the first sentence and decide which of the two words above it belongs in the sentence. Have them write the correct word in the sentence. Repeat procedure with the other sentences. For less able pupils, this exercise should be completed as part of the developmental reading lesson *under teacher supervision.*

Specified skills. The early linguistic programs emphasized sound-symbol relationships. This emphasis was based on the belief that children needed to learn each sound-symbol relationship in a systematic and gradual way. The sounds were never presented in isolation but always within a word. Despite the dictum of linguistic programs that sounds should be presented in words, the early linguistic programs deemphasized comprehension in the beginning stages of reading. They believed that the child's oral language already included the words to be decoded and that there was no need for emphasis on comprehension.

In the more recent statements of psycholinguists, meaning *is* emphasized at all levels. Psycholinguists have not only pointed out the importance of teaching sound-symbol relationships within words but also of teaching decoding in meaningful printed messages. This, they believe, causes the reader to use semantic (meaning), syntactic (sentence grammar), and phonological (sound-symbol) clues interdependently in the decoding of printed messages.

Psycholinguists emphasize the importance of decoding, with not so much adherence to the systematic introduction of sound-symbol relationships as stress on receiving the message. They teach reading within a much broader context, one which includes semantics and syntax. Thus they encourage the use of a much larger vocabulary in the writing of beginning reading materials. The emphasis on reading for meaning has also resulted in an approach to reading that encourages the reader to state specific purposes for reading, to apply the results of the reading to some activity, to rethink the concepts he or she holds, and to establish new concepts.

Most psycholinguists do not emphasize a specific sequence or hierarchy of skills; their analysis of reading emphasizes the interdependence of the skills. For example, the skills that need to be taught to a child should be determined by listening to a child read and then discussing with the child what has been read. Once the skill need is determined, instruction should be planned so that the child focuses on the needed skill and then immediately moves back to application of the skill.

Suppose, for example, that a child, in his or her oral reading, does not seem to be making use of the initial consonant *f* in attempting to decode. That is, the guesses a child made for unknown words seldom began with the sound represented by the consonant *f*. The teacher would plan various kinds of instructional activities to help the child learn the association and the help he or she can get from using that consonant in decoding words. Later, the child may be given practice with materials of special interest to him or her and that stress the technique of using a specific consonant cue in connected reading.

As another example, consider a child who reads very slowly and hesitantly in a word-by-word fashion and attempts to sound out each word carefully. A child who reads like this usually comprehends little of what is sounded. In this case, instruction would be planned to help the child rely on meaning and word order as cues to word recognition. Once the child learns to use such cues, other reading materials should be provided for the child to practice his or her developing strategies independently.

The point that most linguists are making today is that learning to read is not merely the acquiring of a hierarchy or sequence of skills. Instead, it requires that various skills must be used simultaneously. And since many of these skills are similar to those employed by a child in listening, this fact should be capitalized on when teaching a child to read. Most linguists also emphasize that any sequence of skills taught to a child who is learning to read will necessarily be arbitrary.

Specific teaching procedures. Getting children to read for meaning and not for word identification is perhaps the major teaching procedure in linguistic programs. Teachers are encouraged to help the child focus on his or her purpose for reading and the author's message—not on the identification of individual words. They argue that reading is a process that must focus on meaning. The teaching procedures in a linguistic program also encourage the child's oral language development as a basis for learning to read. Children come to school already able to use many of the language skills needed in learning to read, and these skills are demonstrated by the children every day in their listening and speaking activities.

In addition to emphasizing reading for meaning, sound-symbol relationships are introduced through inductive teaching procedures. Children discover the predictable relationships between sounds and symbols through exposure to print. Linguistic teaching methods always introduce sounds as parts of words and never in isolation. If you were influenced by the psycholinguists, you would seldom, if ever, interrupt a child's reading to have him or her learn or practice a word-recognition skill. Rather, you would record the child's miscue and determine at a later time if specific practice in some reading strategy were necessary.

It would be inaccurate to assume that the teaching strategies presented above are endorsed by all linguists and that they are a part of all linguistic programs. Because *linguistics* has become one of the "in words" in reading instruction today, many publishers have labelled their materials as being "linguistically oriented" or as "linguistic programs" or "linguistically correct programs." These terms are sometimes nothing but labels applied to programs. Often, however, these are meaningful identifications of programs that are based on the theories, research, and philosophy of linguistics.

Linguistic programs sometimes look very much like some of the phonics programs described earlier; sometimes the programs use programed workbooks; and there are some linguistic programs that follow a basal reader pattern. What all of this means is that there are a variety of teaching procedures that can be used with linguistic programs.

Control of the language of the reading materials.   Psycholinguists have strongly advocated the use of the language the child brings to school as the structure for beginning reading materials. "The basic form of his language—that used in common discourse and conversation—is his means of communication, expression, thinking, and learning. Experience stories, directions, labels, signs are examples of early reading materials that use common language" (Goodman, 1970).

Goodman goes on to say that before children encounter unfamiliar writing styles, they should be made familiar with those styles through having stories read to them and through oral discussions of concepts they will encounter in their reading. The responsibility for this instruction, according to Goodman (1970), rests with the teacher: "Every teacher of whatever subject and level must be prepared to help children to meet new demands on their reading competence and to develop the special strategies which these demands require."

Although the language patterns in linguistic materials often look different in the various programs, each program is based on linguistic principles. According to Ronald Wardhaugh (1969), materials for reading instruction should be based on the following five linguistic principles:

(1) They must be based on sound linguistic content, that is, on the best available descriptions of language—and of the English language in particular—rather than on random collections of myths. One needs scientific knowledge, not folklore.

(2) They must be based on a sound knowledge of the relationships and differences between sounds and symbols, between speech and writing.

(3) They must be based on a thorough understanding of just what children know about their language as this knowledge reveals itself in what they can do in their language rather than what they can verbalize about their language.

(4) They must differentiate between the descriptive and the prescriptive, particularly when the prescriptives are unrealistic. When the prescriptives refer to standard English, the methods and materials should reflect some decision about the relationship (if any) between teaching reading and teaching a standard spoken dialect. It may well be that standard English orthography is perfectly adequate for teaching reading to speakers of any dialect of English, and more than one linguist known to the writer would be prepared to argue for just such a proposition.

(5) Finally, they must recognize the important active contribution the learner makes in reading, both in trying to make sense of the orthographic conventions of English and in trying to make sense out of sentences. (pp. 88–89)

Linguistic Programs Provide More Language Consistency

If some of your children are likely to profit from a linguistic program because they need practice in sound-symbol relationships or because they need a gradual introduction to integrating various skills, you should begin studying several of the suggested readings listed at the end of this chapter. Such study will provide you with an increased knowledge of what linguistics is all about and will give you a basis on which to devise your own linguistic program. In addition, such study will help you to learn more about language, the basis for all reading instruction. Be sure to include in your reading some of the earlier linguists, such as Fries and Bloomfield and Barnhart.

As we emphasized at the beginning of this section, linguistic programs are the least well defined of all the programs. Indeed, it is perhaps best to state that there is no such thing as a "linguistic program"; rather there are a set of ideas based on the work of different linguistic schools of thought.

The strengths of these ideas have already been stated but can be summarized here:

There is a strong emphasis on the development of reading as a part of a total language (reading, listening, speaking, and writing) program.

Linguists have pointed out the consistencies in sound-symbol relationships and emphasized that these consistent patterns should be introduced first in instructional materials.

Recent linguists have stressed the primary importance of meaning in reading.

The limitations of these ideas are not necessarily those of the linguists' contributions, but are differences of opinion regarding some of the ideas about reading among linguists. The most controversial issue is the deemphasis of meaning in beginning reading material by some of the earlier linguistic programs. While more recent linguists have not done this, several of the published linguistic programs still include reading selections that are almost completely devoid of meaning. These materials can still profitably be used when you have children who need practice in specific skills, especially at the beginning reading level—for example, learning word patterns such as *tan, can, fan, pan, ran.* The materials of the more recent linguistic programs, however, are more likely to utilize the strengths of the approach to achieve the overall objective of reading instruction—helping children get meaning from print.

Programed Materials and Systems Programs

More than likely you have seen instructional programs where a student sits at a computer terminal and types on a keyboard the answers to questions that are printed on a screen. This is referred to as "computer assisted" or "computer guided" instruction, and such programs have been used to teach beginning reading. Computer assisted instruction has been made possible because of three continuing efforts—two in psychology and education, and one in technological engineering.

The first of these has been the development of programed instruction, which is based in large measure on the work of B. F. Skinner. According to Bugelski (1964), "Skinner started with a strong desire to help out in the educational crisis that began in the United States in the 1950s (a shortage of competent teachers) and a conviction that the success he had attained in the control of rat and pigeon behavior revealed the basic principles that underlie successful teaching."

Skinner applied the principles of operant conditioning* to the teaching of various kinds of subject matter. Skinner's work led to the devel-

---

* Operant conditioning is increasing the probability of the occurrence of certain behavioral responses to a specified stimulus, such as a question.

opment of the first teaching machines. These machines showed the learner a question on a screen. The student wrote the answer and then opened a shutter that revealed the correct response. If the answer was correct, the student went on to the next question. If it was incorrect, he or she would come back and try this question at a later time. Thus, the student would continue to go through the questions until each was answered correctly. For every response—even wrong ones—the student was reinforced by seeing the correct response.

The results of Skinner's work encouraged curriculum developers to isolate and analyze the individual skills needed to learn some behavior—such as reading—into a hierarchy of small, sequenced bits. These skills sequences were published in various kinds of programs, including workbook-type materials.

The second effort from education and psychology that further encouraged the development of systems and programed approaches was the behavioral objectives movement. Basically, the theory and practice of developing behavioral objectives grew out of the work of Benjamin Bloom and Robert Mager. Bloom (1971) put forth the idea that learning was facilitated if it was arranged in a series of hierarchies of knowledge and thinking abilities and if these were stated in behavioral terms. Mager (1962) defined and further developed the concept of behavioral objectives. Mager's definition included three basic aspects of behavioral objectives: the condition under which the behavior will be done—external conditions; the type of behavior that is to be learned—terminal behavior; and the acceptable performance level.

The result of the work by Bloom and Mager was that curriculum developers had a taxonomy of behaviors (Bloom) and a set of guidelines for developing specific behaviors (Mager) that could be used to develop instructional programs for Skinner's learning machines. The third development that moved this approach even further came from technological engineering. That was the development of computers that could both quickly provide a student with responses and be developed so that a student's response (right or wrong) to a particular question would trigger the computer to present the next question. For example, if the response was correct, the next question would be the next step in the sequence. However, if the response was incorrect, the next question might be the same question stated differently or there might be some sort of branching program that may provide reteaching or remedial questioning to help the student remember something that may have caused him or her to get the first question wrong.

Systems Programs

These three developments culminated in the development of computer-assisted instructional programs in various curriculum areas, including reading. One computer-assisted program in reading was devel-

oped by Richard Atkinson and Duncan Hansen (1966), who described their program as:

> a computer-based system and curriculum for teaching initial reading completely under computer control. The system and curriculum are organized so that instruction is on an individual basis with each child progressing at his own pace through a subset of materials designed to be best suited to his particular aptitudes and abilities. (p. 5)

There were other computer-assisted programs to teach reading that were developed at about the same time, and several are still available commercially. Although the expense of the computer equipment has limited the adoption of these programs by public schools, the use of behavioral objectives, sequenced instruction, and programed instruction has led to the development of systems approaches.

A systems approach to teaching reading usually includes a set of workbooks, readers, and supplementary aids; and reading skills are taught in a sequenced hierarchy of small bits (behavioral objectives). Systems approaches often include teaching machines. Careful records of each student's progress are kept, and the student progresses through the instruction as he or she masters each step. Systems approaches usually include the use of numerous short tests to determine a student's mastery of one skill or objective before he or she moves on to the next skill or objective.

Special materials.   Programed materials gained their greatest popularity in the early 1960s; and while these materials are still used in some schools and a few new materials are being developed and published, the use of programed materials to teach reading seems to have waned in the past five to ten years. The initial interest in programed materials was probably generated by their unique appearance and the fact that children could work in the materials independently. There has been some concern expressed by educators who believe that programed instruction teaches children isolated bits of information or skills and doesn't necessarily transfer to reading a total selection based on his or her interest.

Programed materials are of two general types: linear and branching. In a linear program, the child goes through all the steps of an instructional unit, one step leading to the next until the goal is reached. (See example below.) In a branching program, when a child makes a mistake, he or she is directed to another section of the materials to learn why the answer was incorrect. After learning the reason for the original mistake,

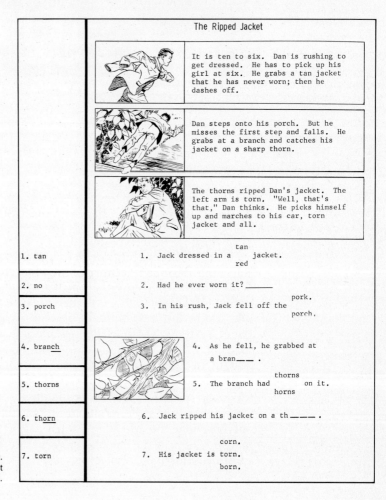

Reprinted from *Programmed Reading* by C. D. Buchanan and Sullivan Associates, copyright 1963, with permission of Webster/McGraw-Hill.

the child returns to the original frame and tries again. Branching programed materials are not abundant.

Workbooks, audio-visual materials—such as filmstrips, films, and audio and video cassettes—skills exercises organized in file boxes, and books are all used in systems and programed approaches. Computers and various kinds of computer input-output terminals are, of course, used in the computer-assisted versions of the programed approaches.

Some basal reader publishers now describe their programs as systems approaches. Generally, they are still basal programs that have included the listing of behavioral objectives for the program, reading-skills charts to keep track of student progress, and tests to determine each student's mastery of the objectives. Some programs also add remedial or corrective (recycling) materials for the students who do not master the skills on their first attempts.

Specified skills. As we have mentioned, most programed materials for teaching reading are linear rather than branching. Thus, the individualization of instruction that occurs in such linear materials is the pace at which the child proceeds through the program. There is only a very limited opportunity to adjust the program to each child's specific needs. Because word-recognition skills can be more easily defined and sequenced, they are emphasized by most systems and programed approaches. However, comprehension, word-recognition, and study skills are included in some programs.

Specific teaching procedures. Student and teacher activities are usually very specifically described with these approaches. Some of the programs can be used without a teacher at all; a monitor need only distribute the materials and see that the students continue at the task. These programs have sometimes been labelled "teacher-proof," implying that there is very little opportunity for the teacher to do something wrong in implementing the program.

The usual teaching procedures with these programs include assessing each student's mastery of the objectives, keeping records of progress on what is often an extensive list of behavioral objectives, and helping students get started in using the materials and assisting those who have difficulty (although few students are ever supposed to have any problems in using correctly programed instruction).

Control of the language of the reading materials. Generally, no specific language structure is used in the materials, although the skills are specifically sequenced for presentation to students. However, there are variations as with the previous programs in this chapter. The Sullivan Associates program, for example, follows a system of language control. The sample page below reveals the systematic introduction of the consonant-vowel-consonant (c-v-c) pattern with very careful vocabulary control.

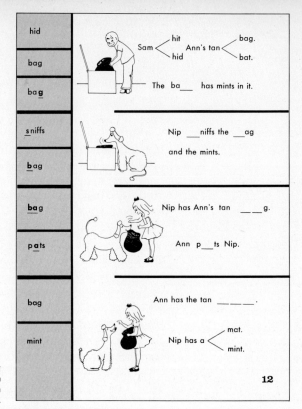

Reprinted from *Programmed Reading*
by C. D. Buchanan and Sullivan
Associates, copyright 1963, with
permission of Webster/McGraw-Hill.

Programed Materials and Systems Programs Can Be Misused

These programs are usually so carefully developed in terms of what teachers and students are to do and so specifically sequenced that they are very easy to use. This ease of use can also lead to misuse if the materials are used only as "busy work" for students.

You may want to consider some parts of the better programed materials to use to put students on their own when they need practice with specific skills. Programed materials do allow students to work independently, but you should not confuse this independence with the concept of individualized instruction.

The major strengths according to the programed instruction proponents are the following:

The skills to be learned are carefully sequenced and the mastery of each skill is almost guaranteed.
Because the programs are almost self-administered by students, the teacher is free to work with students who have special problems.
Students are guided through skills instruction automatically.

These strengths are countered by those who argue that learning to read does not proceed in a hierarchical sequence. They contend that what a student knows, or seems to know, on Monday may be forgotten by Friday. Those who define reading as a global behavior often criticize this approach because they believe reading cannot be broken into a specific set of objectives. Learning each of these objectives, they argue, results not in reading but in the learning of isolated bits. In addition, they argue that most of the systems and programed approaches provide unnatural situations that are quite unlike those of real reading. For example, reading from a computer terminal or filling in a programed workbook is significantly different from reading a story.

Choosing a Program

Now that you have read about each of these seven types of programs for teaching reading, you can see why we introduce this chapter by saying that there are no distinct programs. A basal reader may be written with a modified alphabet, for example; or a phonics program may be written in a programed workbook format and may be based on a linguistic analysis of sound-symbol relationships.

Indeed, the published programs usually combine several of the programs we have described in this chapter, and you should feel free to adopt elements from more than one program.

Before reading about the selection and modification of these programs, it may be useful to review the seven types of programs included in this chapter. Figure 10–2 summarizes the information for you.

Adapting from Various Programs

When you are ready to begin choosing a program; you will probably be choosing parts of various programs to meet the needs of your children. How do you decide what to choose and what to modify? There are three major factors that should influence you in this process. First, you need to consider the characteristics of the learners you are teaching. Second, you should consider your own characteristics. Third, the characteristics of the school and community in which you will be teaching need to be taken into account.

Your learners' characteristics.   Throughout this book we hve been advocating that your reading program be individualized and personalized. We have consistently said that each child needs to have the opportunity to read independently. This does not preclude the use of some leveled text—whatever the philosophy its author adheres to—because many children learn to read best when there is a gradual introduction to new vocabulary. However, a child's placement in such a program is dependent on individual reading development.

Furthermore, you may want to avoid using a synthetic phonics program or a modified alphabet program with any child who is having difficulty with the inconsistencies of sound-symbol relationships and

Figure 10–2 Summary of Seven Types of Programs for Teaching Reading

Programs	Are Special Materials Needed?
Basal	*Yes.* Special materials include student readers and teachers' manuals. Student workbooks, tests, and other supplementary materials are often available.
Individualized Reading	*No.* In this approach, the teacher is encouraged to collect and use a wide variety of reading materials.
Language experience	*No.* In this approach the materials are often student-developed stories based on shared or individual experience.
Phonics	*Yes.* Phonics can be taught using any of a wide variety of materials. However, there are various special phonics programs that come with prepared materials.
Artificial alphabets	*Yes.* The materials are written using special alphabets or language patterns. Sometimes only these—and no supplementary materials—can be used.
Linguistics	*Yes.* Linguistics usually means that children's language patterns and/or regular spelling patterns are employed.
Systems	*Yes.* These are special instructional packages including tests, workbooks, A-V aids, and sometimes computer-assisted instruction.

Are Specified Skills Emphasized?	Are Specific Teaching Procedures Used?	Is The Language of the Reading Materials Controlled?
Yes. Basals usually try to include a wide range of reading skills. Although, the sequence and number of emphasized skills vary, most basal programs build on a systematic introduction of skills in a prescribed order.	*Yes.* Basals usually encourage teachers to use a wide variety of teaching procedures. While specific teaching procedures are described in the teachers' manuals, teachers are encouraged to supplement with other teaching procedures.	*Yes.* Basals usually are developed from "graded word lists" and other controls on the difficulty of the student materials.
No. The emphasis is on teaching the skills that are needed when they are needed.	*No.* Yet, individual student conferences, record keeping concerning student progress, and flexible grouping are common factors in the organization of the program.	*No.* Because a wide variety of materials are used, this is not possible.
No. The emphasis is on comprehension, helping children to see the relationship between language and print.	*Yes.* The procedures for eliciting experience stories from children are fairly well specified. However, the procedures for teaching word-recognition skills are left unspecified.	*No.* The reading materials are based on the oral language patterns of the children being taught.
Yes. The emphasis is on teaching word recognition skills, emphasizing sound-symbol relationships.	*No.* Various teaching procedures can be used.	*Yes.* Instructional materials are usually carefully developed to introduce a sequence of sound-symbol relationships.
To some extent. The materials generally emphasize word-recognition skills more than other skills. However, a variety of skills are taught.	*No.* The varying programs emphasize a wide variety of teaching procedures.	*Yes.* The instructional materials are written in a special alphabet.
Yes. The skills involved initially include attention to regular sound-symbol relationships, and move from simple to complex.	*No.* A wide variety of teaching procedures are used.	*Yes.* The emphasis is on language patterns used by children.
Yes. Usually word recognition skills are emphasized because they can be programed more easily; however, a wide variety of skills are taught.	*Yes.* The instructional package usually specifically tells the teacher what to do.	*Yes.* The skills to be taught are usually arranged in carefully sequenced patterns.

work instead through the learner's strength until the child begins to grasp sound-symbol relationships. With other children you may choose to use a combination of approaches; for example, language experience and a linguistic supplement.

Our point is this: you need to know your children well before you can adapt and adopt from any program.

In Chapter 2 we described many ways of assessing the abilities and interests of the child. There are many questions that you should ask in order to discover this information—among the most important are:

(1) Do the out-of-school activities and experiences of the child match those of the materials he or she will be reading?
(2) What is the language background of the child?
(3) Does the child work well independently, and does he or she like to?

Answers to these and other questions will help you in your goal of creating the best program for each child.

Your characteristics. A major concern in considering your characteristics is to examine your philosophy or definition of reading. A question as broad as this can lead you to an evaluation of programs that will determine whether you want to emphasize one aspect of reading over another. You may, for example, decide to emphasize comprehension—and help children induce phonic generalizations.

You also need to consider your own personality and attitudes about teaching by asking yourself:

(1) Do I work best in a structured or open learning environment?
(2) Does my motivation and enthusiasm increase when I am trying something new and different?
(3) How creative am I? Do I like to construct new materials and to plan child-centered activities?
(4) Can I work effectively in an atmosphere where a great variety of activities are taking place at once, or does such an environment frustrate me as "organized confusion"?

School and community characteristics. Here, too, there are many questions that you ought to consider since schools and communities vary greatly. A few of the more important questions whose answers will influence the development of your reading program are:

(1) Does the staff seem accepting of classrooms where there are a great variety of activities taking place at once?
(2) Are ample reading materials available? Is there a school library? A community library? Are classroom libraries encouraged? Are they tolerated?
(3) Is the school environment flexible or highly structured?

(4) Are teachers encouraged to develop their own programs or is "one program for the entire school" the policy?

It is always wise to make an assessment of the school and community. Even if you think you know which programs you believe in and want to use, you must still make a discrete evaluation of how acceptable they will be in the teaching environment where you are working. If the situation suggests that your program may cause too much of a stir, you don't necessarily have to abandon it completely for one you feel is less effective; it does, however, suggest that you should adapt the program to the prevailing influences. Children do not learn easily in an environment where the teacher is under the gun of professional criticism or is fighting a kind of pedagogical revolution; therefore it is wise to supplement the program accepted by the school with methods you believe will more effectively serve the children you teach. As your uniquely effective presentation of the methods generally accepted by the school produces results, you may find that you are not only influencing your pupils but fellow teachers and administrators as well.

Review the Program and Its Materials

An important part of developing your own reading program is reviewing the myriad of materials in various reading programs. We have divided this review into two sections. The first deals with general considerations in program review and the second with the reading selections the children will be reading; for it is these reading materials themselves that are really the heart of any reading program.

General considerations. The following questions are ones that you should ask yourself as you examine and adapt materials from various program approaches to teaching reading:

(1) Does the program describe itself as complete, offering a range of materials from prereading to intermediate levels?

We certainly believe that no program is complete in itself. The rationale behind this question is not to suggest that only programs that allow you to say *yes* should be used, but rather to lead you to the appropriate gathering of materials.

(2) Are the goals of the program clearly stated so that you can judge whether the materials of the program can be adapted to your goals?

These first two questions are very important to ask, especially if you are a member of a selection committee; but every teacher should be assessing his or her program with such questions. It leads to the kind of analysis that can help the teacher exploit a program and its materials fully—through adaptation, supplements, and so on. By asking your fellow teachers what their goals are and their opinions of the program, you may encourage a growing, schoolwide scrutiny of both the materials and the school's goals.

(3) Are the methods of word analysis utilized in the reading program compatible with your beliefs about the way to teach word analysis?

If *no*, start adding materials based on your beliefs to the existing program—making up practice materials, games, and activities.

(4) Are the events represented in the reading selections familiar in the experience of the pupils in your school and your community?

If the answer is *no*, you have an obligation to help your pupils gain experiences that will help them to identify with their reading. Then expose them to material that *can* have meaning for them.

(5) Are the vocabulary and syntax in the reading selections appropriate for pupils in your school?

Once again, if the answer is *no*, you need to expose your pupils to supplementary materials that *are* appropriate, providing background experiences and vocabulary exercises that can help the children cope with the materials they are expected to read.

(6) If it is a published program, is the publisher's reputation one of responsibility and service?

This is a valuable question for the teacher engaged in the selection of supplementary materials; for you who are assigned an approach, assessing the material before and as you use it should allow you to judge the publisher most objectively.

The children's reading selections. The reading selections read by students are certainly the most important single element in any reading program. Whether it is a basal, linguistic, individualized, phonics, or some other program, the reading selections need to be carefully examined. Listed below are some questions to help guide your review of the reading selections.

(1) Is the principle underlying the sequential introduction of vocabulary (if this is done) clearly stated? Are words introduced on the basis of phonic regularity, frequency of usage, or some other criterion?

(2) How often are new words introduced (for example, one new word for every ten words, or one new word on every page)? How frequently are new words repeated?

(3) Are sufficient words introduced to make possible the writing of meaningful sentences and stories?

(4) Are the sentence patterns of the reading selections similar to the normal speech patterns of the pupils? Are more complex sentence patterns introduced as pupils progress through the series? Are sentence length and complexity controlled?

(5) Are the concepts presented in beginning materials sufficiently within the experience of most pupils? Are concepts in later materials appropriate to the intended age-group?

(6) Are vocabulary and syntax sufficiently regulated in beginning materials to enable the pupil to be successful in his or her first attempts at reading?

(7) Are the words that are introduced in materials designed for initial instruction within the understanding vocabulary of pupils? If a pupil decodes an unknown word correctly, will he or she recognize the word?

(8) Are the stories good with interesting plots, suspense, good style? Are various types of selections included in the readers?

(9) Are stories appropriate in length for the intended age and ability group?

(10) Do the books have attractive formats? Are they likely to motivate interest?

A final consideration. As we have noted above, it is quite possible that you will find yourself teaching in a school where the program has been decided for you. Perhaps a committee of teachers, parents, and administrators decided on the program they thought was best; and every teacher is now expected to use that program. In that event, you need not throw in the towel and merely mimic all the other classrooms. You need to find out what flexibility is allowed.

Second, as we pointed out earlier, most classrooms use a combination of programs anyway. By using materials differently than the "directions indicate" (yet still using the program that has been mandated) and by emphasizing certain skills or teaching techniques—you can come quite close to having the program you want to use. Of all the research findings in education, the one that is almost universally accepted is that the teacher's enthusiasm and belief in what he or she is doing is the greatest single factor in increasing learning.

REFERENCES Adams, Fay; Gray, Lillian; and Reese, Dora. *Teaching Children to Read.* New York: The Ronald Press, 1949.

Allen, Roach Van. "Three Approaches to Teaching Reading." In *Challenge and Experiment in Reading*, edited by J. Allen Figurel, pp. 153–56. International Reading Association Conference Proceedings, 1962.

———, and Allen, Claryce. *Language Experiences in Reading: (LEIR) Teachers' Source Book.* Chicago: Encyclopedia Britannica Press, 1966.

Arnold, Sarah Louise, and Gilbert, Charles B. *Stepping Stones to Literature.* Morristown, N.J.: Silver, Burdett, 1897.

Atkinson, Richard C., and Hansen, Duncan N. "Computer-Assisted Instruction in Initial Reading: The Stanford Project." *Reading Research Quarterly* 7 (Fall 1966): 5–25.

Austin, Mary C., and Morrison, Coleman. *The First R.* New York: Macmillan, 1963.

Bloom, Benjamin S., ed. *Taxonomy of Educational Objectives: The Classification of Educational Goals, Handbook 1: Cognitive Domain.* New York: McGraw-Hill, 1971.

Bloomfield, Leonard, and Barnhart, Clarence. *Let's Read, A Linguistic Approach.* Detroit: Wayne State University Press, 1961.

Bond, Guy L., and Dykstra, Robert. "The Cooperative Research Program in First-Grade Reading Instruction." *Reading Research Quarterly* 2 (Summer 1967): 10–142.

Bugelski, B. R. *The Psychology of Learning Applied to Teaching.* New York: Bobbs-Merrill, 1964.

Cobb, Lyman. *The North American Reader.* New York: B. and S. Collins, 1835.

DeBoer, John J., and Dallman, Martha. *The Teaching of Reading,* New York: Henry Holt, 1960.

Downing, John A. "Research Reports on the British Experiment." In *The i.t.a. Symposium,* edited by John A. Downing et al. Slough, Buckinghamshire: National Foundation for Educational Research in England and Wales, 1966.

Fleming, James T. "Introduction." In *Psycholinguistics and the Teaching of Reading,* edited by James T. Fleming and Kenneth S. Goodman. Newark, Del.: International Reading Association, 1969.

Fries, Charles C. *Linguistics and Reading.* New York: Holt, Rinehart and Winston, 1963.

Fry, Edward. *Reading Instruction for Classroom and Clinic.* New York: McGraw-Hill, 1972.

Goodman, Kenneth S. "Behind the Eye: What Happens in Reading." In *Reading Process and Program,* edited by Kenneth S. Goodman and Olive S. Niles, pp. 1–7. Urbana, Ill.: National Council of Teachers of English, 1970.

Guszak, Frank J. "Questioning Strategies of Elementary Teachers in Relation to Comprehension." In *Elementary Reading Instruction: Selected Materials,* 2d ed., edited by Althea Beery, Thomas Barrett, and William Powell. Boston: Allyn and Bacon, 1974.

Harris, Albert J., and Coleman, Morrison. "The Craft Project: A Final Report." *The Reading Teacher* 22 (January 1969): 335–40.

Heilman, Arthur W. *Phonics in Proper Perspective.* Columbus, Ohio: Charles E. Merrill, 1964.

Laffey, James. *Methods of Reading Instruction.* Newark, Del.: International Reading Association, 1971.

Mager, Robert F. *Preparing Instructional Objectives.* Belmont, Cal.: Fearon Publishers, 1962.

Malone, John R. "The Unifon System." *Wilson Library Bulletin* 40 (September 1965): 63–65.

Mazurkiewicz, Albert J. "The Initial Teaching Alphabet (Augmented Roman) for Teaching Reading." In *New Perspectives in Reading Instruction,* edited by Albert J. Mazurkiewicz. New York: Pitman, 1964.

———. "Teaching Reading in America Using the Initial Teaching Alphabet." *Elementary English* 41 (1964): 766–72.

McDonald, James B.; Harris, Theodore L; and Mann, John S. "Individualized Versus Group Instruction in First Grade Reading." *The Reading Teacher* 19 (May 1966): 643–46, 652.

O'Shea, M. V. *Linguistics in Education.* New York: Macmillan, 1927.

Pei, Mario. *The Story of Language.* New York: J. B. Lippincott, 1965.

Robinson, Helen. M. "News and Comment—Individualized Reading." *Elementary School Journal* 60 (May 1960): 411–20.

Sartain, Harry W. "The Roseville Experiment with Individualized Reading." *The Reading Teacher* 13 (April 1960): 277–81.

Shuy, Roger W., ed. *Linguistic Theory: What Can It Say About Reading?* pp. vi–x. Newark, Del.: International Reading Association, 1977.

Smith, Nila B. *American Reading Instruction.* Newark, Del.: International Reading Association, 1965.

Spache, George D. *The Teaching of Reading.* Bloomington, Ind.: Phi Delta Kappa, 1972.

Stauffer, Russell G. "The Effectiveness of Language Arts and Basic Reader Approaches to First Grade Reading Instruction." In *The First Grade Reading Studies*, edited by Russell G. Stauffer, pp. 140–46. Newark, Del.: International Reading Association, 1967.

————.*The Language-Experience Approach to the Teaching of Reading.* New York: Harper and Row, 1970.

Veatch, Jeannette, and Acinapuro, Philip J. *Reading in the Elementary School.* New York: Ronald Press, 1966.

Wardhaugh, Ronald. "The Teaching of Phonics and Comprehension: A Linguistic Evaluation." In *Psycholinguistics and the Teaching of Reading*, edited by Kenneth S. Goodman and James T. Fleming, pp. 79–90. Newark: Del.: International Reading Association, 1969.

Weintraub, Samuel et al. "Summary of Investigations Relating to Reading, July 1, 1974 to June 30, 1975." *Reading Research Quarterly* 11, no. 3 (1975–1976): 223–563.

FOR FURTHER READING

Anderson, Paul S., ed. *Linguistics in the Elementary School Classroom.* New York: Macmillan, 1971.

Aukerman, Robert C. *Approaches to Beginning Reading.* New York: John Wiley and Sons, 1971.

Bannatyne, Alex. "The Colour Phonics System." In *The Disabled Reader, Education of the Dyslexic Child*, compiled by John Money and Gilbert Schiffman, Baltimore, Md.: Johns Hopkins Press, 1966. Chap. 12.

Davis, Leo G. *k-a-t spelz cat.* New York: Carlton Press, 1966.

Downing, John. *The Initial Teaching Alphabet: Explained and Illustrated.* New York: Macmillan, 1964.

Duker, Sam. *Individualized Reading: Readings.* Metuchen, N.J.: Scarecrow Press, 1969.

Hall, Mary Anne. *The Language Experience Approach for the Culturally Disadvantaged.* Newark, Del.: International Reading Association, 1972.

————. *Teaching Reading as a Language Experience.* Columbus, Ohio: Charles E. Merrill, 1976.

Lee, Dorris M., and Allen, Roach Van. *Learning to Read Through Experience.* New York: Appleton-Century-Crofts, 1963.

Miel, Alice, comp. *Individualized Reading Practices.* New York: Bureau of Publications, Columbia University, Teachers College. 1958.

Sartain, Harry. *Individualized Reading.* Newark, Del.: International Reading Association, 1970.

Spache, George G., and Spache, Evelyn B. *Reading in the Elementary School.* 4th ed. Boston: Allyn and Bacon, 1977.

Veatch, Jeanette. *Individualizing Your Reading Program.* New York: G. P. Putnam's Sons, 1959.

Walcott, Charles C. et al. *Teaching Reading: A Phonic Linguistic Approach to Developmental Reading.* New York: Macmillan, 1974.

Picture Credits

Frontispiece Ken Karp

Chapter 1 p. 3, Greg Gilbert, courtesy *Newsweek;* 7, Library of Congress; 8, Marjorie Pickens; 9, George S. Zimbel, courtesy Educational Facilities Laboratory; 10, James F. Quinn; 17, David S. Strickler/STRIX PIX.

Chapter 2 p. 22, Marion Bernstein; 26, © 1976 Elizabeth Hamlin/STOCK, Boston; 33, George S. Zimbel, courtesy Educational Facilities Laboratory; 35 (*top*), Marion Bernstein; 35 (*bottom*), Marjorie Pickens; 81, David S. Strickler/STRIX PIX.

Chapter 3 p. 110, Marion Bernstein; 128, Marjorie Pickens; 131, Nancy Roser; 137, Suzanne Szasz.

Chapter 4 p. 156, David S. Strickler/STRIX PIX.

Chapter 5 p. 179, Nancy Hays/Monkmeyer Press Photo; 182, Nancy Roser.

Chapter 6 p. 196, David S. Strickler/STRIX PIX; 211, Nancy Roser; 223, George S. Zimbel, courtesy Educational Facilities Laboratory.

Chapter 7 p. 261, 266, David S. Strickler/STRIX PIX; 271, Ken Karp; 286, Marjorie Pickens; 289, David S. Strickler/STRIX PIX; 290, 292, Hugh Rogers/Monkmeyer Press Photo; 300, George S. Zimbel/Monkmeyer Press Photo.

Chapter 8 p. 311, 313, 315, Ken Karp; 318, Bill Anderson/Monkmeyer Press Photo; 343 (*top*), Ken Karp; 343 (*bottom*), David S. Strickler/STRIX PIX.

Chapter 9 p. 384, David S. Strickler/STRIX PIX; 385, Marion Bernstein; 395, Ken Karp; 403 (*top*), Wide World Photos; 403 (*bottom*), Ken Karp; 410, George S. Zimbel, courtesy Educational Facilities Laboratory.

Chapter 10 p. 440, Mimi Forsyth/Monkmeyer Press Photo; 454, David S. Strickler/STRIX PIX; 483, Sam Falk/Monkmeyer Press Photo.

Index

Index

Cullinan, Bernice, 94
Cultural patterns and influences, 36, 37
  representation of in instructional
    materials, 85, 413, 437, 441, 443
  see also Community environment and
    resources

Dale, Edgar, 94, 251n
Dallman, Martha, 457
Dance
  participation in, 95, 96, 144, 283, 293
  see also Movement activities
d'Aulaire, Edgar and Ingri
  Abraham Lincoln, 282
Dawson, Mildred A., 378
DeBoer, John, 457
Dechant, Emerald V., 12, 13
Definitions, 173–74
De Montreville, Doris, 329n
Dewey, John, 88–89
  analysis of thinking, 251–52, 254, 255
Diacritical Marking System (DMS), 469
Diagnostic information, from assessments
  of reading, 77, 117, 165, 194–95,
  217, 475
Diagnostic standardized tests, 77
Diagrams, as graphic aid, 354, 355
Dialect, 51, 95, 161, 162–63, 165, 211, 221
  and learning to read, 455, 475
Dictionary
  picture dictionaries, 237–38, 243, 314,
    315, 322, 408, 456
  use of, 153, 160, 166, 190, 236–40, 273,
    312, 315, 322–23, 329, 408
    skills needed and teaching those
      skills, 239–46 passim, 322
Directions
  understanding and following, 106–07,
    109, 122, 127, 130, 132, 138–40,
    144, 199, 201, 204, 272, 276, 365,
    456
  see also Instructions
DiVesta, Francis J., 155
Doman, Glenn, 88
Dostert, Dennis, 366n
Downing, John A., 468
Drama activities
  participation in, 95, 97, 132, 275, 276,
    279, 284–87, 312–13
  story characters, 144, 285, 286, 287
  see also Puppets
Drawings, *see* Art/art activities; Graphic
  aids
Durkin, Dolores, 89, 90, 91, 109, 373
Durrell, Donald, 105, 109–10, 114
Dykstra, Robert, 426

Eames, Thomas S., 92
Early, Margaret, 52n
Ebony Jr.!, 330
Educational agencies and institutions, and
  availability of instructional
  materials, 32, 260
Eller, William
  Toothless Dragon, 294n
Ellis, A. J., 466
Elson-Gray readers, 429
Emans, Robert, 218, 221
Emotions and feelings
  and child's evaluation of text, 301
  communication of, 133, 283
  development of, 286
Encyclopedia
  activities and games for locating
    information, 326–28
  use of, 268, 314, 315, 323–28, 344, 408
Encyclopedia Britannica Press, 469
Enumeration, 364, 366
  see also Sequence
Ethnic groups
  representation of in instructional
    materials, 85, 413, 437, 441, 443
  see also Cultural patterns and
    influences
Evaluative reading comprehension, 271–
  73, 277–78, 301–02

Facts and details
  directions, following, 106–07, 109, 122,
    127, 130, 132, 138–40, 144, 199,
    201, 204, 272, 276, 365, 456
  identifying and remembering, 271, 272–
    74
  see also Reference books and sources;
    Reasoning
Fader, Daniel, 396
Fairy tales and make-believe, 5, 285, 413
  see also Story characters
Farber, Jerry, 4
Farr, Naunerle, 366n
Farr, Roger, 4, 72n, 79, 80, 85, 108
Females
  interests of vs. those of boys, 413
  representation of in basal readers, 437,
    441, 442–43
Feshbach, Seymour, 108
Field trips, 97, 261–62, 455, 456
Figures of speech, 176–77, 279
Films, use of, 32, 97, 309–10, 316, 485
Filmstrips, use of, 32, 97, 144, 309–10,
  408, 461, 485
Fleming, James T., 475
Flesch, Rudolf, 13, 15

Poetry
   listening and reacting to, 96, 142, 186,
      283, 293, 454
   musical settings for, 129–30, 293
   writing poems, 293
Prefixes, 153, 226–27, 227–28, 230, 323
   see also Affixes
Prereaders
   language awareness, 94–95
   pictures, use of, 183
   reading readiness, 91–93
      see also Reading readiness
Procedures (methods), definition of, 423
Programs, definition of, 423
Programed materials, *see* Systems
      programs
Pronunciation
   deviation in, 94
   dialect and dialect differences, 51, 95,
      161, 162–63, 165, 211, 221, 455, 475
   and dictionary, use of, 240, 244–46, 322,
      323
   and emphasis over meaning, 222
   and teaching word recognition, 161–63,
      165, 190
Psycholinguistics, 475–79 passim
   see also Linguistic programs
Puppets
   activities with, 95–96, 97, 127, 132, 143,
      274–75, 279, 286–87
   kinds and how to make, 285, 287
Puzzles, use of, 88, 136, 141, 144, 187,
      244, 313

Quackenbush, Robert
   She'll Be Comin' Round the Mountain,
      293

Radio, interest in, 260, 285
Ranger Rick, 329, 330
Rankin, Earl F., 73
Readability formulas, 357n, 409, 414, 416,
      431
   Fry formula, 409, 414–16
Readers' Guide to Periodical Literature,
      329–30
Reading, definitions of process, 11–16
Reading achievement test, 109
Reading area (in classroom), 32, 257, 260,
      398, 401, 402, 403, 404
Reading comprehension, 17–18, 250–305
   basal readers' emphasis on, 439
   cloze procedure, 71, 74
   critical, 271–73, 277–78, 299–301
   definitions, 251–52

development of, 253–67 passim, 269
   through arts, 32–33, 284–93
directions and instructions, 106–07, 109,
      122, 123, 127, 130, 132, 138–40,
      144, 199, 201, 204, 272, 276, 280,
      365, 452
evaluative, 271–73, 277–78, 301–02
facts and details, 271, 272–74
and Individualized Reading Program,
      447, 448
purpose determines reading rate, 307,
      356–63 passim
questioning, 273, 276–77, 280, 293–303
reading for meaning, 21, 150, 154, 161–
      63, 165, 166, 182, 188, 190, 475–79
      passim
reading levels, determination of, 38–86
and reasoning, 253, 254, 255, 267–79,
      281–83
testing for, 81–82
Reading levels, 21, 38–86
   capacity, 39n
   and frustration, 38–39, 73
   groups based on, 371, 385–86
   independent, 38, 73
   instructional, 38, 39, 73, 79–80
   publishers' levels, 39n, 79
   testing for, 78, 79–80
      see also Standardized tests; Tests
Reading pacers, 361
Reading programs, 422–96
   adopting from various programs, 487,
      490–91
   basal reading programs, 39, 184, 295,
      378–79, 424, 428–46, 488–89
      see also Basal readers/basal reading
         programs
   beginning reading programs, 107, 109,
      113, 117
   choosing program and summary of
      types, 487, 488–89, 491–93
   comparative studies of, 426–27
   goals, 373–75
   Individualized Reading Program, 446–
      50, 488–89
   and individual needs of child, 8, 371–76
   instructional materials, 371, 372, 373–
      74, 376, 389, 399, 408–20, 488
   interests of child as basis, 96–97, 107,
      246, 257, 371, 372–73, 376, 380,
      381, 382, 413, 490
   language experience programs, 98–105,
      118, 126–28, 198, 199, 450–59, 488–
      89
   linguistic programs, 471–81, 488–89

modified alphabet programs, 465–71, 488–89

phonics programs, 93, 190, 205–25, 424, 458–65, 488–89

space, organization of, 389, 391, 400–07
see also Classroom

students, organization of, 376
group, 76, 78, 82–84, 109, 371–72, 377–78, 380–88
individual, 372, 378–80, 381, 386, 388–96

systems programs, 9–10, 481–89

teachers, organization of, 418–19

time, organization of, 373, 375, 389, 396–400

Reading rate, 307, 356–63
flexibility in, 360–61, 362
mechanical aids, 361
scanning, 358–59, 361, 362, 363
skimming, 357, 358–59, 361–62, 363
speed reading, 362
testing for, 82, 361
timed exercises, 361
word-by-word, 161, 357

Reading readiness, 6, 88–147
and age of child, 88–92
beginning reading program, 107, 109, 113, 117
and language awareness of child, 94–105
and language-rich environment, 95–98, 104, 107
letters/letter names, awareness and development of, 104, 105–06, 134–36, 223–24
and physical development of child, 91–93, 105
tests and informal assessment, 106, 108–26
word awareness and development of, 136–38

Reading records, *see* Records, reading

Reading Research Quarterly, 426

Reading speed, *see* Reading rate

Reading tests, *see* Tests

Reading vocabulary, 312

Reasoning
facts and details, 271, 272–74
main ideas and generalizations, 271, 274–75
and purpose, 269, 270
and reading comprehension, 253, 254, 255, 267–79, 281–83
relationships, 271–72, 275–79

Recordings, *see* Phonographs and

recordings; Tape recorders; Tapes and cassettes

Records, reading, 194, 196, 372, 380, 447
cumulative, 26n
informal reading inventory (IRI), 50–51, 69
of interests, 21–22, 23, 27–30, 50–51
phonic needs, 213–14
skill needs, 387
vocabulary, 194

Reese, Dora, 451

Reference books and sources
locating information, 307–08, 314, 315, 325, 326, 329–37 passim, 357, 363–64
reviewing service, 329n
use of, 268, 269, 273, 314, 315, 321–30, 344, 408
see also Dictionary; Encyclopedia; Newspaper

Relationships
awareness and teaching of, 106–07, 133, 138–39, 175–78, 269, 271–72, 275–80 passim, 307–09, 340–41, 344
as organizational technique in writing, 364, 365–66

Repetition of words, 46

Reversal of words, 46–47

Rhymes, acting out, 284, 285

Rhyming words
and auditory discrimination, 142, 143
testing for, 110, 123

Rhythm activities, 142

Riddles, use of, 133, 186, 204, 205–06, 244, 273, 313

Ridley, John T., 441n

Robinson, Helen M., 251n, 449

Robinson, Violet B., 94

Role playing, 274–75
story characters, children as, 144, 285, 286, 287, 288, 301–02
see also Drama activities

Rosen, Connie, 99

Rosen, Harold, 99

Roser, Nancy L., 72n, 85

Rowls, Michael, 4

Ruddell, Robert, 95

Rude, Robert, 110

Russell, David H., 13, 220

Samuels, S. Jay, 160–61, 183

Sartain, Harry W., 450

Scanning, 358–59, 361, 362, 363

Scarry, Richard
Richard Scarry's ABC Word Book, 126

language experience program and writing experience, 456, 459
listening vocabulary, 312
lists, 191
prereader, 94
reading vocabulary, 312
of school beginner, 210 and n
sight vocabulary, 153, 190–205
speaking vocabulary, 210–11, 312, 441
specialized, and teaching study skills, 306, 308–13
testing for, 80–81, 82, 84, 110, 116–17, 125–26
word notebook, 241–42
writing vocabulary, 312
Vowels, 210, 245
clusters, 210, 219
diphthongs, 210, 212
learning difficulty, 219, 220
phonemes, 212

Wagener, Elaine H.
Poetry for Beginning Readers, 129
Ward, Lynn
The Biggest Bear, 256
Wardhaugh, Ronald, 155, 220, 480
Washburn, Carleton, 89
Weather, study of, 344, 349, 350, 351, 353, 457
Webster, Noah, 428n
American Spelling Book, 221
Weintraub, Samuel, 109, 426
White, E. B.
Charlotte's Web, 265
Wilder, Laura Ingalls
Little House on the Prairie, 256
Wilson Library Bulletin, 323
Women, representation of in basal readers, 437, 441, 442–43
Word awareness, development of, 104, 105–06, 136–38
Word-by-word reader, 161, 357
Word cards, 130, 199–201, 203, 224, 291, 438
Word games, 133, 199–204
see also Games
Word recognition, 16–17, 150–67
in basal readers, 439, 440
cloze procedure, 71, 74, 181, 198
by context analysis, 150, 151, 155–58, 160, 164, 166, 168–90 passim, 195, 198, 439
pictorial clues, 169, 170, 173, 182–84
semantic clues, 155, 157, 161, 164, 169–70, 172–79 passim, 182, 195, 475, 476, 477–78

syntactic clues, 95, 156, 157, 161, 164, 169, 170, 172, 178–82, 195, 436, 475, 476, 477–78
definition of, 150
failure to understand, 157
hesitation, 46
Individualized Reading Program, 448, 450
insertion of word, 45, 46, 47, 51
language experience program, 451, 452, 454
matching words, 112–13, 121
miscues, 44n, 45–47, 51, 66–71 passim, 161–62, 165, 213, 294, 324
modified alphabet programs, 489
omission of word, 45, 46, 47, 51, 165
outside references and sources, 153, 160, 164, 166, 188
by phonic analysis, 151, 152, 153, 158–60, 164, 166, 188, 218, 465, 475, 476, 477–78, 489
see also Phonics/phonic analysis
and pronunciation, 161–63, 165, 190
repetition of words, 46
reversal of order, 46–47
by sight vocabulary, 153, 160, 164, 166, 188
by structural analysis, 153, 160, 164, 166, 188, 190, 225–36, 323
substitution of word, 45, 46, 47, 51, 161–62, 165
systems and programed approach, 485
teaching principles, 160–66, 190, 196–97
testing for, 80–81, 82, 110, 112–13, 121
word pairs, 93
Words
affixes, 226–30, 236
antonyms, 133
awareness of, 104, 105–06, 136–38
base (root), 226, 323
compound, 233, 234–36
contractions, 233–34
inflections, 153, 230, 231, 232
plurals, 230, 231, 232
rhyming, 110, 123, 142, 143
synonyms, 173, 244
Words in Color, 468–69, 470
The World Book Encyclopedia, 323
Writing
organization in, and teaching children to perceive, 363–66
see also Books; Magazines; Newspaper; Poetry
Writing area (in classroom), 290, 398

A 9
B 0
C 1
D 2
E 3
F 4
G 5
H 6
I 7
J